MARKET EVOLUTION

Studies in Industrial Organization

Volume 20

Market Evolution

Competition and Cooperation

edited by

Arjen van Witteloostuijn
University of Limburg,
Maastricht, The Netherlands

KLUWER ACADEMIC PUBLISHERS
DORDRECHT / BOSTON / LONDON

A C.I.P. Catalogue record for this book is available from the Library of Congress

ISBN 0-7923-3350-0

Published by Kluwer Academic Publishers,
P.O. Box 17, 3300 AA Dordrecht, The Netherlands.

Kluwer Academic Publishers incorporates
the publishing programmes of
D. Reidel, Martinus Nijhoff, Dr W. Junk and MTP Press.

Sold and distributed in the U.S.A. and Canada
by Kluwer Academic Publishers,
101 Philip Drive, Norwell, MA 02061, U.S.A.

In all other countries, sold and distributed
by Kluwer Academic Publishers Group,
P.O. Box 322, 3300 AH Dordrecht, The Netherlands.

Printed on acid-free paper

Printed in the Netherlands

Acknowledgments

This book is the result of Professor De Jong's suggestion - then EARIE-president (EARIE is the European Association of Research in Industrial Economics) - to publish a selection of the best papers presented at the annual meeting of the EARIE, held in Stuttgart in September 1992. A volume with collected papers can, of course, be produced only with the help of the contributing authors. Their effort made it possible to bring together a set of high-quality papers reflecting frontier research in modern industrial organization. Moreover, without the editing assistance of Piety van der Nagel and Hans Kerkhof this book would never have been published.

Arjen van Witteloostuijn

July 1994
Maastricht

Contents

CHAPTER 1

The Study of Competition and Cooperation

ARJEN VAN WITTELOOSTUIJN
University of Limburg, Faculty of Economics and Business Administration, Maastricht, The Netherlands

Abstract. This short chapter introduces the book in two ways. First, the future of industrial organization is generally characterized by pointing to two issues: (i) a continuing effort to (game-) theoretically analyze the idiosyncracies of specific competitive settings; and (ii) an intensified search for evidence that relates theory to the real world. Second, two specific themes that are likely to be at the center of IO-research in the decades to come are described: competition *across markets* and *over time*. Both themes have a prominent place in this book, next to contributions on fundamental and policy issues.

I. Introduction

The theory of industrial organization (henceforth IO) studies business strategy and market performance under specific competitive conditions. The key contribution of IO is an elegant and rich theory of competition. The well-established structure-conduct-performance paradigm (Scherer and Ross, 1990) describes the multifaceted (reciprocal) causalities between competitive conditions (structure), business strategy (conduct) and market welfare (performance). Since, say, a decade and a half much IO-modeling is framed in terms of game theory. This so-called "new" theory of industrial organization (Tirole, 1988) has produced a large, if not immense, set of specific models describing the specific outcomes that occur under specific conditions [as is clear from, for example, the Fisher-Shapiro debate in the 1989 issue of the *RAND Journal of Economics* (see below)].[1] Doing so, IO deals with a large range of topics, varying from vertical integration to collusive behavior and innovation to international trade. The 1989 *Handbook of Industrial Organization* (edited by Schmalensee and Willig) collects twenty-six essays that nicely reflect the current state of the art. The current book is a further contribution to this rapidly expanding subfield of economics, which has produced and is still producing an uncountable number of books and papers. This chapter briefly introduces the book. Doing so in a limited number of pages (as not this chapter but the nineteen subsequent chapters may pretend to contain original contributions to IO), the characterization of the field and its future can be but partial and unbalanced. However, a number of features and trends emerges from reviewing the current state of the art, which permits to locate this book's content in the continuing flow of IO-publications.

---

[1]The adjective "new" refers to the game-theoretic modeling of "old" structure-conduct-performance elements. Moreover, what differentiates the "old" from the "new" IO is the former's emphasis on empirical research compared to the latter's focus on theoretical modeling.

Of course, the content of this book too is a reflection of the current state of the art in IO. Many chapters, if not all, describe the idiosyncracies of the specific (game-theoretic) model at hand. For example, Chapters 4 to 7 analyze R&D competition, Chapters 7 and 9 deal with the issue of product differentiation and Chapters 10 and 11 look into the vertical dimension of competition. The analysis of specific settings is clearly useful. Here Shapiro's (1989a: 132) response to Fisher's (1989) critique of IO is worth repeating: "Most fundamentally, I think that Professor Fisher is misguided in seeking a single 'generalizing' theory of oligopoly. First, a very general theory may be of quite limited usefulness if it fails to match real-world conditions. ... Second, a search for a single generalizing theory of oligopoly denies the very richness of business behavior that makes I.O. so interesting. We do have some general themes emerging from the theory of business strategy - the importance of timing and the role of commitment - but to seek a single theory of strategic behavior is both unwise and fruitless".[2] In effect, "[i]ndustrial organization economists are both blessed and cursed: our field encompasses a wide range of business behavior that is a rich arena in which to apply economic principles, but the very richness of business strategy defies simple and general theories. ... A methatheme that emerges from this research is that the predictions of the model concerning the character of the equilibrium of the game tend to be quite sensitive to the exact specification of the firms' strategies and the timing of actions. ... There is no reason to expect or strive for a single unified oligopoly theory that would deliver unique predictions to armchair theorists, independent of the particulars of how competition is played out in a given industry. ... The diversity of predictions in different game-theoretic models reflects our broadening understanding of business strategy. With our game-theoretic tools, we can carefully analyze a much wider range of competitive strategy than was previously possible. The theory tells us the conditions under which different outcomes occur" (*ibidem*: 125-126).[3]

However, although important, game *theory* alone is insufficient. Tirole (1988: 3-4) - being a leading IO-theorist himself - provides an excellent diagnosis of the current state of the art in IO and its future by arguing that "[i]ndustrial organiza-

---

[2]Another interesting research avenue in IO is the interface with the strategic management tradition. This is why Shapiro (1989a) even pleads for replacing the term 'oligopoly theory' by 'theory of business strategy' (*ibidem*: 125). Porter (1980 and 1985) - having won his spurs with fundamental IO-research - is a pioneer in bridging industrial organization and strategic management. The key argument is that the traditional structure-conduct-performance reasoning in IO can be applied to the issue of strategy-making by firms as well - if performance is interpreted as *firm* profitability (or any other measure of firm performance) rather than society's welfare. An interesting outcome of the implied cross-fertilization is, for example, the strategic group concept (Caves and Porter, 1977). Two special issues of the *Strategic Management Journal* - in 1988 and 1991 - indicate that this integration of industrial organization and strategic management is well-established by now. In this book Chapters 12 and 13 are examples of contributions that explore this IO - strategic management interface.

[3]The critique of IO is closely related to the debate on the usefulness (or uselessness) of game theory, which is also reflected in the Fisher-Shapiro communication. In the current context, this issue is beyond the scope of the argument.

tion has become a fairly theoretical field in recent years. At first sight, even a theorist should regret the very high ratio of theory to evidence in a field in which theoretical models are often lacking in generality and in which practical implications are so crucial. While I feel there is an imbalance in the field, I also think the theoretical evolution has been very healthy. ... Furthermore, the theoretical contributions should soon feed back to empirical analysis. They suggest what evidence to look for, separate the endogenous from the exogenous variables, and highlight the hypothesis to be tested. Econometric analysis certainly isn't the only way of doing empirical research in IO. Because of unsatisfactory data, many applied researchers are paying more attention to the development of evidence on firm and industry behavior and performance through detailed case studies[4] ... . Still another method of collecting evidence that can benefit from the theoretical developments is the running of controlled experiments in laboratories. Thus, it is hoped that these three approaches to empirical work will be strengthened by the new theoretical developments". That is, what is needed by now - apart from continuing refinements of game-theoretic models of specific competitive settings - is *empirical* research that links evidence to theory. A nice example of what this undertaking may achieve, is Sutton's seminal *Sunk Costs and Market Structure: Price Competition, Advertising and the Evolution of Competition* (1991). The current book too has a number of contributions that seek to fill the evidence - theory gap, notably the Chapters 4, 5, 8, 10 and 13 to 17.[5] These contributions cover both case study (*e.g.*, Chapter 13) and econometric (*e.g.*, Chapter 15) research.

The above argument indicates the need for two 'general' contributions to IO: first, a continuing effort to (game-)theoretically analyze the idiosyncracies of specific competitive settings and, second, an intensified search for evidence that relates theoretical exercises to real-world phenomena. Both needs are reflected in the contributions to the current book. Moreover, below a picture is painted of 'specific' themes that are likely to (or must?) be at the center of IO-research in the decades to come. First, Section II hints at the importance of two issues in particular: competition (and cooperation, for that matter) *across markets* (or multimarket competition) and *over time* (or market evolution). Both themes have a prominent place in this book. Second, Section III closes this brief introduction of the current book by pointing to the remaining contributions that precede and follow upon the book's core by focusing on a number of fundamental and policy issues, respectively.

---

[4]On this Shapiro (1989a: 126[n]) notes that "the more applied field of corporate strategy has a long and rich history. Economists have much to learn from scholars who have studied corporate behavior and corporate strategy in detail. I hope the learning will be mutual, as economists undertake more case studies to test their theories and as corporate strategy experts integrate game-theoretic insights into their work". This points to a further potential for IO - strategic management cross-fertilization (*cf.* note 1).

[5]The Fisher-Shapiro-Tirole arguments are echoed in the import of the many review articles that have been devoted to Schmalensee and Willig's *Handbook of Industrial Organization* (1989). Five typical examples are Fisher (1991), Klevorick (1991), Peltzman (1991), Porter (1991) and Waterson (1992).

II.   Multimarket Competition and Market Evolution

Much IO focuses on the analysis of competition in an isolated market. Part II (Chapters 4 to 8) contribute(s) to this within-market competition studies.[6] Then, the issue is how competition proceeds within a specific market environment. The particulars of the setting follow from the familiar structure and conduct elements. Particularly crucial are the assumptions of competitive strategy and competitive timing. That is, which variables are subject to decision making (competitive strategy), and in which sequence are strategies effectuated (competitive timing)? The chapters in Part II focus on four competitive strategies: R&D (Chapters 4 and 5), product differentiation (Chapter 7), strategic partnering (Chapters 4 and 6) and information sharing (Chapter 8). As far as the competitive timing is concerned, basically three types of games can be distinguished: static, finite and infinite (both being dynamic) games (Fudenberg and Tirole, 1991). Broadly speaking, modern modeling in IO generally operates a multi-stage framework, which determines the timing structure of the game. For example, Chapter 5 assumes that firms select a partner first (the first-stage game), whereas the strategic alliances compete in the market next (the second-stage game). By now, this within-market and multi-stage competition studies are, probably, the hard core of IO [that is, what Fisher (1989) calls 'oligopoly theory'; see also Shapiro (1989b)]. However, the current book emphasizes two logical extensions of this hard core.

Firstly, many - if not all - firms operate (and probably increasingly so) in multiple markets.[7] That is, what counts is not only competitive strategy (*i.e.*, how to compete - which is the essential question in within-market competition studies) but also corporate strategy (*i.e.*, where to compete) - firms, by operating in many markets, have to handle a portfolio of competitive strategies. Moreover, competitive and corporate strategies are interrelated. This is the issue of multimarket competition (Van Witteloostuijn and Van Wegberg, 1992; see also Chapter 12) or extended rivalry (Porter, 1980; see also Chapter 13), which is central in Part III (Chapters 9 to 13). Multimarket competition has a horizontal and a vertical dimension. Horizontally, on the one hand, a firm may offer a set of products (a multiproduct firm) in a number of countries (a multinational firm). The fact that a firm operates in a number of markets may have specific implications for competition and strategy. Two examples are the opportunities to sustain cooperative behavior (Bernheim and Whinston, 1988; and Van Wegberg, Van Witteloostuijn and Roscam Abbing, 1994) or to pursue reciprocal entry strategies (Calem, 1988; and Van Wegberg and Van Witteloostuijn, 1992): that

---

[6]Part of this within-market competition tradition deals with issues of potential competition (Gilbert, 1989). Then, however, the modeling focuses on an isolated market as well - as the entry threat is assumed to be unidentified (Van Wegberg and Van Witteloostuijn, 1992).

[7]Two remarks are worth making. First, the issue of multimarket competition is well-established in a number of subbranches of IO, notably the literatures on diversified, internationalized and multiproduct firms (Van Witteloostuijn, 1993). Second, the process of European integration indicates the increased relevance of multimarket competition and, for that matter, multimarket cooperation (Van Wegberg, Van Witteloostuijn and Roscam Abbing, 1994).

is, a tit-for-tat strategy can be extended over multiple markets. Chapters 9, 12 and 13 analyze aspects of horizontal multimarket competition. Vertically, on the other hand, a firm has to deal with downstream buyers and upstream suppliers. This relates to such issues as vertical integration, contracting and bargaining. Chapters 10 and 11 focus on this vertical dimension of multimarket competition.

Secondly, firms not only compete across markets, but also over time. Of course, much game theory is dynamic. This is clear from, for example, the many contributions in Parts II and III of this book that start from a multi-stage setting (*e.g.*, Chapters 7 and 12). However, this multi-stage game theory is generally *not* dynamic in the sense that a *series* of (multi-stage) games is analyzed. Moreover, in so far as a dynamic series of games is analyzed, the rules of the game (including the assumptions of competitive strategy and competitive timing) are - by and large - fixed over time. For example, the modeling of cooperative behavior takes generally place within a supergame setting.[8] This is, of course, not to say that this type of dynamic game theory is unimportant. To the contrary: both multi-stage game and supergame modeling is crucial in understanding essential aspects of competition and cooperation. However, the question of how competition evolves over time is important as well. The study of changes in structure-conduct-performance elements over time - or, as a short-cut, the study of market evolution (Boone and Van Witteloostuijn, 1995) - is the focus of Part IV (Chapters 14 to 17). Here, the book concentrates on empirical research in general, and the issue of entry and exit processes in particular.[9] The running thread in this part of the book is a selection metaphor: on the basis of longitudinal datasets the contributions focus on explaining the rates of success (and thus failure) of (new) firms in the face of dynamic competition in Germany (Chapter 17), Portugal (Chapter 16), The Netherlands (Chapter 15) and the U.S. (Chapter 14).

---

[8]The above characterization of 'dynamic' IO is a clear illustration of the (unavoidable?) unbalanced nature of an introductory chapter in a book that covers a broad field of research (see the first paragraph of this chapter). That is, the introductory purpose of this chapter implies that many subtleties cannot be expressed properly. The dynamic branch of game theory - and its applications within IO - is growing rapidly. On this see, for instance, Tirole (1988: for example, Chapters 6 and 9), Shapiro (1989b: 397-408) and Fudenberg and Tirole (1991: particularly Part IV). A case in point is the increasing popularity of learning issues in the context of (evolutionary) game theory. A recent survey is Friedman (1991) - and five recent examples of applications are Budd, Harris and Vickers (1993), Ellison (1993), Kandori, Mailath and Rob (1993), Trefler (1993) and Young (1993). Apart from game theory, stochastic equilibrium modeling of IO-processes gains *momentum* (*e.g.*, Jovanovic and Lach, 1989; and Hopenhayn, 1992). The theory - evidence gap in this area (including both the game-theoretic and stochastic equilibrium variants) is impressive, however.

[9]The study of market evolution in IO has close counterparts in evolutionary economics (Nelson and Winter, 1982) - being based upon a merger of Schumpeter's (1943) process of creative destruction and Simon's (1945) behavioral perspective on organizational functioning - and organizational ecology (Hannan and Freeman, 1989) - being rooted in an organizational sociology that borrows freely from biological ecology. Boone and Van Witteloostuijn (1995) explore this interface.

III.   Fundamental and Policy Issues

Apart from the future potential of empirical research in IO, Tirole (1988: 4) "believe[s] that the intersection between organization theory and IO is one of the most interesting areas for theoretical research in the years to come". Indeed, the issue of the economic theories of management and organization is gaining popularity in the IO-literature (Milgrom and Roberts, 1992) - which is clear from, for example, the many agency, contracting, signaling, and transaction cost studies that appear in frontier IO-journals.[10] Part I of the current book deals with two fundamental issues in this IO - organization theory arena by focusing on two assumptions that almost all IO-studies (including all contributions in Parts II to V in this book) take for granted: the *existence* of firms that *maximize* profits. First, a key question in what may be called organizational economics relates to the explanation of the emergence and existence of firms (or hierachies) next to markets - an issue that Coase (starting with his 1937 article) has put at the center of economic thinking (and which, in part at least, produced his winning of the Nobel prize). Chapter 2 reviews the literature that followed upon (after a decade-long lag) Coase's introduction of the issue, and presents an alternative to the well-established transaction cost argument. Second, the key assumption in IO-modeling - and, for that matter, microeconomics in general - is that firms are driven by profit maximization. This assumption is not controversial within mainstream IO (and microeconomics), but the more so in unorthodox alternatives. This is particularly clear from the behavioral theory of organizations and evolutionary economics (Nelson and Winter, 1982), which both replace the maximizing principle by a satisficing mechanism. Chapter 3 summarizes the debate on the maximization assumption, and reports the results of an empirical test on the basis of a dataset on U.S. hospitals.

A final issue in the book relates to governmental intervention. The performance element in the structure-conduct-performance paradigm is central in much IO-work. Actually, in their influential textbook Scherer and Ross (1990: 2-3) characterize IO by arguing that "[i]n the field of industrial organization, we seek to ascertain how market processes direct the activities of producers in meeting consumer demands, how those processes can break down, and how they adjust, or can be adjusted, to make performance conform more closely to some ideal standard. ... [S]tudies in the field have a direct and continuing influence on the formulation and implementation of public policies in such areas as the choice between private and public enterprise, the regulation or deregulation of public utility industries, the promotion of competition through antitrust and free trade policies, the stimulation of technological progress through patent grants and subsidies, and much else". This is why the performance box in their visual presentation of the structure-conduct-performance paradigm contains such

---

[10]A further case in point is the introduction in 1992 of a new journal under the name of the *Journal of Economics and Management Strategy* (*cf.* note 1). In effect, an argument can be put forward that the organizational economics field has developed into a separate branch of economics - apart from, though closely related to, IO. Recently, for example, the *Journal of Economic Perspectives* published a special issue (1991) on this topic.

benchmarks as efficiency, progress, employment and equity (*ibidem*: 5).[10] Therefore, as this book is firmly embedded in the IO-tradition, it comes as no surprise that many of this book's contributions pay attention to policy implicati-ons - either as an integrated element of the argument or as an afterword (see, for example, Chapters 3 and 4). Moreover, Part V is exclusively devoted to three policy issues that currently attract much attention - in both IO and public debates - for obvious reasons: (i) the restructuring of Eastern Europe (Chapter 18), (ii) the integration of Western Europe (Chapter 19), and (iii) the develop-ment of underdeveloped countries (Chapter 20). Hopefully, these (and the preceding) chapters convincingly reveal that modern IO has something to say on issues that are at the heart of (economic) life.

References

Bernheim, B.D. and M.D. Whinston (1988) 'Multimarket Contact and Collusive Behavior', *RAND Journal of Economics* **21**, 1-26.

Boone, C. and A. van Witteloostuijn (1995) 'Industrial Organization and Organizational Ecology: The Potentials for Cross-Fertilization', *Organization Studies* **15**, forthcoming.

Budd, C., C. Harris and J. Vickers (1993) 'A Model of the Evolution of Duopoly: Does the Asymme-try between Firms tend to Increase or Decrease?', *Review of Economic Studies* **60**, 543-573.

Calem, P.S. (1988) 'Entry and Entry Deterrence in Penetrable Markets', *Economica* **55**, 171-183.

Caves, R.E. and M.E. Porter (1977) 'From Entry Barriers to Mobility Barriers: Conjectural Decisions and Contrived Deterrence to New Competition', *Quarterly Journal of Economics* **91**, 241-261.

Coase, R.H. (1937) 'The Nature of the Firm', *Economica* **4**, 386-405.

Ellison, G. (1993) 'Learning, Local Interaction, and Coordination', *Econometrica* **61**, 1047-1071.

Fisher, F.M. (1989) 'Games Economists Play: A Noncooperative View', *RAND Journal of Economics* **20**, 113-137.

Fisher, F.M. (1991) 'Organizing Industrial Organization: Reflections on the *Handbook of Industrial Organization*', *Brooking Papers on Economic Activity* **22**, 201-240

Friedman, D. (1991) 'Evolutionary Games in Economics', *Econometrica* **59**, 637-666.

Fudenberg, D. and J. Tirole (1991) *Game Theory*, Cambridge, MA: MIT Press.

Gilbert, R.J. (1989) 'Mobility Barriers and the Value of Incumbency', in R. Schmalensee and R.D. Willig (eds), *Handbook of Industrial Organization*, Amsterdam: North-Holland, 475-536.

Hannan, M.T. and J. Freeman (1989) *Organizational Ecology*, Cambridge, MA: Harvard University Press.

Hopenhayn, H.A. (1992) 'Entry, Exit, and Firm Dynamics in Long Run Equilibrium', *Econometrica* **60**, 1127-1150.

Jovanovic, B. and S. Lach (1989) 'Entry, Exit, and Diffusion with Learning by Doing', *American Economic Review* **79**, 690-699.

Kandori, M., G.J. Mailath and R. Rob (1993) 'Learning, Mutation, and Long Run Equilibria in Ga-

---

[10]The issue of society's welfare has intrigued economists ever since the origin of the econo-mics field of science. Here IO is no exception, as is clear from the prominence of welfare-theoretic analyses in much IO-publications. IO shares this interest with all fellow travellers in economics - be it public choice, macroeconomics, labor studies or, in the extreme, welfare economics. This 'normative' attitude is not without danger, however. On this Scherer and Ross (1990: 7), for example, comment that "[m]any aspects of industrial organization analysis are controversial, but none excite economists' disputative juices more than questions of appropriate public policy. At bottom, the debate turns on ideological value judgements as the proper role of government. Here, analysis is futile; *de gustibus non est disputandum*". It is beyond the scope of this chapter (and this book) to unravel the ins and outs of the debate on the (non)existence of value-free IO (or, for that matter, value-free economics and science). Note, however, that this book focuses by and large on the 'positive' approach to IO.

mes', *Econometrica* **61**, 29-56.

Klevorick, A.K. (1991) 'Directions and Trends in Industrial Organization: A Review Essay on the *Handbook of Industrial Organization*', *Brooking Papers on Economic Activity* **22**, 241-280.

Milgrom, P. and J. Roberts (1992) *Economics, Organization and Management*, Englewood Cliffs, NJ: Prentice-Hall.

Peltzman, S. (1991) 'The *Handbook of Industrial Organization*: A Review Article', *Journal of Political Economy* **99**, 201-217.

Porter, M.E. (1980) *Competitive Strategy: Techniques for Analyzing Industries and Competitors*, New York: Free Press.

Porter, M.E. (1985) *Competitive Advantage: Creating and Sustaining Superior Performance*, New York: Free Press.

Porter, R.H. (1991) 'A Review Essay on *Handbook of Industrial Organization*', *Journal of Economic Literature* **24**, 553-572.

Scherer, F.M. and D. Ross (1990) *Industrial Market Structure and Economic Performance*, Boston: Houghton Mifflin.

Schmalensee, R. and R.D. Willig (1989) *Handbook of Industrial Organization* (two volumes), Amsterdam: North-Holland.

Schumpeter, J.A. (1943) *Capitalism, Socialism and Democracy*, London: Allen and Unwin.

Shapiro, C. (1989a) 'The Theory of Business Strategy', *RAND Journal of Economics* **20**, 125-137.

Shapiro, C. (1989b) 'Theories of Oligopoly Behavior', in R. Schmalensee and R.D. Willig (eds), *Handbook of Industrial Organization*, Amsterdam: North-Holland, 329-414.

Simon, H.A. (1945) *Administrative Behavior*, London: McMillan.

Sutton, J. (1991) *Sunk Costs and Market Structure: Price Competition, Advertising and the Evolution of Concentration*, Cambridge, MA: MIT Press.

Tirole, J. (1988) *The Theory of Industrial Organization*, Cambridge, MA: MIT Press.

Trefler, D. (1993) 'The Ignorant Monopolist: Optimal Learning with Endogenous Information', *International Economic Review* **34**, 565-581.

Waterson, M. (1992) 'Book Review of the *Handbook of Industrial Organization*', *Managerial and Decision Economics* **13**, 171-177.

Wegberg, M. van and A. van Witteloostuijn (1992) 'Credible Entry Threats into Contestable Markets: A Multimarket Model of Contestability', *Economica* **59**, 437-452.

Wegberg, M. van, A. van Witteloostuijn and M. Roscam Abbing (1994) 'Multimarket and Multiproject Collusion: Why European Integration May Reduce Intra-Community Competition', *De Economist* **142**, forthcoming.

Witteloostuijn, A. van and M. van Wegberg (1992) 'Multimarket Competition: Theory and Evidence', *Journal of Economic Behavior and Organization* **18**, 273-282.

Witteloostuijn, A. van (1993) 'Multimarket Competition and Business Strategy', *Review of Industrial Organization* **8**, 83-99.

Young, H.P. (1993) 'The Evolution of Conventions', *Econometrica* **61**, 57-84.

PART I

FUNDAMENTAL ISSUES

The Theory of the Firm

Part I deals with two fundamental issues in the IO - organization theory arena by focusing on two assumptions that almost all IO-studies (including all contributions in Parts II to V in this book) take for granted: the *existence* of firms that *maximize* profits. First, a key question in what may be called organizational economics relates to the explanation of the emergence and existence of firms (or hierachies) next to markets. Chapter 2 reviews the literature that followed upon (after a decade-long lag) Coase's introduction of this issue, and presents an alternative to the well-established transaction cost argument. Second, the key assumption in IO-modeling - and, for that matter, microeconomics in general - is that firms are driven by profit maximization. Chapter 3 summarizes the debate on the maximization assumption, and reports the results of an empirical test on the basis of a dataset on U.S. hospitals.

CHAPTER 2

On the Nature of the Firm

CHRISTOS PITELIS

Judge Institute of Management Studies and Queens' College, University of Cambridge

Abstract. This paper assesses critically recent debates on the nature of the firm, paying particular attention to the contribution of transaction costs economics. Following a critical assessment of the contribution by critiques of, and alternatives to, the transaction costs perspective, the paper pursues a dynamic analysis to explain the nature of the firm. The main claims of the paper are that: all employment relationships (including market-type ones) are hierarchical, a fact highlighted if one focuses on production, not just exchange; the issue of the existence of firms is not separable from that of objectives (of its principals); a dynamic existence equals objectives framework suggests that there is merit in considering the multi-person firm-like employment relation (the Coasian firm) as the result of improvements in the benefits from the division of labor afforded through increased control/monitoring in such 'firms'.

I. Introduction

The analysis of the market (price mechanism) has been the near exclusive concern of economics for most of its history. In this mono-institutional world, economic analysis is viewed as the allocation of scarce resources through the price mechanism and, more specifically, the existence, stability and optimality of equilibrium of this allocation. It is only in recent years (mainly post mid-1970s) that economic analysis has started considering it important to discuss the nature and role of other institutional devices for the coordination of economic (and social) activity, most notably the firm and the state, but also the family, customs and norms. In main part, the move towards a poly-institutional economics is due to a 'school of thought' defined as 'new institutional economics' (NIE).[1] The NIE starts from the premise that the existence, form, functions and evolution of capitalist institutions need to be explained and that such explanation is a necessary and potentially very fruitful endeavour of economic analysis. In so doing, NIE has made substantial inroads in most areas of

---

[1]'New' institutional economics consists of work on the nature and evolution of institutions developed from neoclassical (including game theoretic), 'Chicago School', 'public choice' and Austrian perspectives. The neoclassical contribution includes work on 'property rights' (*e.g.*, Alchian and Demsetz, 1972) on economic history (*e.g.*, North, 1981) and on transaction costs and the internal organization of firms and the markets-firms juxtaposition (*e.g.*, Williamson, 1975, 1981 and 1985). Game-theoretic approaches include Schotter's (1981) attempt to explain both political and economic institutions. 'Chicago School' theorists (*e.g.*, Friedman and Friedman, 1980) are interested in the comparative properties of markets versus planning, in particular the state. So does the 'public choice' school and the Austrian school, which is mainly represented by Hayek (*e.g.*, Hayek, 1978). Green (1987) and Mueller (1989) have extensive surveys of the 'public choice' school. The latter also discusses the Austrian and Chicago school approaches. 'New' institutionalism, unlike the 'old' institutionalism (such as the work of Veblen, Commons, Mitchell and Ayres) shares a lot with the mainstream neoclassical perspective [see Hodgson (1989) and Rutherford (1989) for expositions and comparisons between the two].

economic analysis[2] and also in fields such as politics, sociology and 'organization studies' - traditionally regarded as lying outside the scope of economic analysis - thus renewing fears of 'economic imperialism' among other social scientists.[3]

The single most important contribution in the renewal of interest in institutions has been the classic work of Coase (1937) on the nature of the firm. Coase set out to explain the emergence of the firm in terms of market failure. After a very long gestation period Coase's work has been taken up, particularly by Williamson (e.g., 1975, 1985 and 1986) who developed Coase's insight in a full-blown theory of 'transaction costs' (also known as 'governance structures', 'markets and hierarchies' and 'organizational failures'). The premise of this theory is that transaction cost economizing is the most important explanatory variable underlying the emergence and evolution of hierarchies (the firm) from the market.

The sheer size, breadth and potentionally revolutionary implications for mainstream economics - but also politics, sociology and organizational studies - of Williamson's task has given rise to substantial concern and criticism from many quarters. Still, Williamson's research program is alive, kicking and going from strength to strength, as growing interest and contributions in the area confirm. The argument here is that one important reason for the transaction costs success story is that existing critiques are basically *ad hoc* - *i.e.*, they do not originate from a coherent, integrated alternative framework.[4] The task of this paper is to make a first step towards this direction. In Section II the Coase/Williamson perspective and its underlying assumptions are expounded. Following this, the criticisms advanced against it and the proposed alternatives are summarized.

A criticism of the Williamsonian theory is that it attempts to explain the nature of capitalist institutions without explaining the nature of (or even defining the term) capitalism. The starting point in Section III is that such an explanation is a necessary precondition for the analysis of capitalist institutions, and has dramatic implications to the markets-hierarchies perspective. In particular, the claim in this section is that so far as a most important concern of transaction costs economics - the emergence of the 'employment contract' - is concerned, by focusing on the process of capitalist production (as opposed to Williamson's focus on exchange) the market itself can be regarded as a hierarchy! From this perspective, the 'choice' of institutional forms is not one of markets and

---

[2]Williamson (1990) quotes R.C.O. Mathews' list, which includes industrial organization and corporate governance, labor economics, public choice, development and economic history.

[3]See, for example, Donaldson (1990) and also the contributions and debates in Francis, Turk and Williamson (1983), particularly the introduction, and in Aoki, Gustafsson and Williamson (1990), particularly the chapter by Williamson.

[4]Other reasons also exist, notably the prominence of 'efficiency' in the Williamson story, which allows it to be seen as a complement to the neoclassical perspective rather than an alternative - as Williamson (1990) himself acknowledges - and the associated 'policy implications' of this view, for which more is to follow.

hierarchies, but rather market and non-market hierarchies. With the help of this insight previous criticisms of transaction costs economics can be accommodated in a coherent new framework. Viewing the market as a hierarchy renders obsolete the need to explain *first* the emergence of the hierarchy (firm) and *then* to analyze its objectives. This paper suggests that existence and objectives are inseparable - in particular, the objectives of those who own and/or control the firm are the very *raison d'être* of the existence of the firm. This point is raised in Section IV. Section V discusses the objectives of firms within a proposed unified existence-equals-objectives framework. It is suggested that firms exist in order to realize the interests of the principals (employers) which can be seen as long-term profits through expansion/growth, motivated by conflict with labor and rivalry with other firms. Summary, conclusions and policy issues follow in Section VI.

II.   Markets, Hierarchies and the Employment Relation

Coase's concern is to explain the existence of firms. His starting point is that resource allocation in market economies is ordinarily regarded by economic theorists as taking place through the price mechanism. Yet, he observes, economists often employ the assumption that such allocation depends on the entrepreneur-coordinator. The two assumptions, however, are incompatible. In fact, in his view "[i]t can ... be assumed that the distinguishing mark of the firm is the supersession of the price mechanism" (Coase, 1937: 389). If this is so, one has to explain the choice of alternatives, in particular the existence of "islands of conscious power in this ocean of unconscious cooperation" (*ibidem*: 388) - that is, of firms. Coase's own answer is that "the operation of the market costs something and by forming an organization and allowing some 'authority'/'entrepreneur' to direct the resources, certain marketing costs are saved" (*ibidem*: 392). Marketing costs are "the costs of using the price mechanism" (*ibidem*: 403).

Coase mentions a number of such 'marketing costs' - for example, discovering the relevant prices and negotiating and concluding separate contracts for each exchange-transaction. Contracting costs in particular, he observes, are not eliminated but are greatly reduced if the 'factor of production' owner of the firm does not have to make a series of contracts with the other factors of production with whom s/he is cooperating within the firm, but substitutes them with one contract whereby the latter factor agrees to obey the directions of the former factor (the entrepreneur) within certain limits. Within these limits the entrepreneur can direct the other factors of production. In particular, "it is the fact of direction which is the essence of the legal concept of 'employer and employee'" (*ibidem*: 409). To summarize, Coase's argument is that under the assumption that the market pre-exists, the existence of firms implies that the latter reduce costs associated with the price mechanism. Coase's insight is a revolutionary one (and potentially very damaging to the neoclassical tradition) as it provides a reason why planning (including central planning!) may be preferable to the market.

Although some insights resembling those of Coase were developed in the

1960s and early 1970s, particularly by authors in the theory of the trans-national corporation (TNC) - notably Hymer (1960), first published in 1976, and McManus (1972) - it was not until Williamson's (1975) *Markets and Hierarchies* that a serious attempt to develop Coase's insight into a full-blown new 'research program' in economics has started.[5] Williamson's starting point was that of Coase's "in the beginning there were markets" (Williamson, 1975: 20). Given this, the core methodological elements of the markets-hierarchies perspective are that

"1. The transaction is the basic unit of analysis.
2. Human agents are subject to bounded rationality and self-interest.
3. The critical dimensions for describing transactions are frequency, uncertainty and transaction specific investments.
4. Economizing in transaction costs is the principal factor that explains viable modes of contracting; it is the main issue with which organizational design ought to be concerned.
5. Assessing transaction costs differences is a comparative institutional exercise" (Williamson and Ouchi, 1983: 33).

A transaction occurs, for Williamson, "when a good or service is transferred across a technologically separable interface" (Williamson, 1986: 139). Transaction costs are taken to be the costs of running the economic system (Arrow, 1970), which Williamson considers useful to think of in contractual terms.[6] Following Coase (1960), Dahlman (1979) and North (1981), such costs include search and information costs, measurements costs, bargaining and decision costs, and policing and enforcement costs [see also Eggertson (1990)].

Bounded rationality refers to behavior which is "intendedly rational, but only limited so" (Williamson, 1990: 11; quoting Herbert Simon). Limits to rationality arise from limited knowledge, foresight, skill and time. Self interest is of a special type, in that it makes allowance for guile: specifically, agents can be selective in information disclosure and can even distort information. Also, they can try to "mislead, disguise, obfuscate and confuse" (*ibidem*: 12). Self-interest seeking with guile is called 'opportunism' (but also moral hazard and agency). The importance of these two behavioral assumptions, Williamson claims, is profound in that "[g]iven bounded rationality, *all complex contracts are unavoid-ably incomplete*. Given opportunism, *contract-as-promise unsupported by credible commitments in hopelessly naive*" (*ibidem*: 12; emphasis in original). It follows that transactions should be organized so as to economize on bounded rationality, while safeguarding transactions from the hazards of opportunism.

Transaction-specific investment (or asset specificity) refers to the extent to which assets can be redeployed to alternative uses and by different users without loss of productive value. Its forms include site specificity, human asset specificity, physical asset specificity and dedicated assets. The contracting

---

[5]This delay has led Coase to observe that his 1937 paper was much cited, but little used [see, *e.g.*, Coase (1991)].

[6]Kay (1992) observes that these two definitions are not necessarily compatible. He claims that transactions can exist which are not due to any agreement to exchange.

ramifications of these are said to differ (Williamson, 1985). From the three - asset specificity, uncertainty and frequency - the first is claimed to be more important and distinctive. The co-existence of asset specificity, bounded rationality and opportunism creates a situation where market transaction costs are too high *vis-à-vis* those incurred by superseding the market and organizing resource allocation within the firm. Thus, the 'internalization' of the market by the firm is due to the latter's ability to economize in market transaction costs, arising from the co-existence of these three factors. If any of the three factors does not exist, markets can still allocate resources economically (*vis-à-vis* firms). In particular, in the absence of bounded rationality all potential problems can be settled from the outset, thus the market can be relied upon to solve the problems of opportunism and asset specificity. In the absence of opportunism the principle of stewardship (where the transactors can be relied upon to keep promises) can be used instead of a hierarchy. Finally, in the absence of asset specificity (thus sunk costs) contestable markets - *i.e.*, markets characterized by perfectly easy entry and costless exit (see Baumol, 1982) - will exist.[7]

However, Williamson considers the coexistence of all three factors as pervasive, implying the possibility of market supersession by hierarchies. In particular, the advantages of internal organization are that they facilitate adaptive, sequential decision making in circumstances where complex, contingent claim contracts are not feasible and sequential spot markets hazardous. Thus problems from bounded rationality are being reduced. Internal organization also attenuates opportunism, in part due to the ability of authority to stop prolonged disputes, but also because members of a hierarchy are said to feel part of a whole. Convergent expectations are more likely to appear, which reduces uncertainty. Bargaining costs arising from asset specificity can similarly be reduced, through the use of authority. While these economizing aspects of internalization call for the supersession of the market by internal organization (hierarchies), however, Williamson points to the 'high powered' incentives of markets which can be blunted or lost by hierarchies. Thus, there is a trade-off between "high powered incentives and bilateral adaptability" (Williamson, 1990: 15). The advantages of internalization can explain why firms exist. Similarly, the loss of high powered incentives [as well as transaction costs of firms, or management costs: see Demsetz (1988)] can partly explain the boundaries of the firms and thus (given the assumption of pre-existing markets) the market. As Coase (1937) claimed, "[a]t the margin the costs of organizing within the firm will be equal either to the costs of organizing in another firm, or to the costs involved in *leaving the transaction to be 'organized' by the price mechanism*" (Coase, 1937: 404; emphasis added). 'Leaving' here is obviously the crucial word.

The transaction costs/Markets-Hierarchies framework has been applied mainly by Williamson to explain a number of important issues, such as the 'employment relation', vertical integration, the evolution of the multidivisional structure of the firm (the M-form organization) and the conglomerate and TNCs [see, for

---

[7]Note, however, that 'contestable markets' involve the conduct (particularly the price output decisions) of firms - *i.e.*, existing *hierarchies*. This raises question marks on Williamson's claim.

example, Williamson (1981)]. From these the employment relation (Coase's exclusive concern) is our main focus here. The reason for this is that it is *only* this relation which can have a legitimate claim in explaining the *emergence of hierarchies from pre-existing markets*. All others - vertical integration, the M-form, conglomeration and the TNC - presuppose the existence of firms, and thus refer to the functions and/or evolution of hierarchies.[8]

To examine this idea, consider first the case of vertical integration. In Williamson's analysis this is explained within his organizational failures perspective.[9] As Davies (1987) observes, this approach to vertical integration derives directly from Coase's observation that firms will tend to expand (integrate) up to the point where it is equally costly not to! It follows that vertical integration's *raison d'être* in this view is the same as the one explaining the firm's existence. The same arguments used above explain why firms can also be used to explain why vertical integration occurs [see, for example, Williamson (1986)]. Two possibilities arise here that are worth considering. First, a firm which integrates vertically by setting-up its own new supplies and/or distributor is a case of internal expansion. Second, a firm taking over or merging with an upstream or downstream producer is a case of external expansion. Although arguments about opportunist suppliers, frequency of transactions and specific assets and *ex post* bilateral dependencies may be perfectly legitimate explanatory factors of a firm's decision here, the fact is that integration involves an ongoing existing hierarchy which internalizes (further) market transactions. Thus, no explanation of *new* hierarchies from markets is offered.

The case of the M-form organization is very similar. Chandler (1962) was the first to analyze the emergence of the multidivisional structure (the M-form firm), which gradually started replacing the unitary (U-form) firm in the U.S. soon after the Second World War. The organizational structure of the U-form, on the one hand, involved a central office responsible for strategic (long-run) decisions but also for the operational (day-to-day) decisions of the firm and a number of divisions, production, marketing, finance, personnel, *etc*. The M-form, on the other hand, consists of a general office supported by elite staff responsible for the strategic decisions alone and a number of operating divisions, each one of them organized in the way the U-form was. The operational decisions are left with the divisional managers in this structure. Chandler's idea was that the adoption of the M-form was a response to firms' needs for diversification.

---

[8]The particularly important status of the employment relation is pointed out by, for example, Malcolmson (1984) and Picot and Wegner (1988). The latter, for instance, observe that "from the beginning, transaction cost analysis found its most important application in the employment relation" (*ibidem*: 31). The main reason for this, however, that it is only this relation which may be able to explain hierarchies from markets, is not being observed. Kay (1992) does observe that Williamson's (as opposed to Coase's) comparative basis is one of internal markets versus external markets, or hierarchy versus hierarchy, not market versus hierarchy. In this sense, he concludes, Williamson's analysis involves false hierarchies.

[9]Williamson (1985) and Davies (1987) as well as most texts in industrial organization have surveys on other explanations of vertical integration.

Already by 1917 a number of firms were vertically integrated and realized that their know-how could be applied in new product lines (Chandler, 1977). The U-form was creating difficulties when the need arose to administer activities in different markets. The M-form was the step forward, as a firm would only have to add another division in a new product market to achieve its diversification plans. In this sense, Chandler's thesis was that *strategy caused structure*.

In Williamson (1975 and 1981) the story is different. He claims that the *size* of the U-form firm was becoming so large that "bounds on rationality were reached as the U-form structure labored under a communication overload while the pursuit of subgoals by functional parts ... was partly a manifestation of opportunism" (Williamson, 1981: 1555). This was due to the fact that the central office was taking both strategic and operational decisions. The M-form, by creating "semi-autonomous operating divisions (mainly profit centres), organized along product, brand or geographical lines" (*ibidem*: 1555) and with the operating affairs of each being managed separately, was able to reduce managerial opportunism, ease the confusion between strategic and operating goals and, importantly, re-establish the profit motive by re-uniting ownership and control (see Pitelis, 1987). In Williamson's view, the adoption of the M-form was due to its inherent control (transaction cost eliminating) advantages. In this sense, it was size that led to the M-form, or *structure caused strategy*. Whatever the (relative) merits of Williamson's explanation of the M-form structure, here again it is a case of the organizational form of an existing hierarchy. External capital market inefficiencies and/or middle management opportunism as well as 'control loss' problems due to the confluence of operation and strategic decisions along with increasing U-form firm size may well have something to offer on the debate. But this debate is one of hierarchies versus hierarchies, or external versus internal markets (Kay, 1990).

In the case of the conglomerate firm, the arguments are in terms of internalizing the external capital market, due to failures in the latter (Williamson, 1975 and 1981). Internalization increases the availability of information and the ability to control auditing. It also facilitates performance assessment of the M-form-type divisionalized profit centres. Further, transaction costs can be economized by internalizing the production of separate goods. This is due to the possibility that firms will be better able to exploit the quasi-rents from the ownership of specialized resources, either physical capital or human know-how. In both cases, conglomeration - as compared to leasing or selling in the open market - can help reduce market transaction costs arising from opportunism, particularly acute in the case of organizational know-how, due to its tacit and fungible nature (Teece, 1980). Thus, exploiting the quasi-rents from intangible assets can offer an explanation for the conglomerate.[10] Once again, whatever the merits of Williamson's arguments are, it is clear that in this case too what is being explained is the conglomerate divisionalization of existing hierarchies. There is an explanation of why some market transactions are being superseded, but not why hierarchies arise from markets.

---

[10]Clarke (1987) has a more detailed summary of the Williamson/Teece thesis and surveys other explanations of the conglomerate.

Williamson's treatment of the TNC is not extensive (see Williamson, 1981) and is in the same lines as the conglomerate firms [the 'intangible assets' hypothesis: see Pitelis (1991)]. This allows me to conclude in favor of my main point that it is only the *employment relation* that can provide a potentially legitimate claim of explaining *new* hierarchies from markets. Indeed, Coase was aware of this. In his paper it is the employment relation that receives near exclusive attention.[11] It follows that 'failures' of (pre-existing) markets *for labor* can potentially explain the emergence of hierarchies (the firm). Transaction costs explanations of vertical integration, the M-form, conglomerates and TNCs simply explain the (further) internalization of markets by *existing hierarchies*. This raises the question why labor markets fail and what is the exact nature of such labor market failure. To examine this, it is useful to introduce some historical insights.

From a historical point of view, the firm (factory system) has succeeded the putting-out system. In the putting-out system, on the one hand, a merchant-manufacturer 'puts out' raw materials to dispersed cottage laborers to be worked up into (semi) finished products, in most cases by using their own equipment (looms and forges, as the case might be). Material was moved from home to home in batches under the direction of the merchant-manufacturer. In the factory system, on the other hand, the laborers have 'agreed' to accept the employers' authority - *i.e.*, do as they are told - provided that the employers' behavior falls within a 'zone of acceptance'. The 'agreement' (the employment contract) thus replaced the market-type relationship existing under the putting-out system.[12] Why has this happened? In particular, which are the critical factors which led to the replacement of the market-type putting-out system by the factory system?

In Williamson's story the general reasons for this relate to transaction costs economizing. In brief, the main claim is that workers obtain 'idiosyncratic' experiences (job-related skills), which increase their bargaining power *vis-à-vis* employers. This and worker opportunism give rise to transaction costs difficulties of market-type relationships, such as the putting-out system - for example, protracted haggling. The employment relation, however, cannot fully solve the problem of 'asymmetric information' between employers and employees. Given this and employee opportunism, the firm (employer) will

---

[11]More recently, Coase (1991) expresses his regret for this and claims that the firm involves more than the employment relationship. However true this is, there remains the possibility that the employment relation constitutes the *differentia specifica* between single person (or unitary) and multiple person (or unitary) and multiple person (Coase-type) firms. See Pitelis (1993) for a more extensive debate of this.

[12]In real life, the number of institutional arrangements for the 'organization of work' is many more. Williamson (1986), for example, examines six - two entrepreneurial (putting-out and federated), two involving collective ownership (communal-emhs and peer group) and two capitalist (inside contracting and the authority relation) - and compares their relative efficiency properties on the basis of transaction costs economizing. The putting-out versus the authority relationship has received the lion's share in the literature, and it will also be employed in this section. Dow (1987) summarizes other types of transactions, such as informal reciprocity arrangements, franchising, long-term contracts, inside contracting, joint ventures and quasi-vertical integration.

provide incentives to the employee to increase cooperation. For example, in the 'internal labor market' the wage rate is attached to the job, not to the worker. This reduces individual bargaining power, and thus opportunism. Employees accept voluntarily the reduction in their freedom, but retain the right to cancel the authority relationship - *i.e.*, leave the employer. Although 'shirking' (by employees) is not prevented, 'consummate' (as opposed to 'perfunctory') cooperation is encouraged. Employers' opportunism is being reduced for 'reputation' reasons, a point going back to Coase (1937). Cheating firms are becoming known quicker than cheating workers. This and the existence of unions which monitor the firm's commitments, make shirking by firms less likely (Malcolmson, 1982). To conclude, idiosyncratic transactions and asymmetric knowledge necessitate the emergence of the employment relation [see Ricketts (1987) for more on this].

To what extent does the transaction costs story provide an accurate description of the putting-out - factory system relative advantages? Landes (1966) apparently supports the Williamsonian view of workers' opportunism when he describes a typical worker's behavior in the putting-out system as follows: "carouse the Saturday of pay, the Sabbath Sunday, the 'Holy Monday' as well; dragged himself reluctantly back to work Tuesday, warmed to the task Wednesday, and laboured furiously Thursday and Friday to finish in time for another long weekend" (*ibidem*: 59; quoted in Francis, 1983: 107-108). Moreover, in Braverman's (1974) view, the putting-out system was "plagued by problems of irregularity of production, loss of materials in transit and through embezzlement, slowness of manufacture, lack of uniformity and uncertainty of the quality of product" (*ibidem*: 63; also quoted in Williamson, 1986: 237). The main problem, however, Braverman observes, was the inability to change the production processes.

From the above, it follows that - from the employers-merchants' point of view at least - there were good reasons why the market-based putting-out system should be replaced by the authority relation.[13] By making the ability to work (labor power) rather than the quantity of a product the subject of the contract, employers could increase their ability to control quality and, more generally, to monitor the workers. The impetus for the factory system, North (1981) observes, "was monitoring of the production process by a supervisor" (*ibidem*: 169). This monitoring had obvious productivity advantages: the appropriation of the benefits of innovation and the checking of "embezzlement and like deceits" (Williamson, 1985: 210; quoting Marglin, 1975: 51). There is little doubt from the above that, from the merchant-manufacturer's point of view, superseding the putting-out system by a hierarchical organization had obvious efficiency (at least productivity) advantages. This appears to be in line with Williamson's claim that such "changes are driven by efficiency" (Williamson, 1985: 232). To what extent this is true can be better assessed after having considered the critiques and alternatives to the 'Williamsonian

---

[13]It is worth stressing here that the focus on the putting-out system is in order to provide a degree of historical specificity to the analysis. Similar considerations for those for putting-out would apply to the case of 'purer' market-type employment contracts (*e.g.*, of the spot-contracting type).

synthesis'.

III.   Markets and Hierarchies: Critiques and Alternatives

As already suggested, the starting point of the Coase-Williamson framework is the pre-existence of markets - the idea that the market is the natural (or original) means of resource allocation, so that non-market institutions need to be explained. There are conceptual and empirical problems with this assertion, however.

Conceptually, Fourie (1989) observes, market exchanges are nothing but exchanges between existing firms, or between such firms and their customers. The reason for this is that exchange presupposes production. Markets do not produce. Firms (including single-person ones) do. It follows for Fourie that conceptually the firm precedes the market, and not *vice versa*.[14] Historically, moreover, it is far from clear that markets predate hierarchies. Indeed, as the neoclassical economic historian Douglass North (1981) observes, if one focuses on price-making markets (the concern of the transaction costs analysts), hierarchies predate the market. While the first known price-making market - the Athenian 'agora' - dates back to the sixth century BC, hierarchies are known to have existed well before this.

Another line of criticism of the Coase-Williamson scenario concerns the assumption that firms' existence presupposes market failure (of the transaction costs type), and therefore that firms' existence implies the superior efficiency properties of hierarchies *vis-à-vis* markets. There are a number of crucial assumptions in this argument, importantly concerning the process through which an efficient institution (here the firm) replaces an inefficient one (here the market). Rutherford (1989), for example, observes that many institutions tend to contain a self-sustaining pattern of actions: "Once a pattern is established, it may be maintained despite being socially suboptimal" (*ibidem*: 309). It is common among transaction costs theorists to employ 'evolutionary' arguments in order to explain the replacement process. North (1981: 7), for example, suggests that "competition in the face of ubiquitous scarcity dictates that the more efficient institutions ... will survive and the inefficient ones perish". While the above possibility cannot be excluded, it is also possible that competition can lead to monopoly (Marx, 1954; and Rutherford, 1989) and/or wasteful use of resources (Baran and Sweezy, 1966; and Rutherford, 1989). Thus, market

---

[14] The question whether exchange presupposes production or not as well as the issue whether single producers qualify as firms are very complex ones, and depend very crucially on the definitions of exchange and/or firm one is willing to adopt. Von Mises, for example, considers the possibility of 'autistic exchange' (*i.e.*, one's 'exchange' of leisure for hunting) where no change of property rights takes place, since no other individuals are involved (see Hodgson, 1988). Coase's definition of the firm, moreover, is based exclusively on the existence of an entrepreneur-coordinator (of other people's work), and so differs from Fourie's definition. Marx (1973) moreover argues for the inseparability between production, exchange and distribution. In this sense, Fourie's contribution is that it makes clear the need for unambiguous definitions of the terms employed. More importantly, the argument points to the importance of production, which transaction costs economists ignore. For this see below.

inefficiencies (if present) need not necessarily lead to (efficient) firms.[15] Hodgson (1993) pursues this issue further.

A second line of criticism concerning the efficiency argument relates to the nature of efficiency and its beneficiaries: that is, the concept of Pareto efficiency. As suggested above, the move from putting-out to the factory system incorporates productivity gains through, in particular, the reduction of employees' opportunism. It also involves, however, the disappearance of laborers' opportunity to be opportunists! (Francis, 1983). Why should they want to lose this? From Landes' (1966) description, in fact, one would be surprised if 'independent' craftsmen and women were willing to sacrifice their 'independence' and obey employers' orders. It is at least as plausible to expect that laborers would be against such a change. If so, the firm was not efficient in the Pareto sense. Someone became better off, the merchant, while someone became worse off, the laborer [see Francis (1983) and Sugden (1983) for this argument]. A counter to this line of reasoning would be that from a purely pecuniary point of view both laborers and merchants became better off. Although this is a realistic *possibility*, the question arises as to whether the focus of the mainstream theorists on pecuniary costs-benefits should be extended to incorporate 'psychological' costs-benefits (McGuinness, 1987). If so, the preference of the putting-out laborers for 'independence' (which Coase himself acknowledges) would suffice to invalidate the very claim that firms are Pareto efficient *vis-à-vis* markets.

A critique related to the last mentioned criticism of the transaction costs scenario is that the theory ignores, or (more accurately) downplays, the role of power considerations. Such considerations can refer to market power and/or power in its more general sense of the ability of an agent (group) to impose its will on others through coercion and/or 'charisma'. Focusing on market power, I have already pointed out that competition itself can lead to monopoly (Marx, 1954). Monopoly, however, is itself one of the major aspects of (structural) market failure, according to conventional welfare economists [see, *e.g.*, the exposition of Cullis and Jones (1988)].[16] The ability of firms to give rise to (as opposed to solve) market failure has been noted extensively [see, for example, Yamin and Nixson (1984) and Pitelis (1987a)]. Particularly damaging, however, from this point of view is Malcolmson's (1984) observation that market power and transaction costs considerations are inseparable, as it is often the case that firms attain monopoly power by reducing market transaction costs! Considering Williamson's examples of vertical integration, moreover, Malcolmson concludes that "at least *prima facie*, the observed pattern of vertical integration is as consistent with the power argument as with the transaction costs argument.

---

[15]Rutherford (1989) and Kay (1992), among others, have more detailed criticisms of the new institutionalists' reliance on evolutionary processes and 'invisible hand' arguments, while Kay puts particular emphasis on the U-form versus M-firm debate.

[16]The distinction between structural and 'natural' (or cognitive) market failure, whereby the former is due to market power reasons (such as structural barriers to entry) while the latter is the result of transaction costs, is implicit in the Coase-Williamson program. It has been introduced and discussed explicitly by Dunning and Rugman (1985).

Without a separate measure of transaction costs efficiency or of the use of power, one cannot discriminate between the hypotheses" (*ibidem*: 125). Malcolmson's last observation relates to the ability of transaction costs economics to claim that it can offer refutable hypotheses different from those of other perspectives. Methodologically this is being done by varying governance structure while holding the transaction constant (Williamson, 1975). This, however, Dow (1987) observes, is illegitimate as changes in governance structures normally imply changes in the nature of the transaction costs involved: "a 'better' transaction must in some way be a *different* transaction. This undermines the premise that the transaction under discussion remains fixed, while governance structures can be varied to assess the transaction costs of each" (*ibidem*: 18). Sticking to issues of methodology, the reliance of the market-hierarchies scenario on methodological individualism (reductionism) - that is, the attribution of institutions or other social phenomena to individual action alone - has been noted and criticized by, for example, Hodgson (1988), Rutherford (1989) and Donaldson (1990). An alternative would be to explain individual behavior in terms of institutions, or at least recognize some sort of interaction between the two - *i.e.*, adopt as a unit not the individual but the social individual (Hodgson, 1989). Williamson's concept of opportunism, Hodgson observes, does not depart from this tradition, as self interest is a typical feature of 'economic man'.

Besides the adherence to methodological individualism, the concept of opportunism has been attacked from many other sides. First, opportunism may be mediated through culture and/or differing types of economic organizations. Kay (1992), on the one hand, observes that countries like Japan rely more on 'obedience' than opportunism. The need to emphasize 'trust' relations within the firm is discussed by Hodgson (1988) and, in particular, Ouchi (1981) in his 'theory Z'. Picot and Wegner (1988), on the other hand, observe that the 'trust relation' between employers and employees in Japan is mythical. By raising wages with seniority, employers in Japan render the employees' 'exit' option void, thus reducing the incentive to 'shirk'. The Pareto efficiency of this is doubted, given its association with "high levels of dissatisfaction, stress, mental illness, and even suicide rates, as well as an unfair cleavage between regular and subcontract workers" (*ibidem*: 33). When the Japanese system of 'trust relations' had to pass the test of the oil shock of the mid-1970s, employers forced middle aged employees with long service to 'voluntary' resignation! Picot and Wegner quote the president of a leading textile firm as saying that "[w]hen a firm is about to be wrecked, heavier cargoes should be thrown off first to sea" (*ibidem*: 33). Although the above would appear to offer some support to the 'opportunism' idea[17], it does so for *employers*' opportunism. This is in stark contrast to Williamson's emphasis on middle management opportunism (a reason for the M-form in his scenario) and employees' opportunism (a reason for the authority relation)! This asymmetric treatment is also noted by Donaldson

---

[17]The view that Japanese employers behave 'opportunistically' does not in itself invalidate the observation that 'opportunism' fails to account for a number of human actions, such as charity, blood giving, *etc*. These issues are discussed in Hodgson (1988).

(1990) concerning middle level management and, in particular, Dow (1987) concerning employers. In fact, Dow observes, the existence of authority is itself an inducement to employers' opportunism.

Other criticisms of the transaction costs perspective include the idea that firms supplement as well as replace markets (Auerbach, 1988), which is also in line with Hodgson's (1988) 'impurity principle' - *i.e.*, the (necessity of the) co-existence of a variety of institutional forms (impurities) in market economies as information provision devices [see also Schotter (1981)]. The primarily static nature of the perspective has also been noted (McGuinness, 1987; and Pitelis, 1987a), including its total disregard of the macroeconomic structure as a potential explanatory factor of (the existence and/or functions of) institutions (Pitelis, 1991). Brown (1984) and Imai and Itami (1984) observed that the distinction between markets and firms is not as clear-cut as the transaction costs framework implies, as firm-type behavior in markets and interpenetrations of markets and hierarchies can often be found. Cowling and Sugden (1987) suggested that if one focuses on control rather than ownership, certain market-type relations - *e.g.*, TNCs' subcontractors - should be viewed as part of the firm (the TNC), so transactions between TNCs and their subcontractors as intra-firm rather than market transactions. Further critiques concern the operationalizability of transaction costs and its downplaying of production costs (Demsetz, 1988) and also institutional devices in between markets and hierarchies, such as networks (see Thompson, 1991).

Concerning Williamson's particular version of the transaction costs scenario, Demsetz (1988) and Coase (1991) question the importance Williamson attached to asset specificity. Kay (1992) moreover observes that, in the case at least of the TNC, the internalization of specific and non-specific assets is involved (see also Galbraith and Kay, 1986). Dugger (1993) and Pitelis (1991) have pointed to Williamson's failure to extend transaction costs analysis to the theory of the state, despite Coase's own early 1960 contribution [see North (1981) and Eggertson (1990) for more on this].

The above extensive but non-exhaustive coverage is indicative of the strong interest the transaction costs framework has aroused. Alternative perspectives have also been proposed (although not necessarily as a direct response to transaction costs ideas). Most notable among these are the pure neoclassical approach of Alchian and Demsetz (1972) and the radical perspective of Marglin (1974).

The starting point in Alchian and Demsetz (1972) is that there is no difference between the firm and the market, and that the firm *is* essentially a market: "the firm can be considered as a privately owned market; if so, we could consider the firm and the ordinary market as competing types of markets" (*ibidem*: 138)! In a now famous quote, Alchian and Demsetz reject the idea that the firm has the power to settle issues by fiat, by authority or by disciplinary action superior to that available in ordinary markets: "Telling an employee to type this letter rather than to file that document is like my telling a grocer to sell me this brand of tuna rather than that brand of bread" (*ibidem*: 120). Overall, the firm is a nexus of contracts and involves continuous renegotiation of the contracts between employers and employees in terms acceptable to both parties. Thus, there is a perfectly symmetrical relationship. The right to 'exit' implies that firing can be bidirectional. The employer fires the employee, and similarly the employee fires the employer by leaving. If it is the case that firms are private markets, then (how) does the relationship between a grocer and a customer differ from that of a grocer and his employees? The answer Alchian and Demsetz suggest "is the *centralized contractual agent in a team production process* - not some superior authoritarian directive or disciplinary power" (*ibidem*: 120; emphasis in the original). Team production, however, involves metering problems, thus difficulties of rewarding good performance and punishing bad one. To do this, a monitor is required to minimize 'shirking'. To make sure that the monitor is being (self) monitored, she should have the right to claim the residual (profit). Thus, the employer is regarded as a coordinator or orchestrator of a private market (firm). The right to be the residual claimant ensures efficient production (*vis-à-vis* the ordinary market). Competition among potential coordinators, moreover, ensures that team members are not exploited (see Loasby, 1990).

The Alchian/Demsetz challenge has not gone uncriticized. Langlois (1987), for example, refuses to believe that the grocer example is meant literally.[18] He observes that if an employee is *not* doing something, it is precisely to continuously renegotiate contracts. If there is any efficiency value at all in the employer-employee relationship, he continues, it is exactly that it dispenses with this need for continuous renegotiations. This criticism loses a lot of its thrust if renegotiations of contracts are seen as implicit; yet, carrying the 'implicit contract' idea very far can be dangerous. As Hodgson (1988) observes, in the limit one could adopt Samuel Seabury's characterization (and justification) of slavery as an implicit contract between master and slave! Despite shortcomings, the Alchian/Demsetz scenario is valuable in that it re-emphasizes the well-known point that from the perspective of *exchange* and in the purely legal sense there is no essential difference between employers and employees, a point going back to Marx (1954). This equality may be constrained through the actions of one or the other party *within* the process of exchange - as, for example, discussed by Picot and Wegner (1988) - such as the labor market conditions (see Putterman, 1986). More importantly, however, equality in exchange need not imply equality in production, a point pursued in Section IV.

The other major alternative to the transaction costs perspective is Marglin's (1974) account of the rise of the factory. In Marglin's 'What Do Bosses Do?' the main claim is that, in contrast to neoclassical perspectives, the rise of the factory from the putting-out system "had little or nothing to do with the technical superiority of large-scale machinery. The key to the success of the factory, as well as its aspiration, was the substitution of capitalists for workers' control of the production process, discipline and supervision could and did reduce costs *without* being technologically superior" (*ibidem*: 46; emphasis in original). In this sense, Marglin suggests that the reason for the factory system was the desire of capitalists to increase their control over labor. Given workers'

---

[18]It is worth mentioning here that more recently Demsetz (1988) rejects the idea that the Alchian/Demsetz argument (but also transaction costs) can explain the *origin* (as opposed to the extent) of firms.

relatively higher autonomy under the putting-out system, it cannot be presumed that they did also prefer the factory system. Accordingly, the aim or the *raison d'être* of the factory was due to control-distributional and *not* to efficiency reasons. Marglin provides historical evidence, and also cites Stone's (1974) views of the transformation of the steel industry in the U.S. in the late nineteenth century as supportive of his views. His perspective, moreover, has been developed in a number of areas, including the explanation of the M-form organization (see Marginson, 1985) and the TNC (see Sugden, 1983).

Williamson's response to the Marglinian challenge is cautious and rather surprising. First, he accepts that there is 'merit' in all explanations, including 'power' ones. He then re-interprets Marglin's and Stone's analysis in a way consistent with his views, and suggest that "[g]iven ... the large efficiency gains that Stone reports, the efficiency hypothesis (or a combined efficiency-power) hypothesis cannot be rejected" (Williamson, 1985: 236). This is, effectively, Malcolmson's (1984) critique of Williamson! Still, Williamson proceeds, the main problem with power ideas is that power is less operationaliz-able than (even) transaction costs are. So, "[i]nasmuch as power is very vague and has resisted successive efforts to make it operational, whereas efficiency is much more clearly specified and the possibility of an efficiency hypothesis is buttressed by ecological survival tests, we urge that efficiency analysis be made the centrepiece of the study of organizational design" (Williamson and Ouchi, 1983: 30). I have already noted the problems with the Williamson program, including ones concerning operationalization. Similarly, I noted that from the capitalist's point of view (and from a purely pecuniary perspective, even from the worker's point of view) the factory system did have efficiency properties *vis-à-vis* putting-out. Last, I noted that focus on exchange alone does provide some apparent support to Alchian and Demsetz's idea of symmetry between capital and labor. Are they all right? The next section attempts to address this question.

IV.   The Nature of Capitalism, Markets and Hierarchies

In his *Economic Institution of Capitalism* Williamson (1985) fails to define either the term capitalism or institution! A definition of 'institutional environment' and 'arrangements' is offered in Williamson (1990), borrowed from Davis and North (1971). Capitalism, however, still remains undefined! So what is capitalism? A rather uncontroversial definition is that capitalism is a system of commodity production where labor service (or labor power) - that is, the ability of labor (workers, agents, employees) to produce commodities (products intended for sale and not personal use) - is itself a commodity. This can be transacted (purchased and sold) in the market for a compensation - the wage (rate) - by owners (controllers and/or coordinators) of productive means such as physical capital, who then become residual claimants of any 'profit' (revenue minus cost) generated by the transaction by virtue of their coordinating, owning and/or controlling function. These are invariably referred to as employers, capitalists, principals or entrepreneurs. The attractive feature of this definition is that by avoiding to attribute profits to ownership and/or control by employers-capitalists, it can encompass both mainstream and radical (including Marxist) perspectives. It still suffices to make the point, however, that under capitalism there are 'agents' who sell their labor power and 'principals' who buy it and also that for so long as the agents are contracted for, they have to obey the directions (order, authority) of the principal.[19] Why does this happen?

Coase (1937) raised a similar question. He observed that it may be that some people prefer to work under someone, but dismissed this idea in favor of the view that people tend to prefer quite the opposite - *i.e.*, "being one's own master" (*ibidem*: 390). An alternative scenario would be that people realize the benefits from cooperation and the need for supervision during this process of cooperation. In order to achieve the benefits from cooperation, they are prepared to sacrifice part of their autonomy for the duration of the productive process. This is the idea underlying the Alchian/Demsetz argument. A third possibility is that people (agents) are coerced to do so, either legally and/or because of their inability to survive (live what they perceive as a satisfactory life) if they fail to do so. This scenario is favored by the Marxist tradition. Hymer, for example, summarizes this scenario very succinctly: "In its early days, capital allied itself with the central power of the sovereign against the feudal classes. This system, working in complex ways, helped to drive the population off the land to become a free wage labor force in the towns and cities. People became unencumbered by property in the twofold sense: They were free of feudal claims on their time and had no property of their own, and therefore had no alternative to working for others" (quoted in Cohen *et. al*, 1979: 30). Thus, the need to survive, given the absence of property, has led people to work for others in the Marxist scenario.

Whatever the relative merits of these conflicting scenarios (or their synthesis?) may be, a consensus point which emerges is that when one focusus on the process of *production* an asymmetry emerges between agents and principals in that the former have to obey the latter - *i.e.*, sacrifice part of their autonomy. Thus, as far as the production process is concerned, any employment relationship is one of asymmetry: a hierarchical one. This last observation has interesting implications for the discussion of the putting-out versus factory system debate (or, for that matter, for any type of employer-employee relationship, be it market-type or firm-type). In particular, it implies that the existence of a merchant-manufacturer (principal) and the cottage-laborer (agent) in the putting-out system was itself a hierarchical one. The laborer agreed for whatever reason to sacrifice part of her autonomy (as compared, for example, to being self-employed or even a merchant-manufacturer herself) and work for the merchant-manufacturer. In this sense, the market-type putting-out system was itself a hierarchy! The historical evidence does indeed seem to support this simple observation. Landes (1966), for example, observes that, although most domestic weavers owned their looms

---

[19]Note that this argument does not contradict Alchian and Demsetz's (1972) idea that the 'exit' possibility and the ability of employees to 'order' their principals to pay them wages imply a symmetrical relation between the two. It simply points out that for the duration of the production process obeying the principals' directions is part of the employees' contractual requirements.

and nailers their forge, "[t]hey were not, however, independent entrepreneurs selling their products in the open market; rather they were hirelings, *generally tied to a particular employer*, to whom they agreed to furnish a given amount of work at a price stipulated in advance" (*ibidem*: 12; emphasis added; also quoted in Williamson, 1985: 216). Given the hierarchical nature of the putting-out system, the transition from this to the factory system did not involve a transition from a market to a *new* hierarchy but rather (as in the case of vertical integration, conglomerates, the M-form and the TNC) a transition from a *hierarchy* to a different hierarchy. Put more generally, any employment relationship involving an agent working for a principal is a hierarchical one. The transition from the one to the other involves a differential degree of supersession of market-type transactions, but it does not represent a supersession of *the* market by *a* hierarchy. So far as the employment relationship goes, the difference between its various forms is a quantitative and not a qualitative one.[20] The real issue is why any (type of) employment relation prevails at all.

As already suggested, the move from the putting-out to the factory system involved a further loss of autonomy of the agents to the principals, a point acknowledged by Williamson (1985) too. Why did cottage laborers accept this? Unlike the case of the propertyless 'proletarian' discussed by Hymer, in the case of the cottage laborer some capital ownership was there. In this sense, the 'ownership of capital' barrier to entry argument often employed by the Marxists cannot fully explain the cottage laborers' 'acceptance' of the factory system, which involved a further loss of independence. Acknowledging this, Marglin (1983) suggests that it was the 'organizational knowledge' of capitalists which allowed them to win the day - that is, oblige cottage laborers to accept the factory system. Capitalists' motivation to do so was their ability to further their profit by increasing their control over labor. Given their (however obtained) access to organizational knowledge and the conscious attempts on their part to protect it from becoming known to others, they only had to give the all-or-nothing choice to the cottage laborers: 'work for us or starve' was the idea. This is further discussed by Francis (1983) and Sugden (1983).

Marglin's rather instrumentalist account and rigid distinction between cottage laborers and capitalists solve fewer problems than they create. First, the knowledge-equals-power idea still fails to address the possibility of outright coercion by the state and the merchant-capitalists, as raised by Hymer. Second, and more important, the organizational knowledge idea raises the 'ugly' head of the question: how is such knowledge obtained? The answer is not incons-

---

[20]In the limit, even autistic 'exchanges' can be said to involve some loss of autonomy. This however does not involve hierarchy - *i.e.*, loss of autonomy to others. Similarly, the independence of the single person firm is only relative as it is constrained by the need of the person-firm to sell products. Similarly, principals (employers) are constrained by the market, customers, *etc*. Again, however, the relationship is not hierarchical, as it does not involve direct authority by others.

equential; it has dramatic implications for the efficiency properties of capitalism.[21] Consider the following quote from Hymer (1971), for example: "Marshall, like Marx, stressed that internal division of labour within the factory, between those who planned and those who worked (between 'undertakers' and labourers) was the 'chief fact in the form of modern civilization, the 'kernel' of the modern economic problem'. Marx, however, stressed the authoritarian and unequal nature of the relationship based on the coercive power of property ... . Marshall ... argued for the voluntary cooperative nature of the relationship between capital and labour. He argued that ... '[u]ndertakers' were not captains of industry because they had capital; they could obtain capital because they had the ability to be captains of industry. They retained their authority by merit not coercion" (*ibidem*: 57-58). It appears that the importance of the question of organizational knowledge hinges more on the process of its derivation rather than on its existence *per se*.

Marglin's failure to address this question is in part due to his focus on putting-out versus factory systems rather than the issue why firms exist at all (Coase's concern). As a result, Marglin fails to address the important issue, which is not the transition from one form of hierarchy (the putting-out system) to another (the factory system) but rather the very emergence of the putting-out system from the single-producer, who exchanged her products in the market with the products of other producers and/or merchants. In fact, it is this question that Coase addresses - *i.e.*, the emergence of any form of entrepreneurial coordination of production from a non-entrepreneurial one (the price mechanism). As shown, in the putting-out system the 'undertaker' was already there.

One can approach the emergence of the multiperson hierarchical employment contract both logically and historically. Logically, the issue is in effect to explain why *production for exchange*, as opposed to production for own use (self-sufficiency), and therefore to explain why exchange - and thus transactions and transaction costs - prevails at all. Given that an individual's original state of nature is self-sufficiency, one needs to explain why individuals 'exchange' this with a state where they specialize in the production of a limited range of goods, which they then exchange with other similar individuals who produce different goods. An answer which has the supporting weight of no less than Adam Smith, Karl Marx and Alfred Marshall relates to the benefits from specialization and the division of labor. If so, one could legitimately claim that the employment relation in a multiple person-hierarchy emerges because it achieves improvements in the benefits from specialization and the division of labor through, for example, closer monitoring of employees. Although Coase (1937) has entertained such a possibility, he dismissed it on the curious grounds that the price mechanism could itself achieve the integration of activities of specializing agents. However, the real issue is whether or not the multiperson hierarchy could do so more efficiently (from the point of view of the principals)

---

[21] A further issue arises from the possibility that some cottage laborers did manage to become capitalists, a historical fact acknowledged by both Marx (1959) and Marglin (1974). In fact, cottage laborers, through their capital ownership, were already capitalists in germ.

because of its higher monitoring-control advantages. This issue is not addressed by Coase, allowing my hypothesis as a distinct possibility [see Pitelis (1993) for more on this]. Similar considerations apply if one adopts a historical perspective, the main focus in this paper. Namely, the issue here is to explain why historically the merchants might have chosen to replace market-type (spot contracts or putting-out) relationships with their suppliers-employees with the firm-like multiple person hierarchical employment relationship. The reasons, I suggest, can be as follows.

Merchants, like any other transactor, would buy from single producers in order to sell, and thus make a 'profit'.[22] To ensure the existence of a 'profit', they needed to ensure the existence of suppliers. Total reliance on the market (price mechanism) could simply not do. Single producers might choose not to produce for sale, change merchant in their look-out to strike a bargain, *etc*. Putting-out was the 'obvious' solution. The necessary condition for its existence was the need of the merchants for stable suppliers, particularly in the face of expanding markets for their products. The sufficient one was a similar need for stable income on the part of the single producer, as well as their not being (willing and/or able to become) merchants themselves. Obviously, some might have done it, rather than sacrificing their autonomy for the merchants' authority under the putting-out. This is inconsequential. All that matters is that merchants, by virtue of being merchants alone (knowledge of markets, willingness and ability to sell), were able to 'persuade' (or coerce, directly or through the state) some single producers to work for them (see below). The capitalist was born, and so was the multiperson firm (*e.g.*, putting-out). Following this, organizational knowledge of production within the firm was obtained in the process. Given the difficulties associated with the appropriation of its quasi-rents, it was kept secret through strategy, as Marglin (and Marx) discusses.[23] This allowed the merchant-capitalists to maintain the power to organize and control production, whilst the capital barrier was not important[24]. The move to the factory system and the growth of factories increased the

---

[22]For this to happen, merchants should be able to sell for more than they bought - *i.e.*, they should be able to buy a product below its 'value' (the socially necessary labor time of average skill embodied in the product as the labor theory of value would have it) because of the supply/demand and relative scarcity conditions of such products in the markets they were sold. I will not enter the 'value' debate here, as it is inconsequential for my analysis. The *existence* of a pool of merchants by virtue of being merchants suffices to make the point that some 'surplus' (however derived) was present. For different theories of value see, for example, Dobb (1973). A consoling (albeit not uncontroversial) view is Marglin's (1984), who suggests that "the essence of capitalist profit does not lie in exchange - a point of view that is now common to virtually all economic theory" (*ibidem*: 462).

[23]A commonly referred to example is the use of semi-idiotic persons and/or the specialization of tasks for both workers and low-level supervisors.

[24]This is not to say that some capitalists could not fail or that no laborer could become capitalist, but rather that from a systemic point of view organization of production was such that at any particular point in time the vast majority had to work for a small minority, with little mobility between the two groups. This is still the case (see Edwards, 1979).

relative significance of the capital ownership barrier, consolidating the victory of the merchant-capitalist and the capitalist firm. There is some evidence that the state facilitated this process [see, *e.g.*, Galbraith (1987) and Hymer and Resnick (1970), particularly concerning the farmers (land enclosures)].

It follows from this short account that historically too it can be claimed that improvements in the exploitation (of the fruits of the division) of labor could be the driving force behind the emergence and evolution of the Coasian firm. Further, independently of the *ex post* Pareto efficiency (or inefficiency) properties of such evolutionary changes, their initiators (and major beneficiaries) were the principals (to be). This is broadly in line with, and provides a basis for, a startling consensus on the part of a widely diverge array of contributors to the definition of institutions, markets and hierarchies. The neoclassical economic historian Douglass North (1981) observes that "[i]nstitutions are sets of rules, compliance procedures, and moral and ethical behavioural norms designed to constrain the behaviour of individuals *in the interests of maximizing the wealth or utility of principals*" (*ibidem*: 202; emphasis added). The Marxist economist Hymer (1970) regards the 'market' and the 'factory' as "the two different methods of *coordinating the division of labour*. In the factory entrepreneurs consciously plan and organize cooperation, and the relationships are hierarchical and authoritarian, in the market coordination is achieved through a decentralized, unconscious competitive process" (*ibidem*: 57; emphasis added). The 'Austrian' economist and philosopher Von Hayek observes that "the commands as well as the rules which govern an organization *serve particular results aimed at by those who are in command of the organization*" (quoted in Clegg, 1990: 33; emphasis added). Von Mises, moreover, the father figure of the Austrian tradition, defines the market as "the *social system of the division of labour* under private ownership of the *means of production*" (quoted in Hodgson, 1988: 173; emphasis added). To summarize, the transition from the market to the firm (*e.g.*, putting-out first and factory after) was the result of the merchants' (rising capitalist class') desire to further their interests by effecting a more 'efficient' division of labor. The process involved consensus and coercion, including state intervention. *Ex ante* it was often undesirable; *ex post* it was often (Pareto) efficient!

V.   Existence and Objectives

The observation that the employment relation (the firm) is the result of (the merchants') attempts to effect a more 'efficient' division of labor and the related idea that the transition from, for example, putting-out to the factory system was simply a choice between two hierarchies, have this very important implication: it renders inseparable the notions of the existence and objectives of firms. In this paper's scenario, firms exist because of their principals' objectives; objectives lead to existence, existence (is due) to objectives. How this is achieved is a different and very important issue. It is neither necessary nor helpful, however, to attempt to explain existence first and discuss objectives after (as Coase-Williamson do) or to assert exogenous preferences of capitalists first and then attempt to derive the existence of firms as Marglin does.

Existence and objectives are the two sides of the same coin.

As already suggested in the historical account, the aim of the merchants in using the market (and underlying their successful attempt to replace the latter by an employment relationship) was to further their profits.[25] Similarly, the transition from one type of employment relation (putting-out) to another (factory) was due to the merchant-manufacturers' desire to further their profits through a more 'efficient' exploitation of the division of labor. From this it follows that both Williamson and Marglin are simultaneously right and wrong! The drive for profits by merchant-manufacturers would lead them to seek more efficient means of exploiting the division of labor. Through such efficient improvements, profitability and power would also increase. Power and efficiency were linked inseparably. Concerning in particular transaction costs, it is exactly through their reduction that profit, and thus potentially market power, can increase, as observed by Malcolmson (1984). To further profits, principals would try to reduce all types of costs, including transaction and labor costs, the latter by increasing their control over the labor process as indeed both Marglin and Williamson emphasize. In this sense, what is involved here are not two different explanations of the existence of firms, but rather differences in emphasis concerning two sides of the more general objective/reason for existence of firms, the furtherance of profits for the principals.[26]

In this light, the Alchian and Demsetz argument also appears correct, given its exclusive focus on exchange. From a legal point of view, the relationship between principals and agents is one of symmetry. Labor market conditions (affecting the agents' alternatives) as well as actions by principals and agents (affecting the 'exit' conditions of agents) in particular can put limits (constraints) on the relative power of the two parties, but cannot change the fundamental 'equality in the face of the law' between the two. Once, however, one focuses on the production side (once it is recognized, that is, that the agents' only alternative to an employment relation is another employment relation or none at all) the relationship becomes one of asymmetry (hierarchy). In the production process the agent has to obey the principal (or else 'choose' another principal to obey!).

Was the aim to further profits maintained and pursued following the emergence and evolution of the capitalist firm? If so, why? From a Marxist perspective, the answer to the first question would be unequivocally yes. The reason is that, given the labor theory of value (that labor power is the source of economic 'surplus', thus profits), the *conflict* between capitalists and laborers to influence the part of the surplus going to each class would lead capitalists to

---

[25]This is not to deny the importance of other motives, such as control over others, power, prestige, *etc.* In a capitalist economy, however, these can plausibly be suggested to be positively and strongly related to profits. For discussions see, for example, Schumpeter (1942) and Eichner (1976).

[26]The similarity between the two models is also observed in Putterman (1986) who, however, attributes their apparent differences in their different assumptions concerning the conditions of the labor market: "Once market conditions are made explicit ... the radical theory ... translates sensibly into the 'mainstream' terminology" (*ibidem*: 27).

try to increase labor productivity by technological and/or organizational changes. Moreover, Putterman (1986) observes, "even without Marx's value theory, which is not universally insisted upon by contemporary radical economists, the struggle to wrest more work out of labourers for a given wage payment remains at the heart of the study of the labour process, which in turn remains a central focus of research" (*ibidem*: 27; see also Marglin, 1984). Another equally important (and even less controversial) reason for the strive for profits is competition (*rivalry*) among firms themselves to improve their competitive position *vis-à-vis* rivals (thus ensure their survival) by cutting costs. The recognition of the importance of actual and potential competition in maintaining a drive for cost reductions cuts across economic ideologies - Austrian, Marxist and neoclassical [see the discussion in Scherer (1980) and Pitelis (1990)].

The short-run implications of the competition-driven strive for profit is a need by firms to exploit economies of scale, improve organization techniques and (or, so as to) increase the intensity of labor. More important, however, are the long-run implications. To keep being profitable (increase long-term profits) firms will need to expand their markets and, more importantly, in so doing remove the constraints they face in the process of this expansion (see below). Maximizing short-term profits will simply not do.[27] Hymer (1979), Schumpeter (1942) and Sweezy (1981), among others, stress the need of firms to expand simply in order to self-preserve themselves. This suggests that growth can and must be seen as a means of obtaining maximum possible profits in the long term. The existence of uncertainty concerning what exactly 'maximization' of long-term profit entails, reinforces the idea that in order to obtain maximum possible profits the firm needs to grow. Emphasis on growth (*per se* or as a means of maximizing long-term profits) has now received a very wide recognition in the literature [see, for example, Penrose (1959), Marris and Mueller (1980), Eichner (1976) and Chandler (1986)].

Penrose (1959), for example, observes firms' "desire to increase total long run profits" (*ibidem*: 29) and suggests that as investment by firms generates profits, firms will try to expand as fast as they can by taking advantage of (subjectively perceived as profitable) expansion opportunities. In this sense, "it does not mater whether we speak of 'growth' or 'profits' as the goal of the firm's investment activities" (*ibidem*: 30; also quoted in Reynolds, 1989). Trying to grow implies trying to remove any obstacles to such growth. Such, I believe, are of five major categories; first, product market constraints; second, labor market constraints; third, capital market constraints; fourth, technology constraints; and fifth, managerial constraints.

Product market constraints arise from the size of the market and the associated product life cycle. Advertising and selling promotion activities as well as the creation of 'competing' product lines within the industry can help firms to maintain and increase their market share. Diversification into new products is

---

[27]Unless, of course, the long run is seen as a sequence of short runs, as in Kalecki (1971). In this case it could be argued that firms try to maximize long-run profits by trying to maximize profits at any point in time (the short run). Note that in view of uncertainties Kalecki did *not* wish to assume that the firms maximize profits in "any precise sort of manner" (*ibidem*: 44).

required for the solution of the product life cycle problem, as pointed out by Hymer (1971). Vertical integration can, in part at least, be seen as a means of diversifying risks (see Auerbach, 1988). More generally, horizontal integration (mergers) and vertical integration are important means of achieving growth within the industry. Labor market constraints arise from the (non)availability of appropriate workforce and the bargaining position of labor. The response to this is an attempt to further the productive base and (in so doing) reduce labor's power. Constraints on the 'exit' option of laborers are also relevant here (see Picot and Wegner, 1988). Capital market constraints arise from difficulties in raising finance for expansion. Such finance can be found by borrowing from financial institutions and/or by issuing shares and retaining profits. Issuing shares is a discretionary means of socializing corporate ownership in order to raise finance. The Joint Stock Company can therefore be seen as the result of the need of firms to remove the constraints to growth. Moreover, mobilizing further finance can take the form of compulsory occupational pension funds. In this light, the 'pension funds revolution' is also a means of eliminating constraints to growth (see Pitelis, 1987). Pricing policies can be used in such a way so that required finance for expansion becomes available internally, subject of course to entry and other considerations such as take-over threats and loss of control to other principals (see Eichner, 1976; and Pitelis, 1987). Technological constraints to growth are removed through the introduction of more technologically advanced products and/or processes. This allows firms to reduce their costs (including labor costs) either through labor-saving technology and/or through better exploitation of the division of labor. Technological advancement therefore is the *sine qua non* of growth, thus long-term profits. Managerial constraints, finally, have received the lion's share in the literature (see in particular Penrose, 1959). The growth of firms puts definite limits to the ability of management to handle information such that control loss problems arise, as discussed by Williamson (1967), and growth through, for example, diversification can be halted. Organizational changes are the way to solve these problems. In particular, the M-form organization can be seen in this light.

The above scenario is not to suggest that other factors, including transaction costs considerations, are of no value in explaining the evolution of firms and their organizational structures, but rather that they can be seen within a unified objectives-equals-existence framework where growth is the means of achieving long-term profits and where the need to remove the constraints to growth explains dynamically the strategies of firms as well as their organizational structures. The major advantage of such a framework is that it endogenizes the need to change technologies and organizational structures which changes are often seen in the literature as the exogenous sources of profitability increases. Many of these issues are analyzed in the chapters below, notably product market constraints (Chapters 7, 9, 12 and 13), capital market constraints (Chapter 8), labor market constraints (Chapters 10 and 11) and technology constraints (Chapters 4 to 6). First, however, the next chapter deals with the issue of managerial constraints - or, for that matter, the objectives of firms.

VI.   Summary, Conclusions and Policy

This paper's starting point was that any explanation of the nature of capitalist institutions requires an analysis of the nature of capitalism. Given the commodity nature of labor power under capitalism, any employment relation seen from the production side is a hierarchical one. In this sense, the transition from, for instance, the putting-out system to the factory system involved a transition from one form of hierarchy to another. Logically and historically, it can be seen as the result of the desire (of merchant-manufacturers) to increase (their) income (profit) through a more efficient exploitation (of the division) of labor. The same reason can explain the very emergence of an employment relationship at all (along with other reasons, such as the perceived interests by other parties like the state and the laborers). In this light, organizational knowledge can be seen as obtained by merchants in the very process of becoming manufacturers. They maintained it through secrecy. The framework suggests that the existence and objectives of firms are inseparable. Firms exist because of the principals' objective to obtain profits. As such, profits can be obtained both by efficiency improvements and changes in technology and/or organization inimical to labor. Efficiency and power considerations are also inseparable, being different sides of the same coin.

Once multiperson firms exist, conflict of employers with employees and rivalry between different firms sustain the motive to further profits. Expansion and growth by firms is the means of achieving this, particularly given uncertainty. The need by firms to overcome constraints to expansion arising from the product, labor and capital markets as well as technology and organizational-managerial constraints, can help us explain the evolution of capitalist firms. These issues are treated in detail elsewhere (see Pitelis, 1991a).

In concluding, it would appear to be ill-advisable to focus on efficiency aspects alone of the firms evolution, as transaction costs theorists invariable do, or power considerations alone, as Marglin and the 'power school' do. Reality is far more complex than unidimensional theories would have us believe. This raises doubts on the policy implication of the Coase-Williamson scenario, which is one of minimal state intervention in market economies, given the alleged ability of the private sector (price mechanism and firms) to solve its own problems. It also casts doubt on any naive anti-monopolies rhetoric. Chapters 18 to 20 deal with a number of 'modern' policy issues that may indeed require governmental intervention.

References

Alchian, A. and H. Demsetz (1972) 'Production, Information Costs, and Economic Organization', *American Economic Review* **62**, 777-795.

Aoki, M., B. Gustafsson and O.E. Williamson, O.E. (1990) *The Firm as a Nexus of Treaties*, London: Sage.

Auerbach, P. (1988) *Competition: The Economics of Industrial Change*, Oxford: Basil Blackwell.

Baran, P. and P. Sweezy (1966) *Monopoly Capital*, London: Pelican Books.

Baumol, W.J. (1982) 'Contestable Markets: An Uprising in the Theory of Industry Structure', *American Economic Review* **72**, 1-15.

Braverman, H. (1974) *Labour and Monopoly Capital: The Organisation of Work in the Twentieth*

Century, New York: Monthly Review Press.

Brown, W.B. (1984) 'Firm Like Behaviour in Markets: The Administered Channel', *International Journal of Industrial Organisation* **2**.

Chandler, A.D. (1962) *Strategy and Structure*, Cambridge, MA: MIT Press.

Chandler, A.D. (1977) *The Visible Hand: The Managerial Revolution in American Business*, Cambridge, MA: Harvard University Press.

Chandler, A.D. (1986) 'Technological and Organisational Underpinnings of Modern Industrial Multinational Enterprise: The Dynamics of Competitive Advantage', in A. Teichova, M. Levy-Leboyer and H. Nussbaum (eds), *Multinational Enterprise in Historical Perspective*, Cambridge: Cambridge University Press, 30-54.

Clarke, R. (1987) 'Conglomerate Firms', in R. Clarke and T. McGuinness (eds), *The Economics of the Firm*, Oxford: Basil Blackwell, 107-131.

Clarke, R. and T. McGuinness (1987) *The Economics of the Firm*, Oxford: Basil Blackwell.

Clegg, S. (1990) *Modern Organizations*, London: Sage.

Coase, R.H. (1937) 'The Nature of the Firm', *Economica* **4**, 386-405.

Coase, R.H. (1960) 'The Problem of Social Cost', *Journal of Law and Economics* **3**, 1-44.

Coase, R.H. (1960) 'The Nature of the Firm. Meaning, and the Nature of the Firm: Influence', in O.E. Williamson and S.G. Winter (eds), *The Nature of the Firm: Origins, Evolution and Development*, Oxford: Oxford University Press.

Cowling, K. and R. Sugden (1987) *Transnational Monopoly Capitalism*, Sussex: Wheatsheaf.

Cullis, J. and P. Jones (1987) *Microeconomics and the Public Economy: In Defence of Leviathan*, Oxford: Basil Blackwell.

Davies, S. (1987) 'Vertical Integration', in R. Clarke and T. McGuinness (eds), *The Economics of the Firm*, London: Basill Blackwell, 88-106.

Davis, L. and D. North (1971) *Institutional Change and American Economic Growth*, Cambridge: Cambridge University Press.

Demsetz (1988) 'The Theory of the Firm Revisited', in *Ownership, Control and the Firm: The Organization of Economic Activity* **1**, Oxford: Basil Blackwell.

Dobb, M. (1973) *Theories of Value and Distribution since Adam Smith*, Cambridge: Cambridge University Press.

Donaldson, L. (1990) 'A Rational Basis for Criticism of Organisational Economics: A Reply of Barney', *Academy of Management Review* **15**, 394-401.

Dow, G.K. (1987) 'The Function of Authority in Transaction Cost Economics', *Journal of Economic Behavior and Organization* **8**, 13-38.

Dugger, J. (1993) 'Transaction Costs Economics and the State', in C.N. Pitelis (ed.), *Transaction Costs, Markets and Hierarchies*, Oxford: Basill Blackwell, forthcoming.

Dunning, J. and A. Rugman (1985) 'The Influence of Hymer's Dissertation on Theory of Foreign Direct Investment', *American Economic Review* **75**, 228-39.

Edwards, R.C. (1979) *Contested Terrain: The Transformation of the Workplace in the Twentieth Century*, New York: Basic Books.

Eggertson, T. (1991) *Economic Behaviour and Institutions*, Cambridge: Cambridge University Press.

Eichner, A.S. (1976) *The Megacorp and Oligopoly*, Cambridge: Cambridge University Press.

Fourie, F.C.V.N. (1989) 'The Nature of Firms and Markets: Do Transaction Approaches Help?', *South African Journal of Economics* **157**, 142-160.

Francis, A., J. Turk and P. Willman (eds) (1983) *Power, Efficiency and Institutions*, London: Heinemann.

Friedman, M. and R. Friedman (1980) *Free to Choose*, London: Seiker and Warburg.

Galbraith, J.K. (1987) *A History of Economics: The Past as the Present*, London: Penguin Books.

Galbraith, J.K. and N.M. Kay (1986) 'Towards a Theory of Multinational Enterprise', *Journal of Economic Behavior and Organization* **7**, 1-19.

Green, D.G. (1987) *The New Right*, Sussex: Wheatsheaf.

Green, F. (1982) 'Occupational Pension Schemes and British Capitalism', *Cambridge Journal of Economics*, **6**.

Hayek, F.A. (1978) *New Studies in Philosophy, Politics and the History of Ideas*, London: Routledge and Kegan Paul.

Hodgson, G. (1988) *Economics and Institutions: A Manifest for Modern Institutional Economics*, Oxford: Polity Press.

Hodgson, G. (1989) 'Institutional Economic Theory: The Old Versus the New', *Review of Political*

Economy **1**, 249-69.

Hodgson, G. (1993) 'Transaction Costs and the Evolution of the Firm', in C.N. Pitelis (ed.) *Transaction Costs, Markets and Hierarchies*, Oxford: Basil Blackwell, forthcoming.

Hymer, S. (1971/1979) 'The Multinational Corporation and the International Division of Labour', in R.B. Cohen, N. Felton, J. van Liere and M. Nkosi (eds), *The Multinational Corporation: A Radical Approach*, 1979, Cambridge: Cambridge University Press.

Hymer, S.H. (1976) *The International Operations of National Firms: A Study of Foreign Direct Investment*, Cambridge, MA: MIT Press.

Hymer, S. and S.A. Resnick (1970) 'International Trade and Uneven Development', in R.B. Cohen, N. Felton, J. van Liere and M. Nkosi (eds) *The Multinational Corporation: A Radical Approach, Papers by Stephen Herbert Hymer*, 1979, Cambridge: Cambridge University Press.

Imai, K. and H. Itami (1984) 'Interpenetration of Organisation and Market. Japan's Firm and Market in Comparison with the US', *International Journal of Industrial Organisation* **2**.

Kalecki, M. (1971) *Dynamics of the Capitalist Economy*, Cambridge: Cambridge University Press.

Kay, N.M. (1992) 'Markets, False Hierarchies and the Evolution of the Modern Corporation', *Journal of Economic Behavior and Organization* **17**, 315-33.

Landes, D.S. (ed.) (1966) *The Rise of Capitalism*, New York: MacMillan.

Langlois, N.R. (1987) *Economics as a Process: Essays in the New Institutional Economics*, Cambridge: Cambridge University Press.

Loasby, J.B. (1990) 'The Firm', in J. Gosby (ed.), *Foundations of Economic Thought*, Oxford: Basil Blackwell.

Malcolmson, J.M. (1982) 'Trade Unions and Economic Efficiency', *Economic Journal: Conference Papers Supplement*.

Malcolmson, J.M. (1984) 'Efficient Labour Organisation: Incentives, Power and the Transaction Costs Approach', in F. Stephen (ed.), *Firm Organizations and Labour*, London: MacMillan.

Marginson, P. (1985) 'The Multidivisional Firm and Control over the Work Process', *International Journal of Industrial Organization* **3**.

Marglin, S. (1974) 'What do Bosses do? The Origins and Functions of Hierarchy in Capitalist Production', *Review of Radical Political Economics*.

Marglin, S.A. (1983) 'Knowledge and Power', in F.H. Stephen (ed.), *Firms Organisations and Labour: Approaches to the Economics of Work Organisation*, London: MacMillan.

Marglin, S.A. (1984) *Growth Distribution and Prices*, Cambridge, MA: Harvard Economic Studies **55**.

Marris, R. and D.C. Mueller (1980) 'The Corporation, Competition and the Invisible Hand', *Journal of Economic Literature* **77**.

Marx, K. (1954) *Capital* **I**, London: Lawrence and Wishart.

Marx, K. (1954) *Capital* **III**, London: Lawrence and Wishart.

Marx, K. (1973) *Grundrisse*, London: Penguin Books.

McGuinness, T. (1987) 'Markets and Managerial Hierarchies', in R. Clarke and T. McGuinness (eds), *The Economics of the Firm*, London: Basil Blackwell.

McManus, J.C. 'The Theory of the Multinational Firm', in G. Paquet (ed.), *The Multinational Firm and National State*, New York: Collier-MacMillan.

North, D.C. (1981) *Structure and Change in Economic History*, New York: Norton.

Ouchi, W. (1981) *Theory Z*, Reading, MA: Addison-Wesley.

Penrose, T.E. (1959) *The Theory of the Growth of the Firm*, Oxford: Basil Blackwell.

Picot, A. and F. Wegner (1988) 'The Employment Relation from the Transaction Cost Perspective', in G. Duglos, W. Dorow and U. Weismair (eds), *Management Under Differing Labour Markets and Employment Systems*, Berlin: Walter de Gruyter.

Pitelis, C.N. (1985) 'The Effects to Life Assurance and Pension Funds on Other Savings: The Post War UK Experience', *Bulletin of Economic Research*.

Pitelis, C.N. (1987) *Corporate Capital: Control Ownership, Saving and Crisis*, Cambridge: Cambridge University Press.

Pitelis, C.N. (1987a) 'Internationalisation and the Transnational Corporation: A Critique', Unpublished manuscript, Cambridge: University of Cambridge.

Pitelis, C.N. (1987b) 'On the Existence of the State', Unpublished manuscript, Cambridge: University of Cambridge.

Pitelis, C.N. (1990) 'Neoclassical Models of Industrial Organisation', in B. Dankbaar, J. Groenewegen and H. Schenk (eds), *Perspectives in Industrial Organisation*, Boston: Kluwer.

Pitelis, C.N. (1991) 'The Transnational Corporation: A Synthesis', *Review of Radical Political Economics.*

Pitelis, C.N. (1991a) *Market and Non-Market Hierarchies*, Oxford: Basil Blackwell.

Pitelis, C.N. (ed.) (1993) *Transaction Costs, Markets and Hierarchies*, Oxford: Basil Blackwell.

Putterman, L. (1986) *The Economic Nature of the Firm: A Reader*, Cambridge: Cambridge University Press.

Reynolds, P.J. (1989) 'Kaleckian and Post-Keynesian Theories of Pricing: Some Extensions and Implications', *Thames Papers in Political Economy*, London: Thames Polytechnic.

Ricketts, M. (1987) *The Economics of Business Enterprise: New Approaches to the Firm*, Sussex: Wheatsheaf.

Rutherford, M. (1989) 'What is Wrong with the New Institutional Economics (and What is Still Wrong with the Old?)', *Review of Political Economy* 1, 299-318.

Scherer, F.M. (1980) *Industrial Market Structure and Economic Performance* (second edition), Chicago: Rand McNally.

Schotter, A. (1981) *The Economic Theory of Social Institutions*, Cambridge: Cambridge University Press.

Schumpeter, J.A. (1942) *Capitalism, Socialism and Democracy* (fifth edition from 1987), London: Unwin Hyman.

Stone, K. (1974) 'The Origins of Job Structures in the Steel Industry', *Review of Radical Political Economics* 6.

Sugden, R. (1983) 'Why Transnational Corporations?', *University of Warwick Economics Research Paper*, Warwick: University of Warwick.

Sweezy, P. (1981) 'Marxist Value Theory and Crises', in I. Steedman (ed.), *The Value Theory Controversy*, Verso.

Teece (1980) 'Economics of Scope and the Scope of the Enterprise', *Journal of Economic Behavior and Organization* 1, 223-47.

Thompson, G., J. Francis, R. Levacic and J. Mitchell, J. (eds) (1991) *Markets, Hierarchies and Networks*, London: Sage.

Williamson, O.E. (1963) 'Managerial Discretion and Business Behaviour', *American Economic Review* 53, 1032-57.

Williamson, O.E. (1967) 'Hierarchical Control and Optimum Firm Size', *Journal of Political Economy* 75, 123-138.

Williamson, O.E. (1975) *Market and Hierarchies*, New York: Free Press.

Williamson, O.E. (1981) 'The Modern Corporation: Origins, Evolution Attributes', *Journal of Economic Literature* 19.

Williamson, O.E. (1985) *The Economic Institutions of Capitalism*, New York: Free Press.

Williamson, O.E. (1986) *Economic Organisation: Firms Markets and Policy Control*, Sussex: Wheatsheaf.

Williamson, O.E. (1990) 'The Firm as a Nexus of Treaties: An Introduction', in M. Aoki, B. Gustafsson and O.E. Williamson (eds), *The Firm as a Nexus of Treaties*, London: Sage, 1-25.

Williamson, O.E. and W.G. Ouchi (1983) 'The Markets and Hierarchies Programme of Research: Origins, Implications, Prospects', in A. Francis, J. Turk and P. Willman (eds), *Power Efficiency and Institutions*, London: Heinemann.

Yamin, Y. and F.I. Nixson (1984) 'Transnational Corporations and the Control of Restrictive Practices: Theoretical Issues and Empirical Evidence', Unpublished manuscript, Trent Polytechnic.

CHAPTER 3

The Maximization Assumption, Profit Maximization and Not-for-Profit Hospitals

DANIEL DENEFFE
The Fuqua School of Business, Duke University, Durham, USA

and

ROBERT T. MASSON
Department of Economics, Uris Hall, Cornell University, Ithaca, USA

Abstract. This chapter reviews two distinct critiques of the maximizing assumption: (i) the world is too complex for firms to understand sufficiently to be able to solve any type of maximizing problem; and (ii) while firms can be viewed as maximizing entities, the object of their maximization problem is not (solely) profits. We argue that these objections often miss the point and that the profit maximization assumption can frequently be justified on methodological grounds. Only when the simplified objective of profit maximization does not yield sufficiently accurate predictive power, is a case made for a more complex multiple objective function. We discuss some empirical evidence that suggests that a multiple objective function, including both profits and patients treated, is necessitated in the analysis of behavior of U.S. not-for-profit hospitals.

I.   Introduction

A vast literature exists that casts doubts on the usefulness of the standard neoclassical assumption that firms are profit (or present value) maximizing institutions [see Scherer and Ross (1990) for a review]. There exist two distinct objections against the assumption of profit maximization. Some critics not only reject the usefulness of the assumption that firms maximize profits but also, and more fundamentally, reject the view that firms in fact maximize some objective function (profits or otherwise) at all. They argue that there exists too much uncertainty in the world, that the world is too complex for a firm to understand sufficiently to be able to solve any type of maximization problem. Other critics do not question the merit of viewing firms as maximizing entities. They do, however, call in question that the object of the maximization problem of the firm is actually profits. The purpose of this paper is to examine critically the usefulness of the maximization assumption *per se* and the profit maximization assumption in particular. We argue that, as soon as one admits that the decision makers in the firm have *some* objective and thus understand some measure of success, the behavior of the firm can always, and tautologically so, be modeled as the solution to a maximization problem. We also argue that the tautological nature of this exercise does not imply its uselessness, but rather that the object of the tautological formulation is to generate novel and falsifiable insights that can often not be generated without solving the maximization problem. While we admit that it is not accurate to assert that the sole objective of a firm is to maximize profits, the profit maximization assumption may still be justifiable on methodological grounds. Each modeling exercise must simplify and abstract to make sense out of the complex world. Suppose now that the assumption of profit maximization generates reasonably accurate predictions that are better than those generated by any other model that assumes a different single objective of the firm. Under these circumstances, it is clearly preferable to assume that firms maximize profits than any other single objective, and it may be preferable to a model that assumes multiple firm objectives since the increased complexity of such model necessarily reduces its predictive power.

For firms in certain industries, there are important reasons to believe that the profit maximization assumption may in fact not be adequate in that it may actually yield incorrect predictions about the behavior of those firms. This is the case for the hospital industry in the United States, which consists primarily of nominally 'not-for-profit' hospitals. A number of single objectives and multiple objectives for the hospital have been proposed in the literature [see Phelps (1992) for a review]. In this paper, we illustrate how the implications of applying the maximization model can help us to distinguish between these competing hypotheses regarding hospital objectives. Our empirical results indicate that for the not-for-profit hospital industry the predictive inadequacy of two assumptions regarding a single hospital objective (profit maximization or output maximization) may require the researcher to construct a model of hospital behavior that assumes multiple hospital objectives. The increased complexity and hence reduced predictive power is necessitated by the inaccuracy of predictions based upon the single objective assumption. This chapter is organized as follows. In Section II we first discuss the methodological advantages of the maximization assumption in relation to the criticism found in the literature. Section III briefly discusses the merits of the assumption that firms typically try to maximize only profits rather than a multitude of objectives. Section IV presents theoretical reasons and empirical evidence suggesting that models based upon the maximization of a single objective may not be appropriate for predicting the behavior of firms in the hospital sector, and Section V concludes.

II.   Do Firms Maximize?

The usual assumption made in economic theory is that consumers maximize utility and firms maximize profit. These assumptions have been challenged on various grounds. We focus here on the objectives of the firm. For our purposes, these criticisms can be categorized in two distinct groups. The first set of criticisms suggests that the object of a firm's maximization problem may in fact not be profits but rather another goal, such as sales maximization or growth maximization, or multiple goals [for a literature review on firm objectives see, *e.g.*, Scherer and Ross (1990)]. A second set of criticisms disputes a more fundamental assumption, namely the assumption that firms are in fact maximizing entities [see, *e.g.*, Nelson (1991) for a review]. The two sets of criticisms are discussed below. We first turn to the critics who reject the value of the maximization assumption itself.

Nelson (1991), for example, believes that it is simply meaningless to presume that firms can calculate an actual 'optimal strategy' because the world is too complex to comprehend. He speculates whether the assumption that 'actors maximize' helps one to analyze situations where some actors are not even aware of a possibility being considered by others. If we start from the postulate that the world is too complex for firms to understand so that they cannot solve a maximization problem, what do firms then do? There are two possibilities. Either firms simply make random choices in each period and continue this process over time, whether or not some choices have proven to be more effective at achieving a particular goal than others. If this is the case, then firms must in fact be viewed as having no objectives. And if firms have no objectives, then learning (from past choices) can, by definition, not take place. If we use the postulate that firms have no objectives, then there is little role left over for the social scientist. For even if the social scientist were to discover a number of strategies that are more successful under certain conditions at achieving *any* goals, the social scientist would not be able to use that information to predict the behavior of firms. The second possibility is that, while firms may initially make random choices, learning takes place over time. This seems to be the prevalent view among evolutionary theorists [see, *e.g.*, Nelson and Winter (1982) and Nelson (1991)]. Although they reject the assumption of the omniscient neoclassical firm, they typically assume that firms which have made choices that prove profitable will tend to stick to this 'strategy' while firms which consistently loose money will have to revise their choices (or exit the market altogether). The critique of evolutionary theorists of the neoclassical model of maximization is at least partly directed against the tremendous informational requirements of this model. Because many factors relevant to economic decision making (demand, cost, *etc.*) are not known with precision, firm strategies are said not be the solution to a maximization problem, but rather the result from a process of gradual learning.

Implicit in the learning process that the firms in evolutionary theory go through is the notion that these firms at least have *some* criterion of success (profits or otherwise) to assess their past actions. We argue that, as soon as one accepts the postulate that firms attempt to achieve some objective at all (this objective may be 'managerial', such as minimizing effort of top management given a profit constraint), the firm is in fact solving a maximization problem. A 'firm' (or its management) attempting to achieve an objective under uncertainty is best modeled as in fact solving a maximization problem where the economic agent attaches subjective probabilities to uncertain events. Even the behavior of the firms in evolutionary theory can be framed as the solution to a maximization problem. The tremendous informational problems that evolutionary theorists stress may in some cases even make random choices initially the optimal solution to these firms' problem (in other words, there are many solutions to the maximization problem given the information environment). Similarly, the typical non-maximizing models of 'satisficing' behavior (*e.g.*, Simon, 1959) *can* be represented as the solution to a maximization problem (in this case a constrained minimization effort). Here the managers of the firm for instance minimize effort (or attempt to achieve a combination of other goals) subject to achieving a 'satisfactory' rate of return.

Critics will argue that casting each firm's strategy as resulting from the solution to a maximization problem eventually becomes a useless tautological exercise. What is the benefit of 'restating' the problem of a firm where managers, for example, care about personal prestige and power, given some minimum profit constraint, as a maximization problem with some measure of prestige and power (growth or sales?) as its goal and minimum profits as its constraint? We agree that the restatement is inherently tautological. We do, however, claim that the objection against the tautological reformulation misses the point of formulating the firm's problem in such fashion. The goal of the tautological maximization exercise is to derive novel insights that are falsifiable and that could only in principle have been derived without the mathematical (or graphical) maximization problem. An analogy with the analysis of consumer behavior will clarify our point. Almost every observed aspect of consumer behavior can be 'explained' using utility theory. Suppose one were to observe a number of individuals who withdraw money from the bank, put it in their wallet and then empty their wallet in your mailbox. Economists could easily 'explain' this phenomenon. One possible and clearly tautological explanation is that these benevolent individuals' utility functions have 'giving money to you' as an argument (or, presumably more sophisticatedly, that these individuals' utility functions include your 'normal' utility function as an argument). The solution to the maximization problem of these individuals can then easily generate the observed phenomenon.

The example has naturally been chosen to illustrate the lack of explanatory power of utility theory, seen in this way. Inserting giving money to you in the utility function of these individuals and then 'deriving' the fact that people will in fact drop money in your mailbox does not 'explain' anything. It simply restates what one already knows. This lack of explanatory power is a criticism against utility theory that can often be heard in circles outside the field of economics. This criticism misses the point. The goal of utility theory is not to restate the obvious, although in many situations that is in fact what is taking place. The boredom of many undergraduate economics students when going through the chapters of consumer behavior may partially be attributed to the fact that little or none of the 'utility theory' in fact helps them understand something that they did not already know. That consumers who like apples and oranges will buy more oranges and fewer apples if the price of apples increases, does not exactly come as a major surprise and is thus not 'explained' by the formulation of the consumer's problem as a choice between apples and oranges when faced with a budget constraint.

Utility theory in fact only has value when it manages to explain more than the things that one can easily explain without the graphical or mathematical formulation. Its value becomes apparent when the mathematical solution (or its graphical equivalent) to 'the problem of the consumer' generates insights that are initially less intuitive or at least unforseen. Mathematically deriving the labor supply curve of workers whose utility function includes income and leisure reveals that a point may be reached where increases in the wage rate may induce the worker to work less. If this is actually the case, then a theoretical justification has been found for raising taxes at higher levels of wages in order to raise the total numbers of hours worked in the economy. It is not clear that the *possibility* of this policy implication could have been conceived without the formal theoretical setup. Even though this example is still very simple, it illustrates how the methodology of formulating the worker's problem of deciding between how much to work and how much leisure to 'buy' at various wage rates generates an insight that would most likely not have been attained as easily (and certainly not as verifiably) without the graphical or, even more pronouncedly so, the mathematical formulation. That workers who care about income and leisure maximize a utility function that includes income and leisure subject to a constraint is tautological and, in itself, indeed useless. But the fact that the analysis of the maximization of such utility function allows us to understand why a particular phenomenon can exist is certainly not. This is especially the case if such revelation could perhaps not have occurred without the formulation of the worker's problem as a maximization issue. Also, this formulation of the worker's problem generates a prediction about the labor supply curve that is, at least in principle, falsifiable.

The same methodological reasons exist for formulating the maximization problem of the firm, independent of the firm's objective or the informational specifications in the problem. The value of formulating the firm's problem in this fashion lies precisely in discovering the hidden implications of this tautological formulation, not in the formulation itself. Whatever the objective of the firm and the information set that is available to the firm's decision makers, the problem of the firm can always be cast as a maximization problem. The objective of economists interested in firm behavior is to understand the complex reality of the business firm and to make predictions about how firms will react in response to various institutional shocks. The goal of the maximization exercise is to yield new insights and to generate precise predictions (not necessarily one optimal solution) that are inherently falsifiable. Without such falsifiable predictions, no progress in our understanding of firm behavior can be made. The reason for even formulating 'non-maximizing' satisficing behavior as the solution to a maximization problem is that without such formulation no new insights or falsifiable predictions about firm behavior (or even a broad set of predictions) can ever be made. And without such falsifiable predictions the theory cannot, even in principle, be disproved and is thus inherently unscientific [see Camerer (1985) and Saloner (1991)].

III.   What Do Firms Maximize?

A second category of criticisms does not dispute the fact that firms maximize some objective function. Critics do, however, contest the notion that the objective of the firm is to maximize profits as opposed to some other goal or multiple goals [see Scherer and Ross (1990) for a review of alternative goals]. Managers may pursue different goals because (i) the shareholders whose interests managers supposedly represent simply may not have sufficient information to scrutinize the optimality of managerial actions in view of the maximization of company profits or (ii) even assuming that shareholders realize that managers do not fully act in the stockholders' interests, stockholders do not have the ability to impose perfectly operating restraints on managerial behavior [for instance, because of managerial control over the board of directors (see, *e.g.*, Masson and Madhavan (1991)]. Others argue that the informational assumptions made in the theory of the firm found in microeconomic textbooks may be too unrealistic to be useful. We already argued that if this is the case, then methodological requirements ask for a reformulation of the problem as a different, in this case more complex, maximization problem. When uncertainty is introduced into the analysis, the standard assumption is that managerial expectations are rational. Managers are assumed to know the distribution of the random variable of interest and then maximize mathematical expected profits. Critics object to this assumption, because managers may not even be able to formulate the mathematical expected value of profits (*e.g.*, Teece, 1985: 41). While the assumption of rational expectations appears to be quite strong, the question is whether, on average, models based upon rational expectations have a better predictive power than those based upon a different type of expectation formation. As Camerer (1985) has pointed out, assuming that expectations are rational is in fact an extremely *humble* assumption on the part of the researcher: assuming that managers, for example, systematically overestimate or underestimate the expected value of a particular variable of interest seems to give to little credit to the intelligence of the modern manager.

In principle, however, no methodological problem exists in assuming that expectations are not rational or that firms maximize something other than profits. And if models in which firms in fact maximize a utility function that includes, say, the (non-mathematical) expectation of two-period returns, managerial comfort and 'consistency with company tradition' generate better predictions than models based upon profit maximization, then the time has come to switch to such models as our building block to make new falsifiable predictions. The complexity of the world, however, requires the social scientist to simplify and abstract. Given this requirement, the profit maximizing model has been found to be at least a good first approximation in describing business behavior as it has better predictive power than any of the other models that assume a single firm objective (such as sales maximization, growth maximization, *etc.*). While deviations from profit maximization certainly occur, these are more or less kept within reasonable bounds. While many economists would agree that managers also pursue other objectives, these are typically not introduced into the model because of the requirement to simplify the real-world situation. Introducing these additional objectives into the model reduces its predictive power, in the sense that fewer unambiguous predictions can be derived. Given the requirement to simplify and given the fact that the simplified model generates sufficiently accurate predictive power, the removal of these other objectives from the model is typically considered as not strongly distorting reality.

IV. The U.S. Hospital Sector: An Important Deviation from Profit Maximization?

1. THEORETICAL CONSIDERATIONS

For the U.S. hospital industry, there exist reasons to believe that hospitals have other *important* objectives (besides or in place of profits) so that a model that assumes that the hospital is a profit maximizing institution may not have any reasonable predictive power. For one thing, most U.S. hospitals are at least nominally not-for-profit institutions. A theoretical explanation for the existence of the not-for-profit hospital sector is that because of the extreme degree of asymmetric information and the degree of risk aversion on the part of the patients, these patients would rather deal with hospital administrators whom they believe are not acting solely to maximize profits (Rose-Ackerman, 1986; Institute of Medicine, 1986; and Yoder, 1986). If hospitals do not solely maximize profits, what other objectives may they have? Some authors (*e.g.*, Newhouse, 1970) argue that not-for-profit hospitals maximize a utility function that does not even include profits but two other arguments, the quantity and the quality of treatment. Such a maximand is posited from considering the self-interest of the administrators or trustees, but it is also consistent with other motivations (*e.g.*, a pure altruistic desire to serve society). It does, however, not immediately follow from the fact that the law prohibits not-for-profit hospitals from distributing profits to residual claimants that hospitals are in all cases acting solely to maximize social surplus. Some (*e.g.*, the U.S. Department of Justice) have argued that not-for-profit hospitals are in fact for-profit institutions in disguise. For one thing, there is anecdotal evidence that most states make little or no effort to enforce the prohibition on distribution of profits (Hansmann, 1986). In addition, the existence of tax breaks for not-for-profit institutions makes the not-for-profit status very attractive. Still others (Dranove, 1988) have argued that hospitals may have an objective function that includes both profits and the quantity and quality of services provided.

Given the dispute about the objective function of the hospital, the enforcement of policies that treat hospitals as any other product or service firm may well reduce rather than, as intended, increase societal welfare. As an example, the Department of Justice has blocked hospital mergers using the same criteria that it employs to block mergers between, say, two airline companies. If hospitals are, in fact, truly social welfare maximizing institutions, then mergers between two hospitals will not result in higher prices (keeping quality constant) and fewer admissions. Rather, any possible synergies between the two merging hospitals may then be passed on to the patients in the form of lower prices and increased admissions. In that scenario, prohibiting the merger would reduce societal welfare. To the contrary, if one were to observe that hospital behavior is consistent with profit maximizing behavior, then, clearly, no economic rationale exists for granting hospitals certain tax and other privileges. Given that the welfare and distributional effects of health policies crucially depend on the hospital's objective function, and considering the importance of the health sector in the United States (14% of GNP), a better understanding of the hospital's objectives is imperative.

Here, again, the methodological advantages of formally modeling hospital behavior as the solution to a maximization problem become apparent. By formulating the hospital's maximization problem in such a way that it contains a number of objective functions as a special case, precise and empirically falsifiable implications of each of these subproblems can be generated. These falsifiable predictions can then be tested against the data and allow us to delve into the 'meta-problem' of choosing the most appropriate objective function to analyze hospital behavior. Once an adequate objective function with reasonable predictive power is obtained, that objective function itself can then be used to make further falsifiable predictions about the behavior of hospitals when subject to various policy changes. While our results are not entirely conclusive, they at least indicate that there is no empirical foundation for the policy recommendations of either the adherents of the view that the U.S. not-for-profit hospitals solely maximize social welfare or of the skeptics who believe in the profit maximizing objective alone. Our results do indicate that models based upon these single hospital objectives do not generate sufficiently accurate predictive power. The results suggest that a case can be made for analyzing the hospital as an institution that maximizes multiple objectives, despite the increased complexity of such models.

2.   EMPIRICAL METHODOLOGY

The essence of our framework is to consider an objective function in which the hospital derives utility from both profit and output.[1] This allows us to test two polar null hypotheses about the hospital's objective function. The first hypothesis is that only output is maximized, subject to breaking even, as an approximation of second-best social surplus maximization [as in Dranove (1988)], we do not have data on the quality of care]. The second hypothesis is that only profits are maximized. Hospitals treat patients in four different categories: private, Medicare, Medicaid, and charity. We assume that prices (the reimbursement that the hospital receives for treating a particular patient) and the number of patients are exogenously determined for Medicare, Medicaid and charity patients (with the 'price' charged to charity patients being equal to zero). The demand curve for private patients is assumed to be downward sloping. In this theoretical discussion, we assume that all patients require the same treatment. We assume that hospitals do not ration government patients [as in Dranove (1988)]. This is certainly optimal when reimbursement exceeds marginal cost if the hospital obtains utility either from profits, from the quantity of patients treated or from both. As a general matter, this is the case for Medicare patients. The Medicaid patient reimbursement for a particular procedure is typically lower than the Medicare reimbursement, and thus closer to (or perhaps even lower than) marginal cost.

For patients for whom reimbursement is obviously below marginal cost, charity patients, it is reasonable to believe that a systematic refusal to admit these patients may lead a hospital to loose their not-for-profit status. While

---

[1]We briefly sketch our methodology here. Details of the analysis can be found in Deneffe and Masson (1993).

hospitals may reduce their admissions of charity patients if economic conditions deteriorate, one does expect that the hospital's not-for-profit status considerably limits the amount of patient dumping. A 1982 national survey (which includes for-profit hospitals) provides some evidence of the relative insignificance of the phenomenon: only 4% of uninsured patients reported that they had been refused care for financial reasons (Robert Wood Johnson Foundation, 1983). As long as the exogenous variation in charity is sufficiently large relative to the endogenous variation, the assumption of exogeneity may be sufficient for empirical implementation. The same reasoning applies regarding the possible endogenous variation in Medicaid and Medicare patients. (This is essentially the logic of the Hausman test, but we have insufficient data to directly test this assumption.) We also assume that the marginal cost of treatment is non-decreasing. Given these assumptions, we can test our polar hypotheses by analyzing the effects of increases in the number of Medicare, Medicaid and charity patients on the price charged to private patients. These effects are different when the hospital is an output maximizer than when it is a profit maximizing institution. These effects are discussed below for the two polar cases.

(i) The output maximizing hospital

We first assume that the maximum profit that the hospital *can* obtain is positive (*i.e.*, the hospital is not forced to operate at a loss). How does an increase in the number of Medicare patients, keeping everything else constant, affect the hospital's price charged to private patients if the hospital's objective is to maximize the number of patients treated subject to breaking even? As the Medicare price typically exceeds the marginal cost of treatment, an increase in Medicare patients generates a positive incremental profit. Thus, the hospital can obtain a higher level of utility by admitting more private patients through a reduction in its private price and still break even. As far as increased Medicaid admissions are concerned, these typically generate a smaller incremental profit (and perhaps even an incremental loss as the Medicaid price does in fact not cover the marginal cost of care) than an equivalent increase in the number of Medicare patients. Thus, if hospitals strive to maximize output but need to break even, they will not decrease the private price as much in response to an increase in the number of Medicaid as in response to an equal increase in the number of Medicare patients. In fact, the hospital may even raise its price in response to increases in Medicaid admissions. This is the case if it turns out that the Medicaid price does not cover the marginal cost of treatment. Finally, more charity patients always generate incremental losses so that the hospital will always increase its private price when admitting more charity patients in order to recoup those losses.

(ii) The profit maximizing hospital

Admitting more non-private patients may affect the profit maximizing hospital's private price only through its effect on the hospital's marginal cost. If this marginal cost function is constant, then admitting more Medicare, Medicaid or charity patients does not affect the hospital's profit maximizing price charged to private patients. If, to the contrary, the hospital's marginal cost function is rising, then more non-private patients increase the hospital's marginal cost of treating all patients. Analogously to the behavior of a price-discriminating monopolist, the hospital will raise its private price in order to equate marginal revenue from privates to the marginal cost of treating all patients. More importantly, if it can reasonably be assumed that Medicare, Medicaid or charity patients do not require a different amount of hospital resources, then the change in private price in response to an increase in Medicare, Medicaid and charity patients should not depend on the type of non-private patient that is admitted.

3.   RESULTS

We obtained information on 72 not-for-profit hospitals in the state of Virginia, during the period 1986-1987.[2] The specific details of the estimation procedure and the results can be found in Deneffe and Masson (1993).[3] Here, we limit ourselves to the presentation of a summary of the qualitative findings.

Result 1:   Hospitals raise the private price in response to an increase in the number of Medicare patients.

Result 2:   Hospitals raise the private price in response to an increase in the number of charity patients.[4]

Result 3:   Increases in the number of Medicaid patients do not have a statistically significant effect on the private price.

Result 4:   The positive effect of increases in charity patients on the private price is about three times as large as the effect of increases in Medicare patients.

Result 1 allows us to clearly reject the hypothesis that hospitals are output maximizing institutions. Under this hypothesis, an increase in the number of Medicare patients should decrease the private price. We observe the opposite. While results 1 an 2 are consistent with a hospital that maximizes profits and faces an upward sloping marginal cost curve, results 3 and 4 clearly are not. That the effect of an additional charity patient is about three times as large as the effect of an additional Medicare patient is only consistent with profit maximizing behavior if the resource use per charity patient is about three times as large as the resource use per Medicare patient. This clearly seems implausible. We refer the reader to Deneffe and Masson (1993) for the derivations, and note here that it can be shown that these results are much easier to reconcile with a hospital maximizing a utility function that includes both profits and the number of patients treated in each category than with any of the two polar hypotheses above. That is, the restrictions on this utility function that would

---

[2]The data come from an Area Resource File, the Virginia Health Services Cost Review Council, the AHA Annual Survey of Hospitals, and the HCFA Federal Register.

[3]For the estimation, we actually did not have data on the private price but obtained the results using a latent variable estimation technique. Also, in the regressions we looked at the effect of the number of, say, Medicare *patient days* on the private price *per patient day*.

[4]The Medicare effect (result 1) is significant at the 5% level in a two-tailed test. The charity effect is significant at the 1% level.

generate the above results are fairly reasonable.

In the context of the issues discussed in this paper, it is important to mention that the revelation of the consistency of our results with such a restricted utility function is, in itself, a powerful example of the importance of formally modeling the behavior of the hospital as maximizing a utility function including profits and patients treated. Without the relatively complex mathematical derivation of the anticipated effects on the private price of variations in the number of patients in various categories and the emergence of unforeseen effects from the derivation, it would have been very difficult, if not impossible, to reconcile these data with a hospital trying to achieve a (weighted) average of two objectives. Our results are, however, only tentative, and much more work is needed to get a better understanding of hospital objectives.

V.   Conclusions

The literature has questioned the profit maximizing assumption on essentially two grounds. First, the appropriateness of the maximization assumption itself for analyzing firm behavior has been challenged. We have argued that the maximization assumption can be justified on methodological grounds: as long as the decision makers in the firm have *any* objective, then the problem that management faces in trying to attain that objective can always be cast as a constrained or unconstrained maximization problem. The tautological nature of this formulation does not make this exercise useless, since it is not the formulation itself that is important. The value of the exercise is that from the solution to the maximization problem unforeseen and often initially less intuitive insights can be derived regarding the behavior of firms, and that these results can be cast as empirically refutable hypotheses. The second criticism against the profit maximizing assumption is directed toward the object of the maximization problem. The objective of the firm may not be to maximize profits but rather to obtain some other goal. An extensive literature suggesting alternative analytical frameworks has emerged. While each of the alternative specifications captures an element of the complex reality of business behavior, it is the predictive superiority of the profit maximization model over these alternative simple formulations that makes it most appealing for the analysis of business behavior in most industries. In certain institutional settings, the assumption of profit maximization is, however, even more questionable. Profit maximization may, for example, not be appropriate for customer-owned cooperatives, where the objective of the firm is to serve the interests of the co-op members. Nominally non-profit institutions may also have important different objectives. Adhering to the profit maximizing model does, however, not mean that one rejects the existence of other firm objectives. Rather, if these other objectives are considered relatively unimportant compared to the profit objective, then simplification is preferred. If, however, these other objectives are in fact important (instead or in addition to the profit objective), then the simple profit maximizing model may yield qualitatively incorrect predictions and thus may be inherently useless.

Many have argued that decision makers in U.S. not-for-profit hospitals may have other objectives. While a useful model requires simplification and abstraction, the evidence that we presented suggests that the assumption of a single objective (output or profit maximization) may be too strong a deviation from reality to be useful in predicting hospital behavior. As Milgrom and Roberts (1992) point out, "not-for-profit organizations have no owners in the usual sense. In such circumstances, predicting organizational form and behavior requires careful analysis of who has the power to design the organization, who can make decisions, and who can influence these decisions and their implementation". From a modeling perspective, the complex institutional reality of this institution (the existence of multiple stakeholders) may necessitate a formulation that includes multiple and sometimes internally conflicting hospital objectives. The reduced predictive unambiguity resulting from such formulation is then not due to improper modeling, but due to the real-world complexity of this institution. The bottom line is that the case of U.S. hospitals confirms our argument that a flexible application of the maximization principle is a fruitful research strategy. Many of the chapters below reflect other examples of this observation.

References

Camerer, C. (1985) 'Thinking Economically about Strategy', in J.M. Pennings and Associates (eds), *Organizational Strategy and Change*, San Francisco: Jossey-Bass Publishers, 64-75.

Deneffe, D. and R.T. Masson (1993) 'What Do Hospitals Maximize?', *Working Paper*, The Fuqua School of Business, Duke University.

Dranove, D. (1988) 'Pricing by Non-Profit Institutions: The Case of Hospital Cost-Shifting', *Journal of Health Economics* 7, 47-57.

Institute of Medicine (1986) 'Profits and Health Care: An Introduction to the Issues', in B.H. Gray (ed.), *For Profit Enterprise*, Washington DC: National Academic Press, 3-18.

Hansmann, H.B. (1986) 'The Role of Nonprofit Enterprise,' in S. Rose-Ackerman (ed.), *The Economics of Nonprofit Institutions*, New York: Oxford University Press.

Masson, R.T. and A. Madhavan (1991) 'Insider Trading and the Value of the Firm', *Journal of Industrial Economics* 39, 333-354.

Milgrom, P. and J. Roberts (1992) *Economics, Organization and Management*, Englewood Cliffs, NJ: Prentice Hall.

Nelson, R.R. (1991) 'Why Do Firms Differ, and How Does It Matter?', *Strategic Management Journal* 12, 61-74.

Nelson, R.R. and S. Winter (1982) *An Evolutionary Theory of Economic Change*, Cambridge, MA: Harvard University Press.

Newhouse, J.P. (1970) 'Toward a Theory of Nonprofit Institutions: An Economic Model of a Hospital', *American Economic Review* 60, 64-74.

Phelps, C.E. (1992) *Health Economics*, New York: Harper Collins.

Robert Wood Johnson Foundation (1983) *Updated Report on Access to Health Care for the American People*, New Jersey: The Robert Wood Johnson Foundation.

Rose-Ackerman, S. (1986) *The Economics of Nonprofit Institutions*, New York: Oxford University Press.

Saloner, G. (1991) 'Modeling, Game Theory, and Strategic Management', *Strategic Management Journal* 12, 119-136.

Scherer, F. M. and D. Ross (1990) *Industrial Market Structure and Economic Performance*, Boston: Houghton Mifflin Company.

Simon, H. (1959) 'Theories of Decision-Making in Economics and Behavioral Sciences', *American Economic Review* 49, 253-283.

Teece, D.J. (1985) 'Applying Concepts of Economic Analysis to Strategic Management', in J.M. Pennings and Associates (eds), *Organizational Strategy and Change*, San Francisco: Jossey-Bass Publishers, 64-75.

Yoder, S.G. (1986) 'Economic Theories of For-Profit and Not-For-Profit Organizations', in B.H. Gray (ed.), *For Profit Enterprise*, Washington D.C.: National Academic Press, 19-25.

PART II

WITHIN-MARKET COMPETITION

Research and Development, Product Differentiation, Strategic Partnering and Information Sharing

By and large, industrial organization (IO) so far has concentrated on the analysis - either empirically or theoretically - of competition within the context of a single industry or single market. Two old-time themes here are R&D and product differentiation. Chapters 4 and 5 contribute to the well-established literature on R&D and innovation, whereas Chapter 7 compares the competitive impact of differentiation in a Bertrand *versus* Cournot setting. Chapters 6 and 8 apply IO-reasoning and IO-techniques to areas that more recently attracted attention: strategic alliances (Chapter 6) and banking competition (Chapter 8). All five chapters are firmly embedded in modern IO-theory. Additionally, Chapters 4, 5 and 8 respond to the cry in the late 1980s and early 1990s for more empirical work to test modern IO-hypotheses.

CHAPTER 4

Should Cooperative R&D Be Subsidized?: An Empirical Analysis

STEFAN FÖLSTER

The Industrial Institute fo Economic and Social Research, Stockholm, Sweden

Abstract. A popular view in the industrial policy debate is that cooperation among firms' R&D departments should be encouraged. This study presents the first empirical test of the effectiveness of such subsidies using a database of competitors in 45 technological races. The results indicate that subsidies that require cooperation in the form of result-sharing agreements increase the likelihood of cooperation significantly, but they decrease incentives to conduct R&D. Subsidy programs such as EUREKA that require cooperation, but do not require result-sharing agreements, do not increase the likelihood of cooperation. They do, however, increase incentives to conduct R&D somewhat, to about the same extent as subsidies not requiring cooperation.

I. Introduction

Private firms have incentives to conduct R&D activities and sometimes to join forces with other researching firms. Firms' incentives to conduct R&D and to cooperate in R&D may, however, be smaller than the socially optimal incentives. A public subsidy to cooperative R&D may then be an effective tool for bringing private incentives, both to conduct R&D and to cooperate, more in line with social incentives. Among proponents of industrial policy this has become a popular argument in recent years. This chapter provides the first empirical test of the argument.

Empirical studies generally find a large gap between private and social returns to industrial R&D.[1] This reflects several potential sources of market failure. R&D spillovers prevent firms from appropriating all the social gains from R&D. Patents seem to have a relatively small effect on limiting spillovers.[2] Even if there are no R&D spillovers, the innovator's inability to price discriminate makes it difficult to appropriate the entire consumer surplus. A number of recent studies investigates whether cooperative R&D can alleviate the problem of R&D spillovers between firms. Katz and Shapiro (1985 and 1987) show that licensing, which they call *ex post* cooperation, may not solve the problem well. Competing firms will not pay for information that spills over anyway. Further, firms may not be able to appropriate all of the surplus due to their inability to price discriminate in selling licenses. Finally, licensing negotiations suffer from opportunism and asymmetric information. It is difficult for the buyer to evaluate the technology before having access to it, and once the buyer has access he may not want to pay for it any longer.

---

[1]Examples of this literature are Bernstein (1989), Bernstein and Nadiri (1991) and Mansfield *et al.* (1977).

[2]A number of empirical studies finds that patents are not very effective at limiting spillovers in many industries. See, *e.g.*, Mansfield *et al.* (1981) and Levin *et al.* (1987).

Agreement to share results can also be made *ex ante* - that is, before the research is conducted. This can take the form of cross-licensing or patent-pooling agreements. Baumol (1990) argues that such arrangements could increase incentives to conduct R&D, because firms that lag behind face the risk of being excluded from the agreement. Other models, however, lead to less sanguine conclusions (Katz 1986; Katz and Ordover, 1990; Ordover and Willig, 1985; and Grossman and Shapiro, 1986). One concern is that such agreements facilitate collusion in downstream markets. Further, firms that are not members of the agreement may be discouraged from competing. In addition, there is a risk that firms that are a part of the agreement reduce their R&D investments, relying instead on access to other firms' results.

Often cross-licensing or patent pooling is used in research joint venture arrangements, where firms also conduct some of the research together. This may economize on R&D costs by internalizing leakage from R&D and avoiding wasteful duplication. An important issue in these arrangements is how background and foreground knowledge is exchanged among cooperating firms (*e.g.*, Ordover, 1991.[3] There is a risk that firms strategically manipulate the flow of *background* knowledge and results from related projects that are not part of the cooperative agreement. Moral hazard may be detrimental to joint venture arrangements in other ways as well. One is that firms may invest less than promised in the common project. This is especially likely when firm researchers are involved both in the cooperative project and in other projects, so that it becomes hard to check how they allocate their time. Alternatively, firms can let their least promising researchers participate in the cooperative project. Evidence for the existence of such moral hazard is the fact that joint venture agreements often are surrounded by extensive legal negotiations. It is not uncommon that firms leave the agreement after a while, dissatisfied with their partners' committment.

Models of R&D cooperation usually compare joint ventures or licensing with no cooperation. This ignores two common alternatives - mergers and information trading - that may better deal with some of the moral hazard problems of joint ventures and licensing. Mergers imply that either two firms merge entirely or parts of each firm are merged into a new firm, which then independently maximizes profits and so avoids moral hazard problems. Information trading means that firms trade intermediary research results, usually on a regular basis. Typically, information trading often seems to occur informally and without the complex legal apparatus of joint ventures. Often the trade occurs between employees of the firms, regardless of whether the firm explicitly consents to the exchange. Several studies have shown that such informal *information trading* between firms is a common phenomenon (Von Hippel, 1987; and Schrader, 1991).

The European Community (now Union) and a number of other countries are now investing extensively in subsidy programs for R&D joint ventures. An important question is therefore whether joint ventures really are a more efficient form of cooperation than information trading and mergers, which firms tend to choose

---

[3]Foreground knowledge refers to results that arise during the course of the cooperative research, while background knowledge is information that is relevant to the cooperative research, but that firms have acquired independently.

when they are not subsidized. The current popularity of promoting joint ventures in the industrial policy debate is to some extent based on alleged Japanese succeses with such arrangements. A much publicized example is the VLSI (Very Large Scale Integrated circuits) research associations, which generated over one thousand patents and involved close cooperation among firms. This research cooperation was, however, the exception rather than the rule. Odagiri (1992), for example, reviews studies showing that it is quite unusual for firms in a research association to cooperate closely. Rather he conjectures that "research associations have been used by MITI primarily as a means to distribute its subsidies, so as to avoid favouring a particular firm and to minimize the cost of supervising the use of subsidies" (Ogadiri, 1992: 298). The normal form of cooperation in these research associations is instead a form of information trading where participants are under no obligation to reveal all their results. The then European Community has embarked on a number of subsidy programs that require a result-sharing agreement among cooperating firms, such as ESPRIT or RACE. In addition, however, there are programs like EUREKA that are financed by each firms' home government. Under EUREKA firms must cooperate with firms from other countries, but they need not choose a result-sharing agreement. Instead, cooperation frequently takes the form of occasional meetings at which firms reveal as much information as they choose. This implies information trading rather than result sharing.

None of these subsidy programs has been subjected to rigorous empirical analysis, however. From an empirical point of view there are three important questions. First, does a subsidy that requires cooperation actually increase the probability of cooperation? Second, does the subsidy increase incentives to conduct R&D? Third, does the increased cooperation that may be induced by the subsidy increase the efficiency of R&D? In this chapter the first and second questions are analyzed using a database of competitors in 45 technological races. Since firms' choice to cooperate, and in which form to cooperate, is an endogenous decision, it is analyzed with a polychotomous self-selection model. The results indicate that subsidy programs that require cooperation but let firms choose (such as EUREKA) how to cooperate, do not increase the likelihood of cooperation. They do however increase incentives to conduct R&D somewhat, to about the same extent as subsidies not requiring cooperation. Subsidies that require cooperation in the form of result-sharing agreements increase the likelihood of cooperation significantly, but they decrease incentives to conduct R&D. This implies that these subsidies can be socially worthwhile only if result sharing has a large effect on the efficiency of the research conducted.

The Section II shows the relation between the different forms of cooperation's effect on incentives to conduct R&D in a very simple theoretical model. Section III describes the econometric model, and Section IV discusses the results. Section V is a conclusion.

II.   The Model

1.   THE FUNDAMENTALS
This section extends a simple model used by Katz and Ordover (1990) to illustrate the effect of subsidizing joint ventures when firms can choose among information-

trading, merger or licensing as alternatives. Assume that two product-market rivals are engaged in a patent race to obtain a discrete innovation. Let e_1 and e_2 denote each firm's R&D investment level, and e the industry vector of effort levels. The expected profit function for firm i is $v_i(e)$, measured net of its expenditures on R&D.

In the patent-race model the firm that first develops the innovation is the winner of the race. The change in the winning firm's profit due to the innovation is denoted W, and L is the change in the losing firm's profit in comparison with no firm winning. Let $p_i(e)$ be firm i's chance of winning the race when the industry vector of R&D levels is e. Then, the change in firm 1's expected profit due to R&D can be written as

(1) $v_1(e) = p_1(e)W + p_2(e)L - e_1.$

Even though this model is labeled a patent race, it is actually more general. W and L can express profits in a technology race even when no patents are granted but there are other advantages of being first.[4]

Even though different forms of R&D cooperation can lead to the same distribution of results, they generate differing incentives to conduct R&D. The incentive to conduct R&D is determined by the derivative of (1) with respect to e_1. That is,

(2) $\dfrac{\partial V_1(e)}{\partial e_1} = \dfrac{\partial p_1(e)}{\partial e_1}W + \dfrac{\partial p_2(e)}{\partial e_1}L - 1.$

A firm's R&D has two types of external effects. One is the effect on other firms' profits. The other is an effect on consumer surplus. Voluntary cooperation among firms at best internalizes the external effect among firms, but not the effect on consumer surplus. For process R&D and most types of product R&D consumer surplus of additional R&D would be positive. Therefore, the aim of a subsidy is generally to increase incentives to conduct R&D by more than merely internalizing the external effects among firms.

The external effect of an increase in firm 1's e_1 on firm 2 can be modeled by assuming a symmetric externality such that for symmetric e

(3) $\dfrac{\partial p_2(e)}{\partial e_1} = s\,\dfrac{\partial p_1(e)}{\partial e_1}\,.$

Moreover, it is assumed that $\partial p_i(e)/\partial e_i > 0$ and $s(e) \in [-1,1]$. The parameter s expresses the purely statistical tradeoff of an increase in one firm's chance of winning reducing the other firm's chance of winning. In addition, however, s depends on the extent of information leakage between firms and the degree of duplication and complementarity in the research approaches. For example, if two

---

[4]Katz and Ordover (1990) also show that a static model, such as in Spence (1984), in which R&D investment leads to some level of R&D capital, can be described as a generalization of a patent race.

firms follow very different research approaches aiming at the same goal, they may have little use for results leaked from the other firms.

When firms actively cooperate in the research process, they share intermediary information and avoid duplication of research. This will increase the spillover effect, but it will not eliminate it fully, since the statistical effect remains implying that one firm's probability of succeeding decreases if the other firm's probability of succeeding increases. When firms cooperate the spillover is, instead,

$$(3') \quad \frac{\partial p_2(e)}{\partial e_1} = c \frac{\partial p_1(e)}{\partial e_1} .$$

Moreover, it is assumed that $c > s$ and $c(e) \epsilon [-1,1]$.

In order to examine incentives to conduct R&D under different cooperation arrangements the terms W and L have to be given some content. Let $w(2)$ be the change in product-market profits per firm when both firms have the innovation compared to the profits in the the absence of any innovation. If only one firms has the innovation, the change in product market profit is denoted with $w(1)$. Let b denote the profit a firm earns in the product market if it does not have the innovation, but the other firm does.

Firms' joint profits may be greater if they *both* have the invention compared to the case where only one does: $2w(2) > w(1) + b$. This situation may correspond to an oligopoly situation, but it need not. It could describe the case of two domestic firms that compete against foreign firms calculating whether or not to cooperate. On the other hand, the case with $2w(2) < w(1) + b$ describes the situation where the winning firm can derive profits from its monopoly position in a way that two competing firms cannot. In the absence of cooperation the firm's incentive to research is

$$(4) \quad \frac{\partial p_1}{\partial e_1}[w(1) + sb] - 1.$$

2.   INFORMATION TRADING

One form of R&D cooperation is information trading. Trading information also allows firms to coordinate research, so that the spillover coefficient increases from s to c. Since the traded information becomes available to both firms, it is assumed that each firm experiences half of the total increase in the probability of succeeding. Each firm can trade information for what it is worth to the other firm, which is the value of the increased chance of winning apart from the fraction that spills over anyway. That is,

$$(5) \quad \frac{1}{2}\left[\frac{\partial p_1}{\partial e_1}+\frac{\partial p_2}{\partial e_1}\right](w(1)+b) + \left[\frac{1}{2}\left[\frac{\partial p_1}{\partial e_1}+\frac{\partial p_2}{\partial e_1}\right](w(1)+b) - \frac{\partial p_1}{\partial e_1}(sw(1)+b)\right].$$

Simplifying this leads to

(6) $\quad \dfrac{\partial p_1}{\partial e_1}[(1 + c - s)w(1) + cb] - 1.$

Here it is assumed that information trading actually implies an equally efficient way of coordinating R&D as a joint venture. If this would not be the case, then in the extreme the spillover parameter with information trading is s rather than c, and it can easily be seen that the incentive to research is the same as without information trading.

3.   JOINT VENTURES AND MERGERS

Much of the previous studies of R&D cooperation do not distinguish between joint ventures and mergers. We will show here that these studies, doing so, ignore an important moral-hazard problem associated with joint ventures but not with mergers.

Katz and Ordover (1990) model the joint venture as an agreement to share costs and technology.[5] In the absence of moral hazard, and assuming that firms do not conduct any independent research, this implies that firms maximize joint profits. Incentives to research are then

(7) $\quad \dfrac{\partial p_1}{\partial e_1} 2(1 + c)w(2) - 1.$

In the absence of moral hazard this gives the same incentives as a merger would provide.

With extreme moral hazard, however, a firm's research effort cannot be observed by the other firm. This can happen in joint ventures where firms have some independent control over their contribution to the R&D cooperation. Each firm then determines its profit-maximizing e, given that both firms get the innovation if one partner succeeds. The incentive to research is

(8) $\quad \dfrac{\partial p_1}{\partial e_1}(1 + c)w(2) - 1.$

Clearly, moral hazard reduces the incentives to research significantly.[6]

---

[5] A theoretical alternative is to let firms only share costs and not technology. Cost sharing does not necessarily imply an equal splitting of costs. Rather, the optimal cost sharing would let firms cross-subsidize each others' R&D expenditures such that the external effects are internalized. The external effect of firm 1 increasing e_1 is, using relation (3), $\partial v_2/\partial e_1 = \partial p_1 \partial e_1 [sw(1) + b]$. Comparing this with (4) shows that cost sharing increases or decreases research incentives depending on whether s is positive or negative.

[6] An additional category could be basic research, where researchers aim at publishing. Then, the firm has also little independent control over researchers and the moral-hazard problem may be less severe.

4.   LICENSING

The last form of cooperation is *ex post* cooperation, or licensing. Assume that the winning firm licenses the innovation to the losing firm for a fixed fee.[7] When bargaining in the licensing market is efficient, licensing leads to the joint profit-maximizing dissemination of technology, so that both firms obtain the innovation. Let F be the fixed fee paid by the licensee to the licensor. Then, $W = w(2) + F$ and $L = w(2) - F$. The incentive to research is then

$$(9) \quad \frac{\partial p_1}{\partial e_1} [(1 + s)w(2) + (1 - s)F] - 1.$$

5.   EFFECTS OF A JOINT VENTURE SUBSIDY

Assume that a subsidy is given that requires firms to cooperate in a joint venture, being just large enough to induce the firm to abandon its chosen form of R&D cooperation and join the joint venture.

   If moral hazard is not a problem and if firms have chosen information trading, then subsidizing joint ventures reduces the incentives to research if and only if

$$(10) \quad (1 + c)(w(1) + b) - (s\,w(1) + b) > 2(1 + c)\,w(2).$$

This condition is fulfilled only if there are significant negative spillovers c and s and if $w(1)$ is large relative to $w(2)$. A joint venture subsidy reduces incentives to research compared to licensing if and only if

$$(11) \quad 2(1 - s)F > 2(1 + c)\,w(2).$$

Suppose that moral hazard is a significant problem for joint ventures. Then, if firms would have chosen a merger in the absence of a joint venture subsidy, comparing (7) and (8) shows that the subsidy clearly reduces incentives to research. The same is true, comparing (8) and (9), if firms without the subsidy would have chosen licensing.

   If firms would have chosen information trading in the absence of a subsidy, the joint venture subsidy decreases incentives to research only if (8) is smaller than (6): that is, if and only if

$$(12) \quad (1 + c)(w(1) + b) - (s\,w(1) + b) > (1 + c)\,w(2).$$

This condition is easily fulfilled under a wide range of conditions, particularly when s is negative and $w(1)$ is large relative to $w(2)$.

   In conclusion, a joint venture subsidy in the absence of moral hazard stands a good chance of increasing incentives to research, especially when spillovers are moderate and $w(2)$ is large relative to $w(1)$. This well reflects findings in the literature. When joint ventures are affected by moral hazard, however, a joint

---

[7]A fixed fee licensing arrangement can be the only feasible one, because information asymmetries make the monitoring necessary to enforce royalties too costly. Kamien and Tauman (1986) analyze licensing with volume-sensitive royalties.

venture subsidy stands a good chance of reducing incentives to research.

III. The Econometric Specification

Firms' choice of the type of cooperation is endogenous. Models with self-selection among two choices have been commonly used (*e.g.*, Heckman, 1974; and Lee, 1978). The problem studied here, however, requires a model of self-selection among polychotomous choices. This model is an extension of the binary choice model. The presentation below follows Maddala's (1983) exposition.

Firms have five choices of how to cooperate with any other firm. These are indexed as follows: 1 = no cooperation; 2 = information trading; 3 = joint venture; 4 = merger; and 5 = licensing. The type of cooperation describes a relationship rather than a property of a firm. Therefore, one should think of an observation as consisting of the relationship between any two firms. The choices of cooperation can be labeled s, where s = 1,2...5. Let any two firms' combined expected profit from cooperation be V_s. Then a polychotomous variable I can be defined such that

(13) $I = s$ iff $V_s > Max V_j$ ($j=1,2,..5 \wedge j \neq s$).

Let e_{si} be the R&D intensity for the i'th firm choosing cooperation of type s: x_s and z_s are vectors of exogenous variables. Then, the polychotomous choice model can be written as

(14) $e_{si} = x_{si}\beta_s + u_{si}$, and $V_{si} = z_{si}\gamma_s + \eta_{si}$ ($i=1,2,...,N$).

The coefficients in this model can be estimated as follows. The first step is to estimate the coefficients of z_s in the choice equation by a multinomial logit model. This model has been widely used, so it will not be discussed in detail here. One point that deserves to be mentioned, however, is that the multinomial logit model is based on the so-called IIA (Independence of Irrelevant Alternatives) assumption. In some contexts this gives the model the unappealing property that the introduction of new alternatives does not affect the probability of current alternatives being chosen. A test for the independence of irrelevant alternatives indicates that in fact the five alternative forms of cooperation do have independent stochastic errors.[8]

A further potential problem is that the type of cooperation a firm chooses depends on which alternative firms it can cooperate with. Although the number of alternative firms and their size distribution are captured in explanatory variables, their individual characteristics are not. This means that the coefficients are

---

[8]Hausman and McFadden (1984) specify a test for the independence of irrelevant alternatives: T = $(q_A - q_C)'[cov(q_A) - cov(q_C)]^t (q_A - q_C)$, with q_B being the parameter vector estimated on a subset of the full choice set q_C found by excluding one of the five alternatives in estimation. The test statistics calculated for each specification and each dichotomous subset of the model indicated that the independence of irrelevant alternatives assumption could not be rejected. In addition, the system was estimated as an ordered probit model, the binary decisions following the sequence cooperation, no licensing, information trading, cost and result sharing, and merger. This yielded coefficient estimates similar to those for multinomial logit model, but the overall fit was somewhat worse.

estimated conditional on the actual distribution of the characteristics of alternative cooperation partners. This does not, however, affect the argument below since the aim here is to estimate the effect of increased subsidies conditional on the existing distribution of alternative cooperation partners.

For the next step in estimating model (14) let

(15) $a_s = \text{Max} V_j - \eta_s \ (j=1,2,..,5 \ \wedge \ j \neq s)$.

It is then assumed that there is a type I extreme-value distribution with a cumulative distribution function such that

(16) $F(\eta_i < c) = \exp(-\exp(-c))$.

Following Domencich and McFadden (1983) this can be transformed into a distribution function for a_s: $F_s(a) = \text{Prob}(a_s < a)$. This is an essential step, since from (17)

(17) $I = s$ iff $a_s < z_s \gamma_s$.

Then, a_s can be transformed into a standard normal random variable a_s^* with $N(0,1)$ such that

(18) $a_s^* = J_s(a_s) = \Phi^{-1}(F_s(a))$.

Finally, an ordinary least squares regression can be estimated for each category s using the equation

(19) $e_s = x_s \beta_s - \sigma_s \rho_s \phi(J_s(z_s \gamma_s))/F_s(z_s \gamma_s) + \epsilon_s$,

where $\sigma_s^2 = \text{Var}(u_s)$ and ρ_s is the correlation coefficient between u_s and a_s. The coefficients of z_s are replaced by the coefficients estimated in the multinomial logit estimation. The model was estimated using the routines for multinomial logit and ordered probit in Gauss.

IV.   Empirical Estimation

1.   DATA

A large part of the data comes from two interview surveys among Swedish industrial firms that were conducted during 1988 and 1990. These surveys are described in Fölster (1991a and 1991b). Those surveys were concerned with determining the effects of government subsidies for industrial R&D and firms' technological competitiveness in relation to foreign competitors. In these surveys individual R&D projects are identified. For each project aimed at developing a specific technology firms have supplied information on R&D investment levels, potential international competitors and which of the latter actually are engaged in similar R&D. Moreover, patterns of R&D cooperation were identified. Often firms are reluctant to reveal such detailed information. Since the surveys were conducted by an institute, the Industrial Institute of Economic and Social Research, with close ties to industries, and as the surveys were carried out as personal telephone calls to managers or research managers, firms were quite open.

The firms were randomly selected among industrial firms that spend at least 5% of their revenue on R&D. Of the contacted firms 9% refused to participate. The remaining firms were asked to pick a representative sample of three R&D projects. Only in 13 cases did firms respond that they could not pick a representative sample, because they did not want to reveal details of a particular R&D project. In sum, the data should represent a reasonably unbiased sample of research-intensive Swedish industrial firms' R&D projects. The Swedish firms could often supply sufficiently detailed information, even about competitors' projects. To be sure, however, the competitors were contacted as well to confirm the information. Among the foreign competitors the reply rate was considerably lower. Of those contacted 46% responded, but not all supplied detailed information. The response of these firms was however sufficient to ascertain that the Swedish firms' information about their competitors was generally accurate.

All in all 45 technologies are included in the sample. A *technology* is narrowly defined, based on the Swedish firm's project definition. Table 1 shows various characteristics of the technologies, the market structure in each of these *races*, and what forms of cooperation existed.

Table 1.   Description of the data: number of technologies in each field, and average number of competitors and cooperative agreements within each technology

Technology type	# of technologies	Average # of competitors	Average # of cooperative agreements
Medical and biotech	7	12.8	1.4
Communications	4	9.6	1.6
Energy	5	8.2	2.1
Environment	4	16.3	3.1
Information	8	8.1	1.7
Lasers	2	14.6	2.0
New Materials	4	5.7	1.3
Robotics	6	21.2	4.1
Transport	5	12.0	3.6

Table 2 shows how many firms were involved in the various cooperative arrangements, and how many received subsidies. In total 540 firms are included. In most cases the cooperation arrangements fall clearly into one of the five categories. There are some borderline cases, however. A few examples should make this clear. Most joint ventures maintain some restrictions on members' access to technology. In programs such as ALVEY, ESPRIT or the MCC, partners are required to license foreground knowledge to each other. The licenses are, however, royalty-free or available at *reasonable* rates. In spite of these restrictions, however, these programs clearly belong to the category of joint ventures. Many joint venture programs distinguish between *partners* that cooperate on a specific project and *participants* consisting of all firms participating in some project under the program. Here only the partners are classified as firms cooperating in a joint venture, since participants usually have no automatic access to foreground knowledge. Some research partners in joint ventures are usually universities or public research institutes. These are not included as independent partners in the analysis below. Instead, they are counted as part of the common research effort. To the extent that the universities' or institutes' participation is publicly funded, this is counted as a subsidy. The category information trading contains both formal information exchange arrangements - such as those resulting from EUREKA - and informal arrangements that arise among researchers in different firms.

Table 2.   Number of firms involved in cooperative agreements and number of firms subsidized, in percentage of firms competing in one technology

	No coop-eration	Licensing	Information trading	Joint Venture	Merger
Number of firms	217	36	189	66	32
Number of firms that receive a subsidy without cooperation requirement	42	13	39	26	12
Number of firms that receive a subsidy that requires some cooperation	0	0	36	9	0
Number of firms that receive a subsidy that requires a joint venture	0	0	0	37	0

As shown in Table 2, only a small number of firms licensed technologies. One likely reason is that most of the projects are not yet completed, even though the majority of projects have already generated results and patents. Thus, the licensing category is probably incomplete. Each observation in the dataset consists of the relationship between two firms. The variables, shown in Table 3, therefore consist of variables for firm 1, firm 2, the relationship between the firms, the market structure, and the technology. All variables except R&D are included in the multinomial logit analysis of the choice of cooperation. The adjusted OLS-regression, however, contains fewer variables. In particular, the variables concerning the relationship between two firms should not affect R&D intensity and are therefore excluded.

Table 3.   The variables

Firm 1

SALES1	The firm's total sales in related technology in U.S. dollars
TECHCOMP1	The firm's technological competence in the technology at the inception of the project as judged by competitors on a scale of 1 - 10
SUB1	Size of unconditional subsidy to the project in percentage of R&D
SUBCOOP1	Size of subsidy that requires a cooperation of choice in percentage of R&D
SUBSHARE	Size of subsidy that requires result-sharing cooperation in percentage of R&D

Firm 2

SALES2, TECHCOMP2, SUB2, SUBCOOP2 defined as for firm 1, though SUBSHARE is not repeated for firm 2 as these subsidies are always given to all participants in the agreement.

Relation between firms

RD	The two firm's combined R&D investment in the technology in U.S. dollars summed over all years since inception of project (including subsidies)
DISTANCE	Geographical distance between R&D locations of firms
COUNTRY	Dummy with value 1 if the firms are situated in the same country
PREVCOOP	Dummy with value 1 if the firms have cooperated previously on R&D
PREVRELATION	Dummy with value 1 if firms have any other relationship
COMPETITION	Degree of competition in terms of percentage of sales of technology type in common market

Market structure

RIVALS	Number of actual competitors
CONCENTRATION	Herfindahl-index of R&D investments, where cooperating groups are treated as equivalents of a single firm
MSHARE	Sales of the firms in the cooperative agreement as a percentage of the total on common markets

Technology

PROCESS	Dummy with value 1 if the technology concerns development of a process technology rather than a product
DUM1 -DUM45	Dummy variables for each of the 45 technologies

2. RESULTS

Table 4 displays the empirical results for the choice of cooperation mode. For normalization, the coefficients of the exogenous variables are estimated as the difference between the coefficients for each type of cooperation and for non-cooperation.

Table 4.   Maximum likelihood logit estimates of the choice of cooperation mode

Explanatory variables	Information trading	Joint Venture	Merger	Licensing
CONSTANT	11.641	10.431	9.221	6.159
	(2.013)	(1.728)	(1.641)	(1.945)
ln SALES1	- 0.0289	- 0.0002	- 0.0332	- 0.0004
	(0.0159)	(0.0490)	(0.0197)	(0.0632)
TECHCOMP1	- 0.0003	- 0.0001	0.0021	0.0102
	(0.0318)	(0.0421)	(0.1032)	(0.0921)
SUB1	0.0001	0.0001	- 0.0012	0.0023
	(0.0298)	(0.0025)	(0.0346)	(0.0612)
SUBCOOP1	0.0021	0.0015	- 0.0009	0.0061
	(0.0471)	(0.0623)	(0.0723)	(0.0812)
SUBSHARE	- 0.0008	0.0013	- 0.0004	0.00003
	(0.0031)	(0.0002)	(0.0009)	(0.0004)
ln SALES2	- 0.0197	- 0.0013	- 0.0192	- 0.0016
	(0.0111)	(0.0096)	(0.0013)	(0.0173)
TECHCOMP2	- 0.0010	0.0002	- 0.0009	- 0.0008
	(0.0281)	(0.0132)	(0.0092)	(0.0047)
SUB2	0.0000	0.0001	- 0.0004	0.0002
	(0.0025)	(0.0064)	(0.0027)	(0.0051)
SUBCOOP2	0.0016	0.0019	- 0.0008	0.0031
	(0.0018)	(0.0038)	(0.0007)	(0.0041)
ln DISTANCE	0.0391	0.0329	0.0299	0.0095
	(0.0032)	(0.0024)	(0.0093)	(0.0026)
COUNTRY	0.8391	0.4915	1.2692	0.1760
	(0.4219)	(0.8080)	(0.6554)	(0.8701)
PREVCOOP	1.1892	0.0815	0.0048	0.8327
	(0.3819)	(0.1740)	(0.2741)	(0.3811)
PREVRELATION	0.9402	0.0218	0.3920	0.2419
	(0.3197)	(0.0924)	(0.1489)	(0.3714)
COMPETITION	- 0.0151	0.0047	0.0078	- 0.0721
	(0.0013)	(0.0002)	(0.0014)	(0.0096)
RIVALS	- 0.0327	- 0.0419	- 0.0272	- 0.0215
	(0.0052)	(0.0320)	(0.0009)	(0.0041)
CONCENTRATION	0.7191	1.3191	0.6143	- 0.3150
	(0.2918)	(0.0092)	(0.1034)	(0.0762)
MSHARE	0.0000	0.0193	- 0.0127	- 0.0072
	(0.0086)	(0.0032)	(0.0245)	(0.0834)
PROCESS	0.2285	0.3525	0.2248	0.2444
	(0.8870)	(0.8204)	(0.7025)	(0.8288)

ln likelihood	916.44
X^2	642.04
Percentage correctly predicted	55.82

Note: 2475 observations; asymptotic standard errors in parentheses; and coefficients for technology dummies available on request.

The overall fit of the model is quite good, even though many variables are not significant individually. As expected, the variable *Sub1*, indicating subsidies without a cooperation requirement, does not have any significant effect on the choice of cooperation. More surprising is that the variable *Subcoop1*, indicating subsidies that allow a choice of information trading or joint venture, does not significantly increase the probability of choosing either form of cooperation, even though the coefficients have the right sign. The variable *Subshare*, indicating a subsidy with a joint venture requirement, does have a significant effect on the probability of choosing joint venture cooperation.

Table 5 shows the coefficients of the adjusted OLS-regression. Since each observation in the dataset describes the relationship between two firms, the dependent variable is now the logarithm of the sum of the two firms' combined R&D expenditure. This R&D expenditure includes all subsidies, so that it reflects total R&D spending.

Table 5.   Empirical results of the corrected OLS-regresion of R&D intensity over explanatory variables

Explanatory variables	No Cooperation	Information trading	Joint Venture	Merger	Licensing
CONSTANT	11.963	10.492	12.279	12.165	9.196
	(0.913)	(1.243)	(2.998)	(3.514)	(3.613)
ln SALES1	0.611	0.689	0.543	0.737	0.519
	(0.1430)	(0.0271)	(0.0630)	(0.0892)	(0.0781)
TECHCOMP1	0.496	0.518	0.6911	0.4967	0.3617
	(0.0142)	(0.0671)	(0.0936)	(0.1123)	(0.1471)
SUB1	0.0025	0.0021	0.0019	0.0012	0.0023
	(0.0002)	(0.0004)	(0.0007)	(0.0006)	(0.0011)
SUBCOOP1	-	0.0019	0.0009	-	-
		(0.0006)	(0.0007)		
SUBSHARE	-	-	- 0.0008	-	-
			(0.0003)		
ln SALES2	0.591	0.629	0.501	0.787	0.671
	(0.0086)	(0.0196)	(0.0541)	(0.0814)	(0.0883)
TECHCOMP2	0.521	0.571	0.599	0.501	0.411
	(0.0097)	(0.0488)	(0.1945)	(0.0957)	(0.1121)
SUB2	0.0023	0.0022	0.0016	0.0010	0.0015
	(0.0001)	(0.0006)	(0.0009)	(0.0008)	(0.0011)
SUBCOOP2	- 0.0002	0.0017	0.0013	- 0.0008	- 0.0003
	(0.0014)	(0.0008)	(0.0011)	(0.0009)	(0.0011)
RIVALS	0.0362	0.0217	0.0261	0.0314	0.0274
	(0.0017)	(0.0061)	(0.0028)	(0.0049)	(0.0031)
CONCENTRATION	1.693	1.264	1.779	1.195	1.0781
	(0.0417)	(0.0961)	(0.2459)	(0.3971)	(0.4152)
MSHARE	0.814	0.418	0.419	0.318	0.219
	(0.0614)	(0.1636)	(0.3197)	(0.3682)	(0.4281)
r^2	0.532				
F-statistic	9.586				

Note: coefficients for technology dummies available on request.

In Table 5 *Sub1* has significant coefficients in all categories. The size of the coefficients implies that each percentage of R&D expenditures financed by the subsidy increases R&D expenditure with 0.25 percent. This result is compatible with that of previous studies (Fölster, 1991a). *Subcoop1* also has a significant effect of about the same magnitude for firms choosing information trading. Remarkably, *Subshare* has a negative effect on R&D investment.

The effects of the three types of subsidies are summarized in Table 6. There, the average effects of a subsidy of 1 million dollars on the average firm's R&D spending and the choice of the cooperation mode are shown.

Table 6.   Estimated effect of the three types of subsidies on R&D intensity and type of cooperation

Dependent variable	Subsidy without cooperation requirement	Subsidy with cooperation requirement	Subsidy with joint venture requirement
R&D intensity (million $)	0.25	0.19	- 0.08
Information trading (%)	2	2	- 4
Joint Venture (%)	1	2	11
Merger (%)	2	- 1	- 2
Licensing (%)	3	3	- 1

V.   Conclusion

The empirical results indicate that subsidy programs that require cooperation but allow a choice of various cooperative agreements such as EUREKA do not increase the likelihood of cooperating. Moreover, such subsidies increase incentives to conduct R&D to about the same extent as a normal R&D subsidy would. A subsidy that requires a result-sharing agreement, such as MCC or most EU-subsidy programs, significantly increases the chances of cooperating, but seems to decrease incentives to conduct R&D. The empirical results do not show whether this result is a consequence of the increased efficiency of the R&D conducted or whether it arises because the result-sharing agreement reduces competition, creates moral hazard, or causes some other disincentive. A next step, currently being planned, is to follow the firms' progress using patent counts and sales of the technology so as to determine whether the result-sharing agreements increased or decreased research efficiency.

References

Baumol, W. J. (1990) 'Technology-Sharing Cartels', *Working Paper*, C.V. Starr Center, New York University.

Bernstein, J. (1989) 'The Structure of Canadian Interindustry R&D Spillovers and the Rates of Return to R&D.', *Journal of Industrial Economics* 21, 324-347.

Bernstein J. and Nadiri, I. (1991) 'Product Demand, Cost of Production, Spillovers, and the Social Rate of Return to R&D, *NBER working paper # 3625*.

Domencich, T. and McFadden, D. (1975) *Urban Travel Demand: A Behavioural Analysis*, Amsterdam, North-Holland.

Fölster, S. (1991a) *The Art of Encouraging Invention: A New Approach to Government Innovation Policy*. Stockholm, The Industrial Institute for Economic and Social Research.

Fölster, S. (1991b) 'Hinder för teknikspridning i Sverige', in: *Forskning, teknikspridning och produktivitet*, Expertrapport nr 10 till Produktivitetsdelegationen.

Grossman, G. and Shapiro, C. (1986) 'Research Joint Ventures: An Antitrust Analysis', *Journal of Law, Economics, and Organization* 2, 315-37.

Hausman, J. and McFadden, D. (1984) 'Specification Tests for the Multinomial Logit Model', *Econometrica* 52, 1219-40.

Heckman, J. (1974) 'Shadow Prices, Market Wages, and Labor Supply', *Econometrica* 42, 679-94.

Hippel, E. von (1987) 'Cooperation between Rivals: Informal Know-how Trading', *Research Policy* 16, 285-305.

Katz, M. L. (1986) 'An Analysis of Cooperative Research and Development', *RAND Journal of Economics* 17, 527-543.

Katz, M. L. and Ordover, J. A. (1990) 'R&D Cooperation and Competition', *Brookings Papers on Economic Activity*, 137-203.

Katz, M. L. and Shapiro, C. (1985) 'On the licensing of innovations', *RAND Journal of Economics*, 16.

Lee, L. F. (1978) 'Unionism and Wage Rates: A Simultaneous Equation Model with Qualitative and Limited Dependent Variables', *International Economic Review* 19, 415-33.

Levin, R., Klevorik, A., Nelson, R. and Winter, S. (1987) 'Appropriating the Returns from Industrial Research and Development', *Brookings Papers on Economic Activity* 3, 783-820.

Maddala, G. S. (1983) *Limited-Dependent and Qualitative Variables in Econometrics*, Cambridge University Press, Cambridge.

Mansfield, E., Rapoport, J., Romeo, A., Wagner, S. and Beardsley, G. (1977) 'Social and Private Rates of Return from Industrial Innovations', *Quarterly Journal of Economics*, 221-240.

Mansfield, E., Schwartz, M, and Wagner, S. (1981) 'Imitation Costs and Patents: An Empirical Study', *Economic Journal* 91, 907-18.

Ogadiri, H. (1992) *Growth through Competition, Competition through Growth: Strategic Management and the Economy in Japan*, Clarendon Press, Oxford.

Ordover, J. A. (1991) 'A Patent System for Both Diffusion and Exclusion', *Journal of Economic Perspectives* 5, 43-60.

Ordover, J. A. and Willig, R. D. (1985) 'Antitrust for High-Technology Industries: Assessing Research Joint Ventures and Mergers, *Journal of Law and Economics* 28, 311-333.

Schrader, S. (1991) 'Informal Technology Transfer between Firms: Cooperation through Information Trading', *Research Policy* 20, 153-170.

CHAPTER 5

Firm Size and Efficiency in R&D Spending

BART NOOTEBOOM and ROBERT W. VOSSEN[1]

University of Groningen, School of Management & Organization, Groningen, The Netherlands

Abstract. The empirical tradition of Schumpeterian studies of the relation between innovation on the one hand and firm size and market structure on the other is linked with a theoretical tradition in which R&D is modeled as a stochastic race in which the winner takes all. Industry effects are taken into account on the basis of a classification introduced by Pavitt in 1984. The empirical study compares results on a survey of Dutch industry with results on a survey of American industry. For both data bases small firms are concluded to be more R&D-efficient in all Pavitt classes, except Science Based industry.

I.   Introduction

This chapter deals with the well-known (neo-)Schumpeterian issues of the relationships between innovation on the one hand and firm size and market structure on the other (Schumpeter, 1942). The questions addressed in empirical studies on this subject (for surveys see Kamien and Schwartz, 1982; Baldwin and Scott, 1987; and Cohen and Levin, 1989) are traditionally: 1. Are large firms more innovative than small firms?; and 2. Is innovation greater in more highly concentrated industries? With respect to the first question, four arguments have been offered in the literature in favor of an affirmative answer. First, larger firms have larger volumes of sales over which to spread the fixed cost of an innovation, which leads to higher returns on R&D. Second, there may be scale economies in R&D. Third, large firms can more easily obtain finances for risky R&D projects, due to capital market imperfections. Finally, complementarities between R&D and other activities are assumed to be better developed within larger firms. Counterarguments are that large firms may become bureaucratic, less efficient, and that researchers may be less motivated in larger firms, because they do not have as much personal benefit from their efforts as do researchers in smaller firms.

An enormous amount of empirical work has been done on this firm-size effect but, as Cohen and Levin (1989), note, "[t]he most notable feature of this considerable body of empirical research on the relationship between firm size and innovation is its inconclusiveness. ... First, most of the samples used in the regression studies are highly non-random ... . Many of the earlier firm-level studies confined attention to the 500 or 1000 largest firms in the manufacturing sector, and, quite typically, firms that reported no R&D were excluded from the

---

[1]The research reported on is funded by the Netherlands Organization for Scientific Research (NWO) under filenumber 450-227-018. We have made use of the 1988 data base on innovation in the Dutch industry of the University of Amsterdam Foundation for Economic Research (SEO), which was funded by the Netherlands Ministery of Economic Affairs.

sample. Second, the studies vary in the degree to which they control for characteristics of firms (other than size) and industries". With respect to the second Schumpeterian question there are several arguments why monopoly power should be conducive to innovative activity. Firms possessing monopoly power should be more inclined to innovate, because they are better able to realize the rewards from innovation. Also, firms realizing monopoly profits should be better able to finance R&D from internal sources. A counterargument is that a firm already in possession of monopoly power is less motivated to innovate because it does not feel threatened by rivals (*e.g.,* Scherer, 1980). Most empirical studies have found a positive relationship, with a few exceptions (*e.g.,* Williamson, 1965; and Bozeman and Link, 1983). Some of these studies compared aggregated data of industry R&D to industry concentration (Horowitz, 1962; and Hamberg, 1966); others employed firm-level data with concentration ratios corresponding to the industry to which the firm belongs (Phlips, 1971; Rosenberg, 1976; and Shrieves, 1978).

It is generally not clear what is meant by "the influence of firm size or market structure on R&D intensity". Is the focus on intensity in terms of participation or spending, input or output and influence on the speed of success, or on the amount of excess profit, in case of winning the 'race', per unit of time or on the time period over which these monopoly profits can be maintained? In the following sections we shall attempt to shed some light on the questions posed here. In Section II a model is presented which, among other things, makes an *explicit* distinction between R&D participation and R&D spending. In Section III this model will then serve to formulate hypotheses as the basis of an empirical study. The empirical study employs two data sets: a survey of Dutch industry in 1988 in Sections IV to VI, conducted by Kleinknecht *et al.* (1990), and a survey of American industry in 1975 in Sections VII and VIII, which was published in *Business Week* (1976) and used before by Acs and Audretsch (1989 and 1990). For a classification of industries, to control for industry effects, we employ the classification introduced and studied by Pavitt (1984). Section IX concludes the chapter.

II.   Model Specification

For the specification of the model we employ a model proposed by Nooteboom (1991), which was developed from previous work by Dasgupta and Stiglitz (1980 and 1981), Loury (1979) and Lee and Wilde (1980). In this line of modeling the core assumptions are the following:
1. R&D is a race between n contestants, in which the winner takes all (no spill-over);
2. The R&D process is stochastic, with a Poisson incidence of success;
3. The Poisson parameter depends on the intensity of research expenditure (concentration of expenditure in time) according to an S-curve; and
4. Contestants independently maximize expected net returns with respect to the intensity of R&D, assuming that each contestant knows the number of contestants and presumes (conjectural variations) that the other contestants adjust intensity in the same proportion in the selection of the optimal rate of

expenditure as he does.

While previously the models had been used for theoretical analysis only, Nooteboom employed his model as a basis for the empirical study of the Schumpeterian issue of the relation between firm size and innovation, which in the previous literature had been conducted in a theoretically more loose, *ad hoc* fashion. The following features were added to the model:

5. Next to the effect of intensity of R&D expenditure (concentration in time) on the Poisson parameter there is an effect of the level of expenditure (quality of the innovation aimed at) on profits in case the race is won, with decreasing returns. This is the first effect of scale. Contestants now maximize expected net returns with respect to both level and intensity of expenditure.

6. In the relation between level of expenditure and profits (feature 5) an effect of firm size is allowed: small firms may be more or less efficient with respect to the profit/cost ratio of R&D. This is the second effect of scale.

7. Apart from the flow cost of R&D (intensity x level of expenditure), which lasts for as long as the race proceeds, there is a fixed entry cost, regardless of firm size. This yields the third effect of scale.

8. A distinction is made between a model to explain participation in R&D and a model to explain the level of expenditure in case of participation, both as a function of firm size.

Nooteboom (1991) employed the analytical results for an empirical study of *participation* in R&D as a function of firm size. In the present chapter we report on an empirical study of R&D *expenditure* as a function of firm size, for firms conducting R&D. Therefore, we concentrate on the expenditure model here.

The assumptions listed above yield the following R&D production function:

$$(1) \qquad C = a + \int_{0}^{T} \tau c S e^{-it} dt,$$

which is the present value of total R&D expenditure, including a fixed entry cost. The probability distribution of the aggregate Poisson parameter is

$$(2) \qquad F(T) = L e^{-LT} \text{ with } L = \sum_{j=1}^{n} \mu_j .$$

The S-shaped effect of intensity of R&D on speed of R&D, with the point of inflection a function of firm size, is reflected in

$$(3) \qquad d\mu/d\tau > 0 \text{ with } d^2\mu/d\tau^2 > 0 \text{ for } \tau < \tau^*(S) \text{ and } d^2\mu/d\tau^2 < 0 \text{ for } \tau > \tau^*(S).$$

Equation (4) below is just the mathematical specification of assumptions (5) and (6), representing profit as a function of the level of expenditure, with decreasing returns and firm size effect.

$$(4) \qquad b = \beta_0 S^{\beta_2} c^{\beta_1} \text{ with } \beta_0 > 0 \text{ and } \beta_1 < 1.$$

The legenda is in Table 1.

Table 1.   Legenda

C	total R&D expenditure during the race (until someone wins at $t=T$), discounted to the present $(t=0)$
a	fixed threshold cost of entry
T	duration of the race: that is, the time period until the first success among contestants occurs
τ	parameter to express intensity of R&D measured by concentration of R&D expenditure in time ($\tau = 1$ represents a *standard* concentration)
c	level of expenditure, per unit of time for as long as the race lasts, per unit of firm size
S	firm size
i	discount rate
t	time index, where at $t=0$ the decision on expenditure during the race is to be made (once the decision is made, the rate of expenditure is fixed for the duration of the race).
F(T)	cumulative probability distribution of T
μ	Poisson parameter
j	index of contestants
n	number of contestants
τ^{*}	point of inflection in the S-curve dependency of μ on τ
b	flow of profits (entrepreneurial rent) for the winner of the race, discounted to the moment at which the flow of profit starts - *i.e.*, the race ends - per unit of firm size
β_2	parameter indicating a possible firm-size effect on profit/cost efficiency

The implications of the assumptions are given below. The proofs are supplied in the Appendix.

The expected net present value of returns E is

(5) $E = -a + (\mu b - \tau c)S/(L+i)$.

Maximization of E with respect to the decision variables c and τ (level and intensity of expenditure), given the production function, yields the optimum conditions

(6) $c = \{(\mu/\tau)\beta_0 \cdot \beta_1 \cdot S^{\beta_2}\}^{1/(1-\beta_1)}$, and

(7) $d\mu/d\tau = (\mu/\tau)(L + i)/(L + i/\beta_1) < \mu/\tau$.

Equation (7) is illustrated in Figure 1. At the optimum the derivative of μ with respect to τ ($d\mu/d\tau$) is a given percentage less than the slope of the ray from the origin to the optimal point (μ/τ). Firms may differ in their efficiency with respect to the speed of R&D: for a more speed-efficient firm, the point of inflection τ^{*} lies more to the left. At the optimum, the slope of the ray is higher, and the intensity (τ) is lower.

For one, the model yields a basis for an analysis of market structure as measured by the number of contestants n. It follows from (7) that as the number of contestants (n) increases, optimal intensity (τ) decreases, and the derivative $d\mu/d\tau$ and the slope of the ray μ/τ both increase to the point where the slope of the ray equals the derivative (for $n \to \infty$). According to (6) the

Figure 1.   S-shaped effect of τ on μ

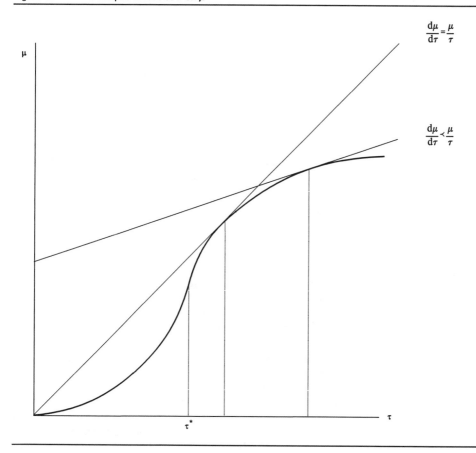

increase of μ/τ yields an increase of the level of expenditure (c). The net effect of an increase of n on the rate of expenditure τc (intensity x level) can be derived as follows. From (6) it follows that

(8) $\mathrm{dlog}\tau c/\mathrm{dlog}n = \{1/(1-\beta_1)\}(\mathrm{dlog}\mu/\mathrm{dlog}\tau - \beta_1)\mathrm{dlog}\tau/\mathrm{dlog}n.$

Therefore, since τ decreases with n (and hence $\mathrm{dlog}\tau/\mathrm{dlog}n < 0$), the rate of expenditure (τc) increases or decreases with n according to whether the elasticity of profits (b) with respect to level of expenditure (c) - *i.e.*, β_1 - is greater or smaller than the elasticity of the Poisson parameter (μ) with respect to intensity (τ). In other words: with a larger number of contestants, which dilutes the chance of winning the race, each contestant goes for higher profitability of winning, while decreasing efforts to win. The net result on the rate of expenditure is an increase (decrease) if the effect of the level of expenditure on profit is greater (smaller) than the effect of the intensity of expenditure on the speed of development.

In the optimum, for firms conducting R&D, the model for annual R&D expenditure is

(9) $K = a/\Theta + kS^{1+\sigma}$ with $k = \tau\{(\mu/\tau)\beta_0\beta_1\}^{1/(1-\beta_1)}$ and $\sigma = \beta_2/(1-\beta_1)$,

where Θ is the number of years over which the entry cost a is amortized. This is the basic model that will be used for the empirical study of R&D expenditure. However, the available observations include only R&D input measured as annual labor input, and hence do not include the amortized fixed entry cost. Thus, parameter a drops from the model: unfortunately, the data cannot be used to test the hypothesis that there is a fixed entry cost. Since the constant term drops from the model, the remainder becomes loglinear so that a loglinear regression of expenditure on firm size can be employed to test hypotheses concerning the parameter β_2: the firm-size effect on profit/cost efficiency of R&D. This is the main point of the present study.

III. Hypotheses

In Section II we briefly indicated some effects of firm size and market structure, the latter in terms of number of contestants n. But there are industry effects as well, coming in through the following parameters: (i) speed of R&D [the S-shaped relation between intensity of R&D and Poisson parameter, reflected in equation (3)]; and (ii) profit/cost opportunities of R&D [parameters β_0, profit/cost ratio and β_1, degree to which there are decreasing returns from level of expenditure, embodied in equation (4)]. Furthermore, firm-size effects are expected to differ between industries: in some industries small firms may be more profit/cost efficient than large firms, and in others less (parameter β_2). The strength of small firms is behavioral: lack of bureaucracy, flexibility, proximity to market demand and motivation. The weakness of small firms lies in resources: limited funds, specialized support, specialist division of labor, and economies of scale and scope (cf. Rothwell, 1985). We hypothesize that small firms are more efficient ($\beta_2 < 0$) in industries where R&D is not dependent on large teams of specialists or other effects of scale or scope. Later we discuss the classification of industries that we employ to test the hypothesis.

The effect of firm size on profit/cost efficiency requires closer scrutiny. The variable b incorporates two aspects: the profits for the winner per unit of time, from the moment he wins the race ($t = T$), and the duration of the period over which profit lasts. This period is called the *protection period*. It may be determined by patent protection, in which case it is fixed and independent of market structure and firm size. However, there is evidence that patent protection is only one of several mechanisms for appropriating entrepreneurial rent as a reward for innovation (cf. Harabi, 1989). Appropriation may be achieved by means of other entry barriers as well: occupation of unique resources, sunkness of costs, switching costs for customers, capacity for credible and rapid price retaliation against entrants, product differentiation, et cetera. Such barriers are likely to depend on industry, market structure and firm size. In this case, the effect of firm size (parameter β_2) or market structure may be interpreted as an effect on the rate of net returns or on the duration of the protection period, or both. With respect to the duration of the protection period large firms are likely to have better opportunities to erect entry barriers, so that we would have $\beta_2 > 0$. Thus, if we find empirically that $\beta_2 < 0$, this is a strong confirmation of the hypothesis that smaller firms are more profit/cost efficient, since the effect can only be weakened by a positive firm-size effect on the duration of the protection period.

One might hypothesize that in some industries small firms are also more speed-efficient than large firms. In the model, this would be represented by a leftward shift of the point of inflection (τ^*) of the S-shaped effect of R&D intensity on the Poisson parameter (see Figure 1). This may have an effect on the parameter k in the expenditure model (9). However, it is not *a priori* clear what the effect of greater speed-efficiency on the parameter k would be: on the one hand, one would expect a higher value for the ratio μ/τ, but, on the other hand, a lower value of intensity τ as a high Poisson parameter can be achieved (yielding a shorter expected period to success) at a lower intensity of expenditure, due to greater efficiency. Thus, the effect of firm size is not clear, and it may depend on the industry. However, to the extent that there is a systematic effect of firm size on parameter k, this will yield an error in the estimate of the parameter σ in (9) and the conclusions with respect to β_2.

We noted that according to the model a larger number of contestants may have a positive or negative effect on the rate of expenditure, depending on the relative values of elasticities of profit and speed of R&D with respect to R&D expenditure. A more concentrated market is expected to have an effect on expenditure for additional reasons. At first sight, we expect a positive effect on the parameter β_0 (profitability of success in R&D), which according to (9) has a positive effect on parameter k due to the well-known conjecture that a more concentrated market yields higher price-cost margins. This is the effect we expect if the protection period for the winner is determined by the patent period. However, if this is not the case - and if protection is determined by other entry barriers - we would expect the presence of fewer and larger competitors (higher concentration) to reduce the protection period, on the assumption that they are better able to circumvent or destroy entry barriers. This would have a negative effect on parameter β_0 and hence parameter k. This may depend on the industry.

Before performing a log-transformation on model (9), we check whether this is consistent with the best way to specify the error term. Important differences in parameter estimates can occur, depending on the assumptions made about this term. The choice is now between the following two alternatives, with error terms u and v,

(10) $K = k.S^\sigma + u$, or

(11) $K = k.S^\sigma.e^v$.

The main underlying issue is whether K is heteroscedastic with a variance depending on S. The additive form (10) is appropriate when K is homoscedastic, while the multiplicative form (11) is appropriate when K is heteroscedastic (*cf.*

Judge *et al.*, 1985). The first equation (10) was estimated, using an iterative nonlinear regression procedure. The variance of the residuals increased with firm size, indicating heteroscedasticity, from which we concluded that (11) is the more appropriate relationship: hence, log-transformation is justified.

The final specification of the model and corresponding hypotheses conclude this section.

(12) $\log K = a_0 + a_1 \log S + a_2 \log n + a_3 \log C4,$

where C4 is the four-firm concentration ratio and n the number of contestants, both on the third-digit SIC-level.

HYPOTHESIS 1:   all coefficients depend on the industry.

HYPOTHESIS 2:   in industries where R&D is not driven by large teams of specialists or other evident effects of scale or scope, small firms are more profit/cost efficient, resulting in $\beta_2 < 0$ and hence $a_1 < 1.0$.

HYPOTHESIS 3: $a_2 <$ or > 0 according to whether the effect of expenditure on profits is higher or lower than its effect on speed.

HYPOTHESIS 4: $a_3 > 0$, implying that market concentration has a positive effect on the rate of R&D expenditure, unless appropriation is achieved by other means than patents.

In the following sections we turn to a discussion of the data and the classification of industries.

IV.   The Data

The main data base used in this study was kindly supplied by Kleinknecht (1990) from his R&D survey conducted in the Netherlands in 1989. We used data on 1292 firms in Dutch manufacturing industry that conducted some form of R&D in 1988. Data were available for individual respondents on SIC-code, firm size and R&D, both measured in terms of employment. Three forms of R&D were distinguished in the survey: R&D in a formal R&D-department, R&D in other departments and R&D put out to contract. Taking these three forms together gives a broad measure of R&D, taking into account the observation that the innovative activity of smaller firms would be structurally underestimated if only formal R&D would be considered (*cf.* Archibugi *et al.*, 1991; and Kleinknecht & Reijnen, 1991). As a proxy of the number of contestants in the R&D-race, the total number of firms with ten or more employees per third-digit SIC-industry was obtained from publications of the Dutch Central Bureau of Statistics (CBS). Finally, the four-firm concentration ratios on the third-digit SIC-level for 1986 were kindly supplied by the Research Institute for Small and Medium Sized Business (EIM) in the Netherlands on the basis of CBS-statistics.

V. Classification of Industries

The number of observations in our sample was not sufficient to estimate different parameters for all second-digit SIC-industry classes. Also, as Kamien and Schwartz (1982) note, "innovation in one area may arise from an industry in an entirely different area, as defined by the Standard Industrial Classification". To still allow for inter-industry differences in all parameters, we used a classification introduced by Pavitt (1984). After analyzing "similarities and differences amongst sectors in the sources, nature and impact of innovations, defined by the sources of knowledge inputs, by the size and principal lines of activity of innovating firms and by the sectors of innovations' production and main use" Pavitt (1984) proposed a taxonomy on the basis of the characteristics of about 2,000 significant innovations and innovating firms in Great Britain from 1945 to 1979. This classification is best described by Table 2, which was directly taken from his article. These four categories of industries also represent classes of technological opportunity. This is an important feature of the environment of a firm that we need to control for, since the opportunity for R&D-based innovations depends on the state of knowledge in relevant fields of science and technology (*e.g.*, Scherer, 1965 and 1967). Finally, we expect that competition through innovation does indeed not confine itself to SIC-classes, but largely takes place within the Pavitt-categories. Firms were assigned to these categories on the basis of their second-digit SIC-codes, as shown in Table 3. With respect to the firm size parameter a_1, we expect a_1 to be smaller than unity in the smaller-scaled industries - 'Supplier Dominated' and 'Specialized Suppliers' - and greater than unity in the larger-scaled industries - 'Scale Intensive' and 'Science Based'.

VI. Empirical Results

As stated in Section III [equation (12), the equation to be estimated is

$$logK = a_0 + a_1 logS + a_2 logn + a_3 logC4.$$

Now, using ordinary least squares regression, the equation was first estimated with sectoral dummies on all four parameters. However, the parameter estimates differed significantly per sector only for a_0 (the constant) and a_1 (parameter of log S), and not for the last two parameters a_2 and a_3 (the parameters of log n and log C4, respectively). So, the sectoral dummies on these two parameters were removed and the regression was run again. Another problem was the high multicollinearity between logn and logC4 (correlation coefficient of -.72, significant at the .1 % level!), causing the estimates of a_2 and a_3 to be unreliable. Hence, only one of these variables could be admitted into the regression equation. LogC4 turned out to be the strongest of the two in terms of t-value and explanatory power, so finally log n was removed from the equation, leading to the following final specification:

(13) $logK = a_0 + a_1 \cdot logS + a_3 \cdot logC4.$

Table 2.   Pavitt's categories

Sectorial technological trajectories: determinants, directions and measured characteristics

Category of firm	Typical core sectors	Determinants of technological trajectories			Technological trajectories	Measured characteristics			
		Sources of technology	Type of user	Means of appropriation		Source of process technology	Relative balance between product and process innovation	Relative size of innovating firms	Intensity and direction of technological diversification
(1)	(2)	(3)	(4)	(5)	(6)	(7)	(8)	(9)	(10)
Supplier dominated	Agriculture; housing; private services traditional manufacture	Suppliers Research extension services; big users	Price sensitive	Non-technical (e.g., trademarks, marketing, advertising, aesthetic design)	Cost-cutting	Suppliers	Process	Small	Low vertical
Production intensive — Scale intensive	Bulk materials (steel, glass); assembly (consumer durables & autos)	PE[a] suppliers; R&D	Price sensitive	Process secrecy and know-how; technical lags; patents; dynamic learning economies;	Cost-cutting (product design)	In-house; suppliers	Process	Large	High vertical
Production intensive — Specialized suppliers	Machinery; instruments	Design and development users	Performance sensitive	design know-how; knowledge of users; patents	Product design	In-house customers	Product	Small	Low concentric
Science based	Electronics/ electrical; chemicals	R&D Public science; PE	Mixed	R&D know-how; patents; process secrecy and know-how; dynamic learning economies	Mixed	In-house; suppliers	Mixed	Large	Low vertical / High concentric

[a] PE = Production Engineering Department

Source: Pavitt (1984)

Table 3. Kleinknecht data

Category of Firm	SIC-code	Description	# Obs
1. Supplier Dominated	22	Textiles	45
	23	Clothing	9
	24	Leather	14
	25	Wood & Furniture	62
	26	Paper	57
	27	Printing	78
	30	Fibres	2

			267
2. Scale Intensive	20/21	Foods, Beverages, Tobacco	173
	28	Oil	6
	31	Rubber & Plastics	69
	32	Building Materials, Eathenware,	
		Glass	65
	33	Metals	18
	34	Metal Products	172
	37	Means of Transport	52

			555
3. Specialized Suppliers	35	Machinery	242
	38	Instruments, Optical Goods	33
	39	Remaining	13

			288
4. Science Based	29	Chemicals	105
	36	Electrical Goods	77

			182
			1292

The results of this regression are summarized in Table 4. These results show that for all but the Science Based category a_1 is significantly smaller than one, which confirms Hypothesis 2 that small firms are more profit/cost efficient. The coefficient is smallest for the Supplier Dominated category, followed by Specialized Suppliers, Scale Intensive and Science Based industries, respectively. Also, separate regressions show different explanatory power of the model per category. The adjusted R-squares are lowest for the smaller-scaled industries (Supplier Dominated: .27; and Specialized Suppliers: .32) and highest for the larger scaled industries (Scale Intensive: .43; and Science Based: .52). This is to be expected from the familiar observation that smaller firms are more heterogenous than large ones. Secondly, a_3 is significantly positive, which affirms Hypothesis 4: market concentration has a positive effect on the rate of R&D expenditure.

Table 4.   Regression with Kleinknecht data

Category of Firm	a_o	a_1	$\sigma(a_1)$	a_3	$\sigma(a_3)$
1. Supplier Dominated	-3.45	.708	.070		
2. Scale Intensive	-3.63	.780	.042	.206	.048
3. Specialized Suppliers	-2.82	.749	.071		
4. Science Based	-3.96	1.005	.071		

Summary statistics:		
F (8, 1283)	=	127.056
R-square	=	$.442^2$
Adjusted R-square	=	.439

VII. A Second Data Set

As a first validation we estimated the model with a second data set. The data were taken from a survey of corporate R&D spending in the United States in 1975, which was published in *Business Week*, June 28, 1976. *Business Week*'s survey, designed to catch nearly all significant R&D expenditures, covers 730 companies that report R&D as a separate item and that have sales in excess of $ 50 million or R&D expenditures in excess of $ 1 million. The total R&D expenditures of the companies in the survey come to $ 14.5 billion, which is 96 % of the NSF-Census estimate of total company-funded R&D in 1975 ($ 15.1 billion). From these data we deleted a few industry groups that could not be assigned to any of the 'Pavitt-categories', like *conglomerates*, *miscellaneous manufacturing*, and a few companies that had reported zero R&D, leaving data on 611 individual companies. The assignment of industries is given in Table 5. Unfortunately, we had no data on industry concentration ratios. Moreover, the *Business Week* classification of industries does not correspond to SIC. However, since the survey covers 96 % of total company-funded R&D, nearly all of the largest companies will probably be in the sample. Hence, we calculated the 'sample-C4' as a proxy of the industry-C4. As before, there were no significant differences per sector in the parameters of logC4, so again the sectoral dummies on this parameter were dropped. The results are summarized in Table 6.

The magnitude of these parameters compared with those obtained with the Kleinknecht data is somewhat different. This is not very surprising if the differences in the data are considered:
1. the filling in of the Pavitt-sectors is not identical;
2. firm size is measured differently (sales *versus* employment);
3. R&D is measured differently (dollars spent *versus* employment);
4. Dutch data *versus* U.S. data;
5. 1975 data *versus* 1988 data;
6. very different average firm size in the samples (*Business Week*: about 20,000 employees; Kleinknecht: about 300!); and

---

[2]The log-transformation has a negative effect on the R-square. If we run a simple linear regression K = a + b.S, the R-square is .77.

Table 5.   *Business Week* data

Category of Firm	#	Description	# Obs
1. Supplier Dominated	15	Leisure Time	13
	21	Paper	15
	23	Publishing	5
	24	Service Industries	31
	27	Textiles & Apparel	22

			86
2. Scale Intensive	1	Aerospace	17
	2	Appliances	7
	3	Automotive	31
	4	Beverages	4
	5	Building Materials	37
	8	Containers	8
	11	Food	33
	16	Metals & Mining	19
	18	Natural Resources & Fuel	19
	20	Oil Service & Supply	13
	22	Personal Care Products	14
	26	Steel	10
	28	Tire & Rubber	15
	29	Tobacco	4

			231
3. Specialized Suppliers	13	General Machinery	50
	14	Instruments	46
	25	Special Machinery	9

			105
4. Science Based	6	Chemicals	51
	9	Drugs	33
	10	Electrical & Electronics	69
	19	Office Equipment & Computers	31
	30	Telecommunication	5

			189
			611

7. for the *Business Week* data we have only a proxy of C4.
Despite all of this, the basic results are exactly the same. Again, for all but the Science Based category a_1 is significantly smaller than one and the coefficient is smallest for the Supplier Dominated category, followed by Specialized Suppliers, Scale Intensive and Science Based industries, respectively. Also, running separate regressions per category leads to the same conclusions with respect to the explanatory power of the model. The adjusted R-square is lowest for Supplier Dominated category (.24), followed by Specialized Suppliers (.65), Scale Intensive (.66) and Science Based (.76). Finally, a_3 is, again, significantly positive.

Table 6.   Regression with *Business Week* data

Category of Firm	a_0	a_1	$\sigma(a_1)$	a_3	$\sigma(a_3)$
1. Supplier Dominated	-4.88	.533	.083		
2. Scale Intensive	-5.43	.905	.042		
				.551	.119
3. Specialized Suppliers	-5.14	.848	.072		
4. Science Based	-5.69	.988	.045		
Summary statistics:	F (8, 597)		= 168.404		
	R-square		= .693		
	Adjusted R-square		= .689		

VIII. Robustness of the Firm Size Parameter

Two tests for robustness of the firm size parameters were performed. First, logC4 was deleted from the model for both data sets and, second, four additional explanatory variables (available only for the Kleinknecht data) were included in the model to see how this would effect the estimates of a_1. The results are summarized in Tables 7 and 8, respectively.

Table 7.   Regression without C4

Category of Firm	Kleinknecht			*Business Week*		
	a_0	a_1	$\sigma(a_1)$	a_0	a_1	$\sigma(a_1)$
1. Supplier Dom.	-2.91	.721	.071	-2.64	.538	.085
2. Scale Intensive	-3.10	.813	.041	-4.18	.903	.042
3. Specialized Sup.	-2.32	.772	.071	-3.09	.857	.073
4. Science Based	-3.14	1.011	.071	-3.38	.963	.046
	Adjusted R-square: .43			Adjusted R-square: .68		

If we compare the parameter estimates in Table 7 with those in Tables 4 and 6, we see no significant change in the firm size parameters a_1 and an increase (especially for the *Business Week* data) in a_0. Next, extra explanatory variables were included in the model for the Kleinknecht data. The following equation was estimated:

$$(14)\quad logK = a_0 + a_1 logS + a_3 logC4 + a_4 logD + a_5 logE + a_6 logP + a_7 logT,$$

where D denotes presence of a separate R&D department (yes/no), E export (<25%, 25-50%, 50-75% or >75% of turnover), P = percentage of 'process R&D' (+1), and T = turnover (less/equal/more than last year). Sectoral dummies were placed on all new variables and (14) was estimated. After this first estimation a number of modifications were made. First, logT and logP had no significant effect in any category, so these two variables were dropped from the model. Second, the parameters of logD and logE were not significantly different per category, so the associated sectoral dummies were also dropped from the model. The result is shown in Table 8.

Table 8.   Regression with additional explanatory variables (Kleinknecht data)

Category of Firm	a_0	a_1 (σ)	a_3 (σ)	a_4 (σ)	a_5 (σ)
1. Supplier Dominated	-3.00	.579 (.062)			
2. Scale Intensive	-3.13	.629 (.038)	.112 (.043)	1.511 (.085)	.203 (.050)
3. Specialized Suppliers	-2.49	.583 (.063)			
4. Science Based	-3.87	.883 (.063)			

Summary Statistics: $F(10,1278) = 168.412$
                              R-square =   .569
                    Adjusted R-square =   .565

From this table we see a positive effect of the presence of a separate R&D department and the percentage of turnover exported. If we compare the estimates of a_0 and a_1 to those in Tables 4 and 7, we see that again a_0 increased, but not as much as in Table 7. Also this time there is a significant change in a_1. For all four categories this parameter has decreased so that even the Science Based category now has a_1 significantly smaller than one. The parameter is still smallest for the Supplier Dominated category, followed by Specialized Suppliers, Scale Intensive and Science Based. Finally, it is noted that logD adds the most explanatory power. Inclusion of logE raises the adjusted R-square from .439 to .457. Subsequently adding logD to the model raises the adjusted R-square from .457 to .565. The additional explanatory variables work empirically, but theoretically they are somewhat *ad hoc*. The presence of a separate R&D department indicates a greater orientation towards R&D, and is correlated with firm size. Export indicates at least some degree of progressiveness of the firm.

From the last two sections we can conclude that the firm size parameter a_1 is quite robust. The inclusion of additional explanatory variables only strengthens the evidence in favor of Hypothesis 2.

IX.   Conclusions

For two very different data sets we find that for all Pavitt sectors except Science Based industry R&D expenditure of firms increases less than proportionately with firm size. According to our underlying theory the implication is that smaller firms are more R&D efficient. As expected, the effect is strongest in Supplier Dominated industries and Specialized Suppliers. Contrary to expectation the effect is also found for Scale Intensive industry. For Science Based industry we find no significant difference between small and large firms. We find a consistent positive effect of industry concentration, as in previous studies, and the effect does not significantly differ between industries. The results of the study are remarkably robust under change of data base and the introduction of additional explanatory variables.

Appendix

Proof of formula (5)

According to (1) we have

$$\text{(A1)} \quad C = a + \int_0^T rcSe^{-it}dt = a + \frac{rcS}{i}(1-e^{-iT}).$$

According to (A1) and (2) the expected present value of costs E(C) is

$$\text{(A2)} \quad E(C) = a + \frac{rcS}{i} \int_0^\infty (1-e^{-iT})Le^{-LT}dT = a + \frac{rcS}{L+i}.$$

The probability of winning the race at time T is the probability of having success at T, while others do not have success until T. According to the Poisson assumption this is

$$\text{(A3)} \quad \mu e^{-\mu T} \cdot e^{-(L-\mu)T}.$$

In case of winning at T profit (profit stream discounted to T) is b.S, so that expected present value of profit E(P) is

$$\text{(A4)} \quad E(P) = bS \int_0^\infty e^{-iT}\mu e^{-\mu T}e^{-(L-\mu)T}dT = \frac{\mu bS}{L+i}.$$

Thus, for expected net present returns from R&D we have

$$\text{(A5)} \quad E = E(P) - E(C) = -a + \frac{(\mu b - rc)S}{L + i} \cdot \text{QED}$$

Proof of formula (6)

Maximization of expected net present value of returns E with respect to c yields as the first-order condition

$$\text{(A6)} \quad \frac{dE}{dc} = \frac{1}{L+i}\left[\frac{\mu\beta_1 b}{c} - r\right] = 0 \text{ iff } c = \frac{\mu\beta_1 b}{r}.$$

Substitution of (4) in (A6) yields

$$\text{(A7)} \quad \frac{dE}{dc} = 0 \text{ iff } c = \left\{\frac{\mu}{r}\beta_1\beta_0 S^{\beta_2}\right\}^{\frac{1}{1-\beta_1}} \cdot \text{QED}$$

Proof of formula (7)

Maximization of E with respect to r yields as the first-order condition

$$\text{(A8)} \quad \frac{dE}{dr} = \frac{1}{L+i}\left\{ b\frac{d\mu}{dr} - c - \frac{(\mu b - rc)}{L+i}\cdot\frac{dL}{dr}\right\} = 0.$$

Concerning $dL/d\tau$ we make the following assumption for Stackelberg conjectural variations:

(A9) $\dfrac{d\log\mu_j}{d\log\mu} = 1$.

In other words, each contestant assumes that each competitor adjusts the Poisson parameter in the same proportion as one does oneself (optimizing with respect to intensity), which yields a symmetric Nash-Cournot equilibrium. As a result,

(A10) $\dfrac{dL}{d\tau} = \sum\limits_{j=1}^{n} \dfrac{d\mu_j}{d\mu}\cdot\dfrac{d\mu}{d\tau} = \dfrac{L}{\mu}\cdot\dfrac{d\mu}{d\tau}$.

From (A8) this yields

(A11) $\dfrac{dE}{d\tau} = \dfrac{1}{(L+i)^2} \left\{ \left[ib + \tau c\dfrac{L}{\mu}\right]\dfrac{d\mu}{d\tau} - c(L+i)\right\}$,

so that $dE/d\tau = 0$ iff

(A12) $\dfrac{d\mu}{d\tau} = \dfrac{L+i}{\dfrac{ib}{c} + \tau\dfrac{L}{\mu}}$.

Substituting the other optimum condition (A6) we find

(A13) $\dfrac{d\mu}{d\tau} = \dfrac{\mu}{\tau}\cdot\dfrac{L+i}{L+i/\beta_1} < \dfrac{\mu}{\tau}$ (since $\beta_1 < 1$) .   QED

References

Acs, Z. and Audretsch, D. (1989) 'R&D, Firm Size and Innovative Activity', *Paper presented at the EARIE-conference*, Budapest.

Acs, Z. and Audretsch, D. (1990) *Innovation and Small Firms*, Cambridge, The MIT Press.

Archibugi, D., Cesaratto, S. and Sirilli, G. (1991) 'Sources of Innovative Activities and Industrial Organization in Italy', *Research Policy* 20, 299-313.

Baldwin, W.L. and Scott, J.T. (1987) *Market Structure and Technological Change*, Chur, Harwood.

Bozeman, B. and Link, A.N. (1983) *Investments in Technology: Corporate Strategies and Public Policy Alternatives*, New York, Praeger.

Cohen, W.M. and Levin, R.C. (1989) 'Empirical Studies of Innovation and Market Structure', in R. Schmalensee and R.D. Willig (eds), *Handbook of Industrial Organization, Volume II*, Amsterdam, North-Holland.

Dasgupta, P. and Stiglitz, J. (1980) 'Uncertainty, Industrial Structure and the Speed of R&D', *Bell Journal of Economics* 11, 11-28.

Dasgupta, P. and Stiglitz, J. (1981) 'Entry, Innovation, Exit', *European Economic Review* 15, 137-158.

Hamberg, D. (1966) *R&D: Essays on the Economics of Research and Development*, New York, Random House.

Harabi, N. (1989) 'Role of Patents in Theory and Practice: Empirical Evidence from Switzerland', *Paper presented at the EARIE-conference*, Budapest.

Horowitz, I. (1962) 'Firm Size and Research Activity', *Southern Economic Journal* 28, 298-301.

Judge, G.G., Griffiths, W.E., Hill, R.C., Lütkepohl, H. and Lee, T.C. (1985) *The Theory and Practice of Econometrics*, Second Edition, New York, Wiley.

Kamien, M.I. and Schwarz, N.L. (1982) *Market Structure and Innovation*, Cambridge, Cambridge University Press.

Kleinknecht, A.H., Reijnen, J.O.N. and Verweij, J.J. (1990) *Innovatie in de Nederlandse Industrie en*

Dienstverlening, Den Haag, Ministerie van Economische Zaken.

Kleinknecht, A.H. and Reijnen, J.O.N. (1991) 'More Evidence on the Undercounting of Small Firm R&D', *Research Policy* **20**, 579-587.

Lee, T. and Wilde, L.L. (1980) 'Market Structure and Innovation: A Reformulation', *Quarterly Journal of Economics* **94**, 429-436.

Loury, G.C. (1979) 'Market Structure and Innovation', *Quarterly Journal of Economics* **93**, 395-410.

Nooteboom, B. (1991) 'Entry, Spending and Firm Size in a Stochastic R&D Race', *Small Business Economics* **3**, 103-120.

Pavitt, K. (1984) 'Sectoral Patterns of Technical Change: Towards a Taxonomy and a Theory', *Research Policy* **13**, 343-373.

Philips, L. (1971) 'Research', Chapter 5 in *Effects of Industrial Concentration: A Cross-Section Analysis for the Common Market*, Amsterdam, North-Holland, 119-142.

Rosenberg, J.B. (1976) 'Research and Market Share: A Reappraisal of the Schumpeter Hypothesis', *Journal of Industrial Economics* **25**, 101-112.

Rothwell, R. (1985) *Innovation and the Smaller Firm*, First International Technical Innovation and Entrepreneurship Symposium, Utah Innovation Foundation, Salt Lake City.

Scherer, F.M. (1965) 'Firm Size, Market Structure, Opportunity and the Output of Patented Inventions', *American Economic Review* **55**, 1097-1125.

Scherer, F.M. (1967) 'Market Structure and the Employment of Scientists and Engineers', *American Economic Review* **57**, 524-531.

Scherer, F.M. (1980) *Industrial Market Structure and Economic Performance*, Second edition, Chicago, Rand McNally.

Schumpeter, J.A. (1942) *Capitalism, Socialism and Democracy*, New York, Harper.

Shrieves, R. (1978) 'Firm Size and Innovation: Further Evidence', *Industrial Organization Review* **4**, 26-33.

Williams, O.E. (1965) 'Innovation and Market Structure', *Journal of Political Economy* **73**, 67-73.

CHAPTER 6

Commitment by Delegation: What Is "Strategic" about Strategic Alliances?

PETER WELZEL[1]

University of Augsburg, Wirtschafts- und Sozialwissenschaftliche Fakultät, Germany

Abstract. The chapter deals with two firms forming a strategic alliance in a three-firm Cournot oligopoly. A standard two-stage game with R&D and output decisions is used. The firms in the alliance carry out a common R&D project by delegating the decision on the level of R&D activity to one of them while remaining competitors in the output game. The results point to the strategic element of such a delegation of power to a competitor. It is the commitment value of forming an alliance that makes it *strategic* in the sense of theoretical industrial organization.

I. Introduction

After the wave of mergers and acquisitions throughout the 1980s, so-called strategic alliances lately became fashionable among firms. A strategic alliance can be defined as a coalition where the partners remain independent firms coordinating some of their activities while being competitors in other areas (for a similar definition see Porter and Fuller, 1986). Recent examples include cooperations among IBM and Siemens to produce a new generation of memory chips, Rolls-Royce and BMW to produce jet engines, and Mitsubishi and Daimler-Benz (the details of which are still being negotiated). Strategic alliances can be found in a variety of forms, ranging from loose technological cooperation and licensing of technology to joint ventures and cross ownership. Trends towards global markets and increased technological complexity are often seen as major reasons for this new development in inter-firm relations. Both trends imply large fixed or sunk costs. An alliance allows to share these costs among the participating firms. Advantages arise from scale economies and learning effects, access to new technologies and new markets, risk sharing and risk spreading, and influencing competition in the market. Since the latter aspect seems to be an ingredient of many real-world alliances and allows for a stylized representation of the other advantages just mentioned, this chapter aims at working out theoretically the notion of forming a strategic alliance to influence competition in an oligopolistic market. One could ask why such cooperations among competing firms are called *strategic*. Apart from the popularity of the adjective, particularly among business people, at least two economic reasons should be considered. First, by forming an alliance the participating firms coordinate their strategies - *i.e.*, their "basic longterm goals and objectives ..., and the adoption of courses of action and the allocation of resources necessary for carrying out these goals" (Chandler, 1962: 13). Second, through an alliance

[1]Paper presented at the 1992 conferences of E.A.R.I.E and the Verein für Socialpolitik. I am grateful to participants of both conferences and to seminar and workshop participants at Sion and Augsburg for their very helpful comments.

the participating firms want to create and/or capture economic rents in markets with perceived interdependence. To reach this goal, a strategic alliance serves as a commitment against competitors.

While these two statements are not necessarily conflicting, this chapter will interpret strategic alliances in the sense of the second angle because it is closer to standard economic reasoning. It will be shown that from a theoretical perspective one important reason for forming such a coalition among competitors is to alter the non-alliance firms' expectations about the alliance's optimal behavior by making a credible commitment, which in turn induces favorable reactions by those rivals outside the alliance. So far, strategic alliances have been analyzed predominantly in the management literature, where papers both on problems of managing an alliance and on specific forms like joint ventures can be found (*cf.* Hamel *et al.*, 1989; Harrigan, 1988; Ohmae, 1989; and Porter and Fuller, 1986). Work on incentives for cooperation was done by Contractor and Lorange (1988) and Buckley and Casson (1988). In the economics literature, older work on cartels is partially relevant for the study of strategic alliances. More recently, cooperative R&D as one particular form of strategic alliances was analyzed in a number of papers (*cf.* Ordover and Willig, 1985; Vickers, 1985a; Katz, 1986; Grossman and Shapiro, 1986; d'Aspremont and Jacquemin, 1988; and Beath *et al.*, 1988). Reynolds and Snapp (1986) examined the effects of joint ventures through partial ownership in rivals on the outcome of a Cournot oligopoly. To show the commitment value of forming a strategic alliance, it is natural to draw upon recent work in theoretical industrial organization. Much of this literature since the late 1970s has focused on firms' commitments in the sense of Schelling (1960) in imperfectly competitive, mostly oligopolistic, markets. In a situation of interdependence, where each competitor knows that the outcome of her actions depends on the actions of other firms, strategic moves to alter the subsequent competitive environment become relevant. To qualify as commitments, such strategic moves have to be irreversible or at least costly to reverse. This alone can guarantee that a firm will behave differently in the later stages of an interaction.

The numerous papers dealing with the issue of tying one's hands to commit to a different behavior pattern share a common structure of two-stage models (for a brief survey see Shapiro, 1989: 381-397). In stage 1 competitors take (strategic) actions which influence stage 2. The equilibrium concept of subgame perfectness ensures that period 1's actions form a commitment for period 2: when deciding on its optimal first-stage choice, each firm correctly anticipates and uses the outcome of stage 2 as a function of the first-stage choices. The distinction between commitment through investing and commitment through contracting provides a useful classification of these approaches to two-stage oligopoly games. Examples of the former are investments in entry-deterring capacity, learning curve, R&D or customers' network (see for detailed references Shapiro, 1989). As for the latter, we can think either of contracts within the firm or contracts with agents outside the firm. Inside the firm, recent work pointed to incentive contracts between owners and managers (*cf.* Vickers, 1985b; Fershtman and Judd, 1987; Fershtman *et al.*, 1991; and Sklivas, 1987) and to profit sharing contracts between owners and employees (*cf.* Stewart, 1989; and Welzel, 1989). Contracts with parties outside the firm can be found when private information is exchanged strategically among competitors (*cf.* Shapiro, 1986) or when technological knowledge is licensed to a competitor (*cf.* Katz and Shapiro, 1985). The case of an owner writing an incentive contract for her manager is particularly interesting for this chapter, since it contains an element of delegation. The literature shows that an owner of an oligopolistic firm can increase her well-being by employing a manager who plays the oligopoly game on behalf of the owner. In what could be called a strategic design of a principal-agent relationship, the owner imposes an objective function on the manager which differs from her own. This is an example where it pays to delegate power to another person. The manager, however, is still part of the firm. In this chapter it will be shown that it can even be beneficial to delegate power to one's own competitor. In fact, this appears to be an important ingredient of so-called strategic alliances. It will be argued that it is this particular feature that makes such an alliance *strategic* from the perspective of theoretical industrial organization. The chapter is organized as follows. In section II a simple two-stage oligopoly model is used to clarify the strategic effects of forming a strategic alliance. In section III the model is slightly modified so to examine the idea of a joint venture. Section IV addresses issues of designing an optimal contract between the firms of the alliance. Section V is a conclusion.

II.   Strategic Effects of Delegation

The model draws on a specification used by d'Aspremont and Jacquemin (1988) to analyze cooperative R&D in a Cournot duopoly. To examine the strategic effects of delegating power in an alliance, the model is extended by assuming that there are three oligopolists producing a homogeneous good. Generalizations to the case of product differentiation are straightforward and do not alter the basic idea of the chapter. Denote by x_i ($i = 1,2,3$) firm i's output. Price p of the good is a linear function of aggregate output x:

(1) $$p(x_1,x_2,x_3) = a-\beta\sum_{i=1}^{3} x_i = a-\beta x.$$

Assume that $a,\beta > 0$ and $x \leq a/\beta$. A standard two-stage oligopoly model is considered. Before deciding on its output x_i in stage 2, each firm i has to determine a level f_i of what will be interpreted as R&D activity. To keep matters simple, there is no asymmetry in the firms' capabilities to do R&D, and spending money on R&D is assumed to buy a cost-reducing process innovation with certainty. Producer i's total cost function consists of production costs and R&D costs. It is given by

(2) $$c_i(x_i,f_i) = (a_i-f_i)x_i+\frac{f_i^2}{2} \text{ with } i=1,2,3.$$

Assume that $0 < a_i < a$ and $f_i < a_i$. R&D activity lowers the initial unit production cost a_i. The price of one unit of R&D is set to 1. The convexity of $c_i(x_i,f_i)$ in f_i should be interpreted as expressing diminishing returns of the underlying R&D

production function. In both stages of the oligopoly game producers act simultaneously as Cournot competitors. Note that an irreversible R&D decision can itself be interpreted as a strategic move before the output game. In the sequel, however, the argument is focused on the fact that forming an alliance between two firms also works as a strategic move.

To examine this more closely, assume that firms 1 and 2 sign an enforcable contract concerning cooperative R&D in stage 1 of the game. In the output game, however, they continue to act as competitors. This appears to be an assumption compatible both with real-world strategic alliances and with competition policy's desire to prevent the firms from cooperating in both stages of the game. The contract specifies whether either firm 1 or 2 is to carry out the common R&D project and how the costs will be shared: *i.e.*, there is full delegation of the R&D decision. The firm which is designated to run the alliance's research program is absolutely free in determining the extent of common R&D. Let f denote the level of R&D activity chosen by the alliance. Under the R&D production function implicit in (2), f will cause R&D expenses of $f^2/2$. Given a share parameter $\mu \in [0,1]$, firms 1 and 2 contribute to the R&D program according to $\mu f^2/2$ and $(1-\mu)f^2/2$, respectively. As for the outcome of the R&D project, both partners benefit in the same way and independently of their contribution to the budget. There are no technological spillovers to or from the firm outside the alliance. This assumption of perfect spillovers inside and no spillovers outside the alliance clearly constitutes a polar case. Inclusion of a more general pattern of spillovers, however, complicates the exposition of the main idea of this chapter and is therefore left to work specialized in the analysis of (asymmetric) spillovers (for a recent contribution in a duopoly framework very similar to the model used here see De Bondt and Henriques, 1992). The cost functions (2) of firms 1 and 2 are then replaced by

$$(3) \qquad c_1(x_1,f,\mu) = (a_1-f)x_1+\mu\frac{f^2}{2}, \text{ and}$$

$$(4) \qquad c_2(x_2,f,\mu) = (a_2-f)x_2+(1-\mu)\frac{f^2}{2}.$$

Note, finally, that the specification of cooperative R&D for process innovation does not imply identical *ex post* production functions for firms 1 and 2 - *i.e.*, perfect spillovers within the alliance are confined to new technologies. Imagine the partners being stuck with their initial equipment which allows them only to share the technological improvements generated by the R&D project. It can easily be verified, however, that the conclusions do not change if firms 1 and 2 possess identical technologies after the R&D project. In stage 2 the firms choose output levels x_i for given R&D levels to maximize profits

$$(5) \qquad \pi_i(x_1,x_2,x_3;\mu,f) = p(x_1,x_2,x_3)x_i-c_i(x_i,f,\mu) \text{ with } i=1,2, \text{ and}$$

$$(6) \qquad \pi_3(x_1,x_2,x_3;f_3) = p(x_1,x_2,x_3)x_3-c_3(x_3,f_3).$$

Both the second-order and stability conditions for a three-firm oligopoly, as presented in Dixit (1986), hold as long as $\beta > 0$. Equations (5) and (6) lead to the following reaction functions in the output game:

(7) $x_i(x_{-i}) = \dfrac{1}{2\beta}(a - \beta x_{-i} - a_i + f)$ with $i = 1,2$, and

(8) $x_3(x_{-3}) = \dfrac{1}{2\beta}(a - \beta x_{-3} - a_3 + f_3)$,

where a subscript "-i" denotes the aggregate value of firm i's competitors for a variable: *i.e.*, $x_{-i} = x - x_i$. Solving for the Nash equilibrium in the output game yields

(9) $x_i(f, f_3) = \dfrac{1}{4\beta}(a - 3a_i + a_{-i} + 2f - f_3)$ with $i = 1,2$, and

(10) $x_3(f, f_3) = \dfrac{1}{4\beta}(a - 3a_3 + a_{-3} - 2f + 3f_3)$.

Substituting (9) and (10) into (5) and (6) results in the profit functions for stage 1, which include optimal behavior in stage 2,

(11) $\pi_i(f, \mu, f_3) = p(x(f, f_3))x_i(f, f_3) - c_i(x_i(f, f_3), f, \mu)$ with $i = 1,2$, and

(12) $\pi_3(f, \mu, f_3) = p(x(f, f_3))x_3(f, f_3) - c_3(x_3(f, f_3), f_3)$.

Suppose, on the one hand, that firm 1 is the one designated by the alliance to carry out the R&D program. It will choose f in stage 1 such that its profit function π_1 is maximized according to (11). This implies for R&D that

(13) $f = \dfrac{a - 3a_1 + a_{-1} - f_3}{2(2\beta\mu - 1)}$.

If, on the other hand, firm 2 is the alliance's researcher, its optimal behavior requires

(14) $f = \dfrac{a - 3a_2 + a_{-2} - f_3}{2(2\beta(1 - \mu) - 1)}$.

Profit maximization by firm 3, which is not in the alliance, is described by

(15) $f_3 = \dfrac{3(a - 3a_3 + a_{-3} - 2f)}{8\beta - 9} = \rho_3(f)$.

In addition to (15), (13)-(14) define reaction functions $\rho_i(f)$ ($i = 1,2$) in (f, f_3)-

space:

(16) $p_1(f) = a - 3a_1 + a_{-1} - 2f(2\beta\mu - 1)$, and

(17) $p_2(f) = a - 3a_2 + a_{-2} - 2f(2\beta(1 - \mu) - 1)$.

Spencer and Brander (1983) pointed to the difficulties in ensuring stability and uniqueness of the equilibrium in a two-stage model. However, given the specification used here, things turn out to be simple (for details see the Appendix). Inspection of second-order and stability conditions for the R&D game imposes a set of restrictions on the parameters of the model which can be summarized as

(18) $\mu \in \left] \dfrac{3}{4}\beta, 1 - \dfrac{3}{4}\beta \right[$.

Note that the stability conditions limit the range of admissible cost-sharing parameters μ. In particular, the extreme cases $\mu = 0$ and $\mu = 1$, where one partner pays for all of the alliance's R&D, are ruled out. Finally, the conditions derived restrict the demand parameter to being *not too small*.

Using the results derived so far it is straightforward, albeit tedious, to calculate the equilibrium values of R&D levels, outputs and profits. Instead, simple reaction curve diagrams are used to work out the economics of delegation in strategic alliances. Given the stability conditions, all reaction curves $\rho_i(f)$ are negatively sloped in (f, f_3)-space. In addition, the slopes of $\rho_1(f)$ and $\rho_2(f)$ exceed in absolute value the slope of firm 3's reaction curve $\rho_3(f)$, which is in the interval $]-1, 0[$. To understand the strategic value of delegating power to a competitor, assume the cost parameters to be ranked according to

(19) $a_1 < a_2$.

It is easy to check that the ranking of a_3 relative to a_1 and a_2 does not affect the results presented in the sequel. If the inequality in (19) is reversed, the conclusions change in a straightforward way. Finally, the special case $a_1 = a_2$, where the firms in the alliance start out with identical technologies, will be addressed in Section IV.

To begin with, assume that firms 1 and 2 agreed to share the costs of R&D evenly - *i.e.*, $\mu = \frac{1}{2}$ - no matter which of them is chosen to carry out the R&D program. From (16) and (17) this implies identical slopes for $\rho_1(f)$ and $\rho_2(f)$. The oligopoly game can then be depicted in (f, f_3)-space as in Figure 1. If, on the one hand, firm 2 were chosen to be the alliance's researcher, the oligopoly would reach its Nash equilibrium in point A. If, on the other hand, the power to set the alliance's R&D level f were delegated to firm 1, point B would be the equilibrium. Figure 1 is drawn under the assumption that cost parameters a_1 and a_2 are relatively similar such that $\rho_1(f)$ and $\rho_2(f)$ are not too far apart. This immediately implies that firm 2 will want to delegate R&D decisions to firm 1 as

Figure 1.   Equilibrium for $\mu = \frac{1}{2}$ and $a_1 < a_2$

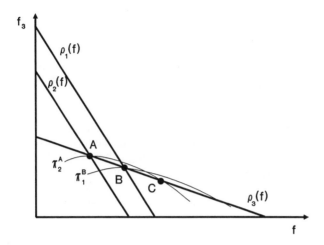

equilibrium B is located on an isoprofit contour strictly superior to π_2^A. Firm 1 will accept this offer because by delegating R&D to firm 2 it could only reach an isoprofit contour strictly inferior to π_1^B.

For the case of equal shares in the R&D budget the model therefore reveals a result similar to the one recently presented by Gatsios and Karp (1991) for a customs union: as long as technologies in the strategic alliance are not too different, the partner with higher production costs will want to delegate the R&D decision to the firm with lower costs, which in turn has an incentive to agree with this proposal. The economics behind this conclusion can be seen from (13) and (14). By participating in the strategic alliance and accepting firm 1's decision for optimal R&D, firm 2 commits to an R&D level it could not credibly choose by itself. Note that firm 3, which remains outside the alliance, faces a reduction in its profits as consequence of the delegation among firms 1 and 2.

If firms 1 and 2 are relatively dissimilar with respect to their cost parameters a_i, a conflict of interest can arise. Imagine $\rho_1(f)$ intersecting $\rho_3(f)$ to the right of point C. If this is the case, producer 2 prefers equilibrium A, whereas producer 1 prefers B. Each one of the firms wants to decide on the common R&D level. This implies that strategic alliances in R&D projects as outlined in the current model are only workable as long as the participating firms are not too dissimilar. So far, the focus was on the case with $\mu = \frac{1}{2}$. Consider now $\mu \neq \frac{1}{2}$. Reaction curves (16) and (17) imply that changes of μ only affect the slopes of firm 1's and 2's reaction curves in (f,f_3)-space. An increase in μ causes an increase in the slope of $\rho_1(f)$ and a decrease in the slope of $\rho_2(f)$ in absolute terms. Producer 1's reaction curve becomes steeper, whereas firm 2's curve becomes flatter. If, on the one hand, in Figure 1 μ is reduced below $\frac{1}{2}$, $\rho_2(f)$ turns to the left and $\rho_1(f)$ turns to the right with the intercepts remaining constant. Point A on $\rho_3(f)$

moves leftwards, whereas point B moves in the direction of C. Both shifts tend to make the delegation of power from firm 2 to firm 1 less attractive. Inspection of the firms' isoprofit contours π_1 and π_2 exhibits changes which work in the same direction: the slope of firm 2's isoprofit contours is increased in absolute value for points to the right of $\rho_2(f)$, which moves point C to the left. If, on the other hand, firm 1's share in the budget increases above $\mu = \frac{1}{2}$, $\rho_2(f)$ turns to the right and $\rho_1(f)$ turns to the left. Delegation of the power to decide on the alliance's R&D expenses becomes more attractive to firm 2. The strategic alliance is more likely to be workable. Again, the changes in the isoprofit contours support this pattern. The π_2's become flatter to the right of $\rho_2(f)$, shifting point C further to the right. Note that for high levels of the cost-sharing parameter μ the incentives to delegate the R&D decision can be reversed. Firm 1's share of the R&D budget becomes so high that it would rather have firm 2 setting a lower f for the alliance. In a modified version of Figure 1 this would be the case if $\rho_1(f)$ and $\rho_2(f)$ intersect above $\rho_3(f)$. Now producer 1 wants its partner 2 to carry out the alliance's R&D program, and firm 2 is willing to accept this offer.

III.   Joint Ventures

In the previous section, a rather extreme form of a strategic alliance was examined so as to work out the effects of delegating power on the oligopoly equilibrium. One might object that full delegation is rarely observed. Real-world firms will always retain some control over what a partner is doing. A slight modification of the model can deal with this issue. Consider now another variety of strategic alliances, where firms 1 and 2 do not delegate the R&D decision to either of them, but set up a separate decision unit for the R&D project. Assume that this research center, which could be called a joint venture, is expected to maximize a weighted sum of stage 2 profits π_1 and π_2. As opposed to the previous analysis this can be interpreted as a partial delegation of power by both firms. Each firm's profit function π_i (i = 1,2) influences the objective function of the R&D decision maker. Let $\tau \in [0,1]$ be the weight of firm 1's profit. The joint venture then maximizes

$$(20) \quad \pi_r(f,\mu,\tau,f_3) = \tau\pi_1(f,\mu,f_3)+(1-\tau)\pi_2(f,\mu,f_3)$$

with respect to f. For $\tau = \frac{1}{2}$ this is equivalent to maximizing $\pi_1 + \pi_2$. The first-order condition leads to the reaction function $\rho_r(f)$ in (f,f₃)-space

$$(21) \quad \rho_r(f) = a+a_1(1-4\tau)+a_2(4\tau-3)+a_3-2f(2\beta(\mu(2\tau-1)+1-\tau)-1).$$

Inspection of ρ_r shows that for all μ permitted by (18) slope and intercept lie in intervals spanned by the slopes of ρ_1 and ρ_2 and the intercepts of ρ_1 and ρ_2, respectively.

Consider, e.g., the situation in Figure 2, where $\mu < \frac{1}{2}$ is assumed. If the management of the joint venture sets f according to (21), equilibrium D will

Figure 2.   Equilibrium with joint venture maximizing $r\pi_1 + (1-r)\pi_2$

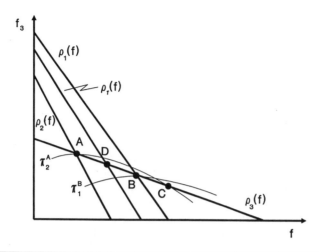

arise. However, both firms prefer the delegation equilibrium B to point D. The result depicted in Figure 2 readily generalizes to all admissible values of μ and r. The conclusions on the slope and intercept of $\rho_r(f)$ imply that setting up a research center to maximize a weighted sum of firm 1's and 2's profits cannot be superior and will normally be inferior to delegating R&D in the model presented here. The two firms in the alliance can do better by full delegation to either of them compared to partial delegation to a joint venture. This conclusion immediately raises the question why in the real world numerous joint ventures are observed, given that this chapter's model reveals that strategic alliances with full delegation are superior. A matter that comes to one's mind when delegation of power among competitors is analyzed, is the problem of moral hazard. In this chapter, moral hazard was assumed to be non-existent. A more realistic setting, however, would have to include stochastic R&D outcomes and non-observable actions of the alliance's researcher. Under full delegation, the firm carrying out the R&D project for the alliance would then have an incentive to choose sub-optimal R&D efforts and blame bad outcomes on adverse stochastic shocks. Joint ventures where both partners retain some control over the common project, are a way to solve this problem. The model's results then point to the price firms pay for this solution: by using partial instead of strategically optimal full delegation, they give up some of the strategic effect of the alliance in order to avoid the problem of moral hazard.

IV.   Optimal Design of a Strategic Alliance

So far, the alliance's cost-sharing parameter μ was taken as given. Under this assumption delegation among the participating firms was shown to be Pareto-superior as long as their technologies were relatively similar. However, when forming an alliance, the prospective partners have to decide on the value of μ. To examine this decision, suppose now an additional stage of the game. In this stage, which is played before the R&D and the output game, producers 1 and 2 reach an agreement on the delegation and set μ. It seems reasonable to assume that firms 1 and 2 act cooperatively in this stage, taking into account the consequences of their decision for subsequent stages of the game. Particularly, they know about the commitment value of the design of their alliance. The best firms 1 and 2 can do is to maximize their joint profit level $\pi_1 + \pi_2$. The previous results (16), (17) and (21) imply that the reaction function $\rho_r(f; \tau = \frac{1}{2})$, which corresponds to maximization of $\pi_1 + \pi_2$ in the R&D game, is located right in the middle between $\rho_1(f; \mu = \frac{1}{2})$ and $\rho_2(f; \mu = \frac{1}{2})$. From Spencer and Brander (1983) and later work on strategic trade policy it is well-known that the most favorable position a duopolist can reach by a strategic move is that of "as-if" Stackelberg leadership. It delivers the profit level a Stackelberg leader would receive given the behavior of his competitor. Denote by π_r the isoprofit contours for joint profits $\pi_1 + \pi_2$ - $i.e.$, the contours corresponding to $\rho_r(f; \tau = \frac{1}{2})$. Point B in Figure 3 is the alliance's most favored point in (f, f_3)-space given firm 3's optimal response $\rho_3(f)$. In B the isoprofit contour π_r^B is tangent to $\rho_3(f)$.

Figure 3.   Choice of optimal cost sharing parameter μ^*

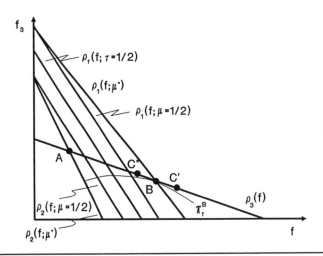

Recalling the previous results on changes of μ, an optimal choice μ^* of the cost-sharing parameter can be suggested. A reduction of μ below the value of $\frac{1}{2}$ causes $\rho_1(f; \mu)$ to turn to the right. By setting μ^* such that $\rho_1(f; \mu^*)$ intersects $\rho_3(f)$ in B and delegating the R&D decision to firm 1, the alliance credibly commits to its most favorable behavior in the R&D game. Note that for point B being located to the left of the intersection between $\rho_3(f)$ and $\rho_1(f; \mu = \frac{1}{2})$, μ^* is above $\frac{1}{2}$.

There is still the question of whether, given μ^*, firm 2 is willing to delegate to firm 1. To avoid cluttering the figure, firm 2's isoprofit contours π_2 are not included in Figure 3. Suppose, instead, C' and C" are alternative points of intersection between $\rho_3(f)$ and isoprofit contour π_2^A running through A. If, on the one hand, C' is the relevant point, there is no conflict of interest between producers 1 and 2. If, on the other hand, C" (which is to the left of B) marks the intersection of $\rho_3(f)$ and π_2^A, firm 2 will prefer to set f for the alliance by itself. However, since in B joint profits $\pi_1 + \pi_2$ of the strategic alliance are maximized, the conflict of interest related to C" does not cause a substantial problem. It can easily be resolved by choosing μ^* such that $\rho_1(f; \mu^*)$ goes through B, delegating the decision to firm 1, and using a lump sum payment from producer 1 to producer 2 as compensation.

The same logic applies to a problem not explicit in Figure 3: will a firm do better by participating in the alliance, given the alliance's optimal choice of μ^*, than by remaining independent and choosing its own R&D level? Again, it has to be pointed out that the partners in the alliance can set μ^* strategically to maximize their joint profit level, and can use a lump sum transfer to ensure Pareto superiority of their contract. Note, finally, that it is even possible for the alliance to reach its most favored equilibrium B by using a reversed delegation decision and choosing a very large value of μ^*. Given a suitable compensating payment among firms 1 and 2 the alliance in principle can use its commitment power by delegating to either one of the two partners. Nevertheless, delegation to the technologically superior firm 1 appears to be the more natural solution, since it implies less compensation and a lower risk of μ^* violating the restriction (18) on the parameters of the model. The analysis in this section also provides insights into the special case of $a_1 = a_2$ not considered so far. Even if firms with identical technologies decide to form a strategic alliance for R&D, there is a commitment value to this decision. For $a_1 = a_2$ the reaction curves $\rho_r(f; \tau = \frac{1}{2})$, $\rho_1(f; \tau = \frac{1}{2})$ and $\rho_2(f; \tau = \frac{1}{2})$ in Figure 3 are identical. However, setting $\mu < \frac{1}{2}$ again turns firm 1's reaction curve to the right and firm 2's curve to the left. By choosing μ optimally, the alliance can reach equilibrium B. As for the algebraic value of the optimal cost-sharing parameter, μ^* can be derived for the case of firm 1 being the alliance's researcher by solving the system

$$(22) \quad \frac{\partial \pi_r \left[f, f_3; \tau = \frac{1}{2} \right]}{\partial f} = \frac{d\rho_3(f)}{df}, \text{ and}$$

$$(23) \quad \pi_r \left[f, f_3; \tau = \frac{1}{2} \right] = \rho_3(f)$$

for (f, f_3), substituting the solution into the definition (16) of $\rho_1(f)$ and solving for μ. A unique solution exists. Since the procedure turns out to be rather tedious and the solution does not provide new insights, the analysis is restricted to the qualitative results presented so far. Note, however, that firms 1 and 2 would have to check their optimal μ^* against the restriction (18) on μ known from the previous section. If μ^* is outside the interval of admissible values, the producers have to solve a second-best problem.

V.   Conclusion

The objective of this chapter was to point to the strategic value of delegating the power for a first-stage decision of a two-stage oligopoly game to a competitor. By forming a strategic alliance prior to the game, two firms make a credible commitment. Such a strategic move alters their competitor's expectation about their subsequent optimal actions, which in turn changes this firm's optimal behavior in a way favorable to the alliance. From the perspective of theoretical industrial organization this can be seen as an economic mechanism which justifies the adjective "strategic" for recently popular strategic alliances.

Using a simple and highly stylized model with R&D and output decisions, insights on both the extent of delegation and the design of financial relations between the partners in the alliance could be gained. Full delegation of the first-stage decision was found to be superior to partial delegation from a strategic point of view, and a way to derive an optimal cost-sharing parameter for the partners in the alliance was outlined. The principal results can be expected to be robust in a more general specification as can be seen by, *e.g.*, adapting a Spence and Brander (1983) setting. There are clearly a huge number of economic issues relevant to strategic alliances beyond the scope of the model presented here. The problem of moral hazard and its effect on the choice between full and partial delegation were already mentioned. Strategic alliances which were modeled as coordinations of a subset of two firms' functions can also be imagined along divisional lines, if two multi-product firms coordinate decisions for a subset of their products. From the literature on capacity as commitment instrument we know that such multiple product market contact can change commitment effects (*cf.* Van Wegberg, Chapter 12). Finally, this chapter has not explicitly dealt with the issue of which of the three firms in the market should be in the alliance. The reasoning in the previous section, however, already pointed out, that any two firms can form an alliance, even if their initial unit production costs are identical. This corresponds to a result derived recently by La Manna (1993) in a somewhat different and simpler framework of technology transfers among firms. What remains as a problem for further research is the question of whether an alliance can be disrupted by an offer from the third firm. La Manna arrives at this conclusion, which taken jointly with his first one should have rather devastating implications for the logical possibility of asymmetric Cournot oligopolies.

Appendix

To analyze stability in the R&D game, the cases of firm 1 playing against firm 3 and firm 2 playing against firm 3 have to be distinguished. Consider, first, the former case. Examination of the usual adjustment mechanism (*cf.* Dixit, 1986) leads to a matrix Γ_1 of partial derivatives of perceived marginal profits:

$$\text{(A.1)} \quad \Gamma_1 = \begin{bmatrix} \dfrac{\partial \gamma_1}{\partial f} & \dfrac{\partial \gamma_1}{\partial f_3} \\[2mm] \dfrac{\partial \gamma_3}{\partial f} & \dfrac{\partial \gamma_3}{\partial f_3} \end{bmatrix} = \begin{bmatrix} -\mu + \dfrac{1}{2\beta} & -\dfrac{1}{4\beta} \\[2mm] -\dfrac{3}{4\beta} & -1 + \dfrac{9}{8\beta} \end{bmatrix}.$$

Necessary and sufficient conditions for stability are trace $\Gamma_1 < 0$ and det $\Gamma_1 > 0$. The first condition holds due to the second-order conditions for profit maximization, which require both $\partial \gamma_1 / \partial f$ and $\partial \gamma_3 / \partial f_3$ to be negative. These second-order conditions imply that

$$\text{(A.2)} \quad \mu > \frac{1}{2\beta} \wedge \beta > \frac{9}{8}.$$

A sufficient condition for det $\Gamma_1 > 0$ is that the own effects on perceived marginal profit dominate the competitor's effect. Therefore,

$$\text{(A.3)} \quad \left[\frac{\partial \gamma_1}{\partial f}\right] > \left[\frac{\partial \gamma_1}{\partial f_3}\right] \wedge \left[\frac{\partial \gamma_3}{\partial f_3}\right] > \left[\frac{\partial \gamma_3}{\partial f}\right] \Rightarrow \mu > \frac{3}{4\beta} \wedge \beta > \frac{15}{8}$$

Going through the same kind of analysis for the case where firms 2 and 3 are the players in the first-stage game, provides two additional conditions:

$$\text{(A.4)} \quad \mu < 1 - \frac{1}{2\beta} \wedge \mu < 1 - \frac{3}{4\beta}.$$

Selecting from (A.2), (A.3) and (A.4) those conditions which are binding generates

$$\text{(A.5)} \quad \beta > \frac{15}{8} \quad \mu \in \left] \frac{3}{4\beta}, 1 - \frac{3}{4\beta} \right[$$

The most restrictive interval for the cost sharing parameter μ which is valid if β is very close to 15/8 is $]0.4, 0.6[$. For higher values of β the interval of admissible values of μ gets wider. Throughout this chapter both β and μ are assumed to meet (A.5)

References

d'Aspremont, C. and Jacquemin, A. (1988) 'Cooperative and Noncooperative R&D in Duopoly with Spillovers', *American Economic Review* **78**, 1133-1137.

Beath, J., Katsoulacos, Y. and Ulph, D. (1988) 'R&D Rivalry vs. R&D Cooperation under Uncertainty', *Recherches Economiques de Louvain* **54**, 373-384.

Buckley, P.J. and Casson, M. (1988) 'A Theory of Co-Operation in International Business', *Management International Review. Special Issue on Cooperative Strategies in International Business*, 19-38.

Chandler, A.D. Jr. (1962) *Strategy and Structure*. Cambridge, MA, The MIT Press.

Contractor, F.J. and Lorange, P. (1988) 'Competition vs. Cooperation: A Benefit/Cost Framework for Choosing Between Fully-Owned Investments and Cooperative Relationships', *Management International Review. Special Issue on Cooperative Strategies in International Business*, 5-18.

DeBondt, R. and Henriques, I. (1992) 'Strategic Investment with Asymmetric Spillovers', *Discussion Paper 9209*, Catholic University of Louvain.

Dixit, A.K. (1986) 'Comparative Statics for Oligopoly', *International Economic Review* **27**, 107-122.

Fershtman, Ch. and Judd, K.L. (1987) 'Equilibrium Incentives in Oligopoly', *American Economic Review* **77**, 927-940.

Gatsios, K. and Karp, L. (1991) 'Delegation Games in Customs Unions', *Review of Economic Studies* **58**, 391-397.

Grossman, G.M. and Shapiro, C. (1986) 'Research Joint Ventures: An Antitrust Analysis', *Journal of Law, Economics and Organization* **2**, 315-337.

Hamel, G., Doz, Y.L. and Prahalad, C.K. (1989) 'Collaborate with your Competitors and Win', *Harvard Business Review*, 133-139.

Harrigan, K.R. (1988) 'Strategic Alliances and Partner Asymmetries', *Management International Review. Special Issue on Cooperative Strategies in International Business*, 53-72.

La Manna, M.M.A. (1993) 'Asymmetric Oligopoly and Technology Transfers', *Economic Journal* **103**, 436-443.

Katz, M.L. (1986) 'An Analysis of Cooperative Research and Development', *RAND Journal of Economics* **17**, 527-543.

Katz, M.L. and Shapiro, C. (1985) 'On the Licensing of Innovations', *RAND Journal of Economics* **16**, 504-520.

Ohmae, K. (1989) 'The Global Logic of Strategic Alliances', *Harvard Business Review*, 143-154.

Ordover, J.A. and Willig, R.D. (1985) 'Antitrust for High-Technology-Industries: Assessing Research Joint Ventures and Mergers', *Journal of Law and Economics* **28**, 311-333.

Porter, M.E. and Fuller, M.B. (1986) 'Coalitions and Global Strategies', in M.E. Porter (ed.), *Competition in Global Industries*, Boston, Harvard Business School Press, 315-343.

Reynolds, R.J. and Snapp, B.R. (1986) 'The Competitive Effects of Partial Equity Interests and Joint Ventures', *International Journal of Industrial Organization* **4**, 141-153.

Schelling, Th.C. (1960) *The Strategy of Conflict*, Cambridge, MA, et al., Harvard University Press.

Shapiro, C. (1986) 'Exchange of Cost Information in Oligopoly', *Review of Economic Studies* **53**, 433-446.

Shapiro, C. (1989) 'Theories of Oligopoly Behavior', in R. Schmalensee, and R.D. Willig (eds), *Handbook of Industrial Organization* **1**, Amsterdam, North-Holland, 3129-3414.

Sklivas, St.D. (1987) 'The Strategic Choice of Managerial Incentives', *RAND Journal of Economics* **18**, 452-458.

Spencer, B.J. and Brander, J.A. (1983) 'International R&D Rivalry and Industrial Strategy', *Review of Economic Studies* **50**, 707-722.

Stewart, G. (1989) 'Profit-Sharing in Cournot Oligopoly', *Economic Letters* **31**, 221-224.

Van Wegberg, M. (1992) 'Capacity as a Commitment Instrument in Multi-Market Competition', *Chapter 12.*

Vickers, J. (1985a) 'Pre-emptive Patenting, Joint Ventures and the Persistence of Oligopoly', *International Journal of Industrial Organization* **3**, 261-273.

Vickers, J. (1985b) 'Delegation and the Theory of the Firm', *Economic Journal* **95** (Supplement), 138-147.

Welzel, P. (1989) 'Strategische Effekte ertragsorientierter Entlohnung in Oligopolen', *Jahrbücher für Nationalökonomie und Statistik* **206**, 61-74.

CHAPTER 7

The Principle of Minimum Differentiation Revisited: Cournot *versus* Bertrand

ALI AL-NOWAIHI and GEORGE NORMAN
Department of Economics, University of Leicester, Leicester, United Kingdom

Abstract. Hotelling was the first to suggest that the competition between oligopolistic sellers would result in consumers being offered products with an excessive sameness. In this chapter we extend his analysis to a case in which demand is elastic and firms compete in quantities. We find that firms are indeed encouraged to adopt excessively agglomerated locations (in some welfare sense). We also find, perhaps contrary to intuition, that some of the non-existence problems that are endemic to cases in which firms choose prices and locations also extend to cases in which they choose quantities and locations. The desire to control the market centre - the principle of minimum differentiation - is self-defeating. This appears to be primarily a result of denying firm the power to price discriminate between consumer locations. Where equilibria can be identified, we show that quantity competition leads to greater product concentration, lower output, higher profits and lower consumer welfare than does price competition.

I. Introduction

There has been a considerable revival of interest in recent years in the models of spatial competition first analyzed by Hotelling (1929) and subsequently extended by Smithies (1941). It has been recognized that these models can shed considerable light on a wide range of non-cooperative oligopolistic problems where the focus of interest is on product selection by competing firms. The main contention from Hotelling's analysis was that when individual demand is perfectly inelastic "[b]uyers are confronted everywhere by an excessive sameness" (Hotelling, 1929: 54). Hotelling also recognized intuitively the modification of his analysis subsequently formalized by Smithies: "The elasticity of demand of particular groups does mitigate the tendency to excessive similarity of competing commodities, but not enough" (Hotelling, 1929: 57).

These conclusions and the great majority of their contemporary extensions have been derived from Bertrand (price-setting) models of competition. While it has been recognized that Cournot (quantity-setting) competition will give rise to very different equilibria (Vives, 1985; and Cheng, 1985), there has been almost no attempt to examine whether an *excessive sameness* characterizes Cournot equilibria. This omission is surprising given the long intellectual history of Cournot competition. There are further reasons for our belief that Cournot equilibria should be investigated for the Hotelling-Smithies models of product choice. First, and most obvious, it is easy to envisage cases in which firms must commit to output in advance of sales, with price being determined by a market-clearing condition. Secondly, the works of Kreps and Scheinkmann (1983) and Vives (1985 and 1986) indicate that if price-competing firms must first precommit to capacity, price competition can lead to the Cournot outcome. It is not yet clear that their results apply fully to spatial models such as that presented in this chapter, but they do imply that Cournot equilibria are likely to be of wider relevance than has thus far been suspected.

The one exception to the neglect of Cournot equilibria of which we are aware[1] is Hamilton, Thisse and Weskamp (1989), but they depart from the Hotelling-Smithies tradition by assuming that the competing firms are able to adopt (third-degree) price discrimination. In this chapter we compare Cournot and Bertrand equilibria for spatial duopolists which are not able to price discriminate between their consumers. The inability to price discriminate may arise, for example, because consumers travel to the seller to collect the goods or, in the product differentiation analogy, because the seller is unable (or unwilling) to customize the product to the individual consumer's desires.

We model quantity-location and price-location choices as two-stage games in which firms chooses quantities or prices in the second stage and locations in the first stage in the belief that the second stage choices will be an equilibrium quantity or price pair for the second-stage subgame. A result familiar in the literature is that when firms do not price discriminate, there are location choices for which there exists no price equilibrium and so no Bertrand-Nash price-location equilibrium because of the temptation to price undercut the rival when the firms are located *near* to each other. We show that a milder form of non-existence arises in the quantity-location game. A quantity equilibrium can be identified for every location choice: but if transport costs are low enough, there exists no Cournot-Nash equilibrium in quantities *and* locations.

A relatively simple intuition underlies this non-existence result. There are two effects at work in determining a firm's location: what might be termed the *market periphery effect* and the *market area effect*. The market periphery effect encourages the firms to separate in order to maintain sales to consumers on the periphery. The market area effect encourages each firm to attempt to invade its rival's market. The nature of the two-stage game makes this effect particularly strong since in the two-stage game the firms anticipate the Nash equilibrium quantities when making their location choices. The nearer to the market centre that firm i locates, the lower is the expected output of firm k implying that agglomeration is encouraged.

When transport costs are low, the market area effect dominates and the principle of minimum differentiation (Eaton and Lipsey, 1975) holds: the firms wish to agglomerate perfectly. However, if the firms are perfectly agglomerated, the lack of any degree of product differentiation intensifies the quantity competition between them. Each firm finds that it will be more profitable to choose a location marginally away from its rival in order to gain exclusive control of its natural market. Such a location lessens competitive pressures between the firms, leads to a restriction of output and increases profit.

The chapter is organized as follows. In Section II we set out the basic model on which the remainder of the analysis is based. Section III presents the quantity-location game and Section IV the price-location game. Some elements of the quantity-location and price-location equilibria are compared in Section V: to facilitate this comparison we confine the models to cases in which equilibrium

---

[1]Since writing this chapter we have been made aware of a similar paper by Hamilton, Klein, Sheshinski and Slutsky (1991).

exists for both classes of model. Our main conclusions are summarized in Section VI.

II.   The Model

Our model is similar to that used by Smithies (1941) with three exceptions. First, we consider both Cournot and Bertrand competition. Second, we concentrate on the *full competition* case (Case D in Smithies): *i.e.*, non-cooperation in locations *and* quantities or prices. Third, we consider two-stage games rather than simultaneous games.

Two firms, indexed 1 and 2, are assumed to choose locations on a linear market normalized to unit length. Their locations, as measured by their distances from the left-hand market boundary, are denoted x_1 and x_2. We assume by convention that firm 1 locates to the left of firm 2 (*i.e.*, $0 \leq x_1 \leq x_2 \leq 1$). They each sell a product that is homogeneous in all characteristics other than the location at which it is available. All production costs are normalized to zero. We confine attention to cases in which both firms are able and willing to supply the entire market.

Consumers are uniformly distributed at unit density over the line market with a consumer's location being indexed s. Each consumer's inverse demand function for the product is linear and is given by $p(s) = 1 - q(s)$, where p is price and q supply. No matter whether we consider Cournot or Bertrand competition, the market areas of the two firms will not overlap unless the firms are perfectly agglomerated: $x_1 = x_2$. Consumers will purchase the good from the firm offering the good at the lower price. In the event of a price tie we assume that demand is equally distributed between the two firms. The price charged by firm i to consumers at s is a f.o.b. price consisting of a mill price p_i plus transport costs $t \mid s\text{-}x_i \mid$, where t is the transport rate assumed linear in distance and quantity transported. Under Cournot competition the price will be set by a market-clearing condition once the firms have set their outputs q_i, while with Bertrand competition the decision variables are the mill prices p_i.

We confine our attention to subgame perfect Nash equilibria in which the firms first choose locations and then quantities or prices. In other words, the competitive game is solved in two stages. The second stage identifies the optimal quantity or price schedules for *any* pair of locations of the firms. In the first stage the equilibrium locations are derived in the belief that the second-stage choices will be an equilibrium quantity or price pair for the second stage subgame. Formal definition of these equilibria are as follows. A pure strategy subgame perfect Nash equilibrium for the two-stage quantity-location game is defined as a pair of locations (x_1^c, x_2^c) and a quantity pair $\left(q_1^c(x_1^c, x_2^c), q_2^c(x_1^c, x_2^c)\right)$ such that

(1) $\Pi_1\left((q_1^c(x_1^c,x_2^c),q_2^c(x_1^c,x_2^c)),x_1^c,x_2^c\right) \geq \Pi_1\left((q_1^c(x_1,x_2^c),q_2^c(x_1,x_2^c)),x_1,x_2^c\right) \ \forall \ x_1 \in [0,1],$

and

$\Pi_2\left((q_1^c(x_1^c,x_2^c),q_2^c(x_1^c,x_2^c)),x_1^c,x_2^c\right) \geq \Pi_2\left((q_1^c(x_1^c,x_2),q_2^c(x_1^c,x_2)),x_1^c,x_2\right) \ \forall \ x_2 \in [0,1],$

where $q_1^c(x_1,x_2)$ and $q_2^c(x_1,x_2)$ are such that

(2) $\Pi_1(q_1^c(x_1,x_2),q_2^c(x_1,x_2),x_1,x_2) \geq \Pi_1(q_1,q_2^c(x_1,x_2),x_1,x_2)$

$\forall\ q_1 \geq 0$ and $x_1,x_2 \in [0,1]$, and

$\Pi_2((q_1^c(x_1,x_2),q_2^c(x_1,x_2)),x_1,x_2) \geq \Pi_2((q_1^c(x_1,x_2),q_2^c(x_1,x_2)),x_1,x_2)$

$\forall\ q_2 \geq 0$ and $x_2 \in [0,1]$.

A pure strategy subgame perfect Nash equilibrium for the two-stage price-location game is defined as a pair of locations (X_1^b,X_2^b) and a price pair $\left(p_1^b(x_1^b,x_2^b),p_2^b(x_1^b,x_2^b)\right)$ such that

(3) $\Pi_1\left((p_1^b(x_1^b,x_2^b),p_2^b(x_1^b,x_2^b)),x_1^b,x_2^b\right) \geq \Pi_1\left((p_1^b(x_1,x_2^b),p_2^b(x_1,x_2^b)),x_1,x_2^b\right)\ \forall\ x_1 \in [0,1]$,

and

$\Pi_2\left((p_1^b(x_1^b,x_2^b),p_2^b(x_1^b,x_2^b)),x_1^b,x_2^b\right) \geq \Pi_2\left((p_1^b(x_1^b,x_2),p_2^b(x_1^b,x_2)),x_1^b,x_2\right)\ \forall\ x_2 \in [0,1]$,

where $p_1^b(x_1,x_2)$ and $p_2^b(x_1,x_2)$ are such that

(4) $\Pi_1\left(p_1^b(x_1,x_2),p_2^b(x_1,x_2),x_1,x_2\right) \geq \Pi_1(p_1,p_2^b(x_1,x_2),x_1,x_2)$

$\forall\ p_1 \geq 0$ and $x_1,x_2 \in [0,1]$, and

$\Pi_2\left((p_1^b(x_1,x_2),p_2^b(x_1,x_2)),x_1,x_2\right) \geq \Pi_2(p_1^b(x_1,x_2),p_2,x_1,x_2)$

$\forall\ p_2 \geq 0$ and $x_2 \in [0,1]$.

III.   Quantity Competition

1.   QUANTITY AND LOCATION

In analyzing equilibria for the quantity subgame we take advantage of the definition in equations (1) of subgame perfect equilibrium for the location stage of the game. We show elsewhere (al-Nowaihi and Norman, 1992) that there can be no location equilibrium such that x_1 and $x_2 > 0.5$ (or < 0.5), since then firm 2 would wish to locate to the left of firm 1 (or firm 1 to the right of firm 2), effectively changing the identities of the firms. We confine our attention, therefore, to cases in which $0 \leq x_1 \leq 1/2 \leq x_2 \leq 1$. We proceed following the logic of Scheinkman induction from the second-style subgame on quantities to the first-stage game on locations.

2.   THE QUANTITY EQUILIBRIUM

In solving the quantity subgame of equations (2) we must distinguish two cases: perfect agglomeration - $x_1 = x_2$ - and non-agglomeration - $x_1 < x_2$. Firstly, take the perfect agglomeration case.

When the firms are perfectly agglomerated, we have a special case of the standard Cournot model: the product is homogeneous in all characteristics. Both firms supply the entire market area and the product price (p) will be determined by aggregate output (q). The quantity dq sold to consumers in the interval ds located at s ($0 \leq s \leq 1$) is dq = $(1 - p - t \mid s - x \mid)$ds from which we derive aggregate demand

(5) $$q = \int_{x=0}^{1} dq = \left[1 - \frac{t}{2} + tx - tx^2 \right] - p.$$

Application of standard Cournot analysis to the demand function (5) gives the following proposition.

PROPOSITION 1: When the duopolists are perfectly agglomerated - $x_1 = x_2 = x$ - the Nash equilibrium for the quantity subgame is

(6) $$q_1^a(x) = q_2^a(x) = \frac{1 - \frac{t}{2} + tx - tx^2}{3} ,$$

and the resulting prices and profits are

(7) $$p^a(x) = \frac{1 - \frac{t}{2} + tx - tx^2}{3} , \text{ and}$$

(8) $$\Pi_i^a(x) = p^a(x)q_i^a(x) = \frac{\left[1 - \frac{t}{2} + tx - tx^2 \right]^2}{9} \quad (i=1,2). \ \square$$

It follows immediately from differentiation of equations (6)-(8) that if the two firms are perfectly agglomerated - $x_1 = x_2 = x$ - then output, price and profit will be greater the nearer are the firms located to the market centre.

Secondly, take the case with non-agglomeration. When the firms are not agglomerated, the products are perceived by consumers as being differentiated by location. There will be no market overlap. Rather, given the outputs q_i of the two firms, the market-clearing condition will determine the mill prices p_i (i = 1,2) and the market boundary x' between the firms, where x': $p_1 + t \mid x'-x_1 \mid = p_2 + t \mid x'-x_2 \mid$ from which

(9) $$x' = \frac{(p_2-p_1)}{2} + \frac{(x_1+x_2)}{2}.$$

Firm 1 (2) will supply all consumers to the left (right) of x'.

The quantity dq_1 sold to consumers in the interval ds located at s ($0 \leq s \leq x'$) is $dq_1 = (1 - p_1 - t \mid s-x_1 \mid)ds$ and the quantity dq_2 sold to consumers in the interval ds located at s ($x' \leq s \leq 1$) is $dq_2 = (1 - p_2 - t \mid s - x_2 \mid)ds$ from which the aggregate quantity sold by each firm is

$$(10) \quad q_1 = \int_{x=0}^{x'} dq_1 = (1 - p_1 + tx_1)x' - \frac{t(x')^2}{2} - tx_1^2, \text{ and}$$

$$(11) \quad q_2 = \int_{x=x'}^{1} dq_2 = (1 - p_2 + t(1 - x_2))(1 - x') - \frac{t(1 - x')^2}{2} - t(1 - x_2^2).$$

These demand functions can be written as the implicit functions

$(10')$ $F(q_1, q_2, p_1, p_2) = 0$, and

$(11')$ $G(q_1, q_2, p_1, p_2) = 0$.

Profit to firm i is, given our normalizations,

(12) $\Pi_i = p_i q_i$ $(i = 1, 2)$,

from which we derive the Cournot reaction functions

$$(13) \quad CR_i : \frac{\partial \Pi_i}{\partial q_i} = p_i + q_i \frac{\partial p_i}{\partial q_i} = 0 \quad (i = 1, 2).$$

Denote by F_n and G_n the partial derivatives of $(10')$ and $(11')$ with respect to the nth argument, and by p_{ii} the partial derivatives $\partial p_i / \partial q_i$ $(i = 1, 2)$. Then,

$$(14) \quad p_{11} = \frac{F_4 G_1 - F_1 G_4}{F_3 G_4 - F_4 G_3}, \text{ and}$$

$$(15) \quad p_{22} = \frac{F_3 G_2 - F_2 G_3}{F_3 G_4 - F_4 G_3}.$$

Substituting for F_n and G_n from the Appendix gives

$$CR_1: 2tDp_1 - \left[1 - p_2 + (1 - x_2) + (1 - x')\right] \cdot \left[(1 - p_1 + tx_1)x' - \frac{t(x')^2}{2} - tx_1^2\right] = 0, \text{ and}$$

$$CR_2: 2tDp_2 - \left[1 - p_1 + tx_1 + tx'\right] \cdot \left[(1 - p_2 + t(1 - x_2))(1 - x') - \frac{t(1 - x')^2}{2} - t(1 - x_2)^2\right] = 0,$$

where $D = F_3 G_4 - F_4 G_3$. These reaction functions can be solved for prices p_i (i =

1,2) as functions of the location pair (x_1,x_2) and the solutions put into equations (10) and (11) to give the Nash equilibrium outputs $q_i^c(x_1,x_2)$ for the quantity subgame.

The complicated nature of the reaction functions makes analytic solution difficult. It is possible, however, to obtain numeric solutions for various values of the transport rate t and location pairs (x_1,x_2). Figure 1 illustrates the reaction functions in quantities for two values of t and a location pair (x_1,x_2). Table 1 provides more detailed information on the nature of the equilibria of the second-stage quantity game.[2] A number of results[3] follows from these simulations.

CONJECTURE 1: For any location pair (x_1,x_2) if firm i is located nearer the market centre than firm k, then
(i)   firm i will produce a greater output than firm k:

$$q_1^c(x_1,x_2) \gtreqless q_2^c(x_1,x_2) \quad \text{if} \quad x_1 \lesseqgtr 1-x_2;$$

(ii)   firm i will charge a higher mill price than firm k:

$$p_1^c(x_1,x_2) \gtreqless p_2^c(x_1,x_2) \quad \text{if} \quad x_1 \lesseqgtr 1-x_2; \quad \text{and}$$

(iii)   firm i will earn greater profit than firm k:

$$\Pi_1^c(x_1,x_2) \gtreqless \Pi_2^c(x_1,x_2) \quad \text{if} \quad x_1 \lesseqgtr 1-x_2. \quad \square$$

There is a strong competitive advantage conferred by a more central location. Conjecture 1 does *not* indicate that a firm will always wish to locate nearer to the market centre than its rival, but the following conjecture indicates at least one set of conditions under which this will be the case.

CONJECTURE 2: Consider any location pair (x_1,x_2) such that $x_1 \leq 1/2$ and $x_2 \geq 1/2$. Let $t_q \cong 0.5104$. For $t < t_q$ firm i's profit is greater the nearer is firm i located to the market centre. $\square$

Location by firm i nearer to the market centre gains consumers from the rival but reduces sales on firm i's market periphery. The lower are transport costs, the weaker will be the sales reduction effect and the more the firm will be encouraged to attempt to invade its rival's territory.

---

[2] We do not provide values for $x_1 = x_2 = 1/2$ for reasons that will become clear below.

[3] Second-order conditions indicate that the reaction functions are monotonic. We conjecture that a unique quantity equilibrium exists for each pair of locations. Simulations have not produced any counterexamples but, of course, an existence proof would be desirable. Results derived from simulations are denoted Conjectures. The simulations were performed using PC-MATLAB. Details are available from the authors on request.

Figure 1a.   Quantity reaction curves: $x_1 = 0.45$, $x_2 = 0.75$ and $t = 0.2$

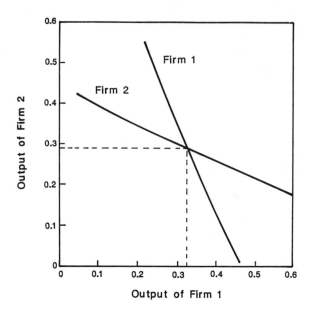

Figure 1b.   Quantity reaction curves: $x_1 = 0.45$, $x_2 = 0.75$ and $t = 0.5$

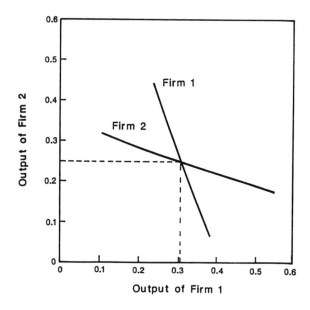

Table 1.   Solutions to the quantity game: (i) t = 0.2

(a) Output

		x_2					
		1.0	0.9	0.8	0.7	0.6	0.5
	0	0.3013	0.2955	0.2886	0.2806	0.2717	0.2617
	0.1	0.3125	0.3067	0.2997	0.2917	0.2826	0.2725
	0.2	0.3225	0.3166	0.3096	0.3015	0.2923	0.2821
x_1	0.3	0.3312	0.3253	0.3182	0.3100	0.3008	0.2905
	0.4	0.3385	0.3326	0.3255	0.3173	0.3079	0.2976
	0.5	0.3444	0.3385	0.3314	0.3232	0.3138	

(b) Price

		x_2					
		1.0	0.9	0.8	0.7	0.6	0.5
	0	0.3474	0.3429	0.3374	0.3308	0.3232	0.3145
	0.1	0.3572	0.3526	0.3471	0.3405	0.3329	0.3242
	0.2	0.3649	0.3603	0.3548	0.3482	0.3406	0.3319
x_1	0.3	0.3706	0.3661	0.3605	0.3539	0.3463	0.3376
	0.4	0.3746	0.3700	0.3644	0.3578	0.3501	0.3414
	0.5	0.3768	0.3722	0.3666	0.3599	0.3522	

(c) Profit

		x_2					
		1.0	0.9	0.8	0.7	0.6	0.5
	0	0.1047	0.1013	0.0974	0.0928	0.0878	0.0823
	0.1	0.1116	0.1081	0.1040	0.0993	0.0941	0.0884
	0.2	0.1177	0.1141	0.1098	0.1050	0.0996	0.0936
x_1	0.3	0.1227	0.1191	0.1147	0.1097	0.1042	0.0981
	0.4	0.1268	0.1231	0.1186	0.1135	0.1078	0.1016
	0.5	0.1298	0.1260	0.1215	0.1163	0.1105	

(d) Consumer Surplus

		x_2					
		1.0	0.9	0.8	0.7	0.6	0.5
	0	0.1820	0.1852	0.1870	0.1874	0.1866	0.1846
	0.1	0.1852	0.1884	0.1901	0.1906	0.1897	0.1876
	0.2	0.1870	0.1901	0.1918	0.1922	0.1912	0.1889
x_1	0.3	0.1874	0.1906	0.1922	0.1924	0.1912	0.1888
	0.4	0.1866	0.1897	0.1912	0.1912	0.1899	0.1873
	0.5	0.1846	0.1876	0.1889	0.1888	0.1873	

(e) Total Surplus

		x_2					
		1.0	0.9	0.8	0.7	0.6	0.5
	0	0.3913	0.3981	0.4020	0.4030	0.4012	0.3967
	0.1	0.3981	0.4047	0.4083	0.4090	0.4068	0.4019
	0.2	0.4020	0.4083	0.4115	0.4119	0.4094	0.4041
x_1	0.3	0.4030	0.4090	0.4119	0.4118	0.4089	0.4032
	0.4	0.4012	0.4068	0.4094	0.4089	0.4056	0.3994
	0.5	0.3967	0.4019	0.4041	0.4032	0.3994	

Notes: Data in sub-tables (a) - (c) are for firm 1. Transposing these sub-tables gives the corresponding data for firm 2. For example, for the location pair (x^i_1, x^k_2) if output of firm 1 is q_{ik}, then
output of firm 2 is q_{ki} .

Table 1 (continued). Solutions to the quantity game: (ii) t = 0.6

(a) Output

		x_2					
		1.0	0.9	0.8	0.7	0.6	0.5
	0	0.2451	0.2358	0.2244	0.2112	0.1967	0.1809
	0.1	0.2710	0.2612	0.2491	0.2351	0.2196	0.2028
	0.2	0.2937	0.2834	0.2707	0.2560	0.2396	0.2218
x_1	0.3	0.3127	0.3021	0.2888	0.2734	0.2561	0.2374
	0.4	0.3274	0.3165	0.3028	0.2868	0.2688	0.2491
	0.5	0.3374	0.3264	0.3124	0.2958	0.2771	

(b) Price

		x_2					
		1.0	0.9	0.8	0.7	0.6	0.5
	0	0.3599	0.3565	0.3513	0.3437	0.3333	0.3194
	0.1	0.3791	0.3757	0.3704	0.3628	0.3524	0.3388
	0.2	0.3900	0.3862	0.3806	0.3726	0.3620	0.3483
x_1	0.3	0.3943	0.3900	0.3828	0.3753	0.3641	0.3499
	0.4	0.3935	0.3885	0.3816	0.3723	0.3604	0.3456
	0.5	0.3884	0.3828	0.3751	0.3649	0.3522	

(c) Profit

		x_2					
		1.0	0.9	0.8	0.7	0.6	0.5
	0	0.0882	0.0841	0.0788	0.0726	0.0655	0.0578
	0.1	0.1027	0.0981	0.0922	0.0853	0.0774	0.0687
	0.2	0.1146	0.1095	0.1030	0.0954	0.0867	0.0772
x_1	0.3	0.1233	0.1178	0.1108	0.1026	0.0933	0.0831
	0.4	0.1288	0.1230	0.1156	0.1068	0.0969	0.0861
	0.5	0.1311	0.1250	0.1172	0.1079	0.0976	

(d) Consumer Surplus

		x_2					
		1.0	0.9	0.8	0.7	0.6	0.5
	0	0.1238	0.1316	0.1365	0.1391	0.1397	0.1384
	0.1	0.1316	0.1390	0.1436	0.1458	0.1460	0.1442
	0.2	0.1365	0.1436	0.1477	0.1495	0.1491	0.1465
x_1	0.3	0.1391	0.1458	0.1495	0.1506	0.1494	0.1458
	0.4	0.1397	0.1460	0.1491	0.1494	0.1471	0.1421
	0.5	0.1384	0.1442	0.1465	0.1458	0.1421	

(e) Total Surplus

		x_2					
		1.0	0.9	0.8	0.7	0.6	0.5
	0	0.3002	0.3184	0.3298	0.3350	0.3341	0.3273
	0.1	0.3184	0.3352	0.3453	0.3489	0.3464	0.3379
	0.2	0.3298	0.3453	0.3538	0.3557	0.3514	0.3409
x_1	0.3	0.3350	0.3489	0.3557	0.3558	0.3494	0.3368
	0.4	0.3341	0.3464	0.3514	0.3494	0.3408	0.3259
	0.5	0.3273	0.3379	0.3409	0.3368	0.3259	

Table 1 (continued). Solutions to the quantity game (iii): t = 0.76

(a) Output

x_1		x_2 1.0	0.9	0.8	0.7	0.6	0.5
	0	0.2254	0.2166	0.2056	0.1926	0.1781	0.1623
	0.1	0.2552	0.2456	0.2335	0.2194	0.2036	0.1865
	0.2	0.2811	0.2708	0.2578	0.2426	0.2256	0.2071
x_1	0.3	0.3023	0.2915	0.2776	0.2614	0.2433	0.2234
	0.4	0.3183	0.3069	0.2924	0.2752	0.2560	0.2349
	0.5	0.3284	0.3167	0.3015	0.2835	0.2632	

(b) Price

x_1		x_2 1.0	0.9	0.8	0.7	0.6	0.5
	0	0.3591	0.3577	0.3546	0.3488	0.3394	0.3257
	0.1	0.3812	0.3796	0.3762	0.3702	0.3608	0.3472
	0.2	0.3920	0.3898	0.3856	0.3789	0.3689	0.3548
x_1	0.3	0.3944	0.3913	0.3861	0.3783	0.3673	0.3524
	0.4	0.3906	0.3865	0.3802	0.3711	0.3589	0.3429
	0.5	0.3820	0.3769	0.3693	0.3589	0.3452	

(c) Profit

x_1		x_2 1.0	0.9	0.8	0.7	0.6	0.5
	0	0.0810	0.0775	0.0729	0.0672	0.0605	0.0528
	0.1	0.0973	0.0932	0.0879	0.0812	0.0735	0.0647
	0.2	0.1102	0.1055	0.0994	0.0919	0.0832	0.0735
x_1	0.3	0.1192	0.1140	0.1072	0.0989	0.0894	0.0787
	0.4	0.1423	0.1186	0.1112	0.1021	0.0919	0.0805
	0.5	0.1254	0.1193	0.1113	0.1017	0.0909	

(d) Consumer Surplus

x_1		x_2 1.0	0.9	0.8	0.7	0.6	0.5
	0	0.1077	0.1164	0.1220	0.1253	0.1267	0.1262
	0.1	0.1164	0.1248	0.1300	0.1329	0.1337	0.1326
	0.2	0.1220	0.1300	0.1348	0.1370	0.1371	0.1350
x_1	0.3	0.1253	0.1329	0.1370	0.1385	0.1376	0.1341
	0.4	0.1267	0.1337	0.1371	0.1376	0.1352	0.1299
	0.5	0.1262	0.1326	0.1350	0.1341	0.1299	

(e) Total Surplus

x_1		x_2 1.0	0.9	0.8	0.7	0.6	0.5
	0	0.2696	0.2912	0.3051	0.3117	0.3114	0.3045
	0.1	0.2912	0.3113	0.3234	0.3281	0.3258	0.3166
	0.2	0.3051	0.3234	0.3336	0.3362	0.3315	0.3198
x_1	0.3	0.3117	0.3281	0.3362	0.3364	0.3291	0.3145
	0.4	0.3114	0.3258	0.3315	0.3291	0.3189	0.3013
	0.5	0.3045	0.3166	0.3198	0.3145	0.3013	

ALI al-NOWAIHI and GEORGE NORMAN

Table 1 (continued). Solutions to the quantity game: (iv) $t = 1.0$

(a) Output

					x_2		
		1.0	0.9	0.8	0.7	0.6	0.5
	0	0.1988	0.1916	0.1821	0.1704	0.1568	0.1417
	0.1	0.2329	0.2246	0.2137	0.2005	0.1853	0.1684
	0.2	0.2621	0.2528	0.2406	0.2259	0.2090	0.1904
x_1	0.3	0.2856	0.2753	0.2618	0.2456	0.2271	0.2067
	0.4	0.3023	0.2912	0.2764	0.2588	0.2387	0.2165
	0.5	0.3116	0.2997	0.2838	0.2648	0.2431	

(b) Price

					x_2		
		1.0	0.9	0.8	0.7	0.6	0.5
	0	0.3523	0.3544	0.3552	0.3532	0.3470	0.3349
	0.1	0.3793	0.3808	0.3808	0.3780	0.3712	0.3588
	0.2	0.3901	0.3903	0.3889	0.3845	0.3761	0.3624
x_1	0.3	0.3897	0.3885	0.3852	0.3789	0.3685	0.3531
	0.4	0.3815	0.3787	0.3736	0.3651	0.3526	0.3353
	0.5	0.3676	0.3633	0.3562	0.3455	0.3309	

(c) Profit

					x_2		
		1.0	0.9	0.8	0.7	0.6	0.5
	0	0.0701	0.0679	0.0647	0.0602	0.0544	0.0475
	0.1	0.0884	0.0855	0.0814	0.0758	0.0688	0.0604
	0.2	0.1023	0.0987	0.0935	0.0868	0.0786	0.0690
x_1	0.3	0.1113	0.1069	0.1008	0.0930	0.0837	0.0730
	0.4	0.1153	0.1103	0.1033	0.0945	0.00842	0.0726
	0.5	0.1146	0.1089	0.1011	0.0915	0.0804	

(d) Consumer Surplus

					x_2		
		1.0	0.9	0.8	0.7	0.6	0.5
	0	0.0895	0.0990	0.1049	0.1087	0.1109	0.1118
	0.1	0.0990	0.1081	0.1137	0.1171	0.1188	0.1189
	0.2	0.1049	0.1137	0.1190	0.1218	0.1226	0.1215
x_1	0.3	0.1087	0.1171	0.1218	0.1238	0.1234	0.1204
	0.4	0.1109	0.1188	0.1226	0.1234	0.1212	0.1156
	0.5	0.1118	0.1189	0.1215	0.1204	0.1156	

(e) Total Surplus

					x_2		
		1.0	0.9	0.8	0.7	0.6	0.5
	0	0.2296	0.2552	0.2718	0.2801	0.2807	0.2738
	0.1	0.2552	0.2792	0.2938	0.2998	0.2978	0.2882
	0.2	0.2718	0.2938	0.3061	0.3095	0.3045	0.2916
x_1	0.3	0.2801	0.2998	0.3095	0.3099	0.3016	0.2849
	0.4	0.2807	0.2978	0.3045	0.3016	0.2895	0.2686
	0.5	0.2738	0.2882	0.2916	0.2849	0.2686	

Our simulations indicate that for any location pair (x_1, x_2) an increase in the transport rate t will reduce the quantity produced by each firm, increase the mill prices and reduce profits. They also provide a benchmark against which we can assess the actual locations the firms choose in the location stage of the quantity-location game. No matter the transport rate, if the firms are located symmetrically (i.e., $x_2 = 1-x_1$), then individual firm profit is maximized when the firms are located inside but "near" the quartiles and total surplus (the sum of total firms' profits and consumer surplus) is maximized when the firms are located symmetrically "near" the quartiles.

Not surprisingly, aggregate output is maximized when the firms are located symmetrically. What is, perhaps, surprising is that the symmetric location pair that maximizes aggregate output is more agglomerated the higher is the transport rate. Low transport costs encourage agglomeration and quantity competition. By contrast, high transport costs imply that sales decline relatively quickly with distance from the firm and so give heavier weight to consumers close to the firm. This moderates somewhat the competitive pressures of proximate locations.

3. THE LOCATION EQUILIBRIUM

The first-order conditions for a location equilibrium are that equations (1) and (13) hold (quantities are optimally adjusted to the location choice). Moreover,

(16) LR_1 : $\dfrac{\partial \Pi_1^c}{\partial x_1} < 0$ for $0 < x_1 < x_2$ and $\dfrac{\partial \Pi_1^c}{\partial x_1} > 0$ for $0 < x_1 < x_2$, and

LR_2 : $\dfrac{\partial \Pi_2^c}{\partial x_2} < 0$ for $x_1 < x_2 < 1$ and $\dfrac{\partial \Pi_2^c}{\partial x_2} > 0$ for $x_1 < x_2 < 1$.

While it is possible to obtain analytic solutions to equations (16), these are so complex as to be intractable. The following series of results can, however, be derived.

CONJECTURE 3: If an equilibrium exists for the two-stage quantity-location game, the two firms are symmetrically located: $x_1^c = x_2^c = x^c$. $\square$

LEMMA 1: For any location pair (x_1^c, x_2^c) such that $x_1^c \leq 0.5$ and $x_2^c \geq 0.5$, the limit as $x_1^c, x_2^c \to 0.5$ of q_i^c, p_i^c and Π_i^c are

(17) $q_i^c \to \dfrac{8 - 13t + \sqrt{97t^2 + 80t + 64}}{48}$,

(18) $p_i^c \to \dfrac{16 + 7t + \sqrt{97t^2 + 80t + 64}}{24}$, and

(19) $\Pi_i^c \rightarrow \dfrac{16 - 58t - 47t^2 + (2 + 5t)\sqrt{97t^2 + 80t + 64}}{288}$. $\square$

Define by t_{max} the maximum economically relevant value of t: the maximum transport rate for which both firms will be willing and able to supply the entire market: $t_{max} \cong 1.8$. Comparison with Proposition 1 gives Lemma 2.

LEMMA 2:
(i)   If t = 0, then
        (a) the locations of the firms are of no consequence and
        (b) $q_i^c = q_i^c$, $p_i^a = p_i^c$ and $\Pi_i^a = \Pi_i^c$ (i=1,2); and

(ii)   if $0 < t < t_{max}$, then $q_i^c \left[\dfrac{1}{2}\right] > q_i^c$, $p_i^a < p_i^c$ and $\Pi_i^a \left[\dfrac{1}{2}\right] < \Pi_i^c$ (i=1,2). $\square$

Lemma 2 points to the central role played by product differentiation in the quantity-location game. If the firms are perfectly agglomerated at (½,½), the products are perceived by consumers as being perfectly homogeneous, there is perfect market overlap and the equilibrium of Proposition 1 applies. If, however, one firm locates marginally away from (½,½), the products of the firms are perceived as being differentiated by consumers and the market overlap disappears: each firm supplies its own "natural" market area. Product differentiation allows the firm that has located away from the market centre to restrict its output, which will lead the rival also to restrict its output. The quantity game will give an equilibrium approximately that of Lemma 1 (approximately, because the two firms are not perfectly symmetrically located) with individual firm (and aggregate) output lower and prices and profit higher than the perfectly agglomerated equilibrium of Proposition 1.

Recall Conjecture 2 in which we define t_q. Conjectures 2 and 3 and Lemmas 1 and 2 allow us to state what might appear on first sight to be a surprising non-existence result for the quantity-location game.[4]

CONJECTURE 4: (i) If t = 0, any location pair (x_1, x_2) in [0,1] is an equilibrium to the location subgame, where the equilibrium for the quantity subgame is given by Proposition 1; and (ii) if $0 < t < t_q$, there exists no equilibrium to the two-stage quantity location game. $\square$

The non-existence problems that are familiar in price-location games when firms are not able to price discriminate between their consumers, extend to quantity-location games.

---

[4]We can prove analytically the weaker result that for t small but greater than zero and for x_i near 1/2 ($x_1 < 1/2$ and $x_2 > 1/2$) the profit function for firm 1 is increasing and for firm 2 is decreasing in x_i: there is no quantity-location equilibrium for this range of values of t (proof is available from the authors on request). We prefer to present Conjecture 4, since it applies to a wider range of values of t. The value for t_q has been determined from the simulations. Greater accuracy is possible but is of little value.

Part (i) of Conjecture 4 is straightforward and needs no comment. An outline proof of part (ii) is as follows. If a location equilibrium exists, it must be symmetric. But if transport costs are low enough $(t < t_q)$, no symmetric location pair $(x_1, 1-x_1)$ with $x_1 < 1/2$ can be an equilibrium: each firm has the incentive to choose a location nearer to the market centre. Thus, the only candidate equilibrium is perfect agglomeration at the centre. But now the products of the firms are perfectly homogeneous. The resulting change in aggregate demand perceived by the two firms leads each to increase output, which reduces profit below the level that would apply if they were not agglomerated. Thus, perfect agglomeration cannot be an equilibrium.

A relatively simple intuition underlies this non-existence result. There are two effects at work in determining a firms' location: what might be termed the *market area effect* and the *market periphery effect*. The market area effect encourages each firm to attempt to invade its rival's market. The nature of the two-stage game makes this effect particularly strong, since in the two-stage game the firms anticipate the Nash equilibrium quantities when making their location choices. The nearer to the market centre that firm i locates, the lower is the anticipated output of firm k implying that agglomeration is encouraged.

The market periphery effect encourages the firms to separate in order to maintain sales to consumers on the periphery [near the left-hand (right-hand) boundary for firm 1 (2)] *provided* that demand is elastic. The *proviso* is important. When $t << t_q$, delivered price is in the *inelastic* portion of the individual demand curve $(p_i + t \mid s - x_i \mid \ < 1/2)$ for the majority of a firm's customers even if the firm is located near to the market centre. Indeed, there are values of $t < t_q$ for which demand is inelastic for *all* a firm's consumers. In these circumstances a location nearer to the market centre will give a higher mill price and so higher revenues and profit: the market area effect dominates. The principle of minimum differentiation (Eaton and Lipsey, 1975) holds and the firms wish to agglomerate. However, once the firms are perfectly agglomerated the lack of any degree of product differentiation intensifies the quantity competition between them. Each firm finds that it is more profitable to locate marginally away from its rival in order to gain exclusive control of its natural market. Such a move lessens competitive pressures between the firms, restricts output and increases profit.

The non-existence result of Conjecture 4 relies on transport costs being sufficiently low such that either firm's profit increases with a location nearer the market centre. For transport costs greater than t_q this condition no longer applies.

CONJECTURE 5: For $t > t_q$ there exists some $(t) - 0 < (t) < 1/2 -$ such that
(i)   if $x_2 = 1/2$, then

$$\frac{\partial \Pi_1^c}{\partial x_1} < 0 \text{ for } x_1 > \frac{1}{2} - \xi(t),$$

$$\frac{\partial \Pi_1^c}{\partial x_1} = 0 \text{ for } x_1 = \frac{1}{2} - \xi(t), \text{ and}$$

$$\frac{\partial \Pi_1^c}{\partial x_1} > 0 \text{ for } x_1 = \frac{1}{2} - \xi(t); \text{ and}$$

(ii)   if $x_1 = 1/2$, then

$$\frac{\partial \Pi_2^c}{\partial x_2} > 0 \text{ for } x_2 < \frac{1}{2} - \xi(t),$$

$$\frac{\partial \Pi_2^c}{\partial x_2} = 0 \text{ for } x_2 = \frac{1}{2} - \xi(t), \text{ and}$$

$$\frac{\partial \Pi_2^c}{\partial x_2} < 0 \text{ for } x_2 > \frac{1}{2} - \xi(t). \quad \Box$$

Conjectures 3, 5 and the location reaction functions (16) then give Conjecture 6.

CONJECTURE 6: For $t > t_q$ there is some $\xi(t) > 0$ such that a location equilibrium (x_1^c, x_2^c) with $x_1^c = x_2^c = x^c = \frac{1}{2} - \xi(t)$ and $\frac{\partial \xi(t)}{\partial t} > 0$ exists. $\quad \Box$

Table 2 presents some values for $\xi(t)$, and Figure 2 illustrates two location reaction functions for cases in which $t > t_q$.

Table 2.   Optimal location for the quantity-location game

t	$\xi(t)$	x^c
0.6	0.0311	0.4689
0.76	0.0797	0.4203
1.0	0.1303	0.3697
1.25	0.1702	0.3298

As expected, the location equilibrium exhibits more agglomeration than would the locations that maximize aggregate profits, consumer surplus or total surplus. Recall the discussion of Conjecture 4. The higher is the transport rate, the greater is the proportion of a firm's customers for whom demand is *elastic*. A location nearer the market centre will reduce sales and revenues for this proportion of the firm's market area, and so moderates the attempts at invasion of the rival's territory. As Conjectures 5 and 6 indicate, if transport costs are high enough the market periphery effect outweighs the market area effect and discourages the firms from agglomerating. This has the immediate effect of guaranteeing the existence of a quantity-location equilibrium.

Figure 2a.   Location reaction curves: t = 1.0

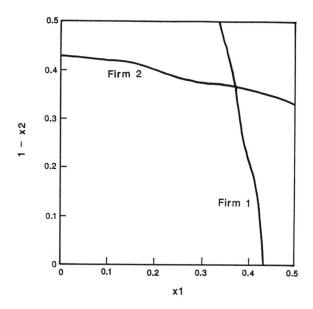

Figure 2b.   Location reaction curves: t = 1.25

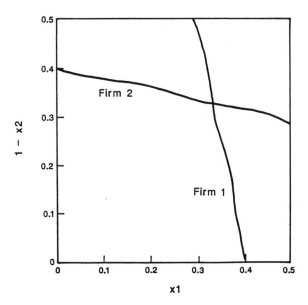

IV.   Price Competition[5]

1.   THE PRICE EQUILIBRIUM

Denote $q_1(R) = \int_0^R (1-p_1-ts)ds$. Then, for the two-stage price-location game the demand function $q_1(.)$ for firm 1 conditional upon the location pair (x_1,x_2) and the price p_2 charged by firm 2 is defined as follows:

(i)   if $p_1 \geq p_2 + t(x_2-x_1)$, then $q_1(.) = 0$;

(ii)   if $p_2 + t(x_2-x_1) > p_1 > p_2-t(x_2-x_1)$, then $q_1(.) = q_1(x_1) + q_1(x'-x_1)$;

(iii)   if $p_1 = p_2-t(x_2-x_1)$, then $q_1(.) = q_1(x_1) + q_1(x'-x_1) + q_1(1-x_2)$; and

(iv)   if $p_1 < p_2-t(x_2-x_1)$, then $q_1(.) = q_1(x_1) + q_1(1-x_1)$.

Here x' is given by equation (9). A similar definition holds for firm 2.

There is a discontinuity in the demand function as p_1 crosses the boundary between conditions (ii) and (iv): if condition (ii) holds, then the two firms split the market; whereas when condition (iv) holds, firm 1 undercuts firm 2 and takes the entire market. The discontinuity in demand gives rise to a discontinuity in firm 1's profit function and so to the possibility that there will exist no price equilibrium for some location pairs (x_1,x_2). Similar non-existence problems have been analyzed for the Hotelling case by, for example, d'Aspremont et al. (1979) and Anderson (1988). We can state Proposition 2 immediately.

PROPOSITION 2: For any location pair (x_1,x_2) such that $x_1 = x_2$ the Nash equilibrium for the price subgame is $p_1 = p_2 = 0$. $\square$

Proof relies on a standard Bertrand argument. Assume, then, that the two firms are not agglomerated: for example, consider location pairs (x_1,x_2) such that $x_1 < x_2$. Applying the same reasoning as for the quantity/location game, we further confine attention without loss of generality to location pairs such that $x_1 < 1/2$ and $x_2 > 1/2$. We proceed in three steps. First, we identify the price equilibrium (p_1^b,p_2^b) given that the firms are in region (ii) of their demand functions. We then check whether firm 1 can feasibly undercut firm 2: does there exist a p_1^u such that $0 < p_1^u < p_2^u-t(x_2-x_1)$? Finally, we check whether price undercutting is both feasible and profitable: that is, whether $\Pi_1^u(p_1^u) > \Pi_1^b(p_1^b)$. First, profit to firm i is given by equations (12) from which we derive the

---

[5]This section is a reformulation of Case D in the analysis by Smithies (1941) in which we specify the price-location game as a two-stage game by contrast to the simultaneous game employed by Smithies.

Bertrand reaction functions[6]

(20) BR_i: $\dfrac{\partial \Pi_i}{\partial p_i} = q_i + p_i \dfrac{\partial q_i}{\partial p_i} = 0$ (i=1,2).

Differentiating the demand functions assuming condition (ii) holds for each firm gives:

$$BR_1: \left[1 - p_1 + tx_1 - \frac{t}{2}x'\right]\left[x' - \frac{p_1}{2t}\right] - \frac{3}{4}p_1 x' - tx_1^2 = 0, \text{ and}$$

$$BR_2: \left[1 - p_2 + t(1 - x_2) - \frac{t}{2}(1 - x')\right]\left[1 - x' - \frac{p_2}{2t}\right] - \frac{3}{4}p_1(1 - x') - t(1 - x_2)^2 = 0.$$

As with the quantity equilibrium, analytic solution is awkward but numeric solutions for and the associated profits are easily generated. Second, given the results of the firsts step, we can identify the undercutting price p_1^u and the associated profit[7]. If $p_1^u > 0$, then price undercutting is feasible. Third, price undercutting increases profit for firm 1 if $\Pi_1^u(p_1^u) > \Pi_1^b(p_1^b)$ for some location pair (x_1, x_2). Then, there is no price equilibrium for that location pair.

Table 3 presents the calculations of p_1^u, p_1^b, and $\Pi_1^u(p_1^u) - \Pi_1^b(p_1^b)$ for a range of values of locations and the transport rate. As might be expected given our knowledge of price-location games, for any transport rate $t > 0$ there are location pairs (x_1, x_2) for which there exists no price equilibrium. This follows from a simple continuity argument: so long as firms 1 and 2 are located *near* to each other, price undercutting will be feasible and profitable for at least one of them. It can also be seen that the higher is the transport rate, the narrower is the set of location pairs (x_1, x_2) for which there exists no price equilibrium. This is merely a restatement of a similar finding by Smithies. For any location pair, the higher is the transport rate, the greater the extent to which firm 1 has to cut its price in order to undercut firm 2 and the less profitable will such undercutting be.

---

[6]There is a further complication that should be investigated. Solution of the reaction functions assumes that the resulting prices are such that $x_1 < x' < x_2$: a condition that will not always hold [see Anderson (1988) for a similar discussion in the Hotelling case]. Our restriction on the ranges of x_1 and x_2 ensures that this condition will always be satisfied.

[7]A similar calculation can be performed for firm 2 with symmetric results.

Table 3.   Price Equilibrium

(i) t = 0.5

(a) p_1^b

					x_2		
		1.0	0.9	0.8	0.7	0.6	0.5
	0	0.3022	0.2940	0.2836	0.2709	0.2557	0.2380
	0.1	0.3144	0.3063	0.2960	0.2834	0.2685	0.2511
	0.2	0.3203	0.3122	0.3020	0.2896	0.2749	0.2579
x_1	0.3	0.3210	0.3129	0.3028	0.2905	0.2760	0.2593
	0.4	0.3174	0.3094	0.2992	0.2870	0.2728	0.2564
	0.5	0.3104	0.3023	0.2923	0.2802	0.2661	

(b) p_1^u

					x_2		
		1.0	0.9	0.8	0.7	0.6	0.5
	0	-0.1978	-0.1356	-0.0797	-0.0290	0.0174	0.0604
	0.1	-0.1560	-0.0937	-0.0378	-0.0129	0.0594	0.1023
	0.2	-0.1164	-0.0540	0.0020	0.0528	0.0992	0.1423
x_1	0.3	-0.0791	-0.0166	0.0396	0.0905	0.1370	0.1802
	0.4	-0.0443	0.0185	0.0749	0.1260	0.1728	0.2161
	0.5	-0.0210	0.0511	0.1079	0.1593	0.2064	

(c) $\Pi_1\left(p_1^u\right) - \Pi\left(p_1^b\right)$

					x_2		
		1.0	0.9	0.8	0.7	0.6	0.5
	0	-0.1751	-0.1432	-0.1124	-0.0821	-0.0519	-0.0213
	0.1	-0.1738	-0.1390	-0.1053	-0.0722	-0.0392	-0.0058
	0.2	-0.1682	-0.1308	-0.0945	-0.0589	-0.0233	0.0126
x_1	0.3	-0.1586	-0.1189	-0.0804	-0.0425	-0.0048	0.0333
	0.4	-0.1456	-0.1040	-0.0637	-0.0240	0.0156	0.0554
	0.5	-0.1300	-0.0870	-0.0452	-0.0041	0.0369	

(ii) t = 0.76

(a) p_1^b

					x_2		
		1.0	0.9	0.8	0.7	0.6	0.5
	0	0.3425	0.3379	0.3305	0.3195	0.3043	0.2842
	0.1	0.3608	0.3558	0.3480	0.3367	0.3215	0.3017
	0.2	0.3674	0.3617	0.3533	0.3415	0.3260	0.3064
x_1	0.3	0.3652	0.3588	0.3497	0.3373	0.3214	0.3017
	0.4	0.3564	0.3494	0.3395	0.3265	0.3101	0.2903
	0.5	0.3426	0.3350	0.3244	0.3109	0.2941	

(b) p_1^u

					x_2		
		1.0	0.9	0.8	0.7	0.6	0.5
	0	-0.4175	-0.3232	-0.2406	-0.1668	-0.0996	-0.0374
	0.1	-0.3461	-0.2522	-0.1703	-0.0972	-0.0306	0.0310
	0.2	-0.2775	-0.1840	-0.1027	-0.0303	0.0355	0.0964
x_1	0.3	-0.2125	-0.1193	-0.0385	0.0333	0.0985	0.1589
	0.4	-0.1517	-0.0585	0.0220	0.0934	0.1581	0.2181
	0.5	-0.0958	-0.0023	0.0784	0.1497	0.2143	

Table 3 (continued).

(c) $\Pi_1\left(p_1^u\right) - \Pi\left(p_1^b\right)$

		x_2					
		1.0	0.9	0.8	0.7	0.6	0.5
	0	-0.1959	-0.1675	-0.1409	-0.1152	-0.0893	-0.0622
	0.1	-0.2095	-0.1755	-0.1438	-0.1128	-0.0816	-0.0490
	0.2	-0.2124	-0.1733	-0.1367	-0.1009	-0.0647	-0.0272
x_1	0.3	-0.2051	-0.1615	-0.1205	-0.0804	-0.0399	0.0020
	0.4	-0.1891	-0.1417	-0.0970	-0.0562	-0.0091	0.0364
	0.5	-0.1667	-0.1163	-0.0686	-0.0220	0.0251	

(iii) t = 1.0

(a) p_1^b

		x_2					
		1.0	0.9	0.8	0.7	0.6	0.5
	0	0.3486	0.3488	0.3467	0.3406	0.3292	0.3108
	0.1	0.3735	0.3726	0.3693	0.3621	0.3498	0.3311
	0.2	0.3814	0.3791	0.3740	0.3652	0.3514	0.3319
x_1	0.3	0.3774	0.3735	0.3667	0.3560	0.3407	0.3202
	0.4	0.3650	0.3596	0.3510	0.3387	0.3219	0.3005
	0.5	0.3464	0.3397	0.3296	0.3156	0.2976	

(b) p_1^u

		x_2					
		1.0	0.9	0.8	0.7	0.6	0.5
	0	-0.6514	-0.5265	-0.4186	-0.3226	-0.2350	-0.1536
	0.1	-0.5512	-0.4274	-0.3209	-0.2265	-0.1404	-0.0603
	0.2	-0.4533	-0.3307	-0.2260	-0.1333	-0.0490	0.0296
x_1	0.3	-0.3594	-0.2379	-0.1348	-0.0440	-0.0387	0.1156
	0.4	-0.2708	-0.1502	-0.0486	0.0407	0.1219	0.1976
	0.5	-0.1892	-0.0689	0.0319	0.1202	0.2005	

(c) $\Pi_1\left(p_1^u\right) - \Pi\left(p_1^b\right)$

		x_2					
		1.0	0.9	0.8	0.7	0.6	0.5
	0	-0.1686	-0.1473	-0.1285	-0.1110	-0.0937	-0.0753
	0.1	-0.2075	-0.1781	-0.1517	-0.1266	-0.1013	-0.0744
	0.2	-0.2282	-0.1910	-0.1574	-0.1250	-0.0922	-0.0573
x_1	0.3	-0.2302	-0.1861	-0.1460	-0.1071	-0.0675	-0.0256
	0.4	-0.2159	-0.1661	-0.1205	-0.0761	-0.0308	0.0170
	0.5	-0.1895	-0.1353	-0.0855	-0.0368	0.0130	

Notes: (i)   Data in sub-tables (a) - (c) are for firm 1. Transposing these sub-tables gives the corresponding data for firm 2: *e.g.*, for the location pair (x_1^i, x_2^k) if price of firm 1 is p_{ik}, then price of firm 2 is p_{ki}.

(ii)   A negative entry in (b) indicates that price undercutting is not feasible. A negative entry in (c) indicates that price undercutting is not profitable.

Figure 3 illustrates the set of location pairs for which there exists no price equilibrium for two values of the transport rate. Region '1' is the set of location pairs (x_1, x_2) for which firm 1 can profitably undercut firm 2 but firm 2 cannot profitably undercut firm 1, and conversely for region '2'. The region marked

'1&2' is the set of location pairs for which either firm can profitably undercut the other.

Figure 3a. Price-undercutting region: t = 0.5

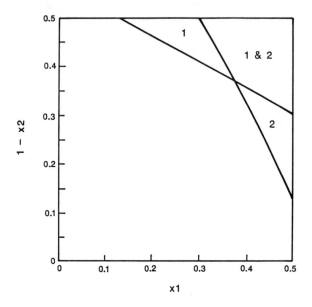

Figure 3b. Price-undercutting region: t = 0.76

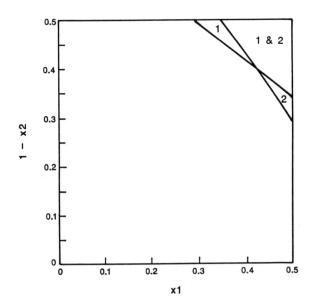

Conjecture 1 applies to those location pairs for which a price equilibrium exists and need not be repeated here. We shall see in the next section that an amended version of Conjecture 2 also applies.

2.   THE LOCATION EQUILIBRIUM

In considering the location equilibrium for the first stage subgame we could follow Anderson (1988: 486) and state that there exists no price-location equilibrium, no matter the transport cost rate, since for either firm there exists locations for which it "cannot know its payoff ... and hence (it) does not have the basis for a rational location decision". There is then no basis for comparison with the quantity-location equilibrium. Alternatively, we can follow Smithies (1941) and analyze those cases for which the location equilibrium in the absence of price undercutting lies in the region for which price undercutting is not profitable. In order to facilitate comparison with the quantity-location case we adopt the latter approach. It is possible to give at least some justification for this approach. The type of equilibrium we are considering is locally stable in that neither firm will consider a marginal change in location. We might also argue that, since the profit function is declining on the boundary of the non-existence region there are reasons for arguing that the equilibrium is globally stable.[8] In view of the somewhat unsatisfactory nature of the resulting price-location equilibrium, however, we shall refer to it below as a *quasi-equilibrium*.

Denote by $\Xi(t)$ the set of location pairs (x_1, x_2) for which a price equilibrium exists, and assume that $x_1^b, 1 - x_2^b < 0.5$. We can then amend our definition of equilibrium for the price-location game formally as follows.

DEFINITION: A quasi-equilibrium for the two-stage price-location game is a location pair $\left(x_1^b, x_2^b\right)$ such that

(i) $\left(x_1^b, x_2^b\right)$ lies in $\Xi(t)$, and

(ii) $\Pi_1^b\left(x_1^b, x_2^b\right) \geq \Pi_1^b\left(x_1, x_2^b\right) \ \forall \ x_1 \, \text{s.t.} \left(x_1, x_2^b\right)$ is in $X(t)$, plus

$\Pi_2^b\left(x_1^b, x_2^b\right) \geq \Pi_2^b\left(x_1^b, x_2\right) \ \forall \ x_2 \, \text{s.t.} \left(x_1^b, x_2\right)$ is in $X(t)$. $\square$

Here the profit functions are given by equations (12) and

(21) $\Pi_i^b(x_1, x_2) = \Pi_i^b\left(x_1, x_2, p_1^b(x_1, x_2), p_2^b(x_1, x_2)\right).$

Analytic expressions in prices can be developed, but once again prove to be intractable. Numerical simulation gives the following result.

---

[8]This might be argued to be the case, for example, if a firm were to apply a low or zero pay-off to locations for which there exists no price equilibrium. Appeal to other forms of behavior, such as the no-mill-price-undercutting assumption first formulated by Lerner and Singer (1937) and subsequently by Eaton and Lipsey (1978) is unsatisfactory: see MacLeod (1985) and Anderson (1986 and 1988).

CONJECTURE 7: Let $t_p \cong 0.7503$. Then,

(i)   if $t = 0$, any location pair (x_1, x_2) is a location equilibrium, with price $p_1 = p_2 = 0$;

(ii)   if $0 < t < t_p$, no location quasi-equilibrium (x_1^b, x_2^b) in $\Xi(t)$ exists; and

(iii)   if $t > t_p$, there exists $\chi(t)$, $0 < \chi(t) < 1/2$ such that analogous conditions to those of Conjecture 5 hold and a location quasi-equilibrium (x_1^b, x_2^b) in $\Xi(t)$ exists with $x_1^b = 1 - x_2^b = x^b = \dfrac{1}{2} - \chi(t)$ and and $\dfrac{\partial \chi(t)}{\partial t} > 0$. $\square$

The set of locations can be partitioned into three subsets:

(i)   those location pairs for which price undercutting is not feasible for either firm $[p_i^u < 0\ (i{=}1,2)]$;

(ii)   those location pairs for which price undercutting is feasible but not profitable $[p_i^u > 0$ but $\Pi_1^u(p_1^u) - \Pi_1^b(p_1^b) < 0\ (i{=}1,2)]$; and

(iii)   those location pairs for which price undercutting is feasible and profitable. $\square$

Set (iii) is the set of location pairs for which there is no price-location equilibrium. For any value of $t < t_p$ at least one firm finds that its profit function is increasing if it chooses a location on the boundary of this non-existence set. As transport costs increase, however, the market periphery effect discussed in the context of quantity competition becomes more dominant, encouraging non-agglomerated locations. In addition, the price reduction necessary to undercut the rival increases, making price undercutting less profitable.

Table 4 presents a range of values of $\chi(t)$ and repeats $\xi(t)$ for comparison.

Table 4. Optimal location for the price-location game

t	$\chi(t)$	$\xi(t)$
0.6	n.a.	0.0311
0.76	0.0925	0.0797
1.0	0.1380	0.1303
1.25	0.1735	0.1702

As can be seen, quantity competition leads to greater location agglomeration than does price competition. This is very much a consequence of the two-stage formulation of the quantity-location and price-location choice: quantity-setting firms are more influenced by the market area effect than are price-setting firms. But in the price-location game locations are again more agglomerated than those that maximize aggregate profits, consumer surplus or total surplus.

V.   Comparison of Quantity-Location and Price-Location Equilibria

We follow convention by taking aggregate consumer surplus as our measure of consumer welfare and the sum of profit and consumer surplus as our measure of total welfare. Table 5 summarizes the main elements of the comparison of the quantity and price equilibria.

Table 5. Comparison of quantity and price equilibria for all (x_1, x_2) in (t)

Quantity	$q^C < q^B$
Price	$p^C > p^B$
Profit	$\Pi^C > \Pi^B$
Consumer Surplus	$CS^C < CS^B$
Total Surplus	$TS^C < TS^B$

Note: superscript C denotes quantity and B price competition.

For any value of the transport rate and for any location pair (x_1, x_2) in $\Xi(t)$ quantity competition benefits producers at the expense of consumers and gives lower aggregate surplus.

Table 6 repeats this comparison but now for the relevant location equilibria. The same results apply as in Table 5.

Table 6. Comparison of quantity and price equilibria at the optimal locations

t		q	p	P	CS	TS
0.76	Cournot	0.2537	0.3535	0.0897	0.1335	0.3128
	Bertrand	0.2798	0.3077	0.0861	0.1609	0.3331
1.0	Cournot	0.2421	0.3622	0.0877	0.1230	0.2983
	Bertrand	0.2567	0.3365	0.0864	0.1372	0.3100
1.25	Cournot	0.2301	0.3677	0.0846	0.1123	0.2815
	Bertrand	0.2377	0.3538	0.0841	0.1192	0.2874

Note. output and profit data are for each firm, and surplus data are aggregate data for the entire market.

VI. Conclusions

The principle advanced by Hotelling that when firms compete in price, consumers will be confronted by products that are excessively similar is intuitively appealing. It was proposed initially on the assumption, first, that the competing firms cannot price discriminate - in the spatial analogue they employ f.o.b. pricing - and, second, that consumer demand is perfectly price inelastic. Smithies subsequently confirmed Hotelling's intuition by extending the analysis to the case where demand is elastic.

We have shown in this chapter that Smithies' conclusions apply perhaps even more strongly to firms that compete in quantities. The desire to control the middle ground - given that the periphery is already controlled - drives firms towards the market centre and away from the socially desirable location choices.

A major problem identified in subsequent formalizations of Hotelling's analysis is that there exists no price equilibrium for a range of potential location choices by firms and consequently there exists no price-location equilibrium.

Since non-existence of equilibrium derives from attempts by non-cooperative firms to undercut each others' prices, it might have been expected that such non-existence results would not arise when firms compete in quantities. We have shown, however, that the non-existence of equilibrium applies, albeit in a weaker form, to quantity-location choice as well.

A quantity equilibrium can be identified for all choices of locations by the firms, but if transport costs are sufficiently low, there is no two-stage quantity-location equilibrium. Low transport costs encourage perfect agglomeration, but perfect agglomeration results in the products being perceived by consumers as perfect substitutes. It is then in the interests of at least one firm to choose a location marginally away from the market centre in order to establish control of its natural market area. By contrast, it has been indicated elsewhere (e.g., Hamilton et al., 1989) that similar non-existence problems do not arise when firms are able to apply third-degree price discrimination.[9]

An important conclusion to be drawn from our analysis, therefore, is that non-existence is a direct consequence of the inability of competing firms to price discriminate rather than a consequence of the competitive setting in which they operate. This is, perhaps, not surprising, since f.o.b. pricing leaves the firm with many fewer degrees of freedom than does discriminatory pricing. We have also shown that the standard welfare comparisons of Cournot and Bertrand equilibria extend to spatial competition. What remains to be done is to compare the welfare properties of the discriminatory and non-discriminatory equilibria when location choice is endogenous.

One further important outstanding issue is an investigation of the extent to which our results and those of other investigators are driven by the precise specification of the strategic game being played by the firms. For example, we have shown (al-Nowaihi and Norman, 1992) that non-existence is not a problem when quantities and locations are chosen simultaneously. There is also the suggestion (Greenhut and Norman, 1992; and Friedman and Thisse, 1991) that if the quantity or price game is specified as a repeated game, the non-existence problem is resolved and perfect agglomeration will characterize the final equilibrium. Of one thing we can be reasonably sure. If firms compete in quantities, they will be encouraged to agglomerate to a greater extent than is socially desirable. This will also be the case when firms compete in prices provided that the strategic setting guarantees the existence of a price equilibrium. It does indeed appear that "cider is too homogeneous" (Hotelling, 1929: 57).

Appendix

Differentiating equations (10) and (11) gives

(A1) $\dfrac{\partial q_1}{\partial p_1} = -\dfrac{1}{2t}(1 - p_1 + tx_1 + tx');\quad \dfrac{\partial q_2}{\partial p_1} = \dfrac{1}{2t}(1 - p_2 + t(1 - x_2) - t(1 - x')),$

---

[9]They also show that perfect agglomeration is the Cournot-Nash equilibrium but not the Bertrand-Nash equilibrium.

(A2) $\dfrac{\partial q_1}{\partial p_2} = \dfrac{1}{2t}(1-p_1+tx_1-tx'); \quad \dfrac{\partial q_2}{\partial p_2} = -\dfrac{1}{2t}(1-p_2+t(1-x_2)+t(1-x')),$

(A3) $\dfrac{\partial q_1}{\partial x_1} = \dfrac{1}{2}(1-p_1-3tx_1+tx'); \quad \dfrac{\partial q_2}{\partial x_1} = -\dfrac{1}{2}(1-p_2+t(1-x_2)-t(1-x')),$ and

(A4) $\dfrac{\partial q_1}{\partial x_2} = \dfrac{1}{2}(1-p_1+tx_1-tx'); \quad \dfrac{\partial q_2}{\partial x_2} = -\dfrac{1}{2}(1-p_2-3t(1-x_2)+t(1-x')).$

Differentiation of equations (10') and (11') gives

(A5) $F_1=1; \; F_2=0; \; F_3=-\dfrac{\partial q_1}{\partial p_1}; \; F_4=-\dfrac{\partial q_1}{\partial p_2},$ and

(A6) $G_1=0; \; G_2=0; \; G_3=-\dfrac{\partial q_2}{\partial p_1}; \; G_4=-\dfrac{\partial q_2}{\partial p_2}.$

Substitution of (A1)-(A6) in equations (13)-(15) and simplifying gives the reaction functions CR_i.

References

al-Nowaihi, A. and Norman, G. (1992) 'Spatial Competition by Quantity-Setting Firms: A Comparison of Simultaneous and Two-Stage Quantity-Location Games', University of Leicester, *Discussion Paper in Economics 92/18*.

Anderson, S.P. (1986) 'Equilibrium Existence in the Circle Model of Product Differentiation', in: G. Norman (ed.), *Spatial Pricing and Differentiated Markets*, London Papers on Regional Science, 16, London: Pion.

Anderson, S.P. (1988) 'Equilibrium Existence in the Linear Model of Spatial Competition', *Economica* **55**, 479-492.

Cheng, L. (1985) 'Comparing Bertrand and Cournot Equilibria: A Geometric Approach', *RAND Journal of Economics* **16**, 146-151.

d'Aspremont, C., Gabszewicz, J. and Thisse, J.-F. (1979) 'On Hotelling's "Stability in Competition"', *Econometrica* **47**, 1145-1150.

Eaton, B.C. and Lipsey, R.G. (1975) 'The Principle of Minimum Differentiation Reconsidered: Some New Developments in the Theory of Spatial Competition', *Review of Economic Studies* **42**, 27-49.

Eaton, B.C. and Lipsey, R.G. (1978) 'Freedom of Entry and the Existence of Pure Profits', *Economic Journal* **88**, 455-469.

Friedman, J. and Thisse, J.-F. (1991) 'Partial Collusion Yields Minimum Product Differentiation', University of North Carolina, *Unpublished manuscript*.

Greenhut, M.L. and Norman, G. (1992) 'Conjectural Variations and Location Theory', *Journal of Economic Surveys* (forthcoming).

Hamilton, J.H., Thisse, J.-F. and Weskamp, A. (1989) 'Spatial Discrimination: Bertrand vs. Cournot in a Model of Location Choice', *Regional Science and Urban Economics* **19**, 87-102.

Hotelling, H. (1929) 'Stability in Competition', *Economic Journal* **39**, 41-57.

Kreps, D. and Scheinkman, J. (1983) 'Quantity Precommitment and Bertrand Competition Yield Cournot Outcomes', *Bell Journal of Economics* **14**, 326-337.

Lerner, A.P. and Singer, H.W. (1937) 'Some Notes on Duopoly and Spatial Competition', *Journal of Political Economy* **45**, 145-186.

MacLeod, W.B. (1985) 'On the Non-Existence of Equilibria in Differentiated Product Models', *Regional Science and Urban Economics* **15**, 245-262.

Smithies, A. (1941) 'Optimum Location in Spatial Competition', *Journal of Political Economy* **49**, 423-439.

Vives, X. (1985) 'On the Efficiency of Cournot and Bertrand Equilibria with Product Differentiation,

RAND Journal of Economics **15**, 546-554.

Vives, X. (1986) 'Commitment, Flexibility and Market Outcomes', *International Journal of Industrial Organization* **4**, 217-230.

CHAPTER 8

Credit Market Structure and Information Sharing Mechanisms

PATRICK VAN CAYSEELE, JAN BOUCKAERT and HANS DEGRYSE[1]

Katholieke Universiteit Leuven, Centrum voor Economische Studiën, Leuven, Belgium

Abstract. This chapter explores the relationship between the credit market structure and the existence of a white and/or black credit register. A black register compiles historical information and no on-line information, as is the case in a white register. Banks enter the market via a two-stage procedure: given they entered, they decide about their number of outlets. We show that in the white register case more but smaller banks arise than under the black register. These findings are tested using a simultaneous equation model. The evidence shows that the model performs fairly well.

I. Introduction

Up to now, the effect of asymmetric information on the performance and organization of the credit market has been analyzed under the assumption that every borrower only applies for one normalized unit of credit per period in only one bank (see, *e.g.*, Bester, 1985; and Stiglitz-Weiss, 1981). This implies that a credit applicant is a mutual exclusive client at a particular bank in a particular period. Alternatively, a credit applicant borrows from more than one bank. The effect of lending within more than one bank upon the organization of the credit market then deserves analysis (Bizer and DeMarzo, 1992).

A priori, the absence of mutual exclusivity does not have to be a problem as long as credit-worthiness is secured. Assessing the credit-worthiness of a borrower is one of the main tasks of a bank. Offering contracts inducing self-selection is one way to ensure this (Bester, 1985 and 1987). In the absence of such self-selection devices banks have to rely on *ad hoc* decision mechanisms, such as credit-worthiness tests (Broecker, 1990; and Bouckaert, Degryse and Van Cayseele, 1991) that estimate the pay-back potential of an applicant.

As individual information about borrowers' credit-worthiness is far from perfect, banks try to improve upon their test-effectiveness by setting up information-sharing mechanisms such as credit registers. A credit register is an organization that collects, stocks, up-dates and distributes information about variables that are related to the credit-worthiness of credit applicants. Members of a credit register are institutions operating in the credit market. They *feed* the register with data related to their own clients. Membership is sustained if there is provision of correct and complete information according to the rules of the register. If that condition is fulfilled, a member is allowed to use information

[1]We are grateful to L. Bettendorf, T. Gehrig and the participants of the workshops at the K.U. Leuven, the EARIE 1992 conference in Stuttgart and the EEA 1992 conference in Dublin. The second author acknowledges the financial support of F.K.F.O. nr. 2.0073.90.

supplied by the other members. This implies that free-riding and fraude are ruled out in one way or another. Throughout the chapter, we assume the credit register reaches this objective.[2]

To illustrate the problem of measuring credit-worthiness we quote the following passage from the 1989 annual report of the Dutch central credit register: "the rise in living standards which set in in the late 1950s resulted in a strong growth in the volume of credit made available to private individuals. At the same time, there was a growing trend for consumer credit to be made available on a nationwide basis. These developments made it almost impossible for lenders to maintain an overview of the amounts lent to each individual ... . A solution to this dilemma was sought in the creation of a central registration system to record the credit data of every borrower". From this passage it is clear that the Dutch lenders opted for a *positive* or *"white"* credit register: the total amount of indebtedness is made public knowledge to every lender participating in the information technology, in order to have a more accurate estimate of the credit-worthiness of an applicant.

As opposed to the Dutch solution for the dilemma, other countries have opted for a *negative* or *"black"* credit register: all borrowers who defaulted in the past are recorded in the register. In Belgium a set of sellers, who sold their products on the instalment system, already in 1941 grouped themselves in order to exchange information on defaulters. Today, a professional organization - linking 95% of the supply in the consumer credit market - manages a negative credit register. Next to this private organization, the central government administers a parallel negative credit register. Every financial service institution operating in the credit market is forced to participate according to the law. *Negative* information is provided to reach a more accurate estimate of one's credit-worthiness.

In both the Dutch and Belgian case the fundamental reason to exchange information on borrowers' characteristics between lenders was the absence of accurate information on borrowers' credit-worthiness. This lack of information really became problematic since in some cases people over-indebted themselves by borrowing from different financial institutions. With this in mind, we model a credit market in which the effect of the two credit registers can be compared. To compare the effects of both credit registers, a model is constructed such that some borrowers visit more than one bank per period of time.[3] This starting point should be self-explaining, otherwise there would be no lack of information on borrowers's total indebtedness. This perspective, in our opinion, clearly adds a dimension to the problem of information sharing in the credit market as already modeled by Pagano and Jappelli (1991). There, borrowers can only visit a monopoly banker operating in their own state, such that borrowing more than one unit of credit within one period of time is impossible. Informational pro-

---

[2]Information-sharing mechanisms in the credit market until now received little or no attention in the industrial organization literature. The only exception to our knowledge is Pagano and Jappelli (1991).

[3]One period of time means the time interval starting from tendering the credit until the time of total repayment.

blems are introduced by migration of borrowers. The introduction of a credit register between different states, and hence banks, becomes an optimal policy. Moreover, credit applicants only look for one unit of credit per period of time. The total indebtedness of a borrower receiving credit then is public knowledge.

In this chapter we investigate the different effects of a black and white credit register, if not of the absence thereof, on the equilibrium market structure when there are two kinds of credit applicants. The first fraction is characterized by its complete safety, whereas its complement is always voluntary defaulting[4] and trying to grab as much money as possible by visiting as much banks as possible. We provide a possible rationale for this specific behavior of over-indebtedness. Unvoluntary default - caused by, *e.g.*, nature - is not considered. The chapter is organized as follows. Section II provides a formulation of the stylized credit market, immediately followed by some results. Section III presents the equilibrium credit market structure. Empirical evidence for the new theory is given in Section IV. Finally, the conclusions follow in Section V.

II.   Formulation of the Credit Market

1.   OVERLAPPING GENERATIONS
From the Introduction we know that a negative register compiles information about defaulters. Hence, it gathers historical information. A positive credit register gathers actual, on-line, information about the total indebtedness of credit-applicants. If we want to compare these two types of credit registers, we need at least two periods per credit applicant. A simple overlapping generations model will suit our purpose. In what follows we formulate our stylized credit market and present some results that we subsequently use to derive the equilibrium market structure in Section III.

2.   THE MODEL
Every credit applicant lives for two subsequent periods, and in both he wants to borrow.[5] Per period we observe two generations of borrowers, indicated as young and old ones. Each generation consists of n/2 credit applicants, with n a strictly positive finite real number. Borrowers have no transportation costs and no time preference.[6] Within each generation there is a fraction $(1-\rho)$ of *honest* borrowers and a fraction ρ, with $0 < \rho < 1$, of *charlatans*.[7] The *honest* borrowers have an extremely high capability to use money in a productive way:

---

[4]Prevention of default has been studied by Allen (1981) but not in the context of over-indebtedness.

[5]The analysis would remain valid when people live and borrow for more than two subsequent periods.

[6]Time preference could be introduced, but this would not alter our results in a fundamental way.

[7]These charlatans are comparable to the charlatans in Greenwald and Stiglitz (1991). There, an exogenous fraction of borrowers are supposed to be crooks.

that is, their capability is so high that they have no incentive to become *charlatans*. The latter have no capability at all, which implies that they spoil money from which they generate utility. An alternative interpretation is found in Crémer (1986), where the agents' characteristics are embedded in their social consciousness. Both fractions are risk neutral and rational in the sense of profit maximizers. As in Sharpe (1990), a borrower's capability persists through time. In our economy borrowers can engage in indivisible, succesful one-unit projects.[8] Every borrower only can engage in one project per period. Per project one unit of money is needed. Borrowers cannot engage in a project and spoil money within the same time interval: spoiling money or engaging in a project is a full-time job.

Borrowers have no collateralizable wealth at the beginning of each period. Any net profit that is left after debt repayment is assumed to be consumed before another loan is demanded in the next period.[9] A borrower is not able to undertake a project if no credit is available to him. Honest borrowers have a lexicographic preference in choosing a credit offer, with the one unit of credit as first element in the preference vector. At the end of each period output is observable to the lender at no cost. Those who engaged in a project can legally be enforced to repay their debt.

Loans are granted by m time-indifferent profit-maximizing banks. In the analysis we neglect any integer problem with m. Deposits are given, and their interest rates are normalized at zero. The cost of borrowing equals $r > 0$ per unit of credit, and is fixed. The gross interest rate, $1 + r$, is smaller than the gross return of a one-unit project. In the first period of their life a honest borrower cannot be screened from a charlatan. Banks, however, are able to distinguish young applicants from old ones. Banks can individually compile information on their own clients, and their memory is unlimited and costless.

We assume there is a pre-game memory when the market starts up. This pre-game memory, taken from Crémer (1986) is to be interpreted as a set of real borrowers who revealed sufficient information to the credit market to arrive immediately in the steady state. Throughout the analysis we follow one generation when young and old.

3.   RESULTS
Given these assumptions are common knowledge to the players, several results follow immediately and hold throughout the chapter.

RESULT 1:   Charlatans mimic themselves as honest borrowers and grab as much money as they can.

Suppose they did not, then they would get no money from the bank, which

---

[8]*Project* should be interpreted in a broad sense, covering consumer expenditure, generating capability to repay.

[9]As Sharpe (1990) remarks, this may seem somewhat unrealistic. The reason is to focus on the fact that past information reveals information whenever one deals with unsecured loans.

would violate profit-maximizing behavior. Moreover, since they cannot generate any positive repayment, they have nothing to loose. This creates an incentive to grab as much money as they can by visiting every bank in the market whenever they can.

RESULT 2:   Banks have a dominant strategy to offer exactly one unit of credit per credit applicant.

Whenever all banks offer less or more than one unit of credit per applicant, every bank i has an incentive to deviate by offering exactly one unit of credit due to the lexicographical preference of honest borrowers. This unilateral deviation implies that bank i receives all honest borrowers, since they only need one unit of credit and all banks but i only get charlatans. This clearly cannot constitute an equilibrium. Given everyone's incentive to deviate towards one unit of credit, no one has an incentive to move to another strategy. That incentive is absent for the same reason as just argumented: one would only attract charlatans given everyone else offered one unit of credit per applicant. This demonstrates existence and uniqueness of the one-unit equilibrium.

RESULT 3:   All banks offer long term contracts and charlatans grab the money in the first period.

To get this result, we move progressively on the basis of the characteristics of the model. We first show that all banks will offer long-term contracts. Every bank can compile information on its own clients in a costless way, implying that a bank will never grant another unit of credit in the second period to applicants who defaulted in the first period. Honest borrowers apply for a unit of credit in each period; since banks are profit maximizers, they offer credit to both young and old borrowers.

Honest borrowers have no incentives to stay with the same bank for both periods, since there are no transportation costs and r is given. Assuming that they redistribute themselves among all banks in the second period, every bank has an incentive to deviate and offer long-term contracts: these are binding in the sense that contingent upon repayment of the debt in the first period, they take their second-period unit of credit at that bank. This allows banks to increase their profits compared to the non-deviating banks due to the particular redistribution scenario. The result is that every bank applies this, dominant, strategy. If the redistribution hypothesis is completely absent, implicit long-term contracts are present as honest borrowers visit the same bank when young and old. We next show that these long-term contracts have an effect on charlatans' behavior. Since banks know that long-term contracts are offered by everyone, a new old credit applicant can never be an honest one! This induces charlatans to grab as much money as they can in the first period only.

RESULT 4:   The absence of a credit register generates the same information to the market participants as a negative register.

From the fact that charlatans visit every bank when young, and since over subsequent time intervals banks stay in the market, a bank knows who is an old charlatan. Hence, a bank does not need a negative register to detect old charlatans. In other words, long-term contracts function as perfect substitutes for a negative credit register.

RESULT 5:   Periods and generations are interchangeable.

At any point in time the credit market is composed of two generations, young and old. In Figure 1 we illustrate periods and generations. Successive generations, G_i, are presented as rows, whereas columns should be interpreted as periods of time, t_i.

Figure 1.   Interchangeable periods and generations

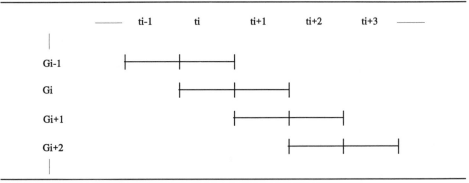

Both rows and columns are exactly composed of one young and one old generation. Rows however follow one generation in time, whereas columns follow the composition of the total population per period of time. Each row is composed by $n/2$ young credit applicants [$pn/2$ charlatans and $(1-p)n/2$ honest borrowers] plus $(1-p)n/2$ old honest borrowers (by Result 3), all of one specific generation. Columns show $(1-p)n/2$ old honest borrowers from generation G_{i-j} and $n/2$ young credit-applicants [$pn/2$ charlatans and $(1-p)n/2$ honest borrowers] from generation G_{i-j+1} at time t_{i-j+1}, where j is any finite natural number. This implies that rows and columns have exactly the same composition. Due to the absence of any discount rate, interchangeability is allowed. Hence, throughout the chapter equilibrium market structures can be interpreted as the result of period-by-period or generation-by-generation analysis.

III.   Credit Market Structure

1.   VARIABLE AND FIXED COST

The banking firm will be modeled as consisting of a variable and fixed component. The variable cost consists of an amount $x_i^* > 0$ (with x_i^* any positive, finite integer number) of outlets with unit cost $F > 0$. The fixed cost $G > 0$ represents a costly banking license and a costly central data file. Both costs are necessary to operate in the market. Every period these costs arise where one can think of them as rental prices. Outlets are equipped with virtual machines linked with the central data file. This central data file compiles every client's credit history in a costless way. There is on-line communication between a particular bank's outlets to check whether or not in the current period a borrower already received a credit in that bank. Hence, a bank consists of a positive credit register with respect to its own outlets. From Result 3 a bank is able to judge whether or not an old applicant is honest and by consequence whether or not a new credit is going to be granted. Whenever there is (no) on-line linkage between different central data files - *i.e.*, between banks - charlatans can(not) be detected from *shopping around* within the same period. Since there is no price competition, banks will maximize profits by optimizing their market share, which is the only variable left that can be manipulated, given the bank entered the market.

Given that the banks know how the credit market is defined in terms of no, white or black information sharing and borrowers' behavior, we assume they enter the market through a two-stage procedure. First they decide whether or not to enter the market. Given that they know the amount m^* of banks that entered, every bank i chooses its optimal amount x_i^* of outlets, which determines its market share. As in Sutton (1991), we solve this optimization problem by backward induction.

Introducing a variable and fixed cost component to the banking firm will not alter the strategic behavior of the borrowers. The only thing that will change is the market structure itself, due to the strictly positive cost components. After the derivation of the equilibrium market structure for a white and black credit register, we will discuss the results.

2.   WHITE CREDIT REGISTER

Given that m banks entered the market, we immediately solve for the optimal amount x_i^* of outlets for bank i. Therefore, we maximize expression (1), representing the expected profit $E\pi_i^w$ i for bank i, with respect to x_i.

$$(1) \quad E\pi_i^w = n \frac{x_i}{\sum_{j=1}^{m} x_j} (1-\rho)r - \frac{n}{2} \frac{x_i}{\sum_{j=1}^{m} x_j} \rho - x_i F - G.$$

Expression (1) is interpreted in the following way. The term $x_i / \sum_{j=1}^{m} x_j$ stands for bank i's market share: since there are $n(1-\rho)$ honest borrowers per period, old and young ones, bank i captures exactly $n(x_i / \sum_{j=1}^{m} x_j)(1-\rho)$ honest borrowers per period, which is Result 3. Each of these borrowers generates a revenue of r. Hence the first term represents revenue on honest borrowers. The second terms equals the amount of charlatans for bank i: since each of them produces a one unit of loss to the bank, the second term represents the total loss due to charlatans. The term $x_i F$ is the total variable cost and G represents the exogenous fixed cost. The first-order conditions with respect to x_i yield for the symmetric case

(2) $x_w^{\bullet} = \dfrac{n(m-1)}{Fm^2} \left[r(1-\rho) - \dfrac{\rho}{2} \right]$,

where $x_w^{\bullet}$ is the optimal amount of outlets per bank for any $m > 1$. The second derivative ensures us that it is a maximum whenever the credit market exists. The total amount $m^{\bullet}$ of banks in the market under the condition of zero expected profits with free entry is found by solving

(3) $E\pi_i^w = \left[\dfrac{1}{m}(1-\rho)r \right] - \dfrac{n}{2m}\rho - \dfrac{n(m-1)}{Fm^2} \left[r(1-\rho) - \dfrac{\rho}{2} \right] F - G = 0$

for m, which equals to

(4) $m_w^{\bullet} = \sqrt{\dfrac{n[2(1-\rho)r-\rho]}{2G}}$.

Comparative statics for the market structure with a white credit register is summarized in Table 1.

Table 1.   Comparative statics white credit register

	n	r	ρ	F	G
$x_w^{\bullet}$	+	+	-	-	0
$m_w^{\bullet}$	+	+	-	0	-

An increase in both the intermediation rate and/or the size of the market creates both more outlets and banks. A higher fraction of charlatans is reflected in less outlets and banks. An increase in F (G) implies less outlets per bank (banks). At the market level we have $\partial x_w^{\bullet}/\partial m \leq 0$ for any $m \geq 2$: an increase in the number of banks entering the market induces every bank to open less outlets. Hence, banks and outlets are substitutes at the market level.

3.   BLACK CREDIT REGISTER

By Result 3 charlatans grab m units of credit when young. Hence, every bank that already entered the market, bears a cost $(n/2)\rho$. This is reflected in the profit function $E\pi_i^b$, b denoting black credit register:

(5) $E\pi_i^b = n\dfrac{x_i}{\displaystyle\sum_{j=1}^{m} x_j}r(1-\rho) - \dfrac{n}{2}\rho - x_i F - G$.

Expression (5) is interpreted as follows. The first term equals the revenue from bank i's honest borrowers, the second term the losses generated by its charlatans, and the last terms represent total variable costs and the exogenous fixed cost, respectively. Derivation with respect to x_i yields the optimal amount x_b^* of outlets, which in the symmetric case equals

(6) $\quad x_b^* = \dfrac{n(m-1)}{Fm^2} [r(1-\rho)].$

A maximum is ensured by a negative second derivative. In the way as for the white register we derive the optimal amount m_b^* of banks for the symmetric case by solving

(7) $\quad E\pi_i^b = n \left[\dfrac{1}{m}(1-\rho)r \right] - \dfrac{n}{2}\rho - \dfrac{n(m-1)}{Fm^2} r(1-\rho)F - G = 0$

for m, which amounts to

(8) $\quad m_b^* = \sqrt{\dfrac{nr(1-\rho)}{G+\dfrac{n}{2}\rho}}.$

For the results of comparative statics we refer to Table I. Again, a higher intermediation rate and size of the market create both more outlets and banks. An increase in F (G) implies less outlets per bank (banks). Again, banks and outlets are substitutes at the market level.

4.   DISCUSSION

From (2) and (6) we notice that if $m^* = 1$, having no outlets is the optimal policy. To operate in the credit market banks have to incur both operational costs F and G. If zero profits are made with $m^* = 1$ and $x^* = 0$, a bank operating in the market obtains negative profits as x has to be at least one. Hence, m^* has to be strictly larger than one for the market to get started.

   We are now able to establish the following proposition.

PROPOSITION: For a given market size n, intermediation rate r, fraction of charlatans ρ, outlet cost F and exogenous fixed cost G, we have that $m_w^* \geq m_b^*$ and $x_w^* \leq x_b^*$. □

Proof: 1) $m_w^* \geq m_b^*$: this is proven if and only if expression (4) $\geq$ (8). This inequality is equivalent to $n(r(1-\rho)-\dfrac{\rho}{2}) \geq G$, which is a necessary condition for the market to get started. This proves that $m_w^* \geq m_b^*$. 2) $x_w^* \leq x_b^*$: by substituting (4) into (2) and (8) into (6), simple algebra shows us that, given the same parametric environment, banks have less outlets in a white regime than under a black one. QED

The intuition of the proposition runs as follows. Whenever there exists a black register, banks only compete for the honest borrowers. A bank always attracts all charlatans, irrespective its amount of outlets. Opening an additional outlet solely attracts an extra fraction of honest borrowers. When a white register is present, opening an extra outlet attracts an extra amount of both honest borrowers and charlatans. This induces a bank in a black register to open more outlets than in a white register. Since every bank in the case of a black register bears the burden of all young charlatans and, in addition, every bank has more outlets, less banks can enter the market.

An interesting question arises what capacity of charlatans both systems of information sharing can bear. The highest bearable proportion of charlatans under the white regime, ρ_w^*, is not unambiguously higher than the highest bearable proportion of charlatans under the black regime ρ_b^*. This indeterminacy follows from two opposite forces. On the one hand, costs under the black regime are larger as a bank has to bear the whole set of charlatans $x_b^* \geq x_w^*$. On the other hand, revenues from the honest borrowers are larger under the black regime since $m_w^* \geq m_b^*$. From these, it is not clear whether $\rho_w^* > \rho_b^*$ or $\rho_w^* < \rho_b^*$.

IV.   Empirical Evidence

1.   A TEST
This section of the chapter adds empirical evidence to the theoretical model. In the first subsection, some data considerations are given. In the next subsection, different regression models are put forward and estimated. The results are presented and discussed in the last subsection.

2.   DATA
Fourty-eight annual observations regarding the consumer credit market were gathered covering eight countries: *i.e.*, Belgium, Finland, France, Germany, Italy, the Netherlands, Spain and Sweden. The distribution of the observations over the countries and years is presented in Table 2, including data on the existence of a white, black or no register together with the period started. Looking at Table 2 we notice that the three different credit registers are encountered. Some countries have no register, while other ones only have a black register. Whenever there is a white register, also a black register exists. Credit registers already appeared in the 1890s. The sample includes not all countries and years due to the lack of availability of all data.

3.   EMPIRICAL MODEL
According to our theoretical model two phenomena should be observed. First, more outlets per bank should be observed with a black or no register *vis-à-vis* a white register. Second, more banks in a white regime (can) enter the market compared to a black or no register. A first test of the central proposition can be performed by regressing the following equations (data sources and definitions of all used variables can be found in the appendix):

Table 2.   Register regimes in 13 countries

Country	Register[c]	Period started	Number of observations	Sample period
Australia	B	1930s	-	-
Belgium	B[b]	1944	7	1983-1989
Finland	B	n.a.	9	1981-1989
France	B	1990	7	1984-1990
Germany	W-B	1920s	10	1981-1990
Greece	N	-	-	-
Italy	N[a]	-	3	1988-1990
Japan	W-B	1960s	-	-
Netherlands	W-B	1960s	6	1981,84,86-89
Spain	N[a]	-	3	1985,1987-1988
Sweden	W-B	1890s	3	1987-1989
U.K.	W-B	1960s	-	-
U.S.	W-B	1890s	-	-

[a] From Pagano & Jappelli (1991): in Spain and Italy black registers exist but only for amounts exceeding personal loans.
[b] In Belgium a white register exists but only for loans larger than 24.000 Ecu.
[c] B = Black; N = No; and W = White.
Source: Pagano and Jappelli (1991); and Beroepsverenging voor Krediet (1990).

(9) $\ln m = c_1 + \alpha \, DUMW$, and

(10) $\ln x = c_2 + \beta \, DUMW$,

where m denotes the amount of banks, x the amount of outlets per bank, c_i constants, α and β are parameters, and DUMW = 1 and DUMW = 0 indicate a white and black register, respectively. Parameter α should be positive, since in a white regime there should be more banks compared to a black or no register. Analogously, β should be negative. The results of estimating equations (9) and (10) are presented in Table 3. The coefficient α shows the expected sign and is statistically different from zero at a 5% level. The coefficient β in (10) has the expected sign, but is not significantly different from zero.

As expressions (2) and (4) plus (6) and (8) demonstrate, banks and outlets are interdependent. Hence, a more rigorous test for the derived properties should be implemented by estimating a system of simultaneous equations. Expressions (2), (4), (6) and (8) show that the most appropriate functional form is a log-linear one. According to the solution method of backward induction m depends on exogenous variables, while x is a function of exogenous variables and m. Our theory focuses entirely on the credit side of a banking market. We know banks also enter the market in order to attract deposits. Therefore, we estimate the following system of equations:

(11) $\ln m = c_1 + a_1 \, DUMW + a_2 \ln RCV + a_3 \ln PC + a_4 \ln RTD$, and

(12) $\ln x = c_2 + \beta_1 \, DUMW + \beta_2 \ln RCV + \beta_3 \ln m$,

with RCV being the revenue on total amount of consumer credit, RTD revenue on total non-bank deposits, PC personnel cost per employee in the banking sector, c_i constants, and a_i, β_i parameters.

From the comparative static results the coefficient of $\ln m$ in equation (12) should be negative, since banks and outlets appear as substitutes at the market level. The variable $\ln RCV$ captures the revenue on the consumer credit market. A higher revenue should induce both more banks and outlets. The deposit activity of banks is measured by the variable $\ln RTD$. The higher RTD, the more banks enter. To measure these revenues the difference between the deposit and lending rate has been splitted up in the following way: the interbank rate minus the deposit rate represents the profit margin of attracting deposits, and the lending rate minus the interbank rate measures the revenue on granting one unit of consumer credit. In addition, we introduced the personnel cost in the bank equation, since banking is highly labor-intensive: entering a market is inversely related with the cost of personnel. Equations (11) and (12) have been estimated separately by OLS and as a system with 2SLS to examine the potential effect of a simultaneous equation bias. The estimation results are presented in Table 3. The results for equation (11) are obviously independent of the estimation procedure. The coefficients of all RHS variables in Equation (11) show the expected sign, except for the register dummy, the latter however not being statistically different from zero. The OLS estimates for equation (12) all have the expected sign, with the register dummy being statistically different from zero at the 10 % level. The 2SLS results for the outlet equation (12') are in the same line, indicating less of a problem with a simultaneous equation bias. Hence, the proposition that less outlets per bank appear in a white regime cannot be rejected. Besides the supply of credit, banks also open outlets to attract deposits. Introducing this deposit activity in equation (12), changes the model into

(11) $\ln m = c_1 + a_1 \, DUMW + a_2 \ln RCV + a_3 \ln PC + a_4 \ln RTD$, and

(13) $\ln x = c_2 + \beta_1 \, DUMW + \beta_2 \ln RCV + \beta_3 \ln m + \beta_4 \ln RTD$.

The results of Equation (11) of course remain the same. The introduction of RTD in (13) has the expected effect on x, since a higher revenue of the deposit activity induces more outlets per bank to be opened. For both the estimation procedures, however, introducing RTD in the outlet equation is at the expense of the significance of the register dummy and a reduction in the effect of RCV and DUMW upon x. The significant estimates for m and RCV provide strong evidence for the comparative static results of our theoretical framework. The

141

Table 3. Estimation results

Dependents	(9) ln m	(10) ln x	(11) ln m	(12) ln x	(12') ln x	(13) ln x	(13') ln x
c1	6.319 (27.504)*	-	-9.095 (3.718)*	-	-	-	-
c2	-	3.142 (13.007)*	-	5.507 (7.287)*	5.993 (7.003)*	2.539 (3.112)*	3.026 (3.239)*
DUMW	0.767 (2.100)*	-0.523 (-1.363)	-0.152 (-0.538)	-0.507 (-1.880)**	-0.536 (-1.859)**	-0.155 (-0.702)	-0.186 (-0.757)
ln RCV	-	-	0.645 (5.800)*	0.454 (4.821)*	0.603 (4.547)*	0.131 (1.370)	0.279 (2.184)*
ln PC	-	-	-3.550 (-4.817)*	-	-	-	-
ln RTD	-	-	0.377 (2.642)*	-	-	0.493 (5.309)*	0.491 (4.769)*
ln m	-	-	-	-1.077 (-8.798)*	-1.386 (-6.264)*	-1.074 (-11.156)*	-1.377 (-7.634)*
R^2	0.087	0.039	0.643	0.654	0.651	0.791	0.783
SER	1.237	1.300	0.800	0.797	0.853	0.627	0.695
SSR	70.408	77.827	27.544	28.004	32.052	16.914	20.803
Procedure	OLS	OLS	OLS	OLS	2SLS	OLS	2SLS
Nx obs	48	48	48	48	48	48	48

t-statistics between brackets.
*(**) Significantly different from zero at the 5% (10%) level.

evidence on the register dummy offers some support for our central proposition. It seems that, next to the deposit activities, sharing information about credit-applicants plays an important role in determining the bank market structure: white registers generate more but smaller banks.

V.   Conclusions

In this chapter we analyzed the effects of different information-sharing mechanisms upon the equilibrium market structure. The credit market was modeled as a two-stage game. In the first stage, banks decide whether or not to enter. In the second stage, banks open outlets in order to maximize profits. We have shown that markets with white credit registers induce more but smaller banks compared to markets with a black credit register. Young dishonest borrowers cannot be prevented from borrowing at every bank whenever there is only a black register. Then, banks only compete for honest borrowers. This induces banks to open more outlets when a black register exists *vis-à-vis* a white register. The cost of this dishonest behavior has its impact on the first stage in the sense that less banks appear when a black register exists. Empirical evidence supports this property of the model. At the market level banks and outlets appear to be substitutes. This property was tested too, by setting up a simultaneous equation model. Empirical evidence also supports this property, as well as the other results derived from the model.

Appendix

Data concerning the amount of banks, total number of outlets and consumer credit volume have been obtained by sending questionnaires to the Central Banks of the respective countries. Data for Finland were obtained from OECD-publications- notably *Bank Profitability, Statistical Supplement, Financial Statements of Banks, 1981-1990, Financial Accounts of OECD countries* and *Financial Statistics Monthly* (Table "Consumer Credit Outstanding"). Data for the total non-bank deposits were taken from OECD (1992), *Bank Profitability, Statistical Supplement, Financial Statements of Banks, 1981-1990.* The revenue of the consumer credit market RCV was calculated as the difference between the lending rate and the interbank rate times the consumer credit volume. The revenue of the deposit activity RTD was calculated as the difference between the interbank rate and the deposit rate times the total non-bank deposits. The lending and deposit rate were taken from *International Financial Statistics*, lines 60p and 60l, respectively. Data for the interbank rate were obtained from *International Financial Statistics* when appropiate (France, 60bs; Germany 60bs; Italy 60b; and Spain 60b). If lines 60b and 60bs were missing or not appropriate, the treasury bill rate, line 60c, was taken (Belgium and Sweden). The data concerning the treasury bill rate for the Netherlands were gathered from OECD *Financial Statistics Monthly* line Treasury paper with remaining maturity of three months. Since the Finnish interbank rate systematically exceeded the lending rate, we took as proxy for the interbank rate the sum of the lending and deposit rate divided by two. The personnel cost per employee PC was calculated as the total staff costs divided by the total number of employees. Both staff costs and the number of employees were taken from OECD (1992), *Bank Profitability, Statistical Supplement, Financial Statements of Banks, 1981-1990.* RCV, RTD and PC have been transformed in millions of Ecu and prices of 1985. Data concerning exchange rates were taken from *Tijdschrift van de Nationale Bank van België,* and price indices from *International Financial Statistics,* line consumer prices 64. Data for DUMW were obtained from Table 2.

References

Allen, F. (1981) 'The Prevention of Default', *Journal of Finance* **36**, 271-276.

Beroepsvereniging voor het Krediet (1991), *Jaarverslag 1990*.

Bester, H. (1985) 'Screening vs Rationing in Credit Markets with Imperfect Information', *American Economic Review* **75**, 850-855.

Bester, H. (1987) 'The Role of Collateral in Credit Markets with Imperfect Information', *European Economic Review* **31**, 887-899.

Bizer, D.S. and DeMarzo, P.M. (1992) 'Sequential Banking', *Journal of Political Economy* **100**, 41-61.

Bouckaert, J., Degryse, H. and Cayseele, P. van (1991) 'Credit-Worthiness Tests and the Performance of a Banking Market', *Financial Economics Research Paper* **8**, Catholic University of Leuven.

Broecker, T. (1990) 'Credit-Worthiness Tests and Interbank Competition', *Econometrica* **58**, 429-452.

Crémer, J. (1986) 'Cooperation in Ongoing Organizations', *Quarterly Journal of Economics* **100**, 33-49.

Greenwald, B. and Stiglitz, J.E. (1991) 'Information, Finance and Markets: The Architecture of Allocative Mechanisms', *N.B.E.R. Working Paper nr. 3652*.

Jaffee, D.M. and Russell, T. (1976) 'Imperfect Information, Uncertainty, and Credit Rationing', *Quarterly Journal of Economics* **90**, 651-666.

Pagano, M. and Jappelli, T. (1991) 'Information Sharing in Credit Markets', *C.E.P.R. Discussion Paper Series 579*.

Sharpe, S.A. (1990) 'Asymmetric Information, Bank Lending, and Implicit Contracts: A Stylized Model of Customer Relationships', *Journal of Finance* **45**, 1069-1087.

Stichting Bureau Krediet Registratie (1990), *Jaarverslag 1989*.

Stiglitz, J.E. and Weiss, A. (1981) 'Credit Rationing in Markets with Imperfect Information', *American Economic Review* **71**, 393-410.

Sutton, J. (1991) *'Sunk Costs and Market Structure'*, The MIT Press, Cambridge, London.

PART III

ACROSS-MARKET COMPETITION

Spillovers Across Country, Factor and Product Markets

Part III focuses on across-market competition. That is, the analysis moves beyond competition (or cooperation, for that matter) in a *single*-market context, where incumbent firms compete either mutually or with unidentified potential entrants. Across-market (or multimarket) competition can operate along both horizontal and vertical lines. With *horizontal* across-market competition, competitive effects spill over different product or geographical markets. This is the issue of Chapter 9, with a specific focus on exchange rate passthrough in an international setting. From a *vertical* angle, competition in a particular product market may be affected by rivalry within and with downstream or upstream markets (or *vice versa*). Here, Chapter 10 deals with the impact of the labor market, whereas Chapter 11 concentrates on buyer-supplier bargaining. Finally, Chapters 12 and 13 offer integrative frameworks of across-market competition from an industrial organization and strategic management perspective, respectively.

CHAPTER 9

Product Differentiation, Market Structure and Exchange Rate Passthrough

STEPHEN MARTIN and LOUIS PHLIPS
Department of Economics, European University Institute, Florence, Italy

Abstract. The impact of changes in the number of foreign/domestic firms, in the extent of product differentiation, and of use of price-setting *versus* quantity-setting behavior on the passthrough of exchange rate fluctuations is examined for trade between oligopolistic markets with and without economies of scale.

I. Introduction

One of the questions addressed in the growing literature on the consequences of imperfect competition for trade flows is the relationship between market structure and the passthrough of fluctuations in exchange rates to domestic prices. Like Dornbusch (1987: 93), we assume an exogenous movement in the nominal exchange rate. This movement causes a change in the relative costs of foreign and domestic firms, leading to a shift of the reaction surfaces of foreign firms and movements along the reaction surfaces of domestic firms. Our model, like that of Dornbusch, allows us to investigate the impact of changes in market concentration, the number of firms, on the magnitude of passthrough effects. We allow foreign goods to be imperfect substitutes or complements for domestic goods, which permits us to examine the way changes in demand relationships affect the passthrough relationship. Extensions of the model examine the impact of price-setting behavior and of economies of scale on exchange rate passthroughs.[1] The plan of the chapter is as follows. Section II describes the basic model, which is then applied to quantity-setting firms in Sections III and IV - focusing on the cases of substitutes and complements, respectively - and price-setting firms in Section V. Section VI analyzes the impact of economies of scale. Section VII is a conclusion.

II. The Basic Model

1. SUBSTITUTABILITY BETWEEN DOMESTIC AND FOREIGN VARIETIES
Consider a partial equilibrium model of trade between two countries, A and B. There are n_A firms in the country A industry and n_B firms in the country B industry. We want to treat the case of differentiated products. Starting from the case of linear (inverse) demand with homogeneous products,

---

[1] For simplicity, we ignore the effects of uncertainty. Hooper and Kohlhagen (1978) and Katz, Paroush and Kahana (1982) incorporate uncertainty in models of exchange rate determination. Neither model is well suited to the examination of the connection between elements of market structure and the nature of passthrough effects.

(1) $p = a - Q,$

a straightforward generalization is to write an inverse demand curve for the variety of a differentiated product group sold by firm A1 in market A as[2]

(2) $p_{A1} = a - \left[q_{A1} + \theta \left[\sum_{i=2}^{n_A} q_{Ai} + \sum_{j=1}^{n_B} x_{Bj} \right] \right].$

In this specification, θ is a product differentiation parameter: $\theta = 1$ implies that products are perfect substitutes [i.e., equation (2) reduces to (1)]; $\theta = 0$ means that goods are completely independent in demand; and $\theta < 0$ covers the case of complementary goods. Without loss of generality, the slope coefficient of q_{A1} is normalized at -1. With a specification of this kind, we ask how changes in θ affect market equilibrium. For our specific purpose, it is natural to ask how changes in θ affect the equilibrium passthrough of exchange rate fluctuations to domestic prices. But (2) has the implication that an increase in θ means (a) foreign goods become better substitutes for variety A1 and simultaneously (b) all other domestic varieties become better substitutes for variety A1. The way a change in θ affects the exchange rate passthrough (and, indeed, other structure-conduct-performance relationships) therefore depends on aspects of both domestic and foreign market structure.

To avoid this convolution of demand-side relationships, when we examine substitute goods we generalize (2) to obtain inverse demand curves which permit the degree of substitutability among domestic varieties and the degree of substitutability between domestic and foreign varieties to differ. That is,

(3a) $p_{Ai} = a - \left[q_{A1} + \theta \sum_{k \neq i}^{n_A} q_{Ak} + \psi \sum_{j=1}^{n_B} x_{Bj} \right]$ with $i = 1, ..., n_A$, and

(3b) $p_{Bj} = a - \left[x_{Bj} + \psi \sum_{i=1}^{n_A} q_{Ai} + \theta \sum_{k \neq j}^{n_B} x_{Bj} \right]$ with $j = 1, 2, ..., n_B$.

P_{Ai} is the country A price and q_{Ai} the country A sales, both of country A firm i; similarly, p_{Bj} is the country A price and x_{Bj} the country A sales of country B firm j. As in (2), θ is a product differentiation parameter, now specific to domestic varieties, lying between zero and one. Parameter ψ, also lying between zero and one, measures the degree of differentiation between domestic and foreign varieties in the country A market. We assume $\theta > \psi$: domestic varieties are better substitutes for one another than are foreign varieties. We begin with the

---

[2]Allowing for notational differences, this is the model of Spence (1976). It can be investigated for its own sake as a generalization of the homogeneous product linear demand case, or it can be rationalized as the outcome of a utility maximization process by a representative consumer with a quadratic utility function. For discussion of the latter approach see Kirman (1992).

case of constant marginal cost. This implies that profit-maximizing behavior in each market can be examined separately. We will henceforth focus on country A. Whether products are strategic substitutes or strategic complements (Bulow, Geanakoplos, and Klemperer, 1985) depends on the sign of, for example,

$$(4) \qquad \frac{\partial}{\partial q_{Ak}}\left[\frac{\partial \pi_{A1}}{\partial q_{A1}}\right] \text{ or } \frac{\partial}{\partial q_{Bj}}\left[\frac{\partial \pi_{A1}}{\partial q_{A1}}\right].$$

If derivatives of the form (4) are negative, an increase in a rival firm's sales reduces the marginal profitability of firm Ai. The varieties are then strategic substitutes. If the derivatives are positive, an increase in a rival firm's sales increases the marginal profitability of firm Ai. For the linear inverse demand curves (3) and constant marginal cost, these derivatives are negatively proportional to θ (if the outer derivative is with respect to a domestic variety) or ψ (if the outer derivative is with respect to a foreign variety). This specification has two advantages. First, demand and strategic substitutability (complementarity) coincide. Second, strategic complementarity ($\psi < 0$) is not ruled out with linear demands, in contrast with the case of linear demand curves and homogeneous commodities (see Kirman and Phlips, 1992: 4).

2.   DEMAND CURVES

Let the country A currency be pounds, the country B currency be dollars, and the exchange rate e the number of pounds per dollar. An increase in e therefore represents a depreciation of the country A currency. Let c_A be the marginal cost of a country A firm, measured in pounds, and c_B the marginal cost of a country B firm, measured in dollars. Finally, t_{BA} is unit tariff and transportation cost (also measured in dollars) incurred shipping from B to A, and $c_B + t_{BA}$ is the marginal cost of a country B firm to supply a unit of output to country A. In what follows, we assume $a > c_A$ and $a > e(c_B + t_{BA})$. Firm Ai's pound profit in country A is

$$(5) \qquad \pi_{Ai} = (p_{Ai} - c_A)q_{Ai}.$$

The dollar profit of country B firm Bj from sales in country A is

$$(6) \qquad \pi_{Bj} = \frac{1}{e}(p_{Bj} - z)x_{Bj}.$$

where for notational convenience we write $z = e(c_B + t_{BA})$.

III.   Quantity-setting Firms

1.   REACTION FUNCTIONS

Consider first the case of substitute goods: $\theta > \psi > 0$. Substituting from the inverse demand curve (3a) in (5) gives an expression for firm Ai's profit in terms of its own output and the outputs of other firms. Maximization of this expression with respect to q_{Ai} gives the equation of firm Ai's quantity reaction function in country A:

$$\text{(7a)} \quad 2q_{Ai} + \theta\sum_{k\neq i}^{n_A} q_{Ak} + \psi\sum_{j=1}^{n_B} x_{Bj} = a - c_A.$$

In the same way, firm Bj's quantity reaction function in country A is

$$\text{(7b)} \quad 2x_{Bj} + \psi\sum_{i=1}^{n_A} q_{Ai} + \theta\sum_{k\neq j}^{n_B} x_{Bj} = a - z.$$

Now impose country-specific symmetry: since all country A firms produce with the same cost and all country B firms produce with the same cost, in equilibrium $q_{Ai} = q_A$ and $x_{Bj} = x_B$. By imposing these conditions outside of equilibrium, it becomes possible to graph condensed reaction curves that determine country A equilibrium. The equations of the condensed reaction curves are

$$\text{(8a)} \quad [2 + (n_A - 1)\theta]q_A + n_B\psi x_B = a - c_A, \text{ and}$$

$$\text{(8b)} \quad n_A\psi q_A + [2 + (n_B - 1)\theta]x_B = a - z.$$

They are graphed in Figure 1. Two types of conditions must be met for the

Figure 1.   Condensed quantity reaction curves: country A

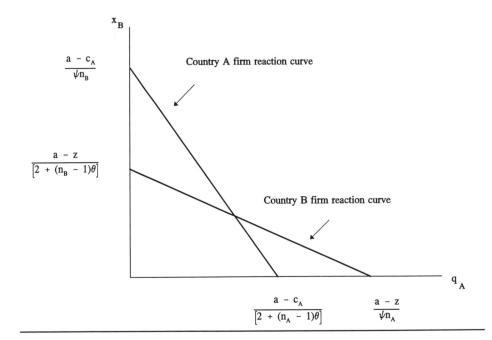

condensed reaction functions to have the indicated configuration, implying positive equilibrium outputs for firms of both countries. For the country A reaction curve to be steeper than the country B reaction curve, it must be that

(9) $DET1 = (2 - \theta)[2 + (n_A + n_B - 1)\theta] + n_A n_B(\theta^2 - \psi^2) > 0.$

For the intercepts of the reaction curves to have the indicated relationship, it must be that

(10a) $[1 + (n_B - 1)\theta](a - c_A) - \psi n_B(a - z) > 0$, and

(10b) $[1 + (n_A - 1)\theta](a - z) - \psi n_A(a - c_A) > 0.$

These conditions are met provided that there is positive demand for each variety if all varieties price at marginal cost,[3] which we henceforth assume. Equilibrium sales are

(11a) $q_A = \dfrac{[2 + (n_B - 1)\theta](a - c_A) - \psi n_B(a - z)}{DET1}$, and

(11b) $x_B = \dfrac{[2 + (n_A - 1)\theta](a - z) - \psi n_A(a - c_A)}{DET1}.$

Country-specific symmetry implies that in equilibrium all country A firms will charge the same price and all country B firms will charge the same price. Substituting from (11) into the equations of the inverse demand curves, we obtain country A equilibrium prices for a Cournot quantity-setting oligopoly with imperfectly substitutable goods:[4]

(12a) $p_A = c_A + \dfrac{[2 + (n_B - 1)\theta](a - c_A) - n_B\psi(a - z)}{DET1}$, and

(12b) $p_B = z + \dfrac{[2 + (n_A - 1)\theta](a - z) - n_A\psi(a - c_A)}{DET1}.$

2.   EXCHANGE RATE COMPARATIVE STATICS
Exchange rate fluctuations translate into proportional fluctuations in $z = e(c_B + t_{BA})$. From (12)

(13) $\dfrac{\partial p_A}{\partial z} = \dfrac{n_B\psi}{DET1} > 0$, and

---

[3]See the equations (23) of the demand curves.

[4]Since $\pi_{A1} = (p_{A1} - c_A)q_{A1}$, the equation of firm A1's reaction curve can be written in implicit form as $p_{A1} - c_A = q_{A1}\partial p_{A1}/\partial q_{A1} = q_{A1}$. Similarly, $p_{Bj} - z = q_B$ as in (12b).

(14) $\quad \dfrac{\partial p_B}{\partial z} = 1 - \dfrac{2 + (n_A - 1)\theta}{DET1}.$

A little algebra shows that

(15) $\quad 1 > \dfrac{\partial p_B}{\partial z} > 0.$

For substitute goods, a depreciation of the home-country currency results in a partial increase in the price of foreign goods and what might be termed a sympathetic increase in the price of competing domestic goods. From (13) and (14) we obtain

(16) $\quad \dfrac{\partial p_B}{\partial z} - \dfrac{\partial p_A}{\partial z} = \dfrac{(2 - \theta)[2 + (n_A + n_B + 1)\theta] + n_B[1 + n_A(\theta + \psi)](\theta - \psi)}{DET1} > 0.$

An increase in e leads to a relative increase in the price of foreign goods.

The magnitude of passthrough effects depends on n_A, n_B, θ, and ψ. From (13)

(17a) $\quad \dfrac{\partial}{\partial n_A}\left[\dfrac{\partial p_A}{\partial z}\right] = -\dfrac{n_B \psi}{DET1^2}[(2 - \theta)\theta + n_B(\theta^2 - \psi^2)] < 0,$

(17b) $\quad \dfrac{\partial}{\partial n_B}\left[\dfrac{\partial p_A}{\partial z}\right] = \psi \dfrac{(2 - \theta)[2 + (n_A - 1)\theta]}{DET1^2} > 0,$

(17c) $\quad \dfrac{\partial}{\partial \theta}\left[\dfrac{\partial p_A}{\partial z}\right] = -2\dfrac{n_B \psi}{DET1^2}[n_A + n_B - 2 + \theta(n_A - 1)(n_B - 1)] < 0,$ and

(17d) $\quad \dfrac{\partial}{\partial \psi}\left[\dfrac{\partial p_A}{\partial z}\right] = n_B\dfrac{(2 - \theta)[2 + (n_A + n_B - 1)\theta] + n_A n_B(\theta^2 + \psi^2)}{DET1^2} > 0.$

On the one hand, as the number of domestic firms increases, the number of firms in the market whose relative costs are not directly affected by exchange rate fluctuations goes up and the magnitude of the passthrough of exchange rate fluctuations to the prices of domestic varieties goes down. Among the other effects which may be laid at the feet of a concentrated market is an enhanced sensibility to exchange rate fluctuations. On the other hand, an increase in n_B increases the passthrough to prices of domestic varieties because it increases the number of varieties whose relative costs are directly affected by exchange rate fluctuations. As θ increases, domestic varieties become better and better substitutes one for another. As a result, the common equilibrium price of domestic varieties falls toward c_A. This means that there is less of a range within which exchange rate fluctuations can affect prices of domestic varieties. As ψ increases, foreign varieties become better substitutes for domestic varieties, so exchange rate fluctuations have a greater impact on p_A. The fact that (17c) and (17d) are of opposite sign explains why $\partial p_A/\partial\theta$ is of ambiguous sign if θ and ψ are constrained to be equal. As regards the pass-through to the country A price of country B varieties, we have from (14)

$$(18a) \quad \frac{\partial}{\partial n_A}\left[\frac{\partial p_B}{\partial z}\right] = -\frac{n_B \psi^2 (2 - \theta)}{DET1^2} < 0,$$

$$(18b) \quad \frac{\partial}{\partial n_B}\left[\frac{\partial p_B}{\partial z}\right] = [2 + (n_A - 1)\theta]\frac{\theta(2 - \theta) + n_A(\theta^2 - \psi^2)}{DET1^2} > 0,$$

$$(18c) \quad \frac{\partial}{\partial \theta}\left[\frac{\partial p_B}{\partial z}\right] = \frac{(n_A - 1)n_A n_B \psi^2 + [2 + (n_A - 1)\theta](n_B - 1)}{DET1^2} > 0, \text{ and}$$

$$(18d) \quad \frac{\partial}{\partial \psi}\left[\frac{\partial p_B}{\partial z}\right] = 2n_A n_B \psi \frac{2 + (n_A - 1)\theta}{DET1^2} > 0.$$

As the number of domestic firms increases, or the number of foreign firms decreases, the impact of exchange rate fluctuations on the prices of foreign varieties decreases. As domestic varieties become better substitutes one for another, and as foreign varieties become better substitutes for domestic varieties, the magnitude of $\partial p_B/\partial z$ goes up.

IV.   Complementary Goods

1.   THE MODEL
We examine the case in which all domestic varieties are substitutes, all foreign varieties are substitutes, but foreign and domestic varieties are complements.[5] For expositional convenience, we substitute $\phi = -\psi$ in the demand curves (3): ϕ lies between zero and one, and is the degree of complementarity between domestic and foreign goods. An increase in ϕ means an increase in the complementarity between foreign and domestic varieties.

2.   EXCHANGE RATE COMPARATIVE STATICS
When foreign and domestic varieties are complements, the condensed reaction curves of quantity-setting firms slope upward. The slope and intercept conditions for the existence of positive equilibrium outputs for firms in both countries are derived in a straightforward way. Equilibrium prices are

$$(19a) \quad p_A = c_A + \frac{[2 + (n_B - 1)\theta](a - c_A) + n_B\phi(a - z)}{DET1}, \text{ and}$$

$$(19b) \quad p_B = z + \frac{[2 + (n_A - 1)\theta](a - z) + n_A\phi(a - c_A)}{DET1}.$$

---

[5]For concreteness, one may consider the case in which n_A domestic firms produce pairs of shoes while n_B foreign firms produce pairs of socks.

Thus,

(20) $\quad \dfrac{\partial p_A}{\partial z} = -\dfrac{n_B \phi}{DET1} < 0$, and

(21) $\quad \dfrac{\partial p_B}{\partial z} = 1 - \dfrac{2 + (n_A - 1)\theta}{DET1}$.

The signs of the comparative static partial derivatives (17b), (17c), and (17d) are reversed. The sign of (17a) is positive if $\theta^2 \ge \phi^2$. Equation (18a) remains negative, and (18d) remains positive if $\theta^2 \ge \phi^2$, and (18c) and (18b) change sign.

V.   Price-Setting Firms

1.   THE MODEL

To model price-setting firms, it is necessary to solve the system of inverse demand curves so as to obtain the implied demand curves. As suggested by (5) and (6), it is convenient to express the quantity demanded as a function of deviations of price from marginal cost. For notational compactness, we will write

(22) $\quad p_{Ai}^{*} = p_{Ai} - c_A$ and $p_{Bj}^{*} = p_{Bj} - z$,

where $z = e(c_B + t_{BA})$. Demand curves are then (see Appendix)

(23a) $(1 - \theta)Dq_{Ak} =$

$$\{[1 + (n_B - 1)\theta](a - c_A) - n_B\psi(a - z)\} + \left[\theta + n_B\frac{\theta^2 - \psi^2}{1 - \theta}\right]\sum_{i \ne k}^{n_A} p_{Ai}^{*} +$$

$$\psi\sum_{j=1}^{n_B} p_{Bj}^{*} - [1 + (n_A + n_B - 2)\theta + (n_A - 1)n_B\frac{\theta^2 - \psi^2}{1 - \theta}p_{Ak}^{*}, \text{ and}$$

(23b) $(1 - \theta)Dx_{Bk} =$

$$\{[1 + (n_A - 1)\theta](a - z) - n_A\psi(a - c_A)\} + \left[\theta + n_A\frac{\theta^2 - \psi^2}{1 - \theta}\right]\sum_{j \ne k}^{n_B} p_{Bj}^{*} +$$

$$\psi\sum_{i=1}^{n_A} p_{Ai}^{*} - [1 + (n_A + n_B - 2)\theta + n_A(n_B - 1)\frac{\theta^2 - \psi^2}{1 - \theta}p_{Bk}^{*},$$

where

$$(24) \quad D = (1 - \theta)[1 + (n_A + n_B - 1)\theta] + n_A n_B \frac{\theta^2 - \psi^2}{1 - \theta} > 0.$$

2. REACTION FUNCTIONS

Return to the case of substitute varieties. Using the demand curves (23a) and (23b) to express profits (5) and (6) in terms of prices, the equations of the price reaction curves of firms A1 and B1 are

$$(25a) \quad 2 \left[1 + (n_A + n_B - 2)\theta + (n_A - 1)n_B \frac{\theta^2 - \psi^2}{1 - \theta} \right] (p_{Ai} - c_A) -$$

$$\left[\theta + n_B \frac{\theta^2 - \psi^2}{1 - \theta} \right] \sum_{i=2}^{n_A} (p_{Ai} - c_A) - \psi \sum_{j=1}^{n_B} (p_{Bj} - z) =$$

$$[1 + (n_B - 1)\theta](a - c_A) - \psi n_B(a - z), \text{ and}$$

$$(25b) \quad 2 \left[1 + (n_A + n_B - 2)\theta + n_B(n_A - 1)\frac{\theta^2 - \psi^2}{1 - \theta} \right] (p_{B1} - z) -$$

$$\psi \sum_{i=1}^{n_A} (p_{Ai} - c_A) - \left[\theta + n_A \frac{\theta^2 - \psi^2}{1 - \theta} \right] \sum_{j=2}^{n_B} (p_{Bj} - z) =$$

$$[1 + (n_A - 1)\theta](a - z) - n_A \psi(a - c_A),$$

respectively. Imposing country-specific symmetry in (25), we obtain the equations of condensed price-reaction functions for country A firms and country B firms in country A:

$$(26a) \quad \left[2 + (n_A + 2n_B - 3)\theta + (n_A - 1)n_B \frac{\theta^2 - \psi^2}{1 - \theta} \right] (p_A - c_A) - n_B \psi(p_B - z) =$$

$$[1 + (n_B - 1)\theta](a - c_A) - \psi n_B(a - z), \text{ and}$$

$$(26b) \quad \left[2 + (2n_A + n_B - 3)\theta + n_A(n_B - 1)\frac{\theta^2 - \psi^2}{1 - \theta} \right] (p_B - z) - n_A \psi(p_A - c_A) =$$

$$[1 + (n_A - 1)\theta](a - z) - n_A \psi(a - c_A).$$

The condensed reaction curves are graphed in Figure 2. From (23) the intercepts of the reaction curves with the lines $p_B = z$, $p_A = c_A$ have the indicated configuration, provided that there is positive demand for each variety if all varieties price at marginal cost.

The existence of equilibrium requires that the slope of the country A firm reaction function be greater than 1, while the slope of the country B firm

Figure 2.   Symmetric reaction curves: country A with $\theta > 0$

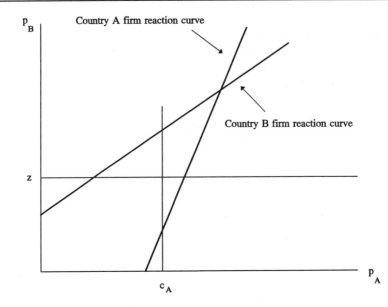

reaction function is less than one. This requires that

$$(27) \quad DET2 = \left[2 + (n_A + 2n_B - 3)\theta + (n_A - 1)n_B \frac{\theta^2 - \psi^2}{1 - \theta} \right]$$

$$\left[2 + (2n_A + n_B - 3)\theta + n_A(n_B - 1)\frac{\theta^2 - \psi^2}{1 - \theta} \right] - n_A n_B \psi^2 > 0,$$

which we henceforth assume.

3.   EXCHANGE RATE COMPARATIVE STATICS

From (26) one obtains the equilibrium prices when firms set prices:

$$(28a) \quad DET2(p_A - c_A) =$$

$$\left\{ \left[2 + (2n_A + n_B - 3)\theta + n_A(n_B - 1)\frac{\theta^2 - \psi^2}{1 - \theta} \right] [1 + (n_B - 1)\theta] - n_A n_B \psi^2 \right\} (a - c_A)$$

$$- n_B \psi \left[1 + (n_A + n_B - 2)\theta + n_A(n_B - 1)\frac{\theta^2 - \psi^2}{1 - \theta} \right] (a - z), \text{ and}$$

(28b) $DET2(p_B - z) =$

$$\left\{ \left[2 + (n_A+2n_B-3)\theta + (n_A-1)n_B\frac{\theta^2 - \psi^2}{1 - \theta} \right] [1 + (n_A-1)\theta] - n_An_B\psi^2 \right\} (a-z)$$

$$-n_A\psi \left[1 + (n_A+n_B-2)\theta + (n_A-1)n_B\frac{\theta^2 - \psi^2}{1 - \theta} \right] (a - c_A).$$

From (28) we have

$$(29a) \quad \frac{\partial p_A}{\partial z} = \frac{n_B\psi \left[1 + (n_A + n_B - 2)\theta + n_A(n_B - 1)\frac{\theta^2 - \psi^2}{1 - \theta} \right]}{DET2} > 0, \text{ and}$$

$$(29b) \quad \frac{\partial p_B}{\partial z} = \frac{\left[1+(n_A+n_B-2)\theta+n_A(n_B-1)\frac{\theta^2-\psi^2}{1-\theta} \right]\left[2+(n_A+2n_B-3)\theta+(n_A-1)n_B\frac{\theta^2-\psi^2}{1-\theta} \right]}{DET2}$$

.

As in the quantity-setting case, (29b) lies between zero and one. Similarly,

$$(30) \quad \frac{\partial p_B}{\partial z} - \frac{\partial p_A}{\partial z} =$$

$$\frac{\left[1+(n_A+n_B-2)\theta+n_A(n_B-1)\frac{\theta^2-\psi^2}{1-\theta} \right]\left[2+(n_A+n_B-3)\theta+n_B(\theta-\psi)+(n_A-1)n_B\frac{\theta^2-\psi^2}{1-\theta} \right]}{DET2} > 0.$$

Whether firms set prices or quantities, an increase in e leads to a relative increase in price of foreign goods.[6]

4.   COMPLEMENTARY GOODS
The condensed reaction curves for price-setting firms slope upward when foreign and domestic varieties are complements. The intercept conditions for equilibrium prices to exceed marginal cost for firms in both countries imply, among other things, that

$$(31a) \quad 1 + (n_A + n_B - 2)\theta + n_A(n_B - 1)\frac{\theta^2 - \phi^2}{1 - \theta} \geq 0, \text{ and}$$

$$(31b) \quad 1 + (n_A + n_B - 2)\theta + (n_A - 1)n_B\frac{\theta^2 - \phi^2}{1 - \theta} \geq 0,$$

---

[6]From (29) it is possible to calculate the comparative static derivatives that correspond to (17) and (18). The resulting expressions are too complex to be signed for general parameter values.

which, in turn, reveal that

(32a) $\dfrac{\partial p_A}{\partial z} = - \dfrac{n_B \phi \left[1 + (n_A + n_B - 2)\theta + n_A(n_B - 1)\dfrac{\theta^2 - \psi^2}{1 - \theta} \right]}{DET2} < 0$, and

(32b) $\dfrac{\partial p_B}{\partial z} =$

$$\dfrac{\left[1 + (n_A + n_B - 2)\theta + n_A(n_B - 1)\dfrac{\theta^2 - \psi^2}{1 - \theta} \right]\left[2 + (n_A + 2n_B - 3)\theta + (n_A - 1)n_B\dfrac{\theta^2 - \psi^2}{1 - \theta} \right]}{DET2} > 0.$$

VI. Economies of Scale

1.   THE MODEL

If increases in output reduce marginal cost, the effect should be to reduce the magnitude of the passthrough of exchange rate fluctuations to domestic prices. The intuition is straightforward: even if an exchange rate movement reduces the revenue that a country B firm earns from its sales in country A, the country B firm will have an incentive to maintain its sales in country A for the sake of the cost reductions that those sales generate. This means that output will fluctuate less than would otherwise be the case. But if economies of scale reduce the impact of exchange rate fluctuations on output, they reduce the impact of exchange rate fluctuations on price.

It suffices to demonstrate this effect in the simplest possible model. Suppose one firm in country A and one firm in country B produce a homogeneous product. Assume tariffs and transportation costs are zero, and let the cost functions of the country A firm and the country B firm be

(33a) $C_A(q_A, x_A) = c_A(q_A + x_A) - d(q_A^2 + x_A^2)$, and

(33b) $C_B(q_B, x_B) = c_B(q_B + x_B) - \delta(q_B^2 + x_B^2)$,

respectively. By assuming $d, \delta > 0$, we obtain a model in which increases in output reduce marginal cost. By making these cost reductions functions of the squares of output in each country, we once again obtain a model in which country A and country B sales decisions can be analyzed separately.[7] We also assume that d and δ are sufficiently small so that both firms produce positive outputs in equilibrium.

---

[7]The leading alternative specification is to let the coefficient of d be the square of total output of the country A firm and the coefficient of δ be the square of total output of the country B firm. Analysis of equilibrium in this case will yield results qualitatively similar to those presented here, but requires simultaneous consideration of all four reaction functions.

2.   QUANTITY-SETTING EQUILIBRIUM

Given our assumption that products are homogeneous, we confine ourselves to the analysis of quantity-setting behavior. The equations of the country A reaction functions are

(34a) $2(1 - d)q_A + x_B = a - c_A$, and

(34b) $q_A + 2(1 - \delta)x_B = a - ec_B$.

Solving (34), equilibrium outputs are

(35a) $q_A = \dfrac{2(1 - e\delta)(a - c_A) - (a - ec_B)}{DET_A}$, and

(35b) $x_A = \dfrac{2(1 - d)(a - ec_B) - (a - c_A)}{DET_A}$,

where $DET_A = 4(1 - d)(1 - \delta) - 1$. We will assume that d and δ are sufficiently small so that $DET_A > 0$.

In equilibrium, total output is

(35c) $q_A + x_A = \dfrac{(1 - 2e\delta)(a - c_A) + (1 - 2d)(a - ec_B)}{DET_A}$.

Substituting the results into the equation of the market demand curve, the Cournot equilibrium price is

(36a) $p_A = c_A + (1 - 2d)\dfrac{2(1 - e\delta)(a - c_A) - (a - ec_B)}{DET_A}$

or, equivalently,

(36b) $p_A = ec_B + (1 - 2e\delta)\dfrac{2(1 - d)(a - ec_B) - (a - c_A)}{DET_A}$.

3.   EXCHANGE RATE COMPARATIVE STATICS

It is easiest to understand the impact of exchange rate fluctuations on equilibrium price by examining the impact of exchange rate fluctuations on equilibrium outputs. From equations (35)

(37a) $\dfrac{\partial q_A}{\partial e} = \dfrac{c_B}{DET_A} - 4\delta(1 - d)\dfrac{a - ec_B}{DET_A^2}$,

(37b) $\dfrac{\partial x_A}{\partial e} = -2(1 - \delta)\dfrac{c_B}{DET_A} + 4\delta(1 - d)\dfrac{2(1 - d)(a - ec_B) - (a - c_A)}{DET_A^2}$, and

$$(37c) \quad \frac{\partial(q_A + x_B)}{\partial e} = 2(1 - d) \left[-\frac{c_B}{DET_A} + 2\delta \frac{2(1 - d)(a - ec_B) - (a - c_A)}{DET_A^2} \right].$$

From equations (37) and for d as well as δ sufficiently small, an increase in e (a depreciation of the country A currency) causes the equilibrium exports of the country B firm to country A to fall, but not by as much as if returns to scale were constant. This reflects a shift in the country B reaction curve and a movement of equilibrium along the country A reaction curve. The equilibrium output of the country A firm rises, but not by as much as if returns to scale were constant. Total output falls, but not by as much as if returns to scale were constant. The presence of economies of scale moderates the impact of exchange rate changes on output. This tends to stabilize country A price:

$$(38) \quad \frac{1}{1 - 2d} \frac{\partial p_A}{\partial e} = \frac{c_B}{DET_A} - 2\delta \frac{2(1 - d)(a - ec_B) - (a - c_A)}{DET_A^2}.$$

A depreciation of the country A currency causes the country A price to rise, but the increase is less than would be the case if returns to scale were constant.

VII. Conclusion

The extent to which exchange rate fluctuations are passed on to domestic prices depends on substitutability/complementarity relationships among varieties produced by domestic and foreign firms and on the extent of economies of scale. When, on the one hand, all varieties are substitutes, the passthrough of exchange rate fluctuations rises with the degree of substitutability. A depreciation of the home country currency causes a relative increase in the prices of foreign varieties. Exchange rate passthroughs are less, all else equal, in unconcentrated markets. If, on the other hand, foreign varieties are complementary to domestic varieties, a depreciation of the home country currency causes a reduction in the price of domestic varieties. This is the expected effect, since such a depreciation causes complementary foreign varieties to become more expensive. Further, if firms are able to reduce marginal cost by increasing output, the impact of changes in the exchange rate on outputs and prices is reduced.

Appendix

Write the system of inverse demand curves (3) as

$$(A1) \quad \begin{bmatrix} p_A^* \\ p_B^* \end{bmatrix} = \begin{bmatrix} (a - c_A)J_A \\ (a - z)J_B \end{bmatrix} - bM \begin{bmatrix} q_A \\ x_B \end{bmatrix},$$

where p_A^* is a column vector of prices of country A varieties and p_B^* is a column vector of prices of country B varieties, measured in deviations from marginal cost. J_A is a column vector of n_A ones; J_B is a column vector of n_B ones. M is the n by n square vector

$$\text{(A2)} \quad M = (1 - \theta)I_n + \begin{bmatrix} \theta J_A J_A' & \psi J_A J_B' \\ \psi J_B J_A' & \theta J_B J_B' \end{bmatrix}$$

for $n = n_A + n_B$. Tedious linear algebra shows that

$$\text{(A3)} \quad M^{-1} = \frac{1}{1 - \theta}I_n - \frac{N}{D}$$

for

$$\text{(A4)} \quad N = \begin{bmatrix} \left(\theta + n_B\dfrac{\theta^2 - \psi^2}{1 - \theta}\right) J_A J_A' & \psi J_A J_B' \\ \psi J_B J_A' & \left(\theta + n_A\dfrac{\theta^2 - \psi^2}{1 - \theta}\right) J_B J_B' \end{bmatrix}$$

and D given by (24). Application of the inverse matrix (A4) to the system of equations (A1) yields the demand curves (23).

References

Brown, D.K. (1989) 'Market structure, the Exchange Rate and Pricing Behavior of Firms: Some Evidence from Computable General Equilibrium Trade Models', *Weltwirtschaftliches Archiv* **125**, 441-463.

Bulow, J.I., Geanakoplos, J.D. and Klemperer, P.D. (1985) 'Multimarket Oligopoly: Strategic Substitutes and Complements', *Journal of Political Economy* **93**, 488-511.

Dornbusch, R. (1987) 'Exchange Rates and Prices', *American Economic Review* **77**, 93-106.

Hooper, P. and Kohlhagen, S.W. (1978) 'The Effect of Exchange Rate Uncertainty on the Prices and Volume of International Trade', *Journal of International Economics* **8**, 483-511.

Katz, E., Paroush, J., and Kahana, N. (1982) 'Price Uncertainty and the Price Discriminating Firm in International Trade', *Journal of International Economics* **223**, 389-400.

Kirman, A.P. (1992) 'Whom or What Does the Representative Individual Represent?', *Journal of Economic Perspectives* **6**, 117-136.

Kirman, A.P. and Phlips, L. (1992) 'Exchange Rate Passthrough and Market Structure', European University Institute, Department of Economics, *Working Paper 92/83*.

Spence, A. M. (1976a) 'Product Differentiation and Welfare', *American Economic Review* **66**, 407-414.

Vives, X. (1984) 'On the Efficiency of Bertrand and Cournot Equilibria with Product Differentiation', *Journal of Economic Theory* **36**, 166-175.

CHAPTER 10

Imperfect Product Competition and the Capital-Labor Ratio of a Unionized Firm: Some Theory and Evidence from Belgian Manufacturing Firms

JACQUES BUGHIN[1]
McKinsey & Company, and Free University of Brussels, Belgium

Abstract. The chapter develops a theory of the firm's capital-labor ratio under unionization of its labor force. Using explicit game-theoretical solutions to union-firm bargaining, it is demonstrated how the firm's product market power interacts with input allocation in such a way that unionism represents a new channel by which the firm's capital intensity is related to imperfect product competition. Some tests are conducted on a panel of Belgian manufacturing firms, which confirm both the effects of market power on the capital-labor ratio as well as the diversity of the union-firm bargaining locus at the industry level.

I. Introduction

Industrial organization models traditionally stress the *strategic* aspect of firms' decisions under imperfect *product* competition. Meanwhile, the evidence has arisen that labor markets are not purely competitive, mainly under the presence of a *unionized* labor force. As stressed by Dowrick (1989) and Bughin (1991) among others, the union-firm bargaining process in the *labor* market may affect the strategic nature of *product* competition. For instance, the firm's product supply depends crucially on whether unions negotiate on the conventional employment demand curve,[2] or whether unions manage to enforce bargaining arrangements to lie on a contract curve.[3]

The effects of union-firm bargaining are however not confined to direct effects on firm output. For example, bargaining may have a significant impact on the firm's debt-equity strategies (Sarig, 1990), the firm's financial beta (Bughin, 1994) or the firm's propensity to invest (Grout, 1984). Here, the focus

---

[1]This is a revised version of a paper presented at the EARIE-meeting, Stuttgart, September, 1992. This version relies on Chapter 9 of my Ph.D. thesis defended at the Université Catholique de Louvain. I want to thank F. Fecher and S. Machin for providing, respectively, the data and the Arellano-Bond DPD package as used in the econometric analysis. Fruitfull discussions with P. Geroski, N. Ireland, A. Jacquemin, H. Sneessens, H. Yamawaki and M. Conyon are acknowledged. The usual disclaimer applies. In any case, the opinions expressed in this paper should not be interpreted as reflecting the views of McKinsey & Co.

[2]This is the case in a 'right-to-manage' type model of bargaining; see Nickell and Andrews (1983).

[3]Refer to the 'efficient bargaining' model of McDonald and Solow (1981).

is on how unionism may affect the optimal determination of the firm's *capital-labor ratio*. There are three motivations for this issue:

a. In many studies, capital-intensity as well as unionism are shown to affect, but as *separate* variables, the firm's performance.[4] This chapter builds a more integrated view of the impact of unionism and capital-intensity on firm's performance by elaborating on the question of the *dependence* between capital-intensity and unionism;

b. There exists a large body of literature on the productivity gap between union and non-union firms (see Freeman and Medoff, 1982). Because labor productivity also depends on capital-intensity, a proper assessment of the productivity gap should consider the *indirect* impact of unionism on those traditional variables that directly affect productivity;[5]

c. Turning to the labor-market side, the *slope and type* of the wage-labor locus is important to explain business cycles. For instance, employment and wage flexibilities are different under a contract curve regime than under the conventional labor demand curve model.[6] Traditionally, inference on the type of bargaining situation faced by the firm has been based on the estimation of normalized employment equations (see, *e.g.*, Alogoskoufis and Manning, 1991). The theoretical model below of the unionized firm's capital-labor ratio shows that the *sign of the relationship* between the firm's capital intensity and the extent of its product rents provides an alternative prediction on the type and slope of the wage-labor bargaining locus faced by the firm.

Notice that the main idea when developing a theory of the firm's capital-labor ratio under unionism is that, as usual, the capital-labor ratio will depend on relative input prices, but the price of labor is no longer exogenous, as is the outcome of a bargaining between the firm and its union. This idea is also found in Clark (1984). However, while this author investigates, only, empirically the impact of unionism *coverage* on the capital-labor ratio, this chapter rather postulates that all firms are unionized - an assumption which is relevant for the great majority of our companies -[7] and then a bargaining situation between the firm and its union is formalized explicitly.

There are several advantages from this procedure. As advocated by many

---

[4]For instance, capital intensity is entered in a performance equation to control for capital requirement in production, as a measure of this entry barrier. Union density is also commonly included to control for the fact that unionization is more probable in concentrated industries, and unions may obtain part of the firm's profit.

[5]Consider the Brown and Medoff (1978) study. They estimate a labor productivity equation of the form: $\text{Ln} (V/L) = \sum_i \beta_{0i} Di + \sum_j \beta_{1j} R_j + \beta_2 \text{Ln} (K/L)_{ij} + \beta_3 U_{ij} + \beta_4 \{\text{Ln} (K/L). U\}_{ij} + e$, where V/L is added value per worker, D and R are industry and regional dummies, K/L is the capital-labor ratio and U represents the unionization rate. This chapter replaces their cross-effect $\{\text{Ln} (K/L). U\}$ by a more appropriate set of variables which might be correlated through union power with the capital-labor ratio.

[6]As advocated by McDonald and Solow (1981), the primary aim of their paper was to present a model of wage rigidity. See also Aoki (1984) on this point.

[7]The unionization rate for blue collar workers is about 90% in Belgian manufacturing.

authors (see, *e.g.,* Dowrick, 1990), union coverage does not provide *per se* any idea of the precise success of the union when bargaining with its employer. On the contrary, an explicit theoretical formalization of union-firm bargaining provides interesting structural forms where, for instance, the inputs substitution induced by the firm's production function implies a *direct* link between oligopoly rents and the capital-labor ratio of the unionized firm. Hence, this chapter's theory adds unionism to the list of factors which might build a link between firm capital-intensity and the nature of competition faced by the firm in its product markets.

The chapter reads as follows. Section II develops a theoretical model of the unionized firm's capital-labor ratio. Section III provides an application to various manufacturing sectors of the Belgian economy. Conclusions are stated in Section IV. To anticipate the results, there is some evidence of a link between the unionized firm's capital-labor and the nature of its product market. Interpreting the results in light of unionism, the bargaining outcome might be found positively-sloped in the wage-employment locus for some sectors, a sufficient condition to assert that bargaining may occur *off* the conventional labor demand curve, as found in other contexts by Bughin (1991 and 1993) and Vannetelbosch (1992).

II.   A Model of the Unionized Firm Capital-Labor Ratio

1.   ASSUMPTIONS

We assume a quantity-setting representative unionized firm which uses a constant returns-to-scale Cobb-Douglas technology - F(K,L) - by means of two homogenous inputs - labor, L, and capital, K - in order to produce a single non-storable good - Q:

(1) $Q = K^\alpha L^\beta \ (\alpha + \beta = 1)$.

A closed analytical expression for the capital-labor ratio is only obtained at the cost of specifying a not too general technology. However, as far as the concern is to show that the link between product competition and the capital-labor ratio of an unionized firm depends on the union-firm bargaining locus, this effect is also obtained with any general revenue function.[8] The firm is a profit maximizer, and its profit function writes:

(2) $\pi = PQ\text{-}wL\text{-}rK$,

where P(.) is the inverse (constant-elasticity) industry demand function with $P' \leq 0$, w is the wage, and r is the competitive capital rental rate.

All workers are unionized and the union utility, U, depends positively on the level of both employment and wage in a modified Stone-Geary form:

---

[8]The only requirement made is the existence of some substitution possibilities between labor and capital. This condition is assumed to hold all along in this chapter.

(3) $U = (w-w_a)^\sigma L^\delta$,

where w_a is the reference (threat-point) wage - that is, the wage below which the union does not accept to negotiate. The parameters δ and σ approximate the union preferences towards employment *versus* wage premium.[9] Labor supply is assumed always higher than L, so avoiding corner solutions in the bargaining game.[10]

The main stream of the union literature generally assumes the existence of two forms of bargaining situation: (i) the 'right-to-manage' model, where the firm retains its management right over labor (Nickell and Andrews, 1983); and (ii) the 'efficient bargaining' model, where the union and the firm bargain over the level of employment in addition to the wage (McDonald and Solow, 1981). In the following, a more general model is considered, which encompasses the two former forms by assuming that bargaining may take place simultaneously both over wage and labor,[11] but that union power over wage is not necessarily the same as that over employment.[12]

The assumed bargaining sequence of the model is of some importance (see Grout, 1984). Here, the sequence is the one where the stock of capital is determined unilaterally by the firm, given the bargaining outcome over wages and employment. The analytical results are however the same for a model with *binding* contracts, where capital is fixed *ex ante* to the bargaining outcome (see Hoel, 1990).[13] Finally, the bargaining over labor is assumed to be *explicit*. A minor strand of the literature has considered the case where negotiations are only implicit over labor, say through manning rules (see Clark, 1990). However, under the maintained assumption of constant returns-to-scale, the capital-labor ratio is the same, either with implicit or explicit bargaining.[14]

---

[9]The Stone-Geary form approximates the union preferences in a *managerial* model of trade unions in which union policy is influenced both by leadership and membership preferences Pemberton (1988). Notice also that because the marginal rate of substitution between L and w is increasing in w (respectively L) holding L (respectively w) constant, both w and L are normal goods.

[10]This assumption is relevant to the extent that unemployment exists in the economy.

[11]This model is emphasized in a sequential framework by Manning (1987).

[12]Even if bargaining is simultaneous, the strategic literature on bargaining has shown that the Nash solution to bargaining - used in this chapter - is only valid when bargaining occurs over one single variable. The model thus formalizes two *separate* simultaneous bargains, and so there is no need to impose union power parameters to be the same in this framework.

[13]Even in the event that capital is fixed *ex ante* and there is an unbinding contract, there is no robust empirical evidence that unions depress investment by increasing the cost of equipment (Wadwhani, 1991).

[14]If the production technology is not homogeneous, the wage-labor locus under implicit bargaining shifts to the *left*. Thus, implicit bargaining may play towards *more* apparent wage-orientation.

2.   THE UNIONIZED FIRM CAPITAL-LABOR RATIO

Traditionally, the optimal capital-labor ratio of a firm facing a Cobb-Douglas technology writes

(4) $K/L = (\alpha/\beta)(w/r)$,

where w and r are generally assumed to be given factor prices. With unionism, w is no longer exogenous to the firm, but is the outcome - as well as possibly labor - of bargaining between the firm and the union. The key question of this chapter now arises: how is the determination of the optimal capital-labor ratio modified when both wages and employment are possibly bargained between the firm and its union? To answer this, remember that the bargaining outcome is subject to the constraint that capital is chosen unilaterally and optimally by the firm. The model is solved in the standard way of backward induction starting with the optimization of capital in the last period. Given (1) and (2), this optimal capital verifies

(5) $P(1\text{-}m)\alpha K^{\alpha\text{-}1}L^{\beta} = r$,

where m is the conventional Lerner index defined on *all* variable inputs (labor and capital), and $m = \varepsilon$ with ε being the inverse of the absolute elasticity of the product demand.

Using the now conventional Generalized Nash bargaining solution for the negotiation outcome over wages and employment (Binmore *et al.*, 1986), the Nash equilibria for wage and labor are such that[15]

(6) $w^{*} = \text{argmax } [(U\text{-}U')^{\tau}(\pi\text{-}\pi')]$,

(7) $L^{*} = \text{argmax}[(U\text{-}U')^{\mu}(\pi\text{-}\pi')]$, and

(5')   s.t. $K^{*} = \left(\dfrac{r}{P(1\text{-}m)\alpha L^{\beta}} \right)^{(1/\alpha\text{-}1)}$,

where τ is the union power over wage, μ is the union power over labor, and U' and π' are the 'fall-back' utility levels (Binmore *et al.*, 1986).

Given that, by definition of the union utility function, U already incorporates the wage fall-back, U' = 0. Since, in addition, the firm engages no production when negotiation breaks down, $\pi' = 0$ may be posited. Further, as shown elsewhere (Clark, 1990; and Bughin, 1991), the specificity of the union's utility function (3), which states that the union utility is *indifferent* to the level of the capital stock, implies that the union-firm contract is *consistent* with the optimal use of capital. The generalized Nash program simplifies to

(8) $w^{*} = \text{argmax}[(U)^{\tau}(\pi)]$, and

---

[15]A ··· means an optimal value.

(9) $L^* = \text{argmax}[(U)^{\mu}(\pi)]$,

while the pair (w^*, L^*) is directly consistent with optimal K, as given by (5').

Notice from (9) that, provided m > 0 and U depends on L, optimal employment is *higher* than if the firm would have chosen *unilaterally* the level of labor. In addition, a combination of (8) and (9) points out to the well-known fact that the marginal revenue product of labor is *lower* than the wage rate. Given the Stone-Geary union utility function, marginal revenue is a combination of both the wage and the threat-point, of which the weight depends on the (relative) union power over labor (see, *e.g.*, Abowd, 1989):

(10) $P(1-m)F'_L(K,L) = \omega = (1-\phi)w + \phi w_a$,

where $\phi = (\delta.\mu/\sigma.\tau)$. Incorporating (10) into (4), the capital-labor ratio of an unionized firm is given by

(11) $K/L = (\alpha/\beta)(\omega/r)$,

which can be restated in a reduced-form by solving explictly for the wage game. For this, the condition (8) is also written as

(12) $\dfrac{\sigma\tau}{w-w_a} + \dfrac{\pi_w^{*'}}{\pi^*} = 0$,

or, knowing from duality theory that $\pi_w^{*'} = -L^*$ and rearranging the terms

(13) $w-w_a = \sigma\tau[(PQ/wL)-1-(K/wL)]$.

Again, using (11), one has

(14) $w-w_a = \sigma\tau w[(PQ/wL)-1-(\alpha/\beta)(\omega/w)r]$.

Recalling that

(15) $(PQ/wL) = [1/(1-m)\beta]$,

and noticing from other work (Bughin, 1991) that

(16) $(PQ/wL) = [1/(1-m)\,\beta + \gamma m]$,

where $[\delta\mu/(1+\delta\mu)]m = \gamma m$ $(0 \leq \gamma \leq 1)$, the reduced-form wage equation (14) is given by (assuming no corner solution)

$$(17) \quad w = \frac{w_a}{1-\sigma\tau\left[\dfrac{1-(1-m)\beta-\gamma m-r(1-m)(1-\beta)}{(1-m)\beta+\gamma m}\right]}.$$

Finally, incorporating (17) into (11) yields the unionized capital-labor ratio

$$(18) \quad K/L = (\alpha/\beta)\psi(w_a/r),$$

with

$$(19) \quad \psi = \phi+(1-\phi)\left[1-\sigma\tau\left[\frac{1-(1-m)\beta-\gamma m-r(1-m)(1-\beta)}{(1-m)\beta+\gamma m}\right]\right].$$

Apparent from (18)-(19) is that the capital-labor ratio of an unionized firm still depends on the output elasticities of inputs of the technology function and on the capital rental rate (r). But the unionized firm's capital-labor ratio also depends on the various parameters which determine the wage outcome such as the elasticity of product demand or the union power parameters. Finally, the impact of the exogenous variables on the capital-labor ratio depends crucially on whether the wage and employment locus is *positively or negatively sloped.*

When union power over labor is higher than union power over employment, it follows from (10) that $\phi \leq 1$ and the wage-employment locus remains downward sloping, as in conventional labor demand curve models. In this latter case, simple algebra reveals that the effect of the exogenous variable on the capital-labor is *unambiguously* signed [see Bughin (1992) for explicit derivation]: $(K/L)_\sigma' \geq 0$; $(K/L)_\tau' \geq 0$; $(K/L)_\beta' \leq 0$; $(K/L)w_a' \geq 0$; $(K/L)_\delta' \leq 0$; $(K/L)_\mu' \leq 0$; and $(K/L)_\varepsilon' \geq 0$. Those partial derivatives are however *ambiguous* when union power is *higher* over employment than over wage, an exception being the partial derivative of (K/L) with respect to ε [where $(K/L)_\varepsilon' \leq 0$ for $\phi \geq 1$ and *vice versa*]. This latter point may only be proven *analytically* given the imposition of a Cobb-Douglas technology for the firm. However, one can reasonably feel that this holds true with more general revenue functions. Take as proven for any revenue function that negotiated wages are positively related to m because product market power expands the feasible portion of the bargaining locus.[16] Then define the variable $\varphi = (w-w_a)/(w)$, which is a positive function of ε. From the definition of the marginal revenue product of labor [see (10)], the capital-labor ratio is amended as

$$(20) \quad K/L = (\alpha^*/\beta^*)\xi(w_a/r),$$

where α^* (respectively β^*) is the capital (respectively labor) elasticity of output, and

---

[16]This is empirically shown in Blanchflower *et al.* (1990).

(21) $\xi = \dfrac{\phi - \varphi(1 - \phi)}{\phi}$,

both to compare with (18)-(19) above, and $(K/L)_\varepsilon' = (K/L)_\theta' \varphi_\varepsilon' \le 0$ for $\phi \le 1$ whatever the revenue function.

Thus, for a wide variety of techologies the sign of $(K/L)_\varepsilon'$ in (20) is *directly* linked to the *slope* of the wage-labor locus, the expectation being that a positive (respectively negative) association between (K/L) and ε is consistent with the wage entering negatively (respectively positively) in the normalized employment equation (10). Finally, note that the union-firm bargaining story yields another rationale as to why the firm's capital-labor ratio might be associated with product market rents, a stylized empirical fact in the industrial organization literature indicating that more concentrated industries use more capital-intensive technology (see, *e.g.*, Scott, 1981). Unionism theory adds that, depending on the bargained wage-employment locus, the association may take *either* sign. Section III wishes to infer the slope of the bargaining outcome in the wage-employment locus by testing from (18)-(19) under which form the firm's capital-labor ratio is related to its oligopoly rents.

3.   REMARKS
3.1   THE FIRM RENTS
The results above have been derived under the assumption of a *monopoly*. More generally, the firm faces an oligopolistic structure in its product market. From industrial organization it is well-known that the mark-up, m, can be related not only to the elasticity of product demand, but also to a function f of variables X:

(22) $m = f(X)$.

X is a vector which generally includes the firm's market share (MS), the price-elasticity of product demand (ε) and a measure of the firm conjectural variation *vis-à-vis* its rivals.[17] In the empirical work below, only MS is an observable. Since in equilibrium - and robust to many alternatives (Harris, 1988) - a *positive* association remains between MS and m, a negative (respectively positive) sign between MS and (K/L) is consistent with an union-firm bargaining locus which is positively (respectively negatively) sloped. A caution that must be taken here is that the market share variable should be (suitably) instrumented. A common reason for this is the Clarke and Davies (1982) objection that the equilibrium profit margin exhibits only a relationship with market share, but is not caused by it. Another reason, related to this chapter's bargaining framework, is that (K/L) and MS are both explained by the same variables (see,

---

[17]See Cowling and Waterson (1976) on this. Of course, if one amends this simple model of symmetric oligopoly to more complex models, other variables emerge as related to monopoly power. As examples, the elasticy of the fringe supply in a model of dominant firms, the elasticities of foreign trade curves in a oligopoly model of international trade or R&D intensity (approximating the extent of differentiation in products).

mutatis mutandis, Nickell *et al.*, 1991).[18]

3.2   ALTERNATIVE THEORIES
Other theories also predict an association between the firm capital-labor ratio and its product market power. Take the *entry barriers* story and the *firm size* argument as examples. One of the most popular theories in the IO-paradigm relates to entry barriers, stating that capital-intensity - as one measure of the degree of sunk costs[19] - may serve as a barrier to potential competitors and may thus prevent firms from profit erosion. Three remarks are however in order here: (i) only a positive association between mark-up and capital-labor ratio is predicted by this theory, whereas the above model may also explain a negative association; (ii) tests on the capital overinvestment story tend to lead to the conclusion that firms do not overinvest in capital, but use other tools as entry barriers (see, *e.g.*, Lieberman, 1988);[20] and (iii) the entry barrier theory assumes (only) a causality from the capital-labor ratio to the firm mark-up, while the above model suggests a simultaneous influence. If, nevertheless, the entry barrier argument is valid, this provides another argument for taking care of the possible endogeneity of the market share variable.

Another explanation of a *positive* association between market share and the firm's capital-labor ratio is the theory of the *size effect*, by which larger size firms - thus, *ceteris paribus*, higher market share firms - tend to use more *capital-intensive* technologies (Mills and Schuman, 1985). Adding an indicator of size in the estimation mainly leads - not surprisingly - to a decrease in *significance* of market share, as a symptom of collinearity between size and market share. Adding a size effect, however, does not change the *magnitude* of the effect of the market share on the capital-labor ratio of the firm.

III.   Evidence

1.   THE SAMPLE
This section provides an application of the theory to various manfacturing sectors of the Belgian economy. The estimation is conducted on a balanced panel of firms with pooling of data from 1978 to 1983. The list of the eight sectors are given in Table 1, including the number of yearly observations per industry. The sectors and the years chosen derive directly from Fecher and Perelman (1989). At this stage, it should be noted that - with the exception of the Metal Product industry - each industry in this sample experienced an

---

[18]To see this, consider an increase in the parameter δ. Then, (K/L) falls, but since $\delta > 0$ also implies overutilization of labor and capital (Q) and, *ceteris paribus*, MS increases as well.

[19]Other constituents of sunk costs are, *e.g.*, advertising (Stonebraker, 1976) and R&D expenditures (Mansfield, 1983).

[20]Theoretically, the underinvestment story is not robust to the incorporation of uncertainty (see Bonanno, 1988).

Table 1.   The sample

	Sector	Number of firms
1	Chemicals	73
2	Metal Products	54
3	Non-Metal Products	102
4	Textile	150
5	Clothing and Leather	55
6	Wood and Furnre	103
7	Food and Tabacco	212
8	Paper and Printing	108

Note: sample size *after* omission of outliers; an outlier is defined as a firm whose estimated marginal revenue product of either labor or capital is negative.

important decline in employment during this period.[21] As put in evidence in Vannetelbosch (1992), the 1978-1983 period is also characterized by high industrial relations conflicts, and the additional fact that motives for union strikes have shifted from wage claims to employment considerations, can be used as a *prior* to infer that the wage-labor locus has shifted towards more *labor orientation*.

1.   DATA

Descriptions of observables are provided in this subsection. Table 2 indicates the source of the statistics. The level of capital, K, is available from financial statements and stands for gross fixed assets net of depreciation deflated by the appropriate sectoral price index. Labor, L, is measured by the yearly number of workers employed. The firm's market share, MS, is computed as the ratio of firm's added value to the aggegate added value of the firm's sector. Market share is not the only indicator of market power, and one often suggests that the structure of the industry plays a great role in sustaining firm profitability. Therefore, a common measure of industry concentration, the Herfindahl index, H, is included. It has been suggested that the conjectural variation parameter is an increasing function of the concentration ratio: yet, the argument is hardly decisive (Nickell *et al.*, 1991). Here, the Schmalensee (1989) stylized fact is checked that profitability tends to be *decreasing* in concentration at given levels of market share, so that the sign of H should be the opposite of the sign of MS,

---

[21]To this end, refer to the table in the Appendix.

Table 2.   Source of statistics

K	NBB
L	ONSS
MS	NBB; INS
H	INS
WA	IRES; NBB; INS
IR	NBB
DR	NBB
PSTR	INS

Legend: NBB = National Bank of Belgium; ONSS = Office National de Securite Sociale; INS = Institut National des Statistiques; and IRES = Institut de Recherches Economiques.

on (K/L).[22] The firm's alternative wage is defined as the wage outside the firm times the probability of finding employment outside the firm. Following common practice, the probability of finding employment is simply proxied by one minus the unemployment rate, UR: so $w_a = W.(1-UR)$ and W is the relevant aggregate real wage.[23] We also assume that the firm cost of capital is a function of both the interest rate, ir, which measures the opportuny cost of investment, and the debt ratio, DR, because cost of debt is generally lower than cost of equity. Concerning, finally, union power and union preferences over wages and labor - the parameters τ, μ, σ and δ - the only observable union measure is the ratio of strikes for employment to the number of strikes for wage claims. This ratio, PSTR, should be more relevant as an indicator of *relative* union preferences, as suggested by Vannetelbosch (1992). Indeed, union power relates to the ability of the union to influence outcomes *during* negotiations, while strikes measure frequencies of breakdown of negotiations.

Notice that traditional measures of union power include unemployment rate and/or the unionization rate. Such approaches might be misleading to the extent that (i) unemployment already influences the union's threat-point (see the definition of the firm's alternative wage above), and (ii) unionization rate *per se* does not tell anything on the union bargaining *success* to influence wage and labor conditions (see Dowrick, 1990). An econometric problem remains, however, by letting union power parameters to be *latent* variables. Since there

---

[22]Other industry variables are also included as determinants of the mark-up in the empirical examination, but none of those variables revealed significance. The variables considered were: industry sales growth (Bradburd and Caves, 1982) and R&D intensity.

[23]Industry wages statistics are only available for the first four sectors; for the other sectors, an index has been constructed from the *sample mean* of industry wage. Results are qualitatively the same when using, for the first four sectors, a sample mean industry wage index.

is good chance that those variables are correlated with the observables,[24] at least firm effects have to be included to minimize the possibily of systematic bias; this is made possible by using the time-series dimension of the data.

2.   THE ECONOMETRIC MODEL

2.1   EMPIRICAL EQUATION

In order to obtain an empirical counterpart to (20), write (as McCurdy and Pencavel, 1986) the capital-labor ratio in terms of an equation defining the unionized firm's inputs *allocation rule*. Remind that, by definition

(23) $\alpha^{\bullet}/\beta^{\bullet} = (K/L)(\partial L/\partial K)$.

Where ∂L (∂K) is the marginal product of labor (capital). Substitute (23) into (20). The capital-labor ratio is identified by

(24) $\partial K/\partial L = \xi[w_a/r]$,

which recovers the property that with purely competitive markets[25] the production of any output verifies the condition that the ratio of marginal products equals the ratio of prices. What this chapter's theory adds is simply the fact that ξ may be different from unity, and may be influenced by union's and firm's market power. Following (24), an equation is derived in log form:

(25) $Ln(\partial K/\partial L) = f + a1.Ln(\xi) + a2.Ln(w_a/r) + \Sigma a3.T$,

where f is a firm-specific effect, T a time dummy common to all firms and from (21) $\xi = g(MS, r, w_a, \sigma, PSTR, ...)$. Assume again a logarithm form for g(.). The final stochastic version of the capital-labor equation then is

(26) $Ln(\partial K/\partial L)_{it} = $ $f_i + b1.Ln(MS)_{it} + b2.Ln(H)_t + b3.Ln(wa/ir)_t + b4.Ln(DR)_{it} + b5.Ln(PSTR)_t + \Sigma_t b6_t.T_t + u_{it}$.

Estimation of (26) requires the knowledge of the *marginal* products of both K and L. The first step in the empirical study is to determine and estimate an accurate representation of the production technology. Among others, the term u represents errors-in-measurement in the dependent variable: assume that u is normally distributed. In addition, $\partial K/\partial L$ is derived from the estimation of a translogarithmic production function. Such an exercise has been already conducted by Fecher and Perelman (1989), using a deterministic production frontier approach on the same data set. The model was re-estimated by use of

---

[24]Refer to the Introduction (Sarig, 1990) to recall that union power may affect the optimal choice of debt. Also, Veugelers (1989) and Bughin (1992) present some arguments for an influence from product market concentration on union power.

[25]That is, $\xi = 1$, which also implies that $w = w_a$.

Instrumental Variables. The Appendix provides some summary findings from this estimation.

2.2   ESTIMATION METHOD

Equation (26) is estimated by differencing out the fixed effects. As the possibility of endogeneity for, say, the market share has been made with some force,[26] a suitable instrumental technique has to be applied for proper estimation. Here, again, the time-series dimension of the data is exploited. Specifically, the Arellano and Bond (1988 and 1991) generalized method of moments is applied, which retains some period lags as optimal instruments. Conditional on u being serially uncorrelated, lags dated t-1 and before of the variables in first-differences may be included in the set of valid instruments of the endogenous variable, together with the exogenous variables of the model. This also implies that the actual period of estimation runs from 1980 to 1983 (inclusive).

2.3   RESULTS

The first column (1) of Table 3 presents results based on (26), while the second column (2) is the result of estimating the equation with the addition of a size measure (S). S is represented by firm's total sales, and is also instrumented. Because the results rely heavily on the absence of serial correlation in the error term, a normality test of this hypothesis is presented at the bottom of each table.[27] Heteroscedastic one-step t-statistics are reported in brackets, following Arellano and Bond (1991).

The following results are to be emphasized. First, in almost all sectors, the effect of incorporating the size variable is primarily to decrease the *significance* of the market share variable on the ratio of marginal value products. This, obviously, reflects *multicollinearity* problems between the size and the market share variables. In the following, we thus concentrate on column (1) of Table 3. Second, the impact of the alternative wage-interest rate ratio on the capital-labor is always positive *and* significant. Except for 'Wood & Furnitures', this elasticity is smaller than one. Remind from this chapter's bargaining theory that the effect of the *alternative wage* on capital-labor is twofold. On the one hand, through the conventional *substitution* effect the alternative wage *increases* the capital-labor ratio; on the other hand, through its indirect effect on the union power[28] it *decreases* the capital-labor ratio. The estimated *positive* elasticities mean that the substitution effect is dominant: yet, the *inelastic* effect of relative input prices on the ratio of marginal products, as a whole, suggests that unions might have used their power to affect employment. Third, the fact that unions have played a role in the determination of the firm's capital-labor ratio is

---

[26]Notice that the industry variables H and w_a could also be potentially endogenous to the capital-labor ratio, although the degree of endogenity is unlikely to be large. As a matter of fact, regressions have been run by endogenizing those variables. Results obtained are extremely close to the ones found in Table 3 hereafter.

[27]For a formal description of the test see Conyon and Machin (1991: 380).

[28]As incorporated in the variable ξ.

revealed by the often significant *depressive* impact of the union strike variable (PSTR) on the firm's capital-labor ratio.[29] The increase in the ratio PSTR during the years in the sample, coupled with a systematic decline in employment for the Belgian manufacturing industries, suggests that unions were

Table 3.   The unionized firm's capital-labor ratio

Chemicals	(1)	(2)	Metal Products	(1)	(2)
MS	-0.03	-0.04	MS	0.07	0.10
	(-1.22)	(-1.36)		(2.12)	(1.88)
H	-0.42	-0.38	H	-0.42	-0.38
	(-1.48)	(-1.67)		(-1.88)	(-1.67)
(w_a/ir)	0.72	0.68	(w_a/ir)	0.72	0.68
	(1.99)	(2.21)		(1.99)	(2.21)
DR	0.03	0.04	DR	0.03	0.04
	(1.98)	(2.00)		(2.98)	(2.70)
S	-	0.04	S	-	0.04
	(-)	(0.06)		(-)	(0.06)
PSTR	-0.04	-0.03	PSTR	-0.10	-0.09
	(-1.99)	(-1.94)		(-1.67)	(-1.73)
R-test	-0.23	-0.99	R-test	1.03	1.09
Non-Metal Products	(1)	(2)	**Textiles**	(1)	(2)
MS	0.25	0.21	MS	-0.20	-0.21
	(1.22)	(0.36)		(-2.12)	(-2.01)
H	0.66	0.64	H	0.89	0.91
	(1.28)	(1.67)		(3.38)	(2.67)
(w_a/ir)	0.87	0.83	(w_a/ir)	0.26	0.28
	(2.65)	(2.69)		(3.03)	(2.89)
DR	0.02	0.002	DR	0.13	0.14
	(1.09)	(1.04)		(1.84)	(1.99)
S	-	0.01	S	-	-0.00
	(-)	(0.32)		(-)	(-0.16)
PSTR	-0.01	-0.03	PSTR	-0.23	-0.20
	(-2.34)	(-2.28)		(-1.65)	(-1.77)
R-test	1.43	1.60	R-test	-1.69	-1.56

[29]This result is relatively robust given that only for two sectors (Clothing and Food) the sign of PSTR on the capital-labor ratio is positive but *insignificant*.

Table 3 (Continued)

Clothing	(1)	(2)	Wood and Furniture	(1)	(2)
MS	0.18	0.17	MS	-0.03	-0.05
	(2.06)	(1.32)		(-1.90)	(-1.64)
H	-1.12	-1.00	H	0.82	0.84
	(-5.99)	(-5.86)		(3.48)	(3.67)
(w_a/ir)	0.30	0.34	(w_a/ir)	1.07	1.04
	(1.74)	(1.71)		(1.55)	(1.60)
DR	0.01	0.04	DR	-0.03	-0.04
	(0.08)	(0.24)		(-1.00)	(-1.12)
S	-	0.04	S	-	-0.12
	(-)	(0.67)		(-)	(-0.66)
PSTR	0.02	0.02	PSTR	-0.06	-0.09
	(1.00)	(1.13)		(-1.09)	(-1.12)
R-test	1.43	1.45	R-test	-1.23	-1.44

Food and Tabacco	(1)	(2)	Paper & Printing	(1)	(2)
MS	-0.11	-0.08	MS	-0.08	-0.12
	(-2.22)	(-1.98)		(-2.43)	(-1.83)
H	0.40	0.39	H	0.38	-0.39
	(2.28)	(2.09)		(1.88)	(1.87)
(w_a/ir)	0.87	0.89	(w_a/ir)	0.41	0.42
	(3.50)	(3.30)		(2.39)	(2.20)
DR	0.10	0.10	DR	0.09	0.08
				(1.98)	(2.00)
S	-	0.02	S	-	-0.00
	(-)	(0.86)		(-)	(-0.01)
PSTR	0.03	0.01	PSTR	-0.08	-0.10
	(0.98)	(0.79)		(-2.00)	(-2.21)
R-test	1.03	0.99	R-test	-0.23	-0.18

Notes: time-dummies, included, not reproduced. R is N(0,1) T-statistics in brackets.

willing to reduce the speed of employment cuts. This might have entailed some kind of labor hoarding, which is reflected in a lower firm's capital-labor ratio. Fourth, the firm's debt ratio is positively correlated with the firm capital-labor ratio, which means that capital-intensive firms in the sample were also the more indebted. Since higher debt ratio may imply *lower* cost of capital, this positive effect implies that a period of high debt has favored substitution of labor for capital. Fifth, the fact that, when both significant (see especially the Textile, Foods and Tobacco, and Paper and Printing sectors), the market share and the concentration variables affect the firm's capital-labor ratio in *opposite* ways, is consistent with the Schmalensee conjecture that MS and the Herfindahl index play opposite effects on the firm's product market power. This is also in accordance with this chapter's bargaining theory that the market share and concentration variables affect the capital-labor ratio primarily through their influence on the firm's oligopoly power.[30]

Finally, according to those five results, one might classify the sectors according to their wage-labor locus as follows.[31]

a. Sectors with *positive* bargaining locus: Textile, Foods & Tobacco, Paper & Printing and, to a lesser extent, Wood & Furnitures;

b. Sectors with *negative* bargaining locus: Metal Products and Clothing; and

c. Sectors with *vertical* bargaining locus: Chemicals and Non-Metal Products.

Given that the conventional labor demand curve model implies a negative, or at the limit an *inelastic*, relationship between labor and wages, sectors with a positive locus provide *indirect* evidence that bargaining takes place *off* the conventional labor demand curve. This confirms the results of Bughin (1991 and 1993) and Vannetelbosch (1992) that union bargaining is not restricted to wage in Belgian manufacturing, and conforts with the evidence that industrial conflicts emerged in the sample period because of union reluctance towards employment decline. Also, the fact that the conventional labor demand curve is rejected in unionized markets is not confined to Belgium, as apparent in Bean and Turnbull (1988), Dowrick (1990) and Paci *et al.* (1991) for the U.K., Christofides (1991) for Canada, and McCurdy and Pencavel (1986) for the U.S.

A final caution is necessary as, for instance, sectors for which the relationship between market share and the firm's capital-labor ratio is the least significant are also the more capital-intensive industries (*i.e.*, Chemicals). This might suggest the *alternative* interpretation that minimum capital requirements are important in those industries, independent from the firm's market share. However, the simple fact that union variables affect the firm's capital-labor ratio suggests that this chapter's theory is not without interest, as it is for sure that unions might have affected substitution possibilities between labor and capital (Clark, 1984).

IV.   Conclusions

This chapter has developed a simple model of the determination of the unionized firm's capital-labor ratio when bargaining is not necessarily restricted to wage, but may include, even indirectly, some aspects related to labor determination. Using the asymmetric Nash solution to model the bargaining outcome, the chapter has highlighted how unions may create some new links between the

---

[30]Notice the *disparities* of estimates across sectors. This is not surprising given that the effects of market share and concentration on firm's product market power depend largely on the conduct in the product market. Further, the effect of market power on the capital-labor ratio is rather complex [recall (19)], and includes the cross-effect with union power, which also appears to be sector-specific, as estimated in De la Croix (1992).

[31]Recall that this classification depends, among others, on the period of the sample.

firm's capital-labor ratio and the extent of the firm's oligopoly rents, being due to the phenomenom of *ability to pay* and unions preferences towards wage and labor. Application of the theory to some Belgian manufacturing sectors has generated some evidence of a relationship between the firm's product market power, union relative preferences towards employment and the firm's capital-labor ratio. Interpreting the results in light of unionism, the bargaining locus appears to be positively sloped for half the sectors of the sample, leading to the conclusion that unionized labor is *not* negotiated on the conventional labor demand curve. Monopoly rents can be suggested as a factor explaining the rate of industry investment (Schiantarelli and Geirgoutsos, 1990). What this chapter's theory adds to this argument is that the ability of unions to affect the process of capital accumulation depends also on the existence of those product rents. Whether product rents boost investment can depend critically on union power and union preferences towards high employment.

Appendix

The technology has been specificied as a translog on three inputs: labor, raw materials and capital. The dependent variable is the firm's total real sale. Estimation has been run with variables taken in first-difference, and using the methodology of IV variables. Results in the following table are computed at the sample mean for the whole period. Those results are entirely comparable to Fecher and Perelman (1989).

Table A.1.   Inside the technology of the firm: some summary findings for eight Belgian industries

	% increase 77-83 in		Elasticity of output with respect to (estimates)		
	Labor	capital	labor	capital	substitution
1	-3.6	-18.3	0.34	0.12	1.71
2	5.03	11.1	0.28	0.07	2.06
3	-23.08	-17.00	0.40	0.15	1.55
4	-12.08	27.09	0.25	0.07	0.99
5	-8.01	18.41	0.21	0.03	0.20
6	-6.00	-2.33	0.33	0.04	0.73
7	-6.1	6.04	0.21	0.04	1.12
8	-2.49	17.08	0.50	0.06	0.60

References

Abowd, J.M. (1989) 'The Effects of Wage Bargains on the Stock Market Value of the Firm', *American Economic Review* **79**, 774-809.
Alogoskoufis, G. and Manning, A. (1991) 'Tests of Alternative Wage-Employment Bargaining Models with an Application to the UK Aggregate Labour Market', *European Economic Review* **35**, 23-39.
Aoki, M. (1984) *The Cooperative Game Theory of the Firm*, Oxford University Press, Oxford.
Arellano, M. and Bond, S. (1988) 'Dynamic Panel Data Estimation Using DPD: A Guide to Users', Institute for Fiscal Studies, London School, *Working Paper* **15**.
Arellano, M. and Bond, S. (1991) 'Some Tests of Specification for Panel Data: Monte Carlo

Evidence and an Application to Employment Equations', *Review of Economic Studies* **18**.

Bean, Ch. and Turnbull, H. (1988) 'Employment in the British Coal Industry: A Test of the Labour Demand Model', *Economic Journal* **98**, 1092.

Binmore, K. , Rubinstein, A. and Wolinsky, A. (1986) 'The Nash Bargaining Solution in Economic Modelling', *RAND Journal of Economics* **17**, 176-88.

Blanchflower, D., Oswald, A. and Garrett, M. (1990) 'Insider Power in Wage Determination', *Economica* **57**, 143-170.

Bonanno, G. (1988) 'Entry Deterrence with Uncertain Entry and Uncertain Observability of Commitment', *International Journal of Industrial Organization* **6**, 351-362.

Bradburd, R.M. and Caves, R.E. (1982) 'A Closer Look at the Effect of Market Growth on Industries Profits', *Review of Economics and Statistics* **64**, 635-645.

Brown, Ch. and Medoff, J. (1978) 'Trade Unions in the Production Process', *Journal of Political Economy* **86**, 355-378.

Bughin, J. (1991) 'Testing Oligopolistic Behavior within an Efficient Wage Bargaining Model, *Universite Catholique de Louvain (UCL) Discussion Paper* **91-04**, Paper presented at the European Economic Association Meeting, Cambridge, September.

Bughin, J. (1992) *Union-Firm Bargaining and Imperfect Product Competition in Belgian Manufacturing*, Ph.D. thesis, UCL.

Bughin, J. (1993) 'Union-Firm Efficient Bargaining and Tests of Oligopolistic Conduct', *Review of Economics and Statistics*, August, 561-565.

Bughin, J. (1994) 'Union-Firm Bargaining and the Influence of Market Power and Production Technology on the Firm Systematic Risk', *Management Science* (forthcoming).

Christofides, L. (1991) 'Non-Nested Tests of Efficient Bargain and Labour Demand Models', *Economics Letters* **32** 91-96.

Clark, A. (1990) 'Efficient Bargains and the McDonald-Solow Conjecture', *Journal of Labor Economics* **8**, 502-526.

Clark, K.B. (1984) 'Unionization and Firm Performance: The Impact of Profits, Growth and Productivity', *American Economic Review* **74**, 893-919.

Clarke, R. and Davies, S. (1982) 'Market Structure and Price-Cost Margins', *Economica* **49**, 227-87.

Conyon, M. and Machin, S. (1991) 'The Determination of Profit Margins in UK Manufacturing', *Journal of Industrial Economics* **39**, 369-382.

Cowling, K. and Waterson, M. (1976) 'Price-Cost Margins and Market Structure', *Economica* **43**, 267-274.

Croix, D. de la (1992) *Union-Firm Bargaining and Equilibrium Unemployment in Quantity Rationing Models*, Ph.D Thesis, UCL.

Dowrick, S. (1989) 'Union-Oligopoly Bargaining', *Economic Journal* **99**, 1123-1142.

Dowrick, S. (1990) 'Wage Pressure, Bargaining and Price-Cost Margin in UK Manufacturing', *Journal of Industrial Economics* **3**, 239-268.

Fecher, F. and Perelman, S. (1989) 'Productivite, progres technique et efficacite: une etude comparative de 14 secteurs industriels belges', *Annales d'Economie et de Statistique* **13**, 103-118.

Freeman, R. and Medoff, J. (1982) 'Substitution between Production Labor and Other Inputs in Unionized and Non-Unionized Manufactoring', *Review of Economics and Statistics* **64**, 220-233.

Grout, P.A. (1984) 'Investment and Wage in the Absence of Binding Contracts in a Nash Bargaining Approach', *Econometrica* **2**, 449-460.

Harris, F.(1988) 'Testable Competing Hypotheses from Structure-Performance Theory: Efficient Structure versus Market Power', *Journal of Industrial Economics* **36**, 267-280.

Hoel, M. (1990) 'Local versus Central Wage Bargaining with Endogenous Investments', *Scandinavian Journal of Economics* **92**, 453-469.

Lieberman, M. (1987) 'Excess Capacity as a Barrier to Entry: An Empirical Appraisal', *Journal of Industrial Economics* **85**, 607-28.

MaCurdy, T.E. and Pencavel, J. (1986) 'Testing between Competing Models of Wage and Employment Determination in Unionised Markets', *Journal of Political Economy* **94**, 3-39.

Manning, A. (1987) 'An Integration of Trade Unions in a Sequential Bargaining Framework', *Economic Journal* **97**, 121-139.

McDonald I.M. and Solow, R. (1981) 'Wage Bargaining and Employment', *American Economic Review* **71**, 896-908.

Mansfield, E. (1983) 'Technological Change and Market Structure: An Empirical Study', *American*

Economic Review, Papers and Proceedings **73**, 205-209.

Mills, D. and Schuman, L. (1985) 'Industry Structure with Fluctuating Demand', *American Economic Review,* 758-767.

Nickell, S. and Andrews, M. (1983) 'Unions, Real Wages and Employment in Britain 1951-79', *Oxford Economic Papers* **35**, 183-206.

Nickell, S., Vainiomaki, J. and Wadwhani, S. (1991) 'Wages, Unions, Insiders and Product Market Power', Institute of Economics and Statistics, University of Oxford, *Paper* presented at a conference on 'Unemployment and Wage Determination', Cambridge, MA.

Paci, P. , Wagstaff, A. and Holl, P. (1991) 'Testing the Efficiency of Wage-Employment Bargaining in U.K. Manufacturing', *City University Discussion Paper*, London.

Pemberton, J. (1988) 'A Managerial Model of the Trade Union', *Economic Journal* **98**, 755-771.

Sarig, O. (1990) 'The Effect of Leverage on Bargaining with a Corporation', *Working Paper*, Tel Aviv University.

Schiantarelli, F. and Georgoutsos, D. (1990) 'Monopolistic Competition and the q-Theory of Investment', *European Economic Review* **34**, 1061-1078.

Schmalensee, R. (1989) 'Inter-Industry Studies of Structure and Performance', in Schmalensee, R. and Willig, R. (eds), *Handbook of Industrial Organization*, North-Holland.

Scott, J. (1981) 'The Pure Capital-Cost Barrier to Entry', *Review of Economics and Statistics* **63**, 444-446.

Stonebraker, R.J. (1976) 'Corporate Profits and the Risk of Entry', *Review of Economics and Statistics* **58**, 33-39.

Vannetelbosch, V. (1992) *Les negociations salariales sont-elles efficientes en Belgique?*, Master thesis, UCL.

Veugelers, R. (1989) 'Wage Premia, Price-Cost Margins and Bargaining Power in Belgian Manufacturing', *European Economic Review* **33**, 169-180.

Wadhwani, S. (1990) 'The Effect of Unions on Productivity Growth, Investment and Employment: A Report on Some Recent Work', *British Journal of Industrial Relations* **28**, 371-385.

CHAPTER 11

Buyer-Supplier Bargaining and Intra-Industry Competition

PAUL W. DOBSON[1]

School of Management and Finance, University of Nottingham, United Kingdom

Abstract. This chapter considers the trading processes between a monopoly supplier and a downstream oligopolistic industry and examines how the degree of downstream rivalry affects both the size and the distribution of profits in the market. With the downstream oligopolists setting the output level and bargaining only over the transfer price, total market profits are primarily determined by the degree of coordination in the final market. If the oligopolists behave in a perfectly competitive manner, then all the available profits are competed away. However, it is shown that strong collusion in the final market can also (perversely) harm the oligopolists, as well as the supplier, by restricting output below the optimal vertical integration level. With price-and-quantity (efficient) bargaining this problem does not arise and the shares of the joint profit-maximizing surplus are distributed simply according to the degree of cooperation between the buyers in bargaining with the supplier.

I. Introduction

This chapter considers trading mechanisms between highly concentrated vertically related industries and examines how differences in the number of firms on each side of the market can affect profits within the market. The analysis concentrates on a market structure which has an upstream monopoly supplying a downstream oligopoly, where outcomes are determined through bargaining.[2] The chapter's main concern is with how the imbalance between the numbers on each side of the market affects the trade between the parties, and more specifically how the degree of the downstream oligopolistic rivalry affects the size and distribution of profits in the whole market. The outcomes from bargaining are shown to depend crucially on the scope and structure of negotiations as well as the degree of cooperation between the buyers in dealing with the single supplier.

The market structure under consideration might occur at a number of places in the production process. For example, a monopoly manufacturer supplying several *dealers*, either wholesalers or retailers, competing with each other in the same output market. In this case, the downstream rivalry takes the form of intrabrand competition. Alternatively, we could imagine oligopolistic firms employing workers organized into an industry-wide labor union, or oligopolistic

---

[1] I would like to thank Mike Waterson, Arjen van Witteloostuijn and participants at the EARIE 19th annual conference, Stuttgart-Hohenheim, for useful comments. Any remaining errors are my own.

[2] Stackelberg (1934) referred to such a market structure as *beschränktes nachfrage-monopol*, literally restricted monopoly (or quasi-monopoly; see Stackelberg, 1952). The opposite case, where an oligopoly supplies a monopolist, has been addressed by several papers in the context of labor markets (*e.g.*, Horn and Wolinsky, 1988a; and Jun, 1989).

manufacturers using a raw material supplied by a monopolist.[3]

In each of these situations it may be more natural for transactions to be determined through bargaining rather than within a vertically integrated structure, especially if the costs of vertical integration are high. For example, the monopolist supplier will not attempt to integrate forwards if the costs incurred outweigh any possible long-run profit advantage, which may well be the case if the input supplied is only one of several used by the downstream firms, or the monopolist supplies large diversified firms. Similarly, the downstream firms may not wish to integrate backwards if the upstream firm is diversified or vertical integration results in diseconomies of scale.[4]

The major focus in this chapter is on trading between the supplier and all available buyers - *i.e.*, monopoly-oligopoly bargaining as considered, for example, by Davidson (1988), Horn and Wolinsky (1988) and Viehoff (1987) - rather than on bargaining processes by which the supplier selects a single trading partner. This latter issue concerning the trading procedure by which a seller trades with a single buyer has received much attention recently (see the surveys by Binmore, Osborne and Rubenstein, 1989; and Osborne and Rubenstein, 1990). Discussion of this issue is left until the final section of the chapter when some comparisons are made between the outcomes where all buyers are supplied and the rather more extreme outcomes which arise when the supplier only chooses to deal with one buyer.

By supplying only one firm, the supplier removes the downstream intra-industry competition. Joint profits can be higher if there are increasing returns to scale downstream or if transaction costs are reduced.[5] However, against this motive to restrict supply to a sole buyer, there are several important reasons why the supplier would wish to supply a number of firms. Firstly, *refusal to supply* is a vertical restraint which may be subject to anti-trust legislation.[6] Secondly, establishing long-term contracts with as many buyers as possible may act as a barrier to entry, helping to maintain the monopoly position of the supplier and keep future profits high. Thirdly, and perhaps more significantly, supplying only one firm establishes a bilateral monopoly situation, which makes the supplier dependent on this buyer. Dependence on a sole buyer may yield unforeseen hazards - *e.g.*, the downstream firm having technical and/or financial

---

[3]The monopoly position in the latter case might be maintained by a patent for the transferred good, or may be due to the supplier being a nationalized industry (this approximates the U.K. electricity industry, where British Coal supplies the two major generating companies PowerGen and National Power).

[4]The organizations may be *incompatible* in the sense that integration could mean that (expensive) internal restructuring becomes necessary to establish effective communication and control channels.

[5]At the very least savings in transportation costs might be expected.

[6]Anti-trust authorities have often been indifferent to this vertical restraint. For example, the recent investigation by the Monopoly and Mergers Commission on the U.K. car retail market led to no action against the local monopoly franchise system operated by car makers.

problems causing trade to stop. Furthermore, the bilateral monopoly situation could lead to future problems if switching costs are high (see Porter, 1980). This problem is most severe if the current potential purchasers leave the market and are not replaced, since then the supplier's future bargaining position will be considerably weakened (especially if a rival supplier appears).

The rest of the chapter is organized as follows. Section II categorizes bargaining processes and discusses the framework of analysis. Section III considers how the degree of downstream oligopolistic rivalry affects price-only bargains, examining the optimal level of cooperation for the downstream firms and the effect that this has on the supplier's profits. Section IV considers efficient bargains where the firms bargain over both transfer prices and quantities, and examines how the buyers can most effectively cooperate in bargaining to secure a high share of the available profits. Finally, Section V concludes the chapter by comparing the results of Section III and IV with the outcomes resulting from trading processes by which a single buyer is selected.

II.   Monopoly-Oligopoly Bargaining

1.   PRICE AND/OR QUANTITY
In analyzing multi-unit bargaining processes the chapter makes a broad distinction based on the scope of bargaining, comparing price-only bargaining with price-and-quantity bargaining. This distinction is the same as made in the labor economics literature, where collective bargaining models take the form of either a *right-to-manage* model (*e.g.*, Nickel and Andrews, 1983) the employers (buyers) unilaterally chosing the employment level (quantity), or an *efficient bargaining* model (*e.g.* McDonald and Solow, 1981) where both wages and employment levels are negotiated over. For convenience, it is assumed throughout the chapter that there are only two potential buyers. This assumption does not affect the arguments presented.

The intuitive feeling might be that since the monopoly supplier is the only source of supply to the buyers it will be in a relatively stronger position, given that the buyers have to compete with each other for purchases and sales. This chapter will consider the supplier's advantage (if any) and examine how it affects profits to the firms in the market. A critical factor turns out to be the form of the supplier's disagreement payoff, representing the opportunities available to the supplier when agreement is not reached with a buyer. Possible forms that this payoff can take are discussed for each bargaining situation.

2.   BARGAINING ONLY OVER THE TRANSFER PRICE
Price-only bargaining in the context of a monopoly supplying an oligopoly has recently been addressed by Davidson (1988) and Horn and Wolinsky (1988b). Both papers assume that the final market is a Cournot-Nash equilibrium and examine outcomes based on simultaneous bargaining between the supplier and each buyer. In Section III this analysis is extended to consider how the degree of rivalry affects outcomes in the market using a conjectural variations model, where the profits each side of the market receives depend on the extent of the buyers' coordination in both their output market and in their bargaining arrange-

ments.

With the objective of each party to maximize profits (net available gains), price-only bargaining results in an inefficient outcome: *i.e.*, joint profits are not maximized. This is a guise of the double marginalization problem associated with successive monopoly where each firm adds its own price-cost margin at each stage of production, but vertical integration or bargaining over quantities generally removes this inefficiency (Spengler, 1950). Nevertheless, even though all parties may recognize the inefficiency, without side payments it may not be in all their interests to move to efficient bargaining. Dowrick (1990) for instance, demonstrates, for a number of collective bargaining structures, that employers earn higher profits when they can set employment levels unilaterally.

It is assumed that the supplier bargains with each buyer separately, so that there are two simultaneous bargains. The outcomes of bargaining are modeled in terms of the (symmetric) Nash bargaining solution, approximating a Rubenstein (1982) dynamic (alternating offers) process (see Binmore, 1982; and Binmore *et al.*, 1986)[7], where subject to the expected outcome in the final product market the bargained price (r_i) between the supplier and the i-th buyer is the solution to

(1) $$\max_{r_i} \left[\pi_i(r_i, r_j) - \overline{\pi}_i \right] \left[\pi_s(r_i, r_j) - \overline{\pi}_s - D_i \right],$$

where i, j = 1, 2, i ≠ j, $\pi_i(r_i, r_j)$ is the i-th buyer's profit function in terms of the transfer prices, $\pi_s(r_i, r_j)$ is the supplier's profit, $\overline{\pi}_i$ and $\overline{\pi}_s$ represent the outside options to each party, and D_i is the payoff to the supplier in the event that agreement can only be reached with the j-th buyer. Assuming that all outside options are normalized to zero, so that $\overline{\pi}_i = 0$ and $\overline{\pi}_s = 0$, and with profit functions specified, the only concern is with defining the disagreement payoff D_i: that is, the amount that the supplier can earn by only dealing with the other buyer when an agreement cannot be reached with the i-th buyer.[8] The larger this is, the larger the share the supplier will receive. Here, three possibilities expressing varying degrees of collaboration between the buyers in bargaining with the supplier are considered. First, as in Davidson (1988), the supplier is able to increase the amount sold to the other buyer in the event of disagreement with the i-th buyer - presumably up to the downstream monopoly level. This represents the buyers acting *competitively* (aggressively) and taking up any opportunity to increase profits, thus making D_i high. The second alternative, following Horn and Wolinsky (1988b) is that the disagreement payoff is based on the anticipated quantity sold to the other buyer. Here the buyers act *independently* and no contingency is made in the bargains to change output should the

---

[7]For instance, the sequence considered by Davidson is for the seller to simultaneously make offers to each buyer and then for each buyer to accept or make a counter-offer, and so on until an agreement is reached or one or more parties refuse to negotiate any further.

[8]The profit functions and disagreement payoffs in this chapter are designed so that the bargaining sets are convex, yielding a unique solution to the Nash bargain.

other firm not reach an agreement.[9] A third possibility is where the buyers behave collusively *(united)* in bargaining and agree that in the event of no agreement between one of them and the supplier, the other will not trade with the supplier thus reducing the supplier's disagreement payoff in (1) to zero. This yields the buyers the greatest profits, but given the individual incentive to cheat it may require a binding contract to be credible.[10]

3. BARGAINING OVER PRICE AND QUANTITY

Negotiated contracts in industrial markets often specify price and quantity, and in the event of the buyer not constrained by the amount of its other complementary inputs both the transfer price and quantity could be bargained over. In such circumstances the parties can remove the inefficiency associated with price-only bargaining. In this chapter price-quantity bargaining is characterized in terms of the Nash bargain, which solves

$$(2) \quad \max_{r_i, x_i} \left[\pi_i(r_i, r_j, x_i, x_j) - \overline{\pi}_i \right] \left[\pi_s(r_i, r_j, x_i, x_j) - \overline{\pi}_s - D_i \right],$$

where x_i is the quantity traded between the supplier and the i-th buyer. The bargain results in the pair (r_i^E, x_i^E). Again, it is assumed that $\overline{\pi}_i$ and $\overline{\pi}_s$ are zero. As in price-only bargaining, three forms of D_i can be considered each expressing a different degree of collaboration between the buyers in bargaining with the supplier. When the buyers cooperate and agree not to trade unless both can make an agreement, then $D_i = 0$. Independent bargaining behavior implies that once an agreement is struck it cannot be altered so that $D_i = \pi_s(r_j^E, x_j^E)$. Competitive bargaining implies that the buyers are willing to establish contingent contracts with the supplier, should the supplier by unable to make an agreement with the other buyer. The contingent contract accounts for the buyer becoming a monopolist and is based on a bilateral monopoly bargain. In the case where the buyers' outputs are substitutes, this severely weakens their position since D_i is high.

In Section IV the outcomes from (2) are examined under these three forms of disagreement payoff. As in Viehoff's (1987) non-cooperative bargaining analysis of efficient bargains between a monopoly and an oligopoly, bargaining results in each party receiving a (half) share of the net profit that their agreement genera-

---

[9]This notion is based on Binmore *et al.* (1986) arguing that the disagreement point should correspond to the stream of income accruing to the parties when they are in a state of disagreement and once an agreement is made it is immediately implemented.

[10]This form of collusive bargaining behavior is considered in preference to the more usual form of the buyers delegating a single representative to negotiate in their joint interests, since - as Bennett and Ulph (1988) and Dobson (1992) have shown - joint bargaining results in lower profits to the buyers than independent bargaining. For whereas separate bargaining allows the supplier to credibly threaten each buyer that in the event of negotiations breaking down the rival buyer could capture the entire market, this disadvantage to the buyers is outweighed by the buyers being better able to (separately) resist the supplier's demands because of the consequences for reduced input purchases (due to a weakened competitive position) if one buyer's costs are raised relative to those of its rival.

tes, but the actual proportion of the total available surplus each party receives is shown to rest on the buyers' degree of collusion during negotiations.

III.   Quantity Determined by the Buyers

In this section bargaining only concerns the transfer price. The buyers unilateral- ly choose the (exchanged) quantity once the transfer prices are agreed. Final market behavior takes the form of quantity setting, where each downstream firm releases a quantity onto the market (and final price is determined by an auctioneer) with the upstream industry supplying any quantity demanded by the downstream firms at the bargained transfer price. The two buyers are assumed to compete in a homogenous final goods duopoly market. The analysis is in terms of conjectural variations, which allows for different degrees of downstre- am rivalry between the extremes of perfect competition and full coordination. To keep the analysis fairly straightforward and enable some simple comparisons to be made, it is further assumed that the downstream firms face a linear demand function and the upstream monopolist produces under constant returns to scale.

The downstream firms face the following linear inverse demand function:

$$p = a - \beta(q_1 + q_2) \text{ with } a, \beta > 0,$$

where p denotes price and a and β are parameters. Each firm's output, q_i, is produced using input, x_i, under constant returns with the units normalized so that $q_i = x_i$ (for i = 1,2). For simplicity it is assumed that the only costs facing the oligopolists are those associated with purchasing the upstream monopolist's goods.

The downstream firms set output and input levels unilaterally to maximize expected profits given the bargained transfer prices and the expected behavior of the other firm (captured by the conjectural variations parameter $dx_j/dx_i = \lambda$). The problem facing each buyer is then[11]

$$\max [a - \beta(x_i + x_j) - r_i]x_i \text{ s.t. } dx_j/dx_i = \lambda \text{ and with } i,j = 1,2, i \neq j,$$

where r_i is the transfer price (per unit) agreed between the i-th firm and the supplier and λ, the conjectural variations parameter, which measures the degree of rivalrous collusion between the two downstream firms in the product market. With symmetric firms $-1 < \lambda < 1$, where $\lambda = -1$ implies competitive behavior, $\lambda = 0$ corresponds to Cournot behavior and $\lambda = 1$ implies full coordination (monopoly behavior). The product-market equilibrium in terms of the bargained transfer prices and (symmetric) conjectural variations can then be shown to be

$$(3) \quad x_i^\lambda = \frac{a(1+\lambda)-(2+\lambda)r_i+r_j}{\beta(3+\lambda)(1+\lambda)} \text{ with } i,j=1,2, \text{ and } i \neq j.$$

---

[11]A simple alternative, without affecting my arguments, would be to introduce fixed costs.

The i-th downstream firm's profit as a function of the bargained prices is then:

$$(4) \quad \pi_i^\lambda(r_i, r_j) = \frac{1}{(1+\lambda)\beta} \left[\frac{a(1+\lambda) - (2+\lambda)r_i + r_j}{3+\lambda} \right]^2$$

and the supplier's profit when facing a constant marginal cost equal to c ($< a$) is

$$(5) \quad \pi_s^\lambda(r_i, r_j) = (r_i - c) \left[\frac{a(1+\lambda) - (2+\lambda)r_i + r_j}{\beta(3+\lambda)(1+\lambda)} \right] + (r_j - c) \left[\frac{a(1+\lambda) - (2+\lambda)r_j + r_i}{\beta(3+\lambda)(1+\lambda)} \right].$$

The preceding bargaining stage is characterized by two separate bargains between the supplier and each oligopolist. From (1) the Nash bargaining solution for the bargain between the i-th firm and the supplier is

$$(6) \quad r_i = \underset{r_i}{\text{argmax}} \left[\pi_i^\lambda(r_i, r_j) \right] \left[\pi_s^\lambda(r_i, r_j) - D_i \right].$$

The term D_i is the disagreement payoff to the supplier if there is no agreement with the i-th firm. From the discussion in Subsection II.1 we have the following forms in descending order of magnitude, reflecting increasing collusion between the buyers in bargaining: (i) $D_i^{c\lambda} = r_j x_j^m - C(x_j^m) = \left[r_j - c \right] \left[\frac{a - r_j}{2\beta} \right]$,

(ii) $D_i^{\lambda} = r_j x_j^\lambda - C(x_j^\lambda) = \left[r_j - c \right] \left[\frac{a(1+\lambda) - (2+\lambda)r_j + r_i}{\beta(3+\lambda)(1+\lambda)} \right]$, and (iii) $D_i^{u\lambda} = 0$. The first of

these relates to the j-th buyer becoming a monopolist should there be no agreement between the i-th firm and the supplier. That is, the other buyer exploits the disagreement and seizes the opportunity to become a monopolist at the expense of the i-th buyer. The second states that the j-th buyer will operate at the anticipated quantity, and consequently goes ahead with production (on the presumption that agreement will be eventually reached with the i-th buyer). The third is where the buyers act united and refuse to trade unless agreement is made with both firms, thus essentially making their outputs complements as far as the supplier is concerned. This final case gives the buyers their strongest position, but their collusive arrangement may need to be supported by a contract to make a joint-action threat credible, given each has an incentive to "cheat" and make an individual agreement with the supplier. The first-order condition for the Nash bargain (6) is

$$(7) \quad \left[\pi_i^\lambda(r_i, r_j) \right] \left[\frac{\partial \pi_s^\lambda(r_i, r_j)}{\partial r_i} \right] + \left[\frac{\partial \pi_i^\lambda(r_i, r_j)}{\partial r_i} \right] \left[\pi_s^\lambda(r_i, r_j) - D_i \right] = 0.$$

Substituting in the outcomes from the product-market equilibrium - *i.e.*, (3), (4) and (5) - it is possible to solve for bargained prices. The outcomes, in respect to each form of D_i, are summarized in Table 1.

Table 1.   Outcomes from price-only bargaining

Supplier's disagreement level	$D_i^{CA} = r_j x_j^m(r_j) - C(x_j^m)$	$D_i^\mu = r_j x_j^A(r_i, r_j) - C(x_j^A)$	$D_i^{UA} = 0$
Transfer prices	$r_i^{CA} = \dfrac{a(1+\lambda) + c(3-\lambda^2)}{4+\lambda-\lambda^2}$	$r_i^\mu = \dfrac{a(1+\lambda) + c(5+3\lambda)}{6+4\lambda}$	$r_i^{UA} = \dfrac{a(1+\lambda) + c(9+5\lambda)}{10+6\lambda}$
Quantity for each buyer	$x_i^{CA} = \dfrac{(a-c)(3-\lambda^2)}{\beta(3+\lambda)(4+\lambda-\lambda^2)}$	$x_i^\mu = \dfrac{(a-c)(5+3\lambda)}{\beta(3+\lambda)(6+4\lambda)}$	$x_i^{UA} = \dfrac{(a-c)(9+5\lambda)}{\beta(3+\lambda)(10+6\lambda)}$
Supplier's profits	$\pi_s^{CA} = \dfrac{2(a-c)^2(1+\lambda)(3-\lambda^2)}{\beta(3+\lambda)(4+\lambda-\lambda^2)^2}$	$\pi_s^\mu = \dfrac{2(a-c)^2(1+\lambda)(5+3\lambda)}{\beta(3+\lambda)(6+4\lambda)^2}$	$\pi_s^{UA} = \dfrac{2(a-c)^2(1+\lambda)(9+5\lambda)}{\beta(3+\lambda)(10+6\lambda)^2}$
Profits for each buyer	$\pi_i^{CA} = \dfrac{(1+\lambda)\left[(a-c)(3+\lambda^2)\right]^2}{\beta\left[(3+\lambda)(4+\lambda-\lambda^2)\right]^2}$	$\pi_i^\mu = \dfrac{(1+\lambda)\left[(a-c)(5+3\lambda)\right]^2}{\beta\left[(3+\lambda)(6+4\lambda)\right]^2}$	$\pi_i^{UA} = \dfrac{(1+\lambda)\left[(a-c)(9+5\lambda)\right]^2}{\beta\left[(3+\lambda)(10+6\lambda)\right]^2}$
Buyers' optimal collusion level	$\lambda_i^{C*} = -0.153$	$\lambda_i^{I*} = 0.597$	$\lambda_i^{U*} = 0.716$
Maximum profits for each buyer	$\pi_i^{CA*} = \dfrac{0.064(a-c)^2}{\beta}$	$\pi_i^{\mu*} = \dfrac{0.081(a-c)^2}{\beta}$	$\pi_i^{UA*} = \dfrac{0.097(a-c)^2}{\beta}$

On comparing the outcomes, increased downstream coordination (as might be expected) is associated with lower output ($\partial x_i/\partial\lambda < 0$) and higher transfer prices ($\partial r_i/\partial\lambda > 0$). There is no monotonic relationship between either the buyers' or the seller's profits and λ. In contrast to the usual oligopoly story that the higher the level of coordination, the higher the level of profits, in this model high values of collusion (i.e., λ close to unity) are associated with lower levels of profits for the oligopolists. For instance, the profits to the oligopolists are only marginally less with the Cournot conjecture ($\lambda = 0$) than the full collusion case ($\lambda = 1$) for the second and third forms of D_i. But with the first form the Cournot profits are significantly larger. This perverse result is due to the inefficiency in bargaining over price only. Since the double marginalization problem is most severe when the oligopolists fully collude (through restricting quantity too much): less product market "collusion" would increase joint market profits, enabling all firms to earn higher levels.

Thus while increased coordination in bargaining increases the buyer's share of the profits, it is not the case, as might have been expected, that increased levels of coordination in the output market always lead to higher levels of available profits. High levels of coordination can result in lower levels of joint profits than more moderate quantity-matching strategies. By colluding through quantity coordination the oligopolists restrict sales and input purchases to raise the price the final consumers pay, but in restricting the quantity the compensation to the monopoly supplier is for higher (bargained) prices, which reduce the oligopolists' profits at high degrees of collusion.[12] In the specified range $-1 \leq \lambda \leq 1$, the supplier and the downstream oligopolists each have concave functions in λ. Profits to all three parties are zero when $\lambda = -1$ (where the intense downstream rivalry competes away all available profits),[13] and rise to a maximum with λ less than unity. The maximum point is different in each of the three cases as well as being different for the supplier and buyers. For example, where the buyers act competitively in bargaining and $D_i^{cА}$ applies, profits are at a maximum for the buyers if $\lambda = -0.1525$ and for the supplier if $\lambda = 0.559$, though joint profits are greatest when $\lambda = 0$ as this results in the efficient quantity being sold $x_1 + x_2 = (a - c)/2\beta$: $i.e.$, the amount a vertically integrated monopolist would produce). Moreover, the oligopolists prefer higher values of λ as their bargaining strength increases. The *optimal* level of product-market coordination, and the associated profits, for the oligopolists increases as D_i falls. As the supplier's position weakens, it is less able to extract higher transfer prices in return for reduced quantity levels, thus reducing the penalty for a high (output-restricting) coordination level.[14]

IV. Efficient Bargaining

In this section the scope of bargaining is increased to cover the quantity traded as well as the transfer price, which results in efficient bargaining in the sense that joint profits are maximized. How these joint profits are split between the parties again rests on how the disagreement payoffs are defined. The outcome from price-quantity bargaining between the supplier and the i-th buyer is described by the following problem:

---

[12]Consequently, the empirical observation of conjectural variation parameters below the level of unity does not necessarily indicate that the firms are not colluding optimally: rather, the firms may have taken inefficiencies arising from bargaining with suppliers into account and acted accordingly.

[13]When the downstream industry becomes very competitive, the benefits to the upstream monopolist of supplying all the firms would seem to be lost. In the absence of any legal restrictions we might expect the supplier to restrict sales to only one firm in such markets. Outcomes from such a situation are considered in Section V.

[14]For instance, if the buyers act independently in bargaining and D_i^U applies, profits are at a maximum for the buyers if $\lambda = 0.597$ and for the supplier if $\lambda = -0.1442$, while joint profits are greatest when $\lambda = 0.281$. In the remaining case where the buyers coordinate their bargaining strategies, the optimal level of coordination in the product market under $D_i^{UА}$ is $\lambda = 0.716$ for the buyers, $\lambda = 0.05$ yields the supplier greatest profits and $\lambda = 0.535$ corresponds to maximum joint profits.

(9) $\max_{r_i, x_i} [R_i(x_i, x_j) - r_i x_i][r_i x_i + r_j x_j - C(x_i, x_j) - D_i],$

where R_i is the i-th firm's revenue function, C the supplier's cost function and D_i the disagreement payoff to the supplier if no agreement is made with the i-th buyer. The solution to this problem has the characteristics

(10) $r_i x_i = \frac{1}{2}[R_i + C + D_i - w_i x_i],$ and

(11) $\frac{\partial R_i}{\partial x_i} = \frac{\partial C}{\partial x_i}.$

The second of these conditions states that the bargain results in an efficient quantity being chosen (equivalent to the quantity set by a vertically integrated monopolist: MR = MC). The first condition states that the transfer $r_i x_i$ is such that the two parties share equally the net profit (*i.e.*, marginal surplus) gained by reaching agreement. This result has also been established by Viehoff (1987) as the outcome from a Rubenstein alternating offers bargaining process.

From (10) the equilibrium transfer is

(12) $r_i x_i = \frac{[2R_i - R_j + C + 2D_i - D_j]}{3}$

and the profits for the supplier and each buyer are

(13) $\pi_s = \frac{[R_i + R_j - C + D_i + D_j]}{3},$ and

(14) $\pi_i = \frac{[R_i + R_j - C - 2D_i + D_j]}{3}$ with $i, j = 1, 2$ and $i \neq j.$

As argued in Subsection II.2, three forms of disagreement payoffs for efficient bargains can be considered depending on the degree of collusion in bargaining between the buyers. When the upstream firms cooperate in bargaining and refuse to trade unless both buyers have an agreement, then $D_i = 0$. If the disagreement payoff is based on the anticipated equilibrium, so that once agreement is made it cannot be changed, then $D_i = r_i x_i^E - C(x_i^E)$. The other possibility is that each bargain takes into account a contingency such that should the supplier fail to make an agreement with firm i, it has a fall-back agreement with firm j equivalent to a bilateral monopoly position. This contingent agreement is based on the following bargain between the supplier and the j-th buyer:

$\max_{r_j^M, x_j^M} [R_j(x_j^M) - r_j^M x_j^M][r_j^M x_j^M - C(x_j^M)],$

where x_j^M is the efficient (JPM) quantity for firm j as a monopolist. The bargain results in the two parties splitting available bilateral monopoly profits equally:

$$\pi_s(x_j^M) = \pi_j(x_j^M) = \frac{1}{2}\left[R_j(x_j^M) - C(x_j^M)\right],$$

so that while bargaining with firm i the supplier can rely on $\pi_s(x_j^M)$ as a disagreement payoff. Table 2 shows the outcomes for each disagreement payoff for both the general and the linear demand-costs case.

Table 2.   Outcomes from price-and-quantity bargaining

Supplier's disagreement level	$D_i^{CE} = \frac{1}{2}\left[R_j(x_j^M) - C(x_j^M)\right]$	$D_i^{IE} = r_j x_j^E(r_i, r_j) - C(x_j^E)$	$D_i^{UE} = 0$
Quantity for each buyer	$x_i^{CE} = \dfrac{(a-c)}{4\beta}$	$x_i^{IE} = \dfrac{(a-c)}{4\beta}$	$x_i^{UE} = \dfrac{(a-c)}{4\beta}$
Transfer prices	$r_i^{CA} = \left[2R_i - R_j + C + R_j(x_j^M) - C(x_j^M)\right.$ $\left. - \frac{1}{2}R_i(x_i^M) + \frac{1}{2}C(x_i^M)\right]/3x_i^E$ $= (a+2c)/3$	$r_i^{U} = \left[R_i + C - C(xj)\right]/2x_i^E$ $= (a+3c)/4$	$r_i^{UA} = \left[2R_i - R_j + C\right]/3x_i^E$ $= (a+5c)/6$
Supplier's profits	$\pi_s^{CE} = \left[R_i + R_j - 2C + \frac{1}{2}R_i(x_i^M)\right.$ $\left. + \frac{1}{2}R_j(x_j^M)\right]/3$ $= 0.167(a-c)^2/\beta$	$\pi_s^{U} = \left[R_i + R_j - C - C(xj)\right]/2$ $= 0.125(a-c)^2/\beta$	$\pi_s^{UA} = \left[R_i + R_j - C\right]/3$ $= 0.083(a-c)^2/\beta$
Profits for each buyer	$\pi_i^{CE} = \left[R_i + R_j - C - R_j(x_j^M) + C(x_j^M)\right.$ $\left. + \frac{1}{2}R_i(x_i^M) - \frac{1}{2}C(x_i^M)\right]/3$ $= 0.042(a-c)^2/\beta$	$\pi_i^{U} = \left[R_i + R_j - C(xi) - C(xj)\right]/2$ $= 0.063(a-c)^2/\beta$	$\pi_i^{UA} = \left[R_i + R_j - C\right]/3$ $= 0.083(a-c)^2/\beta$

In the homogenous symmetric case we can note that the following holds:

$$\pi_s^{CE} = 2\left[\pi_1 + \pi_2\right], \quad \pi_s^{IE} = \pi_1 + \pi_2, \quad \pi_s^{UE} = \frac{1}{2}\left[\pi_1 + \pi_2\right].$$

Clearly, there is an advantage for the supplier to be able to have an alternative (contingent) contract available. The outcome gives the supplier two-thirds of the available profit, leaving the buyers with one-sixth each. This is equal to the payoffs the Shapley value assigns, and complies with the notion that the supply side of the market dominates since there are fewer firms than on the demand side. In the second case, the profits are split equally between each side of the market. This case is therefore equivalent to the outcome from a bilateral monopoly situation (i.e., the same as a single bargain where the buyers had bargained together against the supplier). Here each side of the market makes an equal contribution to available surplus, with each pairing contributing half of this even with disagreement between the supplier and the other buyer. In the remaining case the profits are split between all parties equally. In this situation each party has the same bargaining power because if any one party withdraws from bargaining, all firms receive nothing. From the perspective of the supplier it is as though the buyers make complementary purchases, and this downstream cooperative bargaining behavior - if sustainable - gives the buyers their highest level of profits. This cooperative strategy with separate bargaining is thus more effective than the buyers negotiating jointly with the supplier. Comparing the outcomes for the linear demand-costs case in Table 1 with Table 2, it is observed that the supplier's profits are in all corresponding cases higher when there is bargaining over both the transfer price and the quantity: the supplier would clearly prefer this form of bargaining to price-only bargaining. For the downstream firms the choice depends on their degree of collusion in the input market and how close the value of λ is to their optimal level of collusion in the output market. While the outcome in price-only bargaining is inefficient, when the degree of collusion in the output market is near optimal for the oligopolists then they would prefer this form of bargaining to the corresponding efficient bargaining situation. In this case the greater relative market power of the buyers, by being able to unilaterally control quantity levels, more than compensates for the reduction in available joint (market) profits. Nevertheless, the general advantage of bargaining over both prices and quantity is that it acts as a coordinating device to effectively remove downstream competition in the final market which can compete away profits. The outcome then rests entirely on the arrangements in bargaining which determine the shares of the available surplus to each party.

V.   Discussion and Conclusion

Apart from illustrating the rather obvious point that a wide range of outcomes is possible from bargaining with several parties rather than one party, the results demonstrate that for simultaneous bargains[15] between a monopoly and an

---

[15]One area not investigated in this chapter concerns the case where the supplier wishes to trade with both buyers but bargains with them in sequence rather than simultaneously. This form of bargaining has recently received attention from Horn and Wolinsky (1988b) and Dobson (1994), where it is demonstrated that the supplier can extract even more of the surplus by moving or threatening to move from simultaneous to sequential bargaining.

oligopoly the outcomes are highly sensitive to the degree of cooperation between the downstream firms in both bargaining with the supplier and in setting their output. In general, it is not clear that the fact that there is only one supplier and a number of buyers benefits the monopoly supplier. Only when the buyers do not cooperate in bargaining, would the supplier seem to make substantial gains over the position where it is faced by a single buyer.

To put these conclusions into perspective it is worth drawing some comparisons between these results and the situation where the supplier chooses to supply only one of the buyers, essentially making the buyers bid for the right to supply a monopoly final market. This latter case would seem more appropriate for markets where, for instance, there are significant cost savings to the supplier in supplying a single firm (*e.g.*, transport economies) or there are increasing returns to scale in the downstream industry so that supplying a single firm generates greater joint profits than supplying several firms. Several papers have recently addressed the trading procedure by which a seller deals with a single buyer. This literature is reviewed by Binmore, Osborne and Wolinsky (1989) and Osborne and Rubenstein (1990). Whether the supplier can gain from the presence of more than one buyer critically rests on the specification of the trading procedure. In general, the outcomes from procedures where one side selects only a single trading partner are much more extreme than when the supplier sells to both buyers, with the supplier either gaining the whole or just half of the available surplus. For instance, in both the *random matching* model proposed by Rubenstein and Wolinsky (1990) and the *public price announcements* model of Binmore (1985) the result depends on the type of buyers. When the buyers are (or are close to being) identical, the single seller has a credible outside option when bargaining with one of the buyers which it can use to play-off one buyer against the other to obtain the entire surplus. However, if the buyers are significantly different (say one high-efficiency and the other low-efficiency), the seller does not have such an option and the situation is equivalent to a bilateral monopoly situation with the surplus shared (with the more efficient buyer). Whether the supplier wishes to supply one firm, essentially through a bidding system, or more - *e.g.*, via the independent bargain considered in this chapter - the downstream firms have a clear incentive to take coordinated action in bargaining to maximize their share of the surplus and prevent the supplier from dominating the market. Nevertheless, as with product-market collusion, the success of this collusion in bargaining will rest on their ability to maintain joint action given that each may face a strong incentive to cheat on its fellow competitors. To this end, the institutional setting may play a crucial role.

References

Bennett, J. and Ulph, A. (1988) 'Asymmetries in the Gains to Firms and Unions of Alternative Bargaining Structures', University of Southampton, *Unpublished manuscript*.

Binmore, K. (1982) 'Perfect Equilibria in Bargaining Models', *London School of Economics Discussion Paper* **82-58**.

Binmore, K. (1985) 'Bargaining and Coalitions', in Roth, A. (ed.), *Game-Theoretic Models of Bargaining*, Cambridge, Cambridge University Press.

Binmore, K., Rubenstein, A. and Wolinsky, A. (1986) 'The Nash Bargaining Solution in Economic

Modelling', *RAND Journal of Economics* **17**, 176-88.

Binmore, K., Osborne, M. and Wolinsky, A. (1989) 'Noncooperative Models of Bargaining', *Crest Working Paper* **89-26**, Department of Economics, University of Michigan.

Davidson, C. (1988) 'Multiunit Bargaining in Oligopolistic Industries', *Journal of Labor Economics* **6**, 397-422.

Dobson, P.W. (1992) '"Optimal" Collusion and the Incentive for Merger in Unionized Duopoly', *Unpublished manuscript*, University of Nottingham.

Dobson, P.W. (1994) 'Multifirm Unions and the Incentive to Adopt Pattern Bargaining in Oligopoly', *European Economic Review* **38**, 87-100.

Dowrick, S. (1990) 'The Relative Profitability of Nash Bargaining on the Labour Demand Curve or the Contract Curve', *Economics Letters* **33**, 121-125.

Horn, H. and Wolinsky, A. (1988a) 'Worker Substitutability and Patterns of Unionisation', *Economic Journal* **98**, 484-497.

Horn, H. and Wolinsky, A. (1988b) 'Bilateral Monopolies and Incentives for Merger', *RAND Journal of Economics* **19**, 408-419.

Jun, B.H. (1989) 'Non-cooperative Bargaining and Union Formation', *Review of Economic Studies*, **56**, 59-76.

McDonald, I.M. and Solow, R.M. (1981) 'Wage Bargaining and Employment', *American Economic Review* **71**, 896-908.

Nickell, S.J. and Andrews, M. (1983) 'Unions, Real Wages and Employment in Britain, 1959-79', *Oxford Economic Papers* **35**, 183-206.

Osborne, M.J. and Rubinstein, A. (1990) *Bargaining and Markets*, London, Academic Press.

Porter, M. (1980) *Competitive Strategy*, New York, Free Press.

Rubenstein, A. (1982) 'Perfect Equilibrium in a Bargaining Model', *Econometrica* **50**, 97-110.

Rubenstein, A. and Wolinsky, A. (1990) 'Decentralised Trading, Strategic Behaviour and the Walrasian Outcome', *Review of Economic Studies* **57**, 63-78.

Spengler, J. (1950) 'Vertical Integration and Anti-trust Policy', *Journal of Political Economy* **58**, 347-352.

Stackelberg, H. von (1934) *Marktform und Gleighewicht*, Berlin, Julius Springer.

Stackelberg, H. von (1952) *The Theory of the Market Economy*, Oxford, Oxford University Press.

Viehoff, I. (1987) 'Bargaining Between a Monopoly and an Oligopoly', *Discussion Papers in Economics* **14**, Nuffield College, Oxford.

CHAPTER 12

Capacity as a Commitment Instrument in Multi-Market Competition

MARC VAN WEGBERG[1]
University of Limburg, Department of Economics and Business Administration, Maastricht, The Netherlands

Abstract. In capital-intensive industries, investments in production capacity can be instruments in competition and, in particular, in entry deterrence. The incumbent firm's strategy will take into account the identity of the entrant because new firms pose a different threat than established-firm entrants (*e.g.*, importers). The chapter argues that the appropriate framework is multi-market competition, where firms compete in several - product and factor - markets. The framework integrates both recent game-theoretic modeling as well as an older industrial economics, associated with P.W.S. Andrews. An example of the U.S. steel market illustrates that capacity is a commitment instrument only in a special, historic, setting.

I.   Introduction

Capacity investments provide an input, capital, to production processes. In choosing a capacity level, firms may be guided by the aim to minimize their production costs. Industrial economists, however, have focused on the strategic implications of investments. In particular, they argue that firms may use capacity investments as an instrument in entry deterrence. This may lead to over- or underinvestments relative to the case where cost minimization is the objective. Dixit (1980) summarized this argument in an enticingly simple reaction curve format. A capacity investment transforms variable costs into sunk costs, and thus reduces marginal costs. This shifts the incumbent firm's reaction curve outward: that is, it makes it more aggressive in product market competition with an entrant. Dixit's (1980 and 1986) capacity-commitment models have shown to be a rich framework to study potential entry by different types of entrant and different entry deterrence strategies. This chapter gives an integrated treatment of several games that have been developed in the literature. It will allow an appraisal of the usefulness of capacity investments to entry deterrence in several competitive settings. The approach taken is multi-market competition: *i.e.*, firms compete in several - product and factor - markets. Economists explored the horizontal multi-market setting where firms compete in multiple product or country markets (*e.g.*, Brander, 1981; and Bulow, Geanakoplos and Klemperer, 1985a). Separately, they also explored the vertical multi-market context where firms compete in an input market as well as in the product market (*e.g.*, Salop and Scheffman, 1983). One contribution of this chapter is to offer an integrated approach of both forms of multi-market

[1]I thank Arjen van Witteloostuijn for comments and the audiences of the 19th annual EARIE conference in Stuttgart, September 1992, and the EEA Summer School on New Trade and Growth Theory in Florence, September 1992, for lively discussions.

competition.

Section II discusses why capacity can be a competition instrument in the first place. Section III introduces the basic capacity-commitment model using a multi-market framework. It goes without saying that for cases where capacity is the prevailing commitment instrument, one has to turn to capital-intensive industries. Section IV illustrates the usefulness of a multi-market framework for the U.S. steel industry. The subsequent sections build on the basic model while exploring different competitive settings. Section V focuses on *de novo* entry and Section VI on existing firm entrants (*e.g.*, importers), which implies a horizontal multi-market setting. Section VII discusses cases where incumbent and entrant compete in an input as well as in the product market, which implies a vertical multi-market setting. A firm's investment not only affects its product market competitiveness, but may also influence the input price faced by a second mover or *de novo* entrant. Section VIII summarizes these insights, appraises empirical evidence, and returns to the steel industry example.

II.   Capacity Investments as Instruments in Competition

Initially, economists followed Bain (1962) in thinking that a firm's output level is its instrument in competition, rather than capacity. In particular, Bain's limit price model is based upon the Sylos' postulate that a potential entrant believes that upon entry the incumbent firm will stick to its pre-entry output level. Anticipating this belief, the incumbent firm may choose a pre-entry output level so as to deter entry. If one rejects the Sylos' postulate, the output level becomes an ambiguous instrument in entry deterrence.[2] As Dixit (1980) puts it: "First, faced with an irrevocable fact of entry, the established firm will usually find it best to make an accommodating output reduction. On the other hand, it would like to threaten to respond to entry with a predatory increase in output. Its problem is to make the latter threat credible given the prospective entrant's knowledge of the former fact". The pre-entry output level does not deter entry, therefore, because the entrant expects that upon entry the incumbent firm will adjust its output level.[3,4] Unlike output levels, (pre-entry) capacity investments

---

[2]This is not to say that Bain really believed in the Sylos' Postulate as applying to actual entrants. It merely represents a simplifying assumption which he needed for his analysis.

[3]Notwithstanding this critique, the Sylos' Postulate still appears occasionally. Basu and Singh, (1990) split up the entry decision into an *entry* decision and a *start-up* in the literature decision. Prior to the *entry* decision, the incumbent firm chooses capacity. In between these decisions, the incumbent firm chooses its output level. The entrant holds the Sylos' Postulate, now dubbed a Stackelberg assumption, that the incumbent firm does not revise its output level after the entrant's *start-up* decision. If the potential entrant decides to *enter*, the incumbent firm chooses an output level which deters the entrant from actually starting up production. In this setting, the authors support the use of excess capacity. A similar Stackelberg argument accounts for Spulber's (1981) result of entry deterrence by excess capacity. These papers defy the Spence (1979) lesson that a Stackelberg leadership position cannot be assumed. It has to be derived in a perfect equilibrium from asymmetries in the competing firms' capacity investment processes: a leader has a head start or can expand its capaacity faster than a follower. Leadership has to be credible.

do constitute an irreversible decision. Investments are irreversible if capacity is firm-specific: that is, has no alternative use outside the firm. A market for used capacity may not exist, nor a rental market for new capacity (Dixon 1985: 483). In the extreme case of complete specificity, the opportunity cost of capacity is zero. This argument led to a shift in the entry-deterrence argument from the output level in Bain's theory, to capacity investments and pre-commitments in the game-theoretical literature.

To see what a strategic move may achieve, consider a duopoly with firms 1 and firm 2. Figure 1 illustrates.

Figure 1.   Strategic moves in duopoly competition

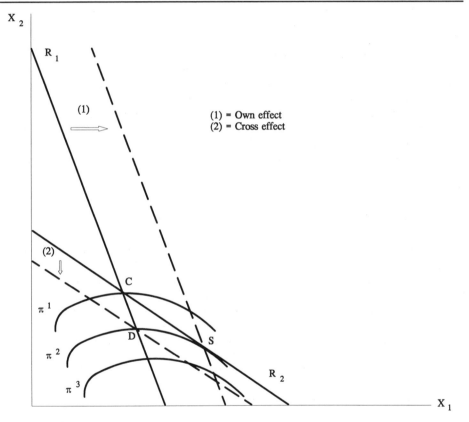

Firm i's output level is x_i and its reaction curve is R_i ($i = 1,2$). The Cournot equilibrium is the intersection C of the reaction curves. The curves π^j ($j = 1,2,3$)

[4]The pre-entry output or price level may signal to a potential entrant that, e.g., the incumbent is a low-cost firm. This information may deter entry by firms who would enter against a high-cost incumbent. Bain's limit price theory has accordingly been developed into a signaling model (e.g., Milgrom and Roberts, 1982).

are some of firm 1's iso-profit curves. The lower the iso-profit curve, the higher firm 1's profit level, as they are associated with lower output levels of firm 2. Given that firm 2 reacts to an output choice by firm 1 by locating along its reaction curve R_2, firm 1 would prefer to locate at the Stackelberg equilibrium S, which is on firm 1's lowest iso-profit curve still tangent to R_2. If firm 1 chooses its output level before firm 2, it might choose the level associated with point S. This carries no weight, however, because of Dixit's argument above. A strategic move - *e.g.*, one which pays off to the firm because it induces rivals to accept outcome S rather than C - has to be irreversible.

The figure suggests two types of strategic move. The capacity-commitment model exploits the idea that firm 1's investment reduces its marginal costs, thereby shifting its reaction curve R_1 outward to R_1', say. As a result, the Cournot equilibrium shifts along R_2 towards the point S. This is the *own effect*. Firm 1 may also try to shift firm 2's reaction curve downward to R_2', say. This shifts the Cournot equilibrium along R_1 towards point D, which is located at the same iso-profit curve as point S. Firm 1 may, as we will see, achieve this if its investments have effects in another - product or factor - market, which in turn affect firm 2 to the effect that, given an output level for firm 1, its marginal costs or revenue change. Firm 1's investment thus has a *cross effect*.

The argument does not explain which instruments firm 1 has for generating a cross effect. To know this, more information is required about both firms. Are they single-product firms? Do they compete with each other in other markets as well? To bring out the underlying mechanism, a full multi-market setting is required.

III.   A Basic Model in a Multi-Market Setting

This section gives the assumptions of the generalized multi-market capacity-commitment model. The basic idea is that an investment reduces marginal costs. Two varieties exist of this argument. The *narrow* definition of capital refers to a given amount of capacity. An upfront capacity investment k_i transforms the production costs $(w+\beta)x_i$ into sunk costs βk_i and variable costs wx_i, where x_i is the output level, w the constant marginal production cost and β the unit capacity cost $(i = 1,2)$. The upfront investment reduces marginal costs from $w+\beta$ to w, therefore, for output levels within the capacity constraint. In a *broad* definition of capital, the commitment instrument is any (in)tangible asset that reduces marginal costs for all output levels. Productive capital and R&D are cases in point. Variable production costs are $C^i(x_i,k_i)$, with

(C1) $C^i_{ki} < 0$ (investments reduce total variable costs), and

$C^i_{xiki} < 0$ (investments reduce marginal costs),

where a subscript C_x refers to a first-order derivative and C_{xx} to a second-order derivative. On the demand side, revenues are $R^i(x_1,x_2)$:

(C2) $R^i_{xj} < 0$ (the products are (im)perfect substitutes), and

$R^i_{xixj} < 0$ (the products are strategic substitutes),

where $j \neq i$ and $i,j = 1,2$. For convenience, homogeneous products and a duopoly are assumed throughout.

In the remainder of the chapter it is assumed that firm 1 makes a pre-emptive investment decision, the so-called first stage of the game. Subsequently, a rival, firm 2, responds by choosing its investment level, and both firms compete in the product market - the second stage of the game. An intuitive explanation of the sequence of these moves is that firm 1 moves first because it is the incumbent firm in the product market, and firm 2 is a potential entrant. The second stage of the game has a Cournot equilibrium with downward sloping reaction curves, since the products are strategic substitutes. Strategic behavior will appear to generate over- or underinvestment, defined relative to a benchmark. The benchmark will be a case where capacity does not have a strategic role, which occurs if the rival does not observe or respond to the firm's investment decision.[5] For example, the benchmark may imply full capacity utilization, with narrowly defined capital, or cost minimization, with broadly defined capital.

Consider a case where each firm's profit function is written as

(1) $\pi^i = R_i^A(x_1,x_2) + V_i^B(x_1,x_2,k_1,k_2)-C^i(x_i,k_i)$,

with revenue R in product market A (i = 1,2). The superscript B refers to a product or factor market and V is a revenue or cost function. The market superscripts A,B will be ignored when convenient. The firm's reaction curve follows from profit maximization, equation (2a), which also determines its investments and thus its marginal costs, equation (2b):

(2a) $\partial\pi^i/\partial x_i = 0 = \partial R^i/\partial x_i + \partial V^i/\partial x_i - \partial C^i/\partial x_i$, and

(2b) $\partial\pi^i/\partial k_i = 0 = \partial V^i/\partial k_i - \partial C^i/\partial k_i$.

The strategic effect of an investment - *i.e.*, the shift of the reaction curve - can be found by totally differentiating the first-order conditions (Dixit, 1986: 111):

(3a)

$$\left(\frac{\partial^2 R^i}{\partial x_i^2}+\frac{\partial^2 V^i}{\partial x_i^2}-\frac{\partial^2 C^i}{\partial x_i^2}\right)dx_i + \left(\frac{\partial^2 R^i}{\partial x_i\partial x_j}+\frac{\partial^2 V^i}{\partial x_i\partial x_j}\right)dx_j + \left(\frac{\partial^2 V^i}{\partial x_i\partial k_i}-\frac{\partial^2 C^i}{\partial x_i\partial k_i}\right)dk_i + \frac{\partial^2 V^i}{\partial x_i\partial k_j}dk_j = 0,$$

and

[5]Fudenberg and Tirole (1984) and Bulow *et al.* (1985a) are the seminal expositions of the benchmark concept in industrial economics. This chapter uses Fudenberg and Tirole's approach.

(3b) $\left(\dfrac{\partial^2 V^i}{\partial k_i \partial x_i} - \dfrac{\partial^2 C^i}{\partial k_i \partial x_i}\right) dx_i + \dfrac{\partial^2 V^i}{\partial k_i \partial x_j} dx_j + \left(\dfrac{\partial^2 V^i}{\partial k_i^2} - \dfrac{\partial^2 C^i}{\partial k_i^2}\right) dk_i + \dfrac{\partial^2 V^i}{\partial k_i \partial k_j} dk_j = 0.$

An investment k_i has an own effect on firm i. Firm j's investment has a cross effect on firm i (via dk_j) only through market B ($\partial^2 V^i / \partial x_i \partial k_j$ and $\partial^2 V^i / \partial k_i \partial k_j$): *the cross effect is a multi-market effect.* Both effects may entail a *direct effect* on a firm's marginal revenue or cost [equation (3a)] or an *indirect effect* through a feedback effect from the output levels on the investment incentives [equation (3b)].[6]

There are three specific cases to be discussed in this chapter. First, $V_B^i = -\beta k_i$, where β is the parametric price of a unit of capital. This case occurs if the factor markets are perfectly competitive on the supply and demand sides. Moreover, there is only one product market, A, which implies that the entrant is a new firm: *i.e., de novo* entry occurs. This is the initial case studied by Dixit (1980). Equations (3a) and (3b) show that firm i's investment only has own effects ($\partial^2 V^i / \partial x_i \partial k_j = \partial^2 V^i / \partial k_i \partial k_j = 0$). Firm 1's investment reduces its *own* marginal cost, in equation (3a) - a direct effect. This raises its output level, which in turn increases its investment by an indirect feedback effect in equation (3b), and reduces firm 2's marginal revenue.

The second case is the *horizontal* multi-market competition case, where the firms sell in related product or country markets. Firm 2 is an established-firm entrant, whose home market is market B. In case of symmetry both firms have $V_B^i = R_B^i (k_1 - x_1, k_2 - x_2) - \beta k_i$, the revenue when firm i sells its excess capacity ($k_i - x_i$) in product market B minus the capacity costs as above. Capacity can be used for sales in either product market, if it is specific to the set of related markets as a whole, rather than to any market in particular. In other words, it may be firm- rather than product-specific.[7] Each firm allocates its sales across markets A and B such that at the margin the (net) revenues of selling a product are equal, $MR_i^A(x_1, x_2) = MR_i^B(k_1 - x_1, k_2 - x_2)$, which implies that the opportunity cost of selling in market A consists of the marginal revenue of selling the product in market B instead. Since k_1 affects firm 1's sales in market B, it affects firm 2's marginal revenue there, which constitutes its marginal cost in market A. This implies the existence of direct and indirect cross effects if $\partial^2 R_i^B / \partial x_i \partial k_j \neq 0$ and $\partial^2 R_i^B / \partial k_i \partial k_j \neq 0$.

In the case of *vertical* multi-market competition, firms compete in an input market as well as in the product market. The input markets may be imperfectly competitive rather than perfectly competitive as in Dixit (1980). For example, $V_i^B = -B(k_1, k_2)$, the sunk costs of acquiring k_i units of capital, given prior investments k_j by the other firm. The incumbent firm may use its market power

---

[6]Dixit (1986: 113) also uses these terms, with a different meaning however.

[7]Note that capacity must be somewhat specific, for otherwise a well developed market for used capacity might exist, as there appears to be for airplanes and trucks. But in this case, an investment is not an irreversible decision.

in the input markets to raise entry costs. For instance, its demand for inputs may affect input prices, which in turn shifts the second mover's reaction curve. This will affect firm 2's investment decision and thus its marginal costs. There is an indirect cross effect ($\partial^2 B/\partial x_i \partial k_j = 0$ and $\partial^2 B/\partial k_i \partial k_j \neq 0$). The mechanisms underlying vertical and horizontal multi-market competition are, therefore, closely related. In both cases firm 1 has a mechanism for a cross effect, which allows it to shift firm 2's reaction curve in market A. Table 1 relates these three cases of interest to an illustrative piece of literature and the sections where they are discussed.

Table 1.   Cross-effects of investments

		Factor markets	
		Perfect competition	Imperfect competition
Entrant	New firm	No cross effect Dixit (1980) Section V	Indirect cross effect Salop and Scheffman (1983) Section VII
	Established firm	Direct and indirect cross effects Calem (1988) Section VI	-

The next section gives an example. This provides an institutional setting that may serve as a background for the subsequent Sections V to VII.

IV.   The U.S. Steel Market

Capacity investments will be the central instrument in competition for capital-intensive industries. Ghemawat (1991: 28) gives a listing of such industries based on research by D.J. Collis: food processing, textile fabrics, basic metals and chemicals, stone and clay, and pulp and paper. Their products are fairly homogeneous commodities, which rules out product characteristics as instruments in competition; the technology is largely mature, which rules out R&D as an important instrument; and the markets are quite concentrated (e.g., Lieberman, 1987: 612). These industries inspired economists to develop the capacity-commitment models with, usually, homogeneous products and given technology.

Especially the steel industry has been studied extensively. In the first part of the century *Big Steel* dominated the U.S. steel industry: *i.e.*, the large, integrated, full-line steel manufacturers - such as U.S. Steel, the largest one, Bethlehem and Armco. U.S. Steel was the long-time price leader since its creation by merger in 1901 (Scherer, 1980: 178-180). These firms' capacity commitments constituted their first-mover advantage. They seem to have (had) few other advantages. Notwithstanding its size, for instance, U.S. Steel did not have a cost advantage over smaller rivals (Scherer, 1980: 239). After the second world war Big Steel faced import competition from foreign manufacturers, who captured nearly 20% of the American market by 1968 (Scherer, 1980: 179) which increased up to 26% in the mid-1980s, (*Fortune*, 9-3-92: 28). The steel industry responded by lobbying for protectionism, which gave rise to a VER (Voluntary Export Restraint) in 1984 such that imports would be limited to 20% of the market, (*The Economist*, 16-5-92: 101-102).

Big Steel faced new domestic competition as well, however. Mini-mills arose, such as Nucor Corp., Birmingham Steel and Chaparral, which make steel from scrap rather than from ore as the integrated steel makers do. The mini-mills derive a cost advantage from being non-unionized, with wages a half and a third of what unionized workers receive (*The Economist*, 16-5-92: 101-102). Nucor, moreover, is a very innovatory firm (*Fortune*, 24-2-1992: 50-55). Big Steel reacted to excess capacity due to import and domestic competition by closing plants. This, however, is a costly affair. The U.S. steel manufacturers pioneered internal labor markets from the mid-1890s on (Elbaum, 1983: 262). By 1980, U.S. steel wages were almost double those in Japan and West Germany (*The Economist*, 16-5-92: 101-102). Employee protection also means that closing plants is costly due to the obligation to fund the pension liability. "One way steelmakers minimize future pension obligations is to sell assets for a song rather than shut them down. Geneva Steel, Weirton Steel, and Gulf States Steel are composed of plants bought from the big integrated outfits" (*Fortune*, 23-3-1992: 29). These *reconstituted mills* are an additional source of new competition. Geneva Steel, for instance, was created in 1987 from a U.S. Steel mill after its new owners gained concessions from the union, which the latter had apparently been unwilling to give to U.S. Steel itself (*ibidem*, 29). This example shows several types of entrants with different strategies. Figure 2 illustrates the setting.

The figure bears a more than passing resemblance to Porter's (1980: 4) *extended rivalry* scheme embedded in a multi-market setting (Van Witteloostuijn and Van Wegberg, 1992). The U.S. steel makers compete with the buyers from their excess capacity (the reconstituted mills) firms using substitutes for iron ore (mini-mills using scrap) and with new entrants (*e.g.*, mini-mills) as well as established-firm entrants (*e.g.*, foreign steel makers). Backward integration entry, by a buyer of steel, occurred when Nucor, originally a producer of steel construction joists, started producing its own steel (*Fortune*, 24-2-1992: 51). A multi-market framework points to the vertical interactions between the steel market and input markets - notably the labor market, the raw materials markets, ore or scrap, and the markets for new and used capacity, the reconstituted mills. It also points to the horizontal interaction between the U.S. steel market and foreign countries, giving rise to import competition. The subsequent sections show how dominant firms, such as Big Steel, may use capacity as an instrument in these competition games.[8]

Figure 2.   Entry in the U.S. steel industry

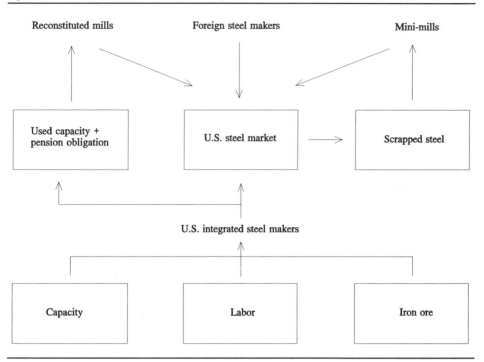

V.   De Novo Entry

The initial capacity-commitment model features *de novo* entry where the potential entrant invests from scratch: *i.e.*, it is not committed to any capacity or output level (Dixit, 1980).[9] The incumbent firm is the first mover in the game: by the time the entrant makes its (investment) move, the first mover has its investments already in place. Both firms are price takers in the capacity input market, with a unit capacity price β.

In the *narrow* definition of capital as capacity, the upfront investment reduces marginal costs from $w + \beta$ to w (see Section III). Consider the special case where entry is profitable if the incumbent firm's marginal cost is $w + \beta$, and unprofitable if equal to w. To deter entry, the incumbent firm may commit

---

[8]Competition among incumbent firms as well as competition by substitutes for steel will be ignored. In the latter case, the assumption is that there is no oligopolistic interaction between steel makers and, say, plastics or ceramics makers.

[9]Other relevant papers are Spence (1977 and 1979), Eaton and Lipsey (1979, 1980 and 1981) and Schmalensee (1981). Dixit (1986) provides an early consolidation.

capacity in order to reduce its marginal cost to w. This implies a capacity such that $x_1^d \leq k_1$, where x_1^d is the duopoly output level if entry occurs. If firm 2 does not enter, firm 1 produces its monopoly output level x_1^m. Since in normal conditions this quantity exceeds the duopoly output level, excess capacity is not required to deter entry: i.e., $x_1^d \leq k_1 \leq x_1^m$. This model shows that the incumbent firm may deter entry even though the entrant knows, contrary to the Sylos' Postulate, that the incumbent firm will reduce its output level in the face of entry. The point is, it will not reduce its output level enough to make entry worthwhile. This gives the meaningful result that although capacity has a strategic role here, this does not mean that excess capacity is required.[10] Lieberman (1987) tests, and rejects, the hypothesis that firms use excess capacity as an entry barrier. His data are a set of 38 chemical products over a 20-year period. Of these products, ten had chronic excess capacity. In only three of these did excess capacity appeared to have been created or used for the sake of entry deterrence. Entry occurred in all but six products; the latter include titanium dioxide, a case to be discussed later.

In the *broad* definition of capital, total costs are $TC^i = C^i(x_i, k_i) + \beta k_i$. Given an output level x_i, total costs are U-shaped in capital with a minimum where $TC^i_{ki} = C^i_{ki} + \beta = 0$. The game is a two-stage one: first firm 1 chooses k_1 and next both firms choose their quantities x_i as well as k_2. Since firm 2 cannot use capital as a commitment instrument, it chooses a capital stock to minimize its costs given its output x_2. In the first stage, firm 1's investment shifts its reaction curve outward by reducing its marginal costs. The result is called an *over(under)investment* relative to a benchmark where capital has no, perceived, commitment value - e.g., because it is not observed by the rival. If the benchmark implies cost minimization, where $C^i_{ki} + \beta = 0$, firm 1 over-(under-)invests if $C^1_{k1} + \beta > (<) 0$ (Dixit, 1980: 104).

The (over)investment result depends upon the type of product market competition. If the products are strategic substitutes (e.g., in a Cournot duopoly), the incumbent firm overinvests and the entrant anticipates this, either by reducing its scale of entry (i.e., Bain's ineffectively impeded entry or partial entry deterrence) or by backing out altogether (i.e., effectively impeded entry or total entry deterrence). Underinvestment results with Bertrand competition (Dixit, 1986) and a competitive product market (Dixon, 1985). In a Japanese recession cartel, over-investment may occur (Matsui, 1989). Hall (1990) tests Dixit's (1980) model, with the broad definition of capital, for the U.S. titanium dioxide industry, with Du Pont as the pre-empting incumbent and its rivals as second movers. Titanium dioxide is a bulk chemical. She finds that in the period 1972-77 Du Pont increased its capacity in an effort to pre-empt at least some of

---

[10]Dixit's model does not, of course, close the book on the *excess capacity* hypothesis. In a rather specific case with convex demand, output levels are strategic complements, at least in a relevant range, rather than strategic substitutes (Bulow, Geanakoplos and Klemperer, 1985b). In that case, the incumbent firm may expand its output upon entry: i.e., $x_1^m < x_1^d$. Excess capacity, since $x_1^d \leq k_1$, is required to deter entry. Eaton and Lipsey (1981) resurrect the excess capacity idea in a dynamic case with finitely durable, *radioactive*, capital. The incumbent firm chooses excess capacity knowing that if entry occurs, its disinvestments take longer the larger its capacity. The incumbent firm does reduce output upon entry but not fast enough to make entry profitable.

its rivals, namely those who had the potential to expand their market share in the future.

VI. Competition in Multiple Product Markets

Andrews (1949), his life-time collaborator Brunner (*e.g.*, 1961), Lydall (1955) and Hines (1957) pointed to existing firms in related markets as highly salient potential rivals. If capital is firm- rather than product-specific, a firm may use its capacity to supply a technically slightly different product to a new, for it, product market, related diversification, or it may start to serve another country market, import competition. The firm may move in fast and at a large scale, display real initiative, and may threaten the core firms in the industry. It bypasses entry barriers that seem unsurmountable to other potential rivals such as new firms (*e.g.*, Brunner, 1961: 250). Established-firm entry may lead to qualitatively different results than *de novo* entry. For example, economies of scale need not be entry barriers, as Bain argued, but may actually induce entry, as in the case of multinational firms (Caves, 1971). With hindsight, this Andrewsian vision of the entry process looks highly modern. Unfortunately, it largely failed to capture the economists' imagination.[11] It took the larger part of a decade for industrial economists to rediscover this vision (Cairns and Mahabir (1988), and to cast it in the analytical mould created by Dixit (1980) and others. This discussion raises the question whether capacity can be used as an instrument to deter entry if the entrants are existing rivals in related markets. Fortunately, this game has been explored quite thoroughly by Calem (1988), Anderson and Fischer (1989) and Venables (1990), who build on the basic model by Brander (1981) and Brander and Krugman (1983).

First consider the basic model (Brander, 1981; and Brander and Krugman, 1983). There are two firms, 1 and 2, denoted by subscripts, and two markets, A and B, denoted by superscripts; firm 1 is the incumbent firm in A and firm 2 in B. The game is a one-stage, two-market Cournot duopoly. Simultaneously each firm chooses sales x_i^j ($i = 1,2$; $j = A,B$) for both markets. Marginal costs are c_i in the home and $c_i + t_i$ in the entry market, where c_i and t_i are constant unit costs. The unit cost t_i is an adjustment cost, transport cost or tariff for selling in the entry market. In each market the products are homogeneous, and the inverse demand function is $p^j(x_1^j + x_2^j)$ ($j = A,B$). The firms treat the two markets as completely separate. Responsible for this are two assumptions: constant returns to scale and the *segmented markets* assumption that prices between the markets may differ in the absence of arbitrage trade. Figure 1 can be interpreted as pertaining to market A. In the Cournot equilibrium (point C) $x_2^c < x_1^c$, as firm 2 has higher marginal costs (by t_2) than firm 1 in market A. Market B offers the mirror image of A. The export level is positive if the monopoly price in its absence exceeds the exporter's marginal cost $c_i + t_i$. Cross-hauling of identical commodities occurs as each firm exports to the other market and *vice versa*.

---

[11]The strategic group theory in Caves and Porter (1977) may be the most tangible offspring. Lydall (1955) and Hines (1957) can be seen as precursors of strategic group analysis by emphasizing mobility between strategic groups rather than new firm entry.

Call this the *one-stage game*.

Now introduce capacity investments. Each firm chooses capacity, k_i ($i = 1,2$) with costs $C(k_i)$. This allows it to produce up to the capacity constraint with marginal costs $c_i(+t_i)$ as above. Output levels exceeding the capacity level are ruled out. If the investment implies complete preproduction, c_i refers to distribution costs and may be zero. Simultaneously firms choose capacity levels k_i and output levels (x_i^j), with the constraint that $\Sigma_j x_i^j \leq k_i$ ($i = 1,2$; $j = A,B$). Call this the *simultaneous game* (Anderson and Fischer, 1989). Assume that capacity will be fully utilized, such that $x_i^B = k_i - x_i^A$. By implication each firm has two decision variables. For instance, given x_2^A and k_2, firm 1 chooses x_1^A and k_1 to maximize its profits

(4a) $\pi_1 = [p^A(x_1^A + x_2^A) - c_1]x_1^A + [p^B(k_1 - x_1^A + k_2 - x_2^A) - c_1 - t_1][k_1 - x_1^A] - C(k_1)$.

A similar equation holds for firm 2. Hence,

(5a) $\partial \pi_1 / \partial x_1^A = 0 = p_x^A x_1^A + p^A - c_1 - p_x^B[k_1 - x_1^A] - [p^B - c_1 - t_1]$,

(5b) $\partial \pi_1 / \partial k_1 = 0 = p_x^B[k_1 - x_1^A] + p^B - c_1 - t_1 - C_{k1}$, and

(5c) $\partial \pi_2 / \partial x_2^A = 0 = p_x^A x_2^A + p^A - t_2 - p_x^B[k_2 - x_2^A] - p^B$.

This determines x_1^A as a reaction function of x_2^A [(5a)] and vice versa for firm 2 [(5c)]. The intersection of the reaction curves defines a Cournot equilibrium. If a firm were to defect from the equilibrium, marginal revenue would fall below the *ex ante* marginal production cost, $c_i + C_{ki}$, but for a small change it will still exceed the *ex post* marginal cost, c_i. Thus the firm will sell all output at the new capacity level. This validates the full capacity utilization assumption above. Because of simultaneity, a firm's capacity decision has no effect on the other firm's output decisions. In the absence of a strategic role, each firm chooses output levels such that marginal revenue equals marginal cost [which follows from (5a) and (5b)]. Capacity just equals the sum of these optimal sales levels. Since this result also holds for the one-stage game, the outcome of the simultaneous game is identical to the one-stage game if the segmented markets and constant returns assumption hold. The latter implies that $C(k_i) = \beta_i k_i$, where the parameter $\beta_i > 0$ ($i = 1,2$).

Strategic moves come in if competition is a two-stage game. In the first *capacity stage*, firms choose k_i. Knowing each other's capacity in the second, *allocation stage*, the firms choose sales levels (x_i^j). This stage is identical to the one-stage game, except for the binding capacity constraint. Call this the *sequential game* (Calem, 1988; Anderson and Fischer, 1989; and Venables, 1990). The second stage entails reaction curves in output levels, identical to equation (5a). Given these second-stage reaction curves, in the first stage both firms choose a capacity k_i ($i = 1,2$). To find their effect, totally differentiate the first-order conditions for both firms to the sales x_i^A and the capacities, k_i. This gives

(6)
$$\begin{bmatrix} p_{xx}^A x_1^A + p_{xx}^B[k_1 - x_1^A] + 2p_x^A + 2p_x^B & p_{xx}^A x_1^A + p_{xx}^B[k_1 - x_1^A] + p_x^A + p_x^B \\ p_{xx}^A x_2^A + p_{xx}^B[k_2 - x_2^A] + p_x^A + p_x^B & p_{xx}^A x_2^A + p_{xx}^B[k_2 - x_2^A] + 2p_x^A + 2p_x^B \end{bmatrix} \begin{pmatrix} dx_1^A \\ dx_2^A \end{pmatrix} =$$

$$\begin{bmatrix} p_{xx}^B[k_1 - x_1^A] + 2p_x^B & p_{xx}^B[k_1 - x_1^A] + p_x^B \\ p_{xx}^B[k_2 - x_2^A] + p_x^B & p_{xx}^B[k_2 - x_2^A] + 2p_x^B \end{bmatrix} \begin{pmatrix} dk_1 \\ dk_2 \end{pmatrix}.$$

Consider first the case where firms use their output levels rather than capacity as competition instruments. If $dk_1 = dk_2 = 0$ and $dx_i^A = -dx_i^B$, then equation (6) gives the slope of the reaction curves R_i in Figure 1. The diagonal elements in the 2x2 matrix G in the left-hand side of equation (6) can be characterized as $G_{ii} = \partial^2 \pi_i / \partial x_i^{A2}$ and the off-diagonal elements as $G_{ij} = \partial^2 \pi_i / \partial x_i^A \partial x_j^A$. This gives the familiar result that the slope of the reaction curve $dx_1^A/dx_2^A = -G_{12}/G_{11}$ (Tirole, 1988: 207). The reaction curves are downward sloping if sign $(G_{ij}/G_{ii}) > 0$. The second-order conditions to equation (6) imply that $G_{ii} < 0$. Also, $G_{ij} < 0$ $(i \neq j)$, if demand is linear $(p_{xx}^j = 0; j = A,B)$ or not 'too' convex (where $p_{xx}^j > 0$). With downward-sloping reaction curves, an increase in x_1^A reduces x_2^A and thus (given k_2) raises x_2^B: by increasing its home market sales, firm 1 reduces the scale of entry in its market. This result is similar to Bain's limit output argument, and the same critique by Dixit (1980) in Section II holds: firm 1 does not have a commitment to increase its home market sales. An irreversible move, an investment, is required.

A change $dk_i > 0$ in equation (6) represents a shift of the reaction curve R_i in Figure 1. Total differentiation of firm 1's profit function gives

(7) $d\pi_1 = \left[p_x^A x_1^A + p^A - c_1 - p_x^B(k_1 - x_1^A) - p^B + c_1 + t_1 \right] dx_1^A + \left[p_x^A x_1^A - p_x^B(k_1 - x_1^A) \right] dx_2^A$

$+ \left[p_x^B(k_1 - x_1^A) + p^B - c_1 - t_1 - \beta_1 \right] dk_1 + p_x^B(k_1 - x_1^A) dk_2.$

The coefficient of dx_1^A equals zero because of equation 5a, which is an application of the envelope theorem. A reduction of firm 2's sales in market A $(dx_2^A < 0)$ raises firm 1's aggregate profits if $p_x^A x_1^A - p_x^B(k_1 - x_1^A) < 0$, which is plausible - e.g., with cross market symmetry, $p_x^A = p_x^B$ (< 0), and home market sales in excess of export sales, $x_1^A > k_1 - x_1^A$. In this case, firm 1 does indeed benefit by reducing the scale of entry, imports, in its market. Equations (6) and (7) solve for dx_i^A, and give $d\pi_1$ as a function of dk_i.

Below, first an interpretation of the model in equations (4) to (7) is provided. In line with Section III, (5c) can be rewritten as equality of the marginal revenues, MR_2^j $(j = A,B)$, net of marginal costs in both markets:

(5c') $p_x^A x_2^A + p^A = p_x^B[k_2 - x_2^A] + p^B + t_2.$

The right-hand side, $MR_2^B + t_2$, is firm 2's opportunity cost of entry in market A.

Whereas with *de novo* entry firm 2's marginal cost of entry $(c_2 + \beta_2 + t_2)$ is exogenous to firm 1, in the case of related-firm entry its opportunity cost of entry is *endogenous* to firm 1, which accounts for a strategic effect of capacity, Calem, 1988, 172. Firm 1's investment changes its allocation dx_1^j (j = A,B). That is, $dk_1 > 0 \rightarrow dx_1^j > 0 \rightarrow dMR_2^j < 0$. The investment reduces firm 2's marginal revenue from export (MR_2^A), which is the classical own effect in Figure 1. It also reduces $MR_2^B + t_2$, which is the cross effect. The investment may *raise* the rival's opportunity cost of entry relative to its marginal revenue from entry if $dMR_2^A < dMR_2^B < 0$. It thereby reduces the scale of entry. Equation (6) demonstrates this. Rewrite its second row into

(6b') $[p_{xx}^A x_2^A + p_x^A]dx_1^A - [p_{xx}^B(k_2 - x_2^A) + p_x^B]dx_1^B = -G_{22}dx_2^A,$

where $dx_1^B = dk_1 - dx_1^A$, the arguments in brackets [] are identical to $\partial MR_2^j/\partial x_1^j$ (j = A,B) and $dk_2 = 0$ (unilateral defection by firm 1). If the left-hand side is negative, firm 1's allocation reduces firm 2's marginal revenue in market A relative to its marginal revenue in market B. This will opt firm 2 to move out of market A - *i.e.*, $dx_2^A < 0$ - which follows from (6b') as $G_{22} < 0$. Firm 1's investment may thus, partially, deter entry in market A by combining the own effect and the cross effect. To see whether this is feasible, equations (6) and (7) will be solved for four special cases.

CASE 1: *Linear demand*. Substitute linear demand, where $p_{xx}^j = 0$ (j = A,B), into equation (6) and use Cramer's rule to find that

(8) $dx_i^A = (p_x^B/(p_x^A + p_x^B))dk_i.$

With unilateral defection by firm 1 ($dk_2 = 0$), it follows that $dx_2^A = 0$. If demand is linear, firm 1 is *unable* to use capacity as a commitment instrument in competition with firm 2 (Calem, 1988: 179; Anderson and Fischer, 1989: 175; and Venables, 1990: 30). The intuition is as follows (Venables, 1990: 36). If firm 1 increases its capacity k_1, it will adjust its allocation (x_1^j) such that marginal revenue falls by the same amount in both markets, thus preserving the equality in equation (5a). With linear demand, marginal revenue is linear and downward sloping in quantity: $MR_1^j = p^j + p_x^j x_1^j$, where p_x^j is constant and j = A,B. Assume symmetric demand for the sake of the argument. Thus the reduction in marginal revenue does not depend upon the level of quantities, which may differ as $x_1^A > x_1^B$ if $t_1 > 0$, but only on the change in output levels. An identical reduction in marginal revenues requires identical sales' expansion in markets A and B: $dx_1^A = dx_1^B$ [which equation (8) confirms if $p_x^A = p_x^B$]. But, again with linear demand, this reduces firm 2's marginal revenues in both markets by an identical amount. Thus firm 2 has no incentive to adjust its allocation if demand is linear. Substitute $dx_2^A = 0$ in equation (7) to find that

(9) $d\pi_1 = [p_x^B(k_1 - x_1^A) + p^B - c_1 - t_1 - \beta_1]dk_1.$

The firms are in equilibrium if the expression in brackets equals zero - *i.e.*, if marginal revenue equals marginal cost: $p_x^B(k_1 - x_1^A) + p^B = c_1 + t_1 + \beta_1$. Since this is also the condition of the one-stage and the simultaneous games, it follows that their equilibrium outcomes pertain in this two-stage game as well. Capacity does not qualify as a commitment instrument if demand is linear.

CASE 2: *Cross-market symmetry.* Assume symmetry of the cost and demand functions. That is, $c_i = c$, $t_i = t$, $\beta_i = \beta$ and $p^j(x) = p(x)$ ($i = 1,2$ and $j = A,B$). It seems acceptable to assume that the associated equilibrium is symmetric: that is, $k_i = k$ ($i = 1,2$), $p_{(x)(x)}^j = p_{(x)(x)}$ ($j = A,B$), $x_1^A = x_2^B = k_2-x_2^A$ and $x_2^A = x_1^B = k_1-x_1^A$. It follows that $x_1^A+x_2^A = k$. Substitute these assumptions in equations (6), using Cramer's rule, and (7) to get

(10a) $dx_2^A = \frac{1}{4}(p_{xx}/p_x)(x_1^A-x_2^A)dk_1$,

(10b) $dx_1^A = \frac{1}{2}dk_1-dx_2^A$, and

(10c) $d\pi_1 = p_x(x_1^A-x_2^A)dx_2^A + [p_x(k_1-x_1^A) + p-c-t-\beta]dk_1$.

Substitute equation (10a) in (10c) to find that

(11) $d\pi_1 = [\frac{1}{4}p_{xx}(x_1^A-x_2^A)^2 + p_x(k_1-x_1^A) + p-c-t-\beta]dk_1$.

If demand is linear (*i.e.*, $p_{xx} = 0$), firm 1 is unable to affect firm 2's output level by its investment decision [equation (10a)]. If there is intra-market symmetry ($x_1^A = x_2^A$), firm 1 is both unable [equation (10a)] and unwilling [equation (10c)] to affect firm 2's output level. In either case, the equilibrium is attained: *i.e.*, $d\pi_1/dk_1 = 0$ if $p_x(k_1-x_1^A)+p = c+t+\beta$ [that is, combining this with equation (5c') if in each market marginal revenue equals the, *ex ante*, marginal cost]. Since this is the condition underlying the simultaneous equilibrium, the simultaneous game outcome holds. No entry deterrence occurs, and again capacity has no commitment value. In the simultaneous game the intra-market symmetry, $x_1^A = x_2^A$, implies absence of transport costs: $t = 0$. The adjustment, transport, cost t may indicate the product- (location-) specificity of the firm's capacity. If $t = 0$, capacity is non-specific: it can without costs be used for either, product or country, market. Non-specific capacity is, therefore, not a commitment, which is consistent with the basic idea in capacity-commitment models: "If capital is to be used as a vehicle for commitment, it is then clear that the capital must be product-specific in some degree" (Eaton and Lipsey, 1981: 594). If $p_{xx} \neq 0$ and $x_1^A-x_2^A \neq 0$, equilibrium is attained if $p_x(k_1-x_1^A) + p-c-t-\beta = -\frac{1}{4}p_{xx}(x_1^A-x_2^A)^2$. If demand is concave - *i.e.*, if $p_{xx} < 0$, this implies that $p_x(k_1-x_1^A)+p > c+t+\beta$: that is, marginal revenue exceeds the (*ex ante*) marginal cost. Production, therefore, falls short of the outcome in the simultaneous game. Each firm under-invests relative to the simultaneous game. If demand is convex (*i.e.*, if $p_{xx} > 0$), then $p_x(k_1-x_1^A)+p < c+t+\beta$: sales exceed the level in the simultaneous game, and firms overinvest relative to it. For intuitive explanations of these results, turn to two special cases of the symmetry case. They follow the same route as Anderson and Fischer (1989).[12] That is, start with a possible outcome, a benchmark, and then find out whether this constitutes an equilibrium in the sequential game.

CASE 3: *The simultaneous equilibrium.* Anderson and Fischer (1989) explore the simultaneous equilibrium outcome. Due to equation (5b), equation (10c) simplifies to

$$(12) \quad d\pi_1 = p_x(x_1^A - x_2^A)dx_2^A.$$

Consider somewhat product-specific capital ($t > 0$) such that $x_1^A - x_2^A > 0$. Since $p_x < 0$, it follows from equation (12) that $\text{sign}(d\pi_1) = -\text{sign}(dx_2^A)$. If an investment by firm 1 induces firm 2 to opt out of firm 1's home market into its own home market B, firm 1's aggregate profits increase. There is a prisoners' dilemma as both firms would benefit if each would back out to its home market. This result gives the rationale for the *spheres-of-influence* hypothesis (Scherer, 1980: 340-342; and Bernheim and Whinston, 1990). Multi-market firms may tacitly collude to raise their profits by staying out of each other's home markets, implying spheres of influence. To see whether $dx_2^A < 0$, turn to equations 10(a and b). Since, from equation (10a), $\text{sign}(dx_2^A) = -\text{sign}(p_{xx}dk_1)$, the following cases exist. If demand is concave (*i.e.*, $p_{xx} < 0$), $\text{sign}(dx_2^A) = \text{sign}(dk_1)$. If firm 1 were to increase k_1, firm 2's marginal revenue in market A would increase more than in market B. Firm 2 reacts to this by re-allocating output (given its capacity) out of its home market B into market A. *Entry induces reciprocal entry.*[13] The net effect in Figure 1 is that firm 2's reaction curve in market A, R_2, shifts upward. This move may be very unwelcome to firm 1, as total output increases in its most profitable market, the home market A. In this case, firm 1 contracts its capacity relative to the simultaneous outcome. Underinvestment deters entry - *i.e.*, reduces x_2^A [equation (10a)] - which raises profits [equation (12)]. Trade ($= x_1^B + x_2^A$) decreases as well, which implies a, small, move towards spheres-of-influence. If demand is convex (*i.e.*, $p_{xx} > 0$), firm 1's overinvestment reduces x_2^A by equation (10a), which raises firm 1's profits by equation (12) (Anderson and Fischer, 1989: 178; and Venables, 1990: 36). Entry by firm 1 into market B induces firm 2 to, partially, exit from market A. Entry deterrence in A by entry into B, therefore, indicates a paradox which has been called *counter-competition* (Watson, 1982; and Van Witteloostuijn and Van Wegberg, 1992). That is, R_2 in figure 1 shifts downward and firm 1 overinvests relative to the simultaneous equilibrium. The next question is whether entry is completely deterred.

---

[12]Explicit solutions of the second stage and first stage of the game are cumbersome and difficult to interpret. I am unable to prove that capacity investments are strategic substitutes - *i.e.*, that the first-stage reaction curves in capacity are downward sloping.

[13]For other models of this phenomenon of interdependent entry decisions see Bulow *et al.*, (1985a) and Van Wegberg and Van Witteloostuijn (1993).

CASE 4: *Entry deterrence.* If entry is deterred, $x_1^A = k_1 = k$, $x_1^B = 0$, $x_2^B = k_2$ $= k$, and $x_2^A = 0$. This is again a special case of the symmetry benchmark. Substitute these assumptions in equations 10(a and c) to get

(13a) $dx_2^A = \max\{0, \tfrac{1}{4}(p_{xx}/p_x)kdk_1\}$, and

(13b) $d\pi_1 = p_x kdx_2^A + [p-c-t-\beta]dk_1$.

Equation (13a) takes into account that $x_2^A = 0$, such that a change can only be positive. If, on the one hand, demand is linear, a deviation from the benchmark by firm 1 will not affect firm 2's output level [equation (13a)]. The same holds if demand is convex ($p_{xx} > 0$) and firm 1 expands its capacity. In both cases, firm 1 will expand its output level in order to export to market B, which is profitable if the monopolist's price p exceeds the marginal export cost, $c+t+\beta$ [equation (13b)]. This is the same condition underlying the one-stage Brander (1981) trade model. Capacity, therefore, fails to deter entry. If, on the other hand, demand is concave ($p_{xx} < 0$), an investment by firm 1 and associated entry induces reciprocal entry by firm 2: $dx_2^A > 0$ [equation (13a)]. This in turn reduces firm 1's entry profit by $p_x kdx_2^A$, where k is firm 1's sales level in market A [equation (13b)]. Entry, that is, has an opportunity cost based on marginal production costs $(c+t+\beta)$ plus home market profits foregone. The entry profit is wiped out completely if $\tfrac{1}{4}p_{xx}k^2+p-c-t-\beta \le 0$. This condition implies *very* concave demand and *high* transport costs t, such that the monopoly price is close to the marginal export cost.[14] Complete entry deterrence is feasible only in this special case.

See Table 2 for a summary of the results of all four cases, assuming that $t > 0$.

Table 2.   Competition in two symmetric product markets

Demand curve	p_{xx}	Firm i's investment	Importer's market share (*e.g.*, m_2^A)
Concave	< 0	$k_i < k_i^S$	$0 \le m_2^A < m_2^{A,S}$
Linear	0	$k_i = k_i^S$	$m_2^A = m_2^{A,S}$
Convex	> 0	$k_i > k_i^S$	$0 < m_2^A < m_2^{A,S}$

Call m_i^A firm i's market share in market A - *i.e.*, $m_i^A = x_i^A/(x_1^A+x_2^A)$; k_i^S is firm i's equilibrium capital stock in the simultaneous game; and m_i^S the associated market share. The main implication from these models is that import competition undermines the commitment value of capacity. Only if $t > 0$ and demand is

---

[14]The argument explores first stage defection, $dk_1 \ne 0$, while ignoring second stage defection, i.e., given k, $dx_1^A < 0 < dx_1^B$. From equation (5a), such defection is profitable if $\partial\pi_1/\partial x_1^A < 0$, i.e., if $p_x k+t < 0$. I assume, therefore, that this does not hold, i.e., $k \le t/(-p_x)$.

convex does firm 1 overinvest, some, capacity to deter entry - *i.e.*, to reduce firm 2's sales in market A. In another special case, with concave demand, both firms underinvest and may completely deter entry. The use of capacity as an entry-deterring instrument against, for instance, import competition is highly circumscribed. This result differs rather starkly from the original capacity-commitment model. It tallies rather well with Big Steel's vulnerability to import competition after the war (see Section IV).

The reason for these results is two-fold. First, the sequence of moves is different than in the *de novo* capacity-commitment model. In the latter model, the incumbent firm is the first mover: it invests before the entrant does. In a real-world setting, such as in international trade, entrants are often established firms in other, product or country, markets. In this case, incumbent firm and potential entrant play symmetrical roles. Both commit to capacity simultaneously, each in its own home market. Second, capital is not completely product-specific. As equation (5c') shows, the correct opportunity cost of selling at home is the marginal revenue abroad, rather than the marginal production or distribution cost. A capacity investment may reduce the marginal *production* cost, from $\beta + c$ to c, but it does not *per se* reduce the opportunity cost. Hence, it fails to make the incumbent firm aggressive in its home market. The entrant knows this, and thus does not keep out of this market. The possibility of *output shifting* undermines the commitment to the product market (Calem, 1988; and Anderson and Fischer, 1989). Capacity may have an indirect effect, though, by changing the entrant's opportunity cost, which is its home market marginal revenue, $MR_2^B + t_2$. In particular, the incumbent firm's investment may raise the entrant's opportunity cost of entry *relative* to its marginal revenue of entry, thereby reducing its scale of entry. The next section explores cases where the pre-emptive firm raises its rival's costs in *absolute* terms.

VII. Vertical Multi-Market Competition

1.   ABSOLUTE COST ADVANTAGES

Bain (1962) mentioned absolute cost advantages as one class of entry barriers, which moreover were particularly important in the steel industry. He traced these advantages to input market conditions: *i.e.*, they arise if entry raises factor prices, incumbents secure factors at lower prices than entrants, or established firms have access to better factors than entrants (Bain, 1962: 14). He treats these cost differences as given to firms. However, a far-seeing incumbent firm may exploit these input market conditions in order to raise entry costs. If inputs need to be acquired prior to production, the incumbent firm may as it were ambush the entrant in the input market rather than in the product market. In a paper which was not enough appreciated at the time Lydall (1955: 304) argued that "the cost of launching a new product on the market depends on the policy of existing firms. Lydall (1955: 310) explains the *endogenous entry cost* by arguing that entrants usually face imperfect factor markets, dominated by established firms. He cites technical knowledge and goodwill as examples. Lydall's (1955: 301-302) vision is not unlike an, imperfectly, contestable market. Translated in modeling terms, his argument is that the incumbent firm deters entry by quoting a price p with $c < p \leq c + E(z)$, where c is the firm's average cost and $E(z)$ the entrant's unit entry cost. The incumbent firm's instruments z - such as advertising, patenting, *et cetera* - raise the entry cost. An investment z (> 0) is profitable if $\max_z\{E(z)D(c + E(z))-z\} > 0$, where D(.) is the market demand function, the profit margin p-c equals $E(z)$ and in the absence of investments profits are zero [*i.e.*, $p = c$ and $E(0) = 0$].[15] In short, Lydall shows that the incumbent firm deters entry by raising the entrant's cost.

In two influential papers, Salop and Scheffman (1983 and 1987) re-invented and extended Lydall's view. They argue that a dominant firm may prey upon its rivals by raising their costs. Numerous instruments can be used, but the authors refer in particular to the dominant firm's market power in input markets. The cost-raising strategies imply that both the fringe's and the dominant firm's costs increase. The dominant firm's profits increase if price rises more than its own average costs (Lydall, 1955: 308; Williamson, 1968: 94; and Salop and Scheffman, 1987: 23). Moreover, the fringe's profits decrease (*cost predation*) or may increase as well (input market *collusion*) (Dixit, 1986: 115; and Salop and Scheffman, 1987: 24). A dominant incumbent firm may thus improve its competitiveness in the product market by exploiting a first-mover advantage or market power in the input market. This is salient only if the dominant firm and its, potential or actual, rivals participate in the same input market. It may not hold if the rivals are located in different regions or countries. Moreover, if the entrants are established firms, they may already own the required assets. The cost-raising strategy seems to aim at small rivals, a competitive fringe, or new, *de novo*, potential rivals. Below, the focus will first be on the intermediate product market, then on the capital goods market, and finally on the labor market. These cases focus on imperfect competition on the demand side of a factor market.

2.   COMPETITION IN THE INTERMEDIATE PRODUCTS MARKET

The dominant buyer of an intermediate product may affect the price charged to rival buyers by the sheer quantity of its purchases. For example, the dominant U.S. aluminum supplier Alcoa may have *overbought* bauxite in order to raise its rivals' costs (Krattenmaker and Salop, 1986: 236).[16] The quantity of bauxite which Alcoa buys in the open market depends, in turn, on its vertical integration. In a make-or-buy context an investment reduces the demand for intermediate goods in the external market. A dominant incumbent firm may use its investments as an instrument to affect the external intermediate input price if

---

[15]Baumol, Panzar and Willig (1982: 293-296) present a model along these lines where z may indicate advertisements.

[16]Lopatka and Godek (1992) criticize the view that Alcoa raised the costs of electricity and bauxite to (potential) rival suppliers. They show that Alcoa was not a dominant buyer of these inputs. They misconstrue the cost-raising argument as implying the purchase of inputs which one does not use (*ibidem*: 314). The model in this chapter re-iterates that the issue rather is the purchase of more, or less, inputs than one would buy absent the cost-raising motive. But given a stock of inputs, one will generally utilize them fully, as production will imply zero marginal costs as far as these inputs are concerned.

the associated input market is imperfectly competitive. This argument will be explored in a variety of the cost-raising models in Salop and Scheffman (1983 and 1987) and Dixit (1986).[17] Firm i (= 1,2) can invest in capital k_i to reduce the variable production costs $C^i(q_i,k_i)$. The quantity q_i refers to the firm's production of an intermediate input. The input can also be purchased in an external market, in a quantity of y_i units at price α. With a fixed proportions technology, one may normalize such that one unit of output requires one intermediate input: $x_i = q_i + y_i$, where x_i is the final good output. Profits are as in equation (1) with $V_B^i = -\beta k_i - \alpha y_i$:

(14) $\pi^i = R^i(x_1,x_2) - C^i(q_i,k_i) - \beta k_i - \alpha y_i$ with $x_i = q_i + y_i$.

The intermediate product market is competitive on the supply side, with a supply function $\alpha = A(y_1 + x_2)$, where A is a continuously differentiable function. In order to focus on market power in this market, assume that both firms are price takers in the capital goods market. Thus β is a parameter. The first mover, firm 1, is partially integrated, along the lines of equation (14). Firm 2, the second mover, is a new or small firm, which purchases all its inputs. Its profits are $\pi^2 = R^2(x_1,x_2) - \alpha x_2$. In the first stage, firm 1 chooses k_1; in the second stage, firm 1 chooses y_1 and q_1, and firm 2 chooses x_2. Profit maximization in the second stage entails the first-order conditions:

(15a) $\partial\pi^1/\partial y_1 = 0 = R^1_{y1}(y_1 + q_1, x_2) - A_{y1}(y_1 + x_2)y_1 - A(y_1 + x_2)$;

(15b) $\partial\pi^1/\partial q_1 = 0 = R^1_{q1}(y_1 + q_1, x_2) - C^1_{q1}(q_1,k_1)$; and

(15c) $\partial\pi^2/\partial x_2 = 0 = R^2_{x2}(y_1 + q_1, x_2) - A_{x2}(y_1 + x_2)x_2 - A(y_1 + x_2)$.

The second-order maximization conditions are (suppressing arguments)

(C3) $R^1_{y1y1} - A_{y1y1}y_1 - 2A_{y1} < 0$;

       $R^1_{q1q1} - C^1_{q1q1} < 0$;

       $R^2_{x2x2} - A_{x2x2}x_2 - 2A_{x2} < 0$.

The first-order conditions implicitly define reaction curves. In the first stage, firm 1 anticipates on the shift of these reaction curves induced by its capacity investments k_1. To find these shifts, totally differentiate equations (15):

---

[17] The link between vertical integration and cost-raising is well known (*e.g.*, Salinger, 1988).

(16) $$\begin{bmatrix} R^1_{y_1y_1}-A_{y_1y_1}y_1-2A_{y_1} & R^1_{y_1q_1} & R^1_{y_1x_2}-A_{y_1x_2}y_1-A_{x_2} \\ R^1_{q_1y_1} & R^1_{q_1q_1}-C^1_{q_1q_1} & R^1_{q_1x_2} \\ R^2_{x_2y_1}-A_{x_2y_1}x_2-A_{y_1} & R^2_{x_2q_1} & R^2_{x_2x_2}-A_{x_2x_2}x_2-2A_{x_2} \end{bmatrix} \begin{pmatrix} dy_1 \\ dq_1 \\ dx_2 \end{pmatrix} = \begin{pmatrix} 0 \\ C^1_{q_1k_1} \\ 0 \end{pmatrix} dk_1 .$$

Call the 3X3 matrix D and its determinant Δ. In order to get stability of the Cournot-Nash equilibrium in equation (15) assume that $\Delta > 0$ (Dixit, 1986: 110). Before solving (16), solve dq_1 as a function of dy_1, dx_2, and dk_1, and substitute, to get

(17) $$\begin{bmatrix} R^1_{y_1y_1}-A_{y_1y_1}y_1-2A_{y_1}-\dfrac{R^1_{y_1q_1}R^1_{q_1y_1}}{R^1_{q_1q_1}-C^1_{q_1q_1}} & R^1_{y_1x_2}-A_{y_1x_2}y_1-A_{x_2}-\dfrac{R^1_{y_1q_1}R^1_{q_1x_2}}{R^1_{q_1q_1}-C^1_{q_1q_1}} \\ R^2_{x_2y_1}-A_{x_2y_1}-A_{y_1}-\dfrac{R^2_{x_2q_1}R^1_{q_1y_1}}{R^1_{q_1q_1}-C^1_{q_1q_1}} & R^2_{x_2x_2}-A_{x_2x_2}x_2-2A_{x_2}-\dfrac{R^2_{x_2q_1}R^1_{q_1x_2}}{R^1_{q_1q_1}-C^1_{q_1q_1}} \end{bmatrix} \begin{pmatrix} dy_1 \\ dx_2 \end{pmatrix}$$

$$= -\dfrac{C^1_{q_1k_1}}{R^1_{q_1q_1}-C^1_{q_1q_1}} \begin{pmatrix} R^1_{y_1q_1} \\ R^2_{x_2q_1} \end{pmatrix} dk_1 .$$

The formula shows that firm 1's investment dk_1 works both ways: it shifts its own reaction curve, the top row, which is the own effect in Figure 1, and it shifts firm 2's reaction curve, the bottom row, which coincides with the cross effect. The reason is that firm 1's investment reduces its marginal production costs, the own effect, which induces it to buy less in the external market. This in turn affects firm 2's marginal costs, the cross effect. Applying Cramer's rule on equation (16) gives $dx_2/dk_1 = \Delta^{-1}C^1_{q_1k_1}\{(R^2_{x_2y_1}-A_{x_2y_1}x_2-A_{y_1})R^1_{y_1q_1}-R^2_{x_2q_1}(R^1_{y_1y_1} -A_{y_1y_1}y_1-2A_{y_1})\}$. Simplify this by taking into account that with homogeneous products $R^2_{x_2y_1} = R^2_{x_2q_1}$, $R^1_{y_1q_1} =R^1_{y_1y_1}$, $A_{x_2y_1} = A_{y_1y_1} = A_{yy}$ and $A_{y_1} = A_y$. That is,

(18) $dx_2/dk_1 = -\Delta^{-1}C^1_{q_1k_1}\{A_{yy}(x_2R^1_{y_1q_1}-y_1R^2_{x_2q_1}) + A_y(R^1_{y_1q_1}-2R^2_{x_2q_1})\}$.

Total differentiation of firm 1's profit function gives

(19) $d\pi^1 = (R_{y_1}-A_{y_1}y_1-A)dy_1 + (R^1_{q_1}-C^1_{q_1})dq_1 + (R^1_{x_2}-A_{x_2}y_1)dx_2-(C^1_{k_1} + \beta)dk_1 = 0$.

The coefficients of dy_1 and dq_1 equal zero because of equation (15). For convenience, assume that $A_{yy} = 0$ such that A_y is a constant. Rewrite revenues: $R^i = x_ip(x_1+x_2)$, where p(.) is the downward-sloping inverse demand function for a homogeneous good. Then, $R^1_{y_1q_1}-2R^2_{x_2q_1} = (x_1-2x_2)p_{xx}$. It follows that the sign$(dx_2/dk_1) = $ sign$(A_y(x_1-2x_2)p_{xx})$. This gives the result that a strategic or indirect effect of k_1 on x_2 is absent if and only if (i) there are constant returns in in the intermediate product market ($A_y = 0$), (ii) firm 2 is sufficiently small ($x_1 = 2x_2$), or (iii) demand is linear ($p_{xx} = 0$). The implication for firm 1's profits is

$$(20) \quad d\pi^1 = -\{(R^1_{x2}-A_{x2}y_1)\Delta^{-1}C^1_{q1k1}A_y(x_1-2x_2)p_{xx} + (C_{k1} + \beta)\}dk_1.$$

The optimal capital stock implies that the coefficient of dk_1 equals zero: $i.e.$,

$$(21) \quad C_{k1} + \beta = -(R^1_{x2}-A_{x2}y_1)\Delta^{-1}C^1_{q1k1}A_y(x_1-2x_2)p_{xx}.$$

Note that $R^1_{x2} < 0$ [condition (C2)]. $R^1_{x2}-A_{x2}y_1$ will be negative if A_{x2} is either positive or negative but small in absolute size. Moreover, $C^1_{q1k1} < 0$ [condition (C1)]. The determinant Δ is positive. In that case, $\text{sign}(C_{k1} + \beta) = -\text{sign}(A_y (x_1-2x_2)p_{xx}) = -\text{sign}(dx_2/dk_1)$. In the case of Big Steel, overinvestment and thus excessive integration will occur in the following case. The fringe rivals are small, $i.e.$, $x_1-2x_2 > 0$. Demand for steel may well be concave, $i.e.$, $p_{xx} < 0$. The reason is that steel has substitutes, $e.g.$, aluminium, plastics, and ceramics. If the steel price increases above a threshold, users may switch to a substitute. If these thresholds hover around a similar steel price, steel demand may trail off strongly at that price. If below that price demand is inelastic, demand may be concave. Decreasing returns may exist in the raw material market ($A_y > 0$), if low-cost ore deposits are scarce. As a result, firm 1 will over-invest ($C_{k1} + \beta > 0$), relative to the case where firm 1 minimizes its production costs ($i.e.$, $C_{k1} + \beta = 0$). Figure 3 illustrates the case.

Figure 3.   An intermediate (I) and final (F) product market

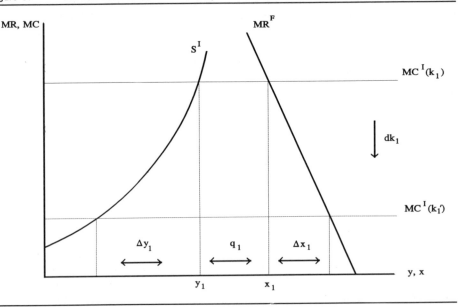

Given firm 2's scale of entry, MR^F is firm 1's marginal revenue and S^I is the supply curve of the intermediate input. An investment by firm 1 reduces its marginal production cost MC^I (the figure assumes constant returns). The firm will raise its production of the intermediate input, q_1, while buying less intermediate inputs ($\Delta y_1 < 0$). Because of the reduced marginal cost it raises its supply by Δx_1. The entrant suffers from the fall in the market price (as $\Delta x_1 > 0$) but benefits from the reduced market price of the intermediate product (as $\Delta y_1 < 0$). The own and cross effect partly cancel out in this case. The net effect may be negative, as a concave demand curve implies that an increase in output can cut price quite strongly. The entrant may reduce the scale of its entry. The commitment value of capital therefore entails a strategic overnvestment.[18] With convex demand, the entrant might benefit, in which case the firm may underinvest and *overbuy* in order to raise the entrant's costs and reduce its output level, as $dx_2/dk_1 > 0$.

If there are constant returns to scale in the intermediate product market (*i.e.*, $A_y = 0$), firm 1's make-or-buy decision and associated investment level cannot be used as instruments in competition. This result differs from the Dixit (1980) model, where in the absence of market power in input markets firm 1 does commit to capital in order to deter firm 2's entry. The reason is that in Dixit (1980) an investment reduces the firm's marginal cost. In the above model, however, partial integration implies that the firm's marginal cost equals the price of the externally acquired intermediate product, α. If $A_y = 0$, the marginal cost of buying inputs is pegged at a parametric α, which destroys the own effect. An investment reduces the firm's marginal in-house production cost, C^1_{x1}, which changes the firm's *make-or-buy* decision, y_1 versus q_1, but it does not affect its marginal production cost, α, and its total production, x_1. Firm 1 chooses k_1 and x_1 to minimize production costs without strategic implications.

3.   COMPETITION IN THE CAPITAL GOODS MARKET

Now suppress the intermediate product market altogether in order to focus on the capital goods market. If final good suppliers compete in, new, capacity, they may be confronted with capacity constraints in the capital goods industry. This provides the setting for Ghemawat's (1990) *snowball effect*, where two firms simultaneously bid for a given supply of, *e.g.*, newly produced capital goods. Prior to the bid, there is an asymmetry as one firm is larger than the other one. If the large firm wins the bid, industry concentration increases, which raises industry profits relative to the case where the small firm wins and industry concentration may decline. The difference in these profits may give the large firm the largest incentive to win the bid. Like the snowball, it grows ever larger.

Ghemawat argues that his model applied for investments by Du Pont in titanium dioxide. In 1975 Du Pont considered two strategies: maintain its share

---

[18]Mr. Dixit points out, personal communication, that firm 1 may commit to buying external resources by entering into a long-run contract with external suppliers. A contract may indeed substitute for an overinvestment in capital goods as a commitment instrument. Some well-known problems stand in the way of a contract as a commitment, however. First, contracts may be renegotiable and, second, firm 1 might sell excess resources, acquired by the contract, to other parties (*e.g.*, to a new entrant).

of U.S. industry capacity at 43% or grow to 55%. It expected the growth strategy to lead to *higher* prices in the long run than the maintain strategy. This illustrates that Du Pont increased its capacity in order to raise its market power over smaller rivals. Another example, where indeed an auction occurred, is given by Lieberman (1987: 623). In 1957 the U.S. government auctioned a large low-cost magnesium plant. Prior to the auction, Dow Chemical, the dominant supplier, stockpiled magnesium ingot. By 1957 the stock was up to approximately two years of U.S. domestic consumption. Dow proved the sole bidder of the auction and bought it for less than the original construction cost. Subsequently, it closed the plant for four years in order to draw down the stockpile.

A model has cost functions as in equation (1) with $V_B^i = -B(k_1 + k_2)k_i$, which reflects a continuously differentiable supply function $\beta = B(k_1 + k_2)$. The capital goods market is competitive on the supply side. If there are decreasing returns to scale (*i.e.*, $B_k > 0$), the situation reflects capacity constraints in the capital goods industry in similar vein as the Ghemawat (1990) model. In the first stage of the game, firm 1 chooses k_1 as before. In the second stage, firm 1 chooses x_1 and firm 2 chooses x_2 and k_2 simultaneously.[19] Firm 2's capacity choice has no strategic effect on firm 1's output choice: that is, firm 2 chooses k_2 to minimize its costs. Firm 1's choice of k_1 is driven by three motivations: to minimize its costs, to pre-empt firm 2, and to raise firm 2's costs. Consider the second stage first. Call $\mu^i := R^i_{xi} - C^i_{xi}$ ($i = 1,2$) and omit the arguments for convenience. Then, $\mu^i_i = R^i_{xixi} - C^i_{xixi}$ and $\mu^i_j = R^i_{xixj}$. The first-order conditions for profit maximization, $\partial\pi^i/\partial x_i = \partial\pi^2/\partial k_2 = 0$, read

(22) $\mu^i = 0$, $i = 1,2$, and

$$C^2_{k2} + B_{k2}k_2 + B = 0.$$

The second-order maximization conditions are

(C4) $\mu^i_i < 0$ ($i = 1,2$), and

$$C^2_{k2k2} + B_{k2k2}k_2 + 2B_{k2} > 0.$$

In the first stage, firm 1 explores the effect of dk_1 on the second-stage decision variables by totally differentiating equations (22). This gives

(23) $\mu^1_1 dx_1 + \mu^1_2 dx_2 - C^1_{x1k1} dk_1 = 0,$

$\mu^2_1 dx_1 + \mu^2_2 dx_2 - C^2_{x2k2} dk_2 = 0$, and

$C^2_{k2x2} dx_2 + (B_{k2k1}k_2 + B_{k1}) dk_1 + (C^2_{k2k2} + B_{k2k2}k_2 + 2B_{k2}) dk_2 = 0.$

---

[19]This implies the simplifying assumption that although investment decisions (k_1 and k_2) are sequential, pricing in the capital input market occurs simultaneously, $\beta = B(k_1 + k_2)$. Introducing time in the capital input markets makes for, at least, more cumbersome notation.

Rewrite equations (23) as a linear system of dx_1, dx_2 and dk_2 in dk_1. Call Δ the determinant of the matrix, which is positive in order to guarantee stability of the equilibrium in (22). Cramer's rule gives us

(24) $dx_2/dk_1 = \Delta^{-1}\{-\mu^1{}_1 C^2{}_{x2k2}(B_{k2k1}k_2 + B_{k1}) - \mu^2{}_1 C^1{}_{x1k1}(C^2{}_{k2k2} + B_{k2k2}k_2 + 2B_{k2})\}$, and

$dk_2/dk_1 = \Delta^{-1}\{-(\mu^1{}_1\mu^2{}_2 - \mu^2{}_1\mu^1{}_2)(B_{k2k1}k_2 + B_{k1}) + \mu^2{}_1 C^1{}_{x1k1}C^2{}_{k2x2}\}$.

The B_{k2k1} factor shows firm 1's cost-raising competition, the cross effect, and the $C^1{}_{x1k1}$ factor the own effect. To find the optimal k_1, firm 1 totally differentiates its profits:

(25) $d\pi^1 = \mu^1 dx_1 + R^1{}_{x2} dx_2 - B_{k2}k_1 dk_2 - [C^1{}_{k1} + B_{k1}k_1 + B]dk_1 = 0$.

Investments have a rival's cost-raising effect, an own effect (indirectly through dx_2 and dk_2) as well as cost-minimization effect (directly through dk_1). Substitution of equations (22) and (24) in (25) gives the total effect. For convenience, assume that the second derivative, B_{kk}, equals zero such that the first derivative, B_k, is constant. Rewrite 25 into

(26) $C^1{}_{k_1} + B_k k_1 + \beta =$

$$\frac{1}{\Delta}\left[-B_k\left(R^1{}_{x_2}(\mu^1_1 C^2{}_{x_2k_2} + 2\mu^2_1 C^1{}_{x_1k_1}) + k_1\mu^2_1 C^1{}_{x_1k_1}C^2{}_{k_2x_2}\right) - R^1{}_{x_2}\mu^2_1 C^1{}_{x_1k_1}C^2{}_{k_2k_2} + B^2_k k_1(\mu^1_1\mu^2_2 - \mu^2_1\mu^1_2)\right].$$

Stability of the product market competition implies that $\mu^1{}_1\mu^2{}_2 - \mu^2{}_1\mu^1{}_2 > 0$ (Dixit, 1980: 104). Conditions (C1) and (C2) imply that $R^1{}_{x2}(\mu^1{}_1 C^2{}_{x2k2} + 2\mu^2{}_1 C^1{}_{x1k1}) + k_1\mu^2{}_1 C^1{}_{x1k1}C^2{}_{k2x2}$ is negative, and $(B_k)^2 k_1(\mu^1{}_1\mu^2{}_2 - \mu^2{}_1\mu^1{}_2)$ is positive. Moreover, $-R^1{}_{x2}\mu^2{}_1 C^1{}_{x1k1}C^2{}_{k2k2}$ is positive if

(C5) $C^i{}_{kiki} > 0$ (decreasing returns to investments).

This gives rise to the following cases. If $B_k > 0$, the left-hand side is positive. Thus $C^1{}_{k1} + B_k k_1 + B > 0$, which implies overinvestment relative to cost minimization. Thus if there are decreasing returns in the capital goods industry, the first mover overinvests both in order to pre-empt the second mover and to raise the costs at which it acquires capacity. This tallies with Ghemawat's, (1990) result. If $B_k = 0$, the left-hand side is still positive. This implies overinvestment - that is, the outcome is identical to Dixit's (1980: 103-104) model. If $B_k < 0$, there are increasing returns in the capital goods industry. This may give firm 1 an incentive to underinvest. This runs counter, however, to the commitment motive. If B_k is sufficiently strong, the left-hand side in equation (26) may be negative, with underinvestment as net outcome.

3.   COMPETITION BY RAISING WAGE COSTS

Nelson (1957) argues that labor unionization resulting in higher wage rates might raise the quasi-rents of coal mines. In general, he shows that industry profits, quasi-rents, can increase if variable costs increase, even if the product market and factor markets are competitive (*i.e.*, if firms are price takers) and if firms are symmetric. His analysis is short-run: that is, entry is barred, and capital is fixed. An increase in marginal (wage) costs raises the market price, and thus the industry producer surplus, given an upward-sloping marginal cost curve. In the long run, of course, entry and investments, substituting for labor, will reduce the quasi-rent until it just covers the fixed capital costs. The short-run assumption implies that some imperfection, in factor and or product markets, must be assumed. Moreover, the increase of the cost must be an unanticipated shock, rather than deliberate firms' policy. Otherwise more firms would have entered the market initially, expecting to recover their capital outlays from the windfall gain. Firms will only then raise the wage rates deliberately if at least one of three assumptions fails: perfect competition in the product market, perfect competition in the factor markets, and symmetric firms. This presumption will be tested against some other papers. Williamson (1968) explored the Pennington case in the U.S. bituminous coal industry, where large coal mines and the United Mine Workers union conspired to raise the fringe firms' wage costs. They were able to do so since a wage (increase) agreed upon with the union, was imposed upon all U.S. coal mines. Since the small mines were less capital-intensive than the large ones, a wage increase would raise the former's unit costs more. This induced exit of small producers such as the Pennington mine. Exit would raise the market price, which may have overcompensated the large mines for the increase in their own wage rates, such that their profits increased. It may pay to raise one's wage costs, therefore, provided one uses more capital-intensive techniques than some rivals.

Gollier (1991) proposes to integrate Williamson's theory into modern labor economics, insider-outsider theory, and industrial organization, entry deterrence. His attempt is valiant but the implementation seems deficient. His model has n homogeneous incumbent firms and one potential entrant. Labor is the only input, sunk costs are absent, and the product market is competitive. In the second stage of the game, the entrant decides about entry taking, given the industry-wide wage rate w and price p. Each incumbent firm, i = 1..n, negotiates with a firm-specific union about an insiders' wage rate w^i ($\geq$ w) and insiders' employment level. In the first stage of the game, the incumbent firms negotiate with a union to set an industry-wide wage rate (w). Incumbent firms have a motive to raise the industry-wide wage rate w above a market wage (w'): by doing so, they raise the entrant's cost. This reduces its output level and raises the market price [see Figure 2 in Gollier (1991: 401)]. This is, however, inconsistent with perfect competition where firms by definition assume that the effect of an individual firm on the market price is negligible. In the special case where Gollier (1991: 404) assumes that incumbent firms ignore the effect of the entrant's output level on the market price, he correctly shows that incumbents will not raise the industry-wide wage rate above the market wage rate.

Gollier's paper underplays the importance of asymmetry between incumbents and entrant. Assume symmetry in that each firm has access to the same technology. In that case, if $w^i > w$, the incumbents' unit costs exceed those of the entrant (*e.g.*, Varian, 1984: 44). With perfect competition in the product market, the incumbents' output and profit levels will be less than the entrant's. The worst incumbents can do, therefore, is to set w such that $w = w^i$. In this symmetry case, any step taken to hurt the entrant hurts the incumbents in the same way. Entry deterrence will not occur, therefore. Entry deterrence will occur only if the entrant is "very inefficient with respect to the incumbent's technology" (Gollier, 1991: 399). This is an *ad hoc* imperfection in the factor markets, considering that incumbent firms are assumed homogeneous. Moreover, if the entrant is inefficient, why bother with it if its output level is even smaller than those of the atomistic incumbents? These results appear to support the argument that cost-raising competition, in the labor market, requires either imperfect competition in the product market such that incumbent firms really gain if entry is deterred, an imperfectly competitive factor market (*e.g.*, if incumbents own factors unavailable to entrants) or asymmetric firms (*e.g.*, in terms of information, sequence of moves).[20] A model explores a special case, where all three conditions occur. It integrates Williamson's insights with labor economics, albeit in a perfunctory way, and industrial organization. It explores a lead by Dewatripont (1987: 152).

The dominant firm (1) chooses capital (k_1) and a wage rate w. The latter is subject to a lower boundary w^m, the market wage. The wage rate w is imposed upon fringe firms as well. This is where, implicitly in the model, the union plays its role. Assume one second mover, firm 2.[21] It chooses an investment and employment level, unobserved by firm 1. Both firms compete in the product market as a Cournot duopoly with a homogeneous product, say steel. In the absence of a strategic motive to influence firm 1 by a choice of investment or employment level, firm 2 chooses the cost-minimizing technique and invests accordingly. Firm 1 may overinvest in order to pre-empt firm 2 by reducing its marginal cost. By choosing a high wage ($w > w^m$) it may raise firm 2's marginal costs more than its own if its capital-intensity exceeds firm 2's level. Firm 1's profits are $\pi_1 = R^1(x_1,x_2)-wl_1-\beta k_1$, where $x_1 = F(k_1,l_1)$, and firm 2's profits are $\pi_2 = R^2(x_1,x_2)-C^2(w,x_2)$, where $C^2(w,x_2) = \min_{l2,k2}\{wl_2+\beta k_2\}$ subject to $x_2 = F(k_2,l_2)$. Given k_1, firm 1's short-run cost function is such that $l_1 = g(k_1,x_1)$ with $F(k_1,g(k_1,x_1)) \equiv x_1$. Obvious conditions to impose on g(.) are $g_k < 0$, $g_x > 0$ and $g_{x1k1} < 0$: investments reduce marginal wage costs. In the first stage of the game, firm 1 chooses its investment and wage rate. In the second stage, profit maximization implies the first-order conditions

---

[20]Ghemawat (1991) argues that an imperfect factor market is a *sine qua non* for strategic, committed, competition. Dixon (1985) shows that if the product market is competitive, there is indeed scope for strategic action, provided that firms invest in capital prior to competing in the product market. Investment decisions are assumed irreversible, which points to a factor market imperfection, and there is no rental market for capital.

[21]If the union and the dominant firm decide to maximize their joint interests (*e.g.*, with efficient bargaining), they act as an integrated firm which supplies an input, labor, to a fringe firm (2) with which it competes in the product market. This setting is conducive to a price squeeze on firm 2, which is similar to the situation in this section.

(27) $\partial\pi_1/\partial x_1 = 0 = R^1_{x1}-wg_{x1}$, and

$\quad\quad \partial\pi_2/\partial x_2 = 0 = R^2_{x2}-C^2_{x2}.$

The second-order conditions are

(C6) $R^1_{x1x1}-wg_{x1x1} < 0$, and

$\quad\quad R^2_{x2x2}-C^2_{x2x2} < 0.$

Equation (23) implies reaction curves. In the first stage, firm 1 anticipates these. It chooses k_1 to shift its own reaction curve outwards, and w to shift both its own and firm 2's reaction curve inwards. Total differentiation of equation (27) gives

(28) $$\begin{bmatrix} R^1_{x_1x_1} -wg_{x_1x_1} & R^1_{x_1x_2} \\ R^2_{x_2x_1} & R^2_{x_2x_2}-C^2_{x_2x_2} \end{bmatrix} \begin{pmatrix} dx_1 \\ dx_2 \end{pmatrix} = \begin{bmatrix} g_{x_1}dw +wg_{x_1k_1}dk_1 \\ C^2_{x_2w}dw \end{bmatrix}.$$

Assume that the determinant Δ at the left-hand side of the matrix $(= [R^1_{x1x1}-wg_{x1x1}][R^2_{x2x2}-C^2_{x2x2}]-R^1_{x1x2}R^2_{x2x1}) > 0$: *i.e.*, own effects on revenue exceed cross effects. Cramer's rule gives

(29) $dx_2 = \Delta^{-1}([R^1_{x1x1}-wg_{x1x1}]C^2_{x2w}dw-R^2_{x2x1}[g_{x1}dw + wg_{x1k1}dk_1]).$

Totally differentiate firm 1's profit function:

(30) $d\pi_1 = [R^1_{x1}-wg_{x1}]dx_1-gdw-[wg_{k1}+\beta]dk_1+R^1_{x2}dx_2.$

The coefficient of dx_1 equals zero because of the first-order condition. Substitute (29) in (30):

(31)

$$d\pi_1 = \left(\frac{R^1_{x_2}}{\Delta}[R^1_{x_1x_1} -wg_{x_1x_1}]C^2_{x_2w} -\frac{R^1_{x_2}}{\Delta}R^2_{x_2x_1}g_{x_1} -g \right) dw - \left(wg_{k_1} +\beta +\frac{R^1_{x_2}}{\Delta}R^2_{x_2x_1}g_{x_1k_1}w \right) dk_1.$$

If the firm sets out from a situation where $w = w^m$ and k_1 minimizes costs (*i.e.*, $wg_{k1}+\beta = 0$), then $dk_1 > 0$ raises profits as $-\{wg_{k1}+\beta+R^1_{x2}\Delta^{-1}R^2_{x2x1}g_{x1k1}w\} = -R^1_{x2}\Delta^{-1}R^2_{x2x1}wg_{x1k1} > 0$. A wage increase, $dw > 0$, raises profits if the (positive) cost-raising effect on firm 2, $R^1_{x2}\Delta^{-1}[R^1_{x1x1}-wg_{x1x1}]C^2_{x2w}$, exceeds the (negative) direct effect that firm 1's marginal costs increase ($-g < 0$) with the indirect effect that this raises firm 2's output ($-R^1_{x2}\Delta^{-1}R^2_{x2x1}g_{x1} < 0$). This is the ore likely the more labor-intensive firm 2 is: *i.e.*, the more impact the industry wage has on its marginal costs by a higher C^2_{x2w}, and the more capital-intensive firm 1 is (that is, the smaller g and g_{x1}). Firm 1 is more capital-intensive than firm 2 as it is the first mover: it pre-empts firm 2 by an overinvestment. This creates an asymmetry which allows firm 1 to benefit from a wage increase which hurts firm 2.[22]

VIII. Appraisal

The chapter shows that analytically Dixit's (1980 and 1986) approach can accommodate a wide range of multi-market situations. The multi-market framework shows that an incumbent firm may try to beat the entrant between hammer and anvil, so to speak, by reducing the marginal revenue of entry (the own effect) while raising the marginal (opportunity) cost of entry (the cross effect). See Table 3 for a summary.

Table 3.   The place and instrument of competition

	Focus of competition	
Locus of competition	Reduce rival's revenue	Raise rival's costs
Product market	x	-
Rival's home market	x	x
Rival's input market	-	x

It also demonstrates the importance of the precise setting of competition, similar to Porter's (1980) extended rivalry (cf. Reid et al., Chapter 13). This suggests that any models to be tested should be context-specific. For this reason, case studies as Ghemawat (1984 and 1990) and Hall (1990) on the U.S. titanium dioxide industry are interesting. Ghemawat and Caves (1986) and Smiley (1988), on the other hand, are incapable of tailoring their models to specific industries because of the diversity of their data. Ghemawat and Caves (1986) have a test on PIMS data pertaining to North American manufacturing firms of non-durables. They show that capital-intensity has a significantly negative impact on profitability. This does not seem to accord with the capital-commitment story. Smiley (1988: 173) questioned managers about entry deterrence, and finds that in the case of new products "[e]ntry deterrence through advertising is most often followed 'frequently' (32%), followed by R&D preemption, building a reputation for toughness, use of the learning curve, and

---

[22]In Williamson's (1968) analysis the difference in capital-intensity was exogenous: mines with rich coal deposits, with wide seams, would be capital-intensive and mines with poor deposits, narrow seams, would prefer labor-intensive techniques. The prior commitment of leading firms was thus in ownership of the, scarce, rich deposits.

capacity preemption. Again, the two price preemption policies are used least often (3% and 2%)". This suggests that capacity pre-emption is not terribly important to managers. But its importance may differ starkly across industries. Evidence, therefore, seems inconclusive. According to the foregoing analysis, this is indeed to be expected. The overview offered by this chapter suggests that the commitment value of capacity depends on six factors: (1) the competitiveness and the returns to scale on the supply side of the input markets; (2) the first- and second-mover's buyer market power in the input markets; (3) the product- or firm-specificity of capital (*e.g.*, transport and adjustment costs); (4) the slope of the demand curve; (5) the identity of the entry threat; and (6) the sequence of moves. A change along any dimension may completely overturn the commitment value of capacity. Even if conditions (1) to (6) are suitable, moreover, a firm may prefer a substitute commitment instrument (see, *e.g.*, note 17). These outcomes point to the hazards of capacity commitments.

Firstly, entry barriers are also exit barriers. Steel firms derive their commitment partly from the huge (psychological, social and political) costs involved with cutting capacity and employment. These exit barriers imply that overcapacity can plague the industry for years (*e.g.*, Morrison, 1988). The associated losses reduce the commitment value of capital. Secondly, a commitment strategy may turn into *clay feet* when the institutional setting changes (Yip, 1982: 29). For instance, a firm 1's wage cost-raising strategy against firm 2 holds only if firm 2 is active in the same labor market as firm 1. This condition obviously failed to hold for foreign importers into the U.S. steel market. Importers, therefore, undermined the wage-cost increasing approach by U.S. Big Steel. Steel makers from developing countries such as Korea benefit from low wages. As they gained market share, excess capacity arose in Big Steel. Given the threat of lay-offs, new domestic firms were able to gain union concessions. Excess capacity induced entry, by reconstituted mills, rather than deterring it. Big Steel's rigid labor practices had turned into its clay feet as it could not, timely, accommodate changes in the U.S. labor market. In an uncertain world firms face a trade-off between flexibility and pre-commitment (Spencer and Brander, 1993). The upshot of the chapter, therefore, is that capacity's use as a commitment instrument is highly precarious.

References

Anderson, S.P. and Fischer, R.D. (1989) 'Multi-market Oligopoly with Production before Sales', *Journal of Industrial Economics* **38**, 167-182.
Andrews, P.W.S. (1949) *Manufacturing Business*, London, MacMillan.
Bain, J.S. (1962) *Barriers to New Competition*, Cambridge MA, Harvard University Press.
Basu, K. and Singh, N. (1990) 'Entry-deterrence in Stackelberg Perfect Equilibria', *International Economic Review* **31**, 61-71.
Baumol, W.J., Panzar, J.C. and Willig, R.D. (1982) *Contestable Markets and The Theory of Industry Structure*, New York, Harcourt Brace Jovanovich.
Bernheim, B.D. and Whinston, M.D. (1990) 'Multimarket Contact and Collusive Behavior', *RAND Journal of Economics* **21**, 1-26.
Brander, J. (1981) 'Intra-industry Trade in Identical Commodities', *Journal of International Economics* **11**, 1-14.
Brander, J. and Krugman, P. (1983) 'A "Reciprocal Dumping" Model of International Trade',

Journal of International Economics **15**, 313-321.

Brunner, E. (1961) 'A Note on Potential Competition', *Journal of Industrial Economics* **9**, 248-250.

Bulow, J.I., Geanakoplos, J.D. and Klemperer, P.D. (1985a) 'Multimarket Oligopoly: Strategic Substitutes and Complements', *Journal of Political Economy* **93**, 488-511.

Bulow, J.I., Geanakoplos, J.D. and Klemperer, P.D. (1985b) 'Holding Idle Capacity to Deter Entry', *Economic Journal* **95**, 178-182.

Cairns, R.D. and Mahabir, D. (1988) 'Contestability: A Revisionist View', *Economica* **55**, 269-276.

Calem, P.S. (1988) 'Entry and Entry Deterrence in Penetrable Markets', *Economica* **55**, 171-183.

Caves, R.E. (1971) 'International Corporations: The Industrial Economics of Foreign Investment', *Economica* **38**, 1-27.

Caves, R.E. and Porter, M.E. (1977) 'From Entry Barriers to Mobility Barriers: Conjectural Decisions and Contrived Deterrence to New Competition', *Quarterly Journal of Economics* **91**, 241-261.

Dewatripont, M. (1987) 'Entry Deterrence under Trade Unions', *European Economic Review* **31**, 149-156.

Dixit, A. (1980) 'The Role of Investment in Entry-deterrence', *Economic Journal* **90**, 95-106.

Dixit, A. (1986) 'Comparative Statics for Oligopoly', *International Economic Review* **27**, 107-122.

Dixon, H. (1985) 'Strategic Investment in an Industry with a Competitive Product Market', *Journal of Industrial Economics* **33**, 483-499.

Eaton, B.C. and Lipsey, R.G. (1979) 'The Theory of Market Pre-emption: The Persistence of Excess Capacity and Monopoly in Growing Spatial Markets', *Economica* **46**, 149-158.

Eaton, B.C. and Lipsey, R.G. (1980) 'Exit Barriers are Entry Barriers: the Durability of Capital as a Barrier to Entry', *Bell Journal of Economics* **10**, 721-729.

Eaton, B.C. and Lipsey, R.G. (1981) 'Capital, Commitment, and Entry Equilibrium', *Bell Journal of Economics* **12**, 593-604.

Elbaum, B. (1983) 'The Internalization of Labor Markets: Causes and Consequences', *American Economic Review* **73**, 260-265.

Fudenberg, D. and Tirole, J. (1984) 'The Fat-Cat Effect, The Puppy-Dog Ploy, and the Lean and Hungry Look', *American Economic Review Papers and Proceedings* **74**, 361-366.

Ghemawat, P. (1984) 'Capacity Expansion in the Titanium Dioxide Industry', *Journal of Industrial Economics* **33**, 145-163.

Ghemawat, P. (1986) 'Sustainable Advantage', *Harvard Business Review*, 53-58.

Ghemawat, P. (1991) *Commitment: The Dynamic of Strategy*, New York: The Free Press.

Ghemawat, P. and Caves, R.E. (1986) 'Capital Commitment and profitability: An Empirical Investigation', in Morris, D.J. *et al.* (eds), *Strategic Behaviour and Industrial Competition*, 1986, Oxford: Clarendon Press, 37-57.

Gollier, C. (1991) 'Wage Differentials, the Insider-Outsider Dilemma, and Entry-Deterrence', *Oxford Economic Papers* **43**, 391-408.

Hall, E.A. (1990) 'An Analysis of Preemptive Behavior in the Titanium Dioxide Industry', *International Journal of Industrial Organization* **8**, 469-484.

Hines, H.H. (1957) "Effectiveness of 'Entry' by Already Established Firms", *Quarterly Journal of Economics* **71**, 132-150.

Krattenmaker, Th.G. and Salop, S.C. (1986) Anticompetitive Exclusion: Raising Rivals' Costs to Achieve Power over Price, *Yale Law Journal* **96**, 209-293.

Lieberman, M.B. (1987) 'Excess Capacity as a Barrier to Entry: An Empirical Appraisal', *Journal of Industrial Economics* **35**, 607-627.

Lopatka, J.E. and Godek, P.E. (1992) Another Look at *Alcoa*: Raising Rivals' Costs Does not Improve the View, *Journal of Law & Economics* **35**, 311-329.

Lydall, H.F. (1955) 'Conditions of New Entry and the Theory of Price', *Oxford Economic Papers* **7**, 300-311.

Matsui, A. (1989) 'Consumer-benefited Cartels under Strategic Capital Investment Competition', *International Journal of Industrial Organization* **7**, 451-470.

Milgrom, P. and Roberts, J. (1982) 'Limit Pricing and Entry under Incomplete Information: An Equilibrium Analysis', *Econometrica* **50**, 443-459.

Morrison, C. (1988) 'Subequilibrium in the North American Steel Industries: A Study of Short Run Biases from Regulation and Utilisation Fluctuations', *Economic Journal* **98**, 390-411.

Nelson, R.R. (1957) Increased Rents from Increased Costs: A Paradox of Value Theory, *Journal of Political Economy* **65**, 387-393.

Porter, M.E. (1980) *Competitive Strategy: Techniques for Analyzing Industries and Competitors*, New York, The Free Press.

Salinger, M.A. (1988) 'Vertical Mergers and Market Foreclosure', *Quarterly Journal of Economics* **94**, 345-356.

Salop, S.C. and Scheffman, D.T. (1983) 'Raising Rivals' Costs', *American Economic Review* **73**, 267-271.

Salop, S.C. and Scheffman, D.T. (1987) 'Cost Raising Strategies', *Journal of Industrial Economics* **36**, 19-34.

Scherer, F.M. (1980) *Industrial Market Structure and Economic Performance*, Chicago, Rand McNally.

Schmalensee, R. (1981) 'Economics of Scale and Barriers to Entry', *Journal of Political Economy* **89**, 1228-1238.

Smiley, R. (1988) 'Empirical Evidence on Strategic Entry Deterrence', *International Journal of Industrial Organization* **6**, 167-180.

Spence, A.M. (1977) 'Entry, Capacity, Investment and Oligopolistic Pricing', *Bell Journal of Economics* **8**, 534-544.

Spence, A.M. (1979) 'Investment Strategy and Growth in a New Market', *Bell Journal of Economics* **10**, 1-19.

Spencer, B.J. and Brander, J.A. (1993) 'Pre-Commitment and Flexibility: Applications to Oligopoly Theory', *European Economic Review* **36**, 1601-1626.

Spulber, D.F. (1981) 'Capacity, Output, and Sequential Entry', *American Economic Review* **71** 503-514.

Tirole, J. (1988) *The Theory of Industrial Organization*, Cambridge MA: MIT Press.

Varian, H.R. (1984) *Microeconomic Analysis*, New York, W.W. Norton.

Venables, A.J. (1990) 'International Capacity Choice and National Market Games', *Journal of International Economics* **29**, 23-42.

Watson, C.M. (1982) 'Counter-competition Abroad to Protect Home Markets', *Harvard Business Review*, 40-42.

Wegberg, M. van, and Witteloostuijn, A. van (1993) 'Credible Entry Threats into Contestable Markets: A Symmetric Multimarket Model of Contestability', *Economica* **59**, 437-452.

Williamson, O.E. (1968) 'Wage Rates as a Barrier to Entry: The Pennington Case', *Quarterly Journal of Economics* **82**, 85-117.

Witteloostuijn, A van, and Wegberg, M. van (1992) 'Multimarket Competition: Theory and Evidence', *Journal of Economic Behavior and Organization* **18**, 273-282.

Yip, G.S. (1982) *Barriers to Entry*, Lexington, MA, Lexington Books.

CHAPTER 13

Extended Rivalry and Competitive Advantage in the New Small Firm[1]

LOWELL R. JACOBSEN
Department of Business Administration and Economics, William Jewell College, United Kingdom

GAVIN C. REID
Department of Economics and Centre for Research into Industry, Enterprise, Finance and the Firm (C.R.I.E.F.F.), University of St. Andrews, United Kingdom

MARGO E. ANDERSON
C.R.I.E.F.F., University of St. Andrews, United Kingdom

Abstract. The strategic behavior and growth of the new small firm is analyzed using field work evidence. An assessment of extended rivalry - embracing suppliers, substitutes and customers - is undertaken to *flesh-out* the appraisal of competitive advantage. Firms are grouped by low, medium and high concentration markets. In the low concentration cases, firms had struggled in imperfectly competitive, atomistic markets to achieve limited competitive advantage through product differentiation. In the medium concentration cases, firms were better placed to achieve competitive advantage by being niche players in a secure competitive fringe. In the high concentration cases, firms looked to achieve appreciable competitive advantage by targeting segments within exclusive and highly profitable markets. In no case was the outcome of the strategy adopted inevitable.

I. Introduction

This chapter explores the strategic behavior and growth of new small firms using longitudinal evidence obtained by field work methods. An assessment of extended rivalry - embracing suppliers, substitutes, and customers - is undertaken to provide an empirically rich characterization of the extent (if any) of competitive advantage in the new small firm. The methodology adopted is not that of positive economics, but of *grounded theory*.[2] In a previous paper (Jacobsen, Reid and Anderson, 1992), the impact of existing and potential rivals on the new small firm was examined. It was found that it was largely such rivals that significantly dictated, or even defined, the market niche filled by the new small firm. This, in turn, largely influenced its degree of competitive advantage. These findings may be interpreted as supporting a narrow Mason/Bain *structuralist* paradigm, emphasizing the primacy of the impact of structure on performance. Nevertheless, when the field work data are marshal-

---

[1]We should like to thank Ed Steinmueller (Stanford University), Bhasker Jyoti Das (Purdue University) and Tom Watkins (Webster University) for comments on an earlier draft of this chapter. The authors remain responsible for any errors of omission or commission that it may contain.

[2]See Reid (1987a: Chapter 3), where the grounded theory approach is explicated, and the status of case study analysis as a scientific method is explored. The field research techniques used are explained in Reid (1987b).

led into case study form using both numerical and textual (or *thick*) information, it is apparent that the import of a firm's behavior in effecting competitive advantage cannot too readily be dismissed. The very individual, and occasionally idiosyncratic, characteristics and behavior exhibited within the sample of small firms necessarily begged for a more thoughtful consideration of the conduct link than in our previous paper. It is quite clear that a robust profit-seeking mentality is typical of the owner-manager, so broadly speaking this aspect of conduct is an operational constant. However, the specific form this conduct takes varies widely according to the circumstances of the new small firm, which provides the focus of this chapter. The nascent or very immature firm necessarily confronts a particularly uncertain environment. Its own actions have a marked influence on the outcome of its quest for competitive advantage (if not sheer survival). Typically there is no market environment in which the small firm can afford to be other than actively involved in ensuring survival, at least, and prosperity, if feasible. Indeed, it is generally acknowledged that the prospects of the new firm operating beyond five years are not good and this is often attributed to the inadequate acquisition and deployment of managerial skills.

The chapter is organized as follows. Section II introduces the sample of a varied set of sixteen firms. In Section III the analytical framework, derived from Porter (1980), is presented. Section IV interprets the observations in terms of the Porter framework. Section V is a conclusion.

II.   The Sample

A summary view of the characteristics and growth of the sixteen firms under consideration is provided in Table 1. The firms in Table I were selected from the initial study's sample of 88 new firms, which ranged over more than 30 Standard Industrial Classifications. The 16 firms exhibited in Table 1 were a judgement sample aiming to reflect the diversity of the main sample, and of course its gathering required the further participation of the owner-managers. In the event, each firm chosen had a unique character compared to other members of the sub-sample. Indeed, each firm came from a different industry. In terms of size, total assets range from 0 to 1.78 million pounds sterling and the number of full-time employees varies from 0 to 90.[3] Highly successful, less successful and unsuccessful firms are represented, as are three levels of market concentration (*i.e.*, low, medium and high). Of course, all of the firms are alike in that they are *new* - *i.e.*, established within three years of our first contact with the firms in 1985. Furthermore, it should be noted that because all of the firms are

---

[3]These, and other general characteristics, are typical of the sample as a whole. For example, the average number of employees in 1985 for the sub-sample in Table 1 was nine, and for the whole sample was eight. Details of the data obtained in 1985 are in Jacobsen (1986), Reid (1987a and 1987b) and Reid and Jacobsen (1988). Details of the data obtained in 1988 are in Reid (1991) and Reid (1993), with the latter giving a general account of the complete data base. In each of the three investigations the authors devised and employed distinctly different field research instruments, resulting in the collection of both numerical and textual (or 'thick') data.

small, they are free of the agency problems which arise in larger enterprises.[4]

Table 1.   Growth and key attibutes of new small firms

Firm	Product Market	Market Concentra-tion	Start Year	Assets (000's)[a] Start	1985	1988	Employees[b] 1985	1988
1	Blind Cleaning	Low	1984	16	16	n.a.	2	n.a.
5	Knitwear Manufacturing	Low	1983	1.5	7	n.a.	5	5
9	Auto Repair	Low	1984	5	9	6	2	2
10	Industrial Cleaning	Low	1984	10	30	54.6	6	10
13	Holiday Tours	Low	1984	4	15	15	3	6
30	Wine Distribution	Low	1984	8	27	52	2	4
61	Theatre Props Manufacturing	Low	1985	nom	7	n.a.	4	n.a.
11	Food Manufacturing	Medium	1982	130	130	-[c]	47	0
17	Computer Software Manufacturing	Medium	1983	5	100	1,780	15	90
25	Electronics	Medium	1984	2.5	20	70	5	39
34	Bulk Bag Manufacturing	Medium	1984	5	50	385	27	57
52	Fencing Manufacturing	Medium	1983	15	50	46	3	6
54	Printing	Medium	1983	nom	180	-[c]	5	0
2	Security Blankets Manufacturing	High	1982	70	105	177	15	16
15	Cosmetics	High	1984	16	65	1,500	8	14
32	Acrobatic Aeroplane Manufacturing	High	1984	35	35	-[c]	1	0

n.a.   : Not available
nom   : Nominal (*i.e.*, less than one hundred pounds).
[a]   Assets are denominated in British pounds and refer to book value at nominal prices (1988 prices may be expressed in 1985 values using the deflator 1.13).
[b]   Only full-time employees counted.
[c]   Zero assets (sold or out of business).

[4]Larger enterprises may be subject to the divorce of ownership and control first emphasized in the pioneering work of Berle and Means (1933).

III.   Analytical Framework

Here we modify the competitive strategy framework developed by Michael
Porter (1980, 1985 and 1990) to the small firms' context and use it in the
analysis of the evidence. The Porter framework, in the words of Teece (1984:
94), is "a translation, redirection, and refinement of the Mason/Bain structure-conduct-performance paradigms". In its emphasis on the pursuit by individual
firms of competitive advantage (in the sense of above average performance) the
conduct of the firm is a focus of interest. This schema is unique in that it treats
suppliers, substitutes and customers along with the more familiar potential and
existing rivals as the fundamental forces of competition impinging on the firms.
This broader scope of competition (referred to as *extended rivalry*) could be
viewed prescriptively by the individual firm in order to systematically assess its
own relative strengths and weaknesses as well as its industry positioning. Here
we use this extended rivalry analysis to give content to the competitive strategies as actually used by the firms, which involves enquiring into the appropriateness of categories like *cost leadership* to firms in this sample. Of course, firms
may overtly use this framework to formulate a competitive strategy with a view
to gaining competitive advantage. However, this is unlikely, as owner-managers
cannot be assumed to have knowledge of this prescriptive framework. That
competitive advantage is sought by them, however, is not denied. Competitive
advantage, according to Porter (1985: 3), "grows fundamentally out of the
value a firm is able to create for its buyers that exceeds the firm's cost of
creating it". What we are doing is using Porter's prescriptive framework as a
way of organizing evidence on, and drawing lessons from, the competitive
strategies used by the actual firms.

   In Porter's analysis competitive advantage is realized through three generic
competitive strategies: overall cost leadership, differentiation and focus. A firm
that follows the first strategy is intent on being the lowest-cost producer, in an
absolute sense, in its market. Sources of cost advantage include, for example,
scale economies, preferential access to inputs and tight overhead control.
Typically, the pursuit of such a strategy requires a large market share. The
strategy of differentiation requires a firm to offer such a distinct product that it
is considered markedly differentiated in the market, thus commanding a higher
value-added/price ratio. Naturally, a large share in the wider product market is
unlikely to be a realistic objective for such firms, given their emphasis on
seeking exclusivity for their product image. Finally, a firm that subscribes to a
focus strategy is concerned with catering to a specific market niche such as a
certain buyer group, geographic market and/or product segment. In serving such
a target, emphasis is placed on low cost, differentiation, or both. Given the
fledgling status and diminutive size of the new small firms under consideration,
a focus strategy of some sort is commonly pursued.

   As this chapter is concerned with the impact of *extended rivalry* on the new
firm, it seems appropriate to consider further the import of *extended rivals* as
competitive forces. Extended rivals are of three types: suppliers, producers of
substitutes and customers. Suppliers exert competitive pressure to the extent
they can raise the prices and/or reduce the quality of goods or services purcha-

sed. A supplier group is powerful if: (1) it is producing in markets which are more concentrated than the markets in which its customers are selling; (2) the threat of alternative or substitute products is minimal; (3) the firm's industry is not a significant customer of the supplier group, implying that such firms are not particularly dependent on suppliers; (4) the suppliers' product is an important input to the firm's good(s); (5) suppliers are able to differentiate their products (e.g., emphasizing service), thus increasing the firm's dependency on them; and (6) the threat of forward integration by the supplier group is credible.

Substitute products present themselves as a more elusive competitive force than actual or potential rivals, as they originate in other industries, which means their presence is not necessarily easily detected in a timely manner. Porter (1980: 23) states that "identifying substitute products is a matter of searching for other products that can perform the same function as the product of the industry". Therefore, it is imperative for the firm to understand fully its product, and this not simply from the perspective of its own industry. A firm's customers or buyers are an important competitive force to the extent that they can exert bargaining power. Such power is high when: (1) customers' concentration is high - i.e., particular customers account for a significant share of the total sales; (2) the product the customer buys accounts for a large proportion of this customer's costs; (3) the products bought are largely homogenous; (4) the customer's switching costs of changing firms are low; (5) the customer's profits are low, thus causing greater sensitivity to price; (6) customers pose a credible threat of backward integration; and (7) customers are relatively well informed about demand, actual market price, et cetera.

IV.   The Evidence

1.   THE VARIABLES

In assessing the evidence regarding extended rivalry, it is useful to consider these new small firms in the context of the level of concentration in their markets (i.e., low, medium and high). This approach takes cognizance of the earlier compelling evidence (Jacobsen, Reid and Anderson, 1992) of the causal relationship between market concentration and the extent of a new small firm's measurable competitive advantage, as gauged by changes in total assets and full-time employees over a three-year period. Table 2 organizes the sample of new small firms in accordance with their market concentration levels. The effects of suppliers are considered in terms of their consequences for competitive advantage (positive, negative or neutral). The types of substitutes which influence competitive advantage are categorized (e.g., close, inferior, et cetera). The power of customers is identified as lying in one of three categories. In the case of category A, customer bargaining leverage is significant and generally reduces the new firm's competitive advantage. At the same time price sensitivity is high, which reduces the new firm's 'elbow-room' in pricing and also diminishes competitive advantage. Firm 1 (blind cleaning) provides such an example. Some of this firm's customers were large institutions like hospitals, which had tight costing systems. They were price sensitive and as large purchasers were willing and able to exercise leverage over supplying firms.

Table 2.   Extended rivals and strategies adopted

Firm	Product Market	Market Concentration	Effects of Suppliers[a]	Types of Substitutes[b]	Power of Customers[c]	Strategy Adopted[d]
1	Blind Cleaning	Low	A	C	A	FLC
5	Knitwear					
	Manufacturing	Low	B	A	A	FD
9	Auto Repair	Low	A	C	C	FD
10	Industrial Cleaning					
	Holiday Tours	Low	A	A	A	FDLC
13	Wine Distribution	Low	A	C	C	FD
30	Theatre Props	Low	A	B	A	FDLC
61	Manufacturing					
	Food Manufacturing	Low	A	C	C	FD
11	Computer Software	Medium	B	B	C	FD
17	Manufacturing					
	Electronics	Medium	B	D	C	FD
25	Bulk Bag	Medium	A	D	B	FD
34	Manufacturing					
	Fencing	Medium	B	D	B	FDLC
52	Manufacturing					
	Printing	Medium	A	B	C	FDC
54	Security Blankets	Medium	C	C	C	FDC
2	Manufacturing					
	Cosmetics	High	C	B	B	FDLC
15	Acrobatic Aeroplane	High	A	A	B	FDLC
32	Manufacturing					
		High	C	B	B	FDLC

[a] Suppliers   A - Positive
                 B - Negative
                 C - Neutral

[b] Substitutes   A - Close
                   B - Inferior
                   C - None Available
                   D - Creating

[c] Customers   A - Customer Leverage
                   Price Sensitivity
                 B - Customer Leverage
                   Price Sensitivity
                 C - Unique

[d] Strategy   FD - Focus on differentiation

                FLC - Focus on Low Cost

                FDLC - Focus on Differentiation and
                   Low Cost

In the case of category B, customer bargaining leverage is slight and price sensitivity low. Firm 2 (security printers blankets) provides such an example.

Principal purchasers of this highly specialized, patent-protected product, above all emphasized product quality. Their own product quality crucially depended on the quality of Firm 2's product, thus diminishing price sensitivity. Furthermore, patent protection removed the threat of backward integration, thus diminishing their customer leverage. Consequently, customers were a positive influence on Firm 2's pursuit of competitive advantage. Finally, category C is a catch-all category for cases in which competitive advantage is neither unambiguously positively or negatively affected by customers. Firm 17 (computer software) provides such an example. Customers often had placed bespoke orders which made their leverage limited as substitution was impossible, but they were very price sensitive, and haggled about price, because they were highly technically informed. We will now consider *seriatim* the analysis of competitive advantage and extended rivalry in low, medium and high concentration markets, respectively.

2.   LOW CONCENTRATION

Those firms operating in low concentration industries could be regarded as monopolistically competitive in that they faced stiff competition from a large number of similar small rivals, all producing similar products and commanding insignificant market shares. Product differentiation was generally mild, and significant excess capacity was the norm. Moreover, entry and exit barriers (*e.g.*, capital requirements and product differentiation) tended to be low and were easily overcome. Notwithstanding the admirable growth experienced over three years in terms of assets and employees by Firm 10 (industrial cleaning) and Firm 30 (wine distribution), most struggled to achieve competitive advantage (as one would expect with such low entry and exit barriers). Despite their general difficulty in generating notable competitive advantage, these firms [with the exception of Firm 5 (knitwear manufacturer)] indicated that their suppliers were a positive competitive force. Generally, these firms in low concentration markets expressed an awareness of the large number of suppliers who were willing to offer *similar* (if not standardized) products or inputs of like quality and price. Switching costs tended to be low, so that in some cases choosing a different supplier was, as one owner-manager observed, 'as easy as picking up the telephone'. Nevertheless, these firms tended not to 'play-off' suppliers against one another and chose to sustain stable relations with particular suppliers. Quick and reliable delivery coupled with easy credit terms were the hallmark of chosen suppliers. Keeping inventory costs at a bare minimum and optimizing cash flows were identified as the principal concerns of these firms. The threat of forward integration was perceived as absent, perhaps due to the suppliers' recognition that their firms were competing in low concentration markets where survival, not competitive advantage, was the primary objective.

Interestingly, only Firm 10 (industrial cleaning) and Firm 30 (wine distribution), who were the most successful of the new firms in low concentration markets, seemed to have a keen awareness of how substitutes could and did affect their own products. Firm 30, the wine distributor, gained access to professional research studies concerning anticipated changes or trends in the consumption of alcoholic and related beverages (*e.g.*, beer, wine coolers, bottled water and wine). These results were pored over and analyzed before committing the firm to wine. Firm 10 (industrial cleaning) countered the emergence of new industrial cleaning substitutes with strategies involving greater salesmanship and promotional activity. The other firms, rightly or wrongly, took a more cavalier approach to substitutes, contending that they were not a threatening competitive force, given the bespoke nature of their product or the perceived inferiority of known substitutes. No firm enjoyed the luxury of having customers who exerted little bargaining leverage *and* had low price sensitivity. Far from it, customers tended to be sophisticated in terms of their knowledge of the market and their use of bargaining power. Often these customers were large, well-established firms, which were capable of providing high-volume orders and steady trade for these new firms. The downside of this relationship is that concentration of customers increases their bargaining power. For example, Firm 9, an auto repairer, admitted that one large auto dealer provided 'almost half of total trade', and felt this conferred bargaining leverage on the dealer. Moreover, several of the firms voiced real concern over the perceived capability of some customers to backward integrate. Even though they have yet to do so, their capacity to do so demonstrably increases bargaining leverage.

The key to countering significant customer bargaining leverage was generally thought to be to pay close attention to product and service reliability, as well as to nurture personal relationships with customers. Over time it is necessary to expand the customer base and become less reliant on particular customers (*i.e.*, to consciously seek to reduce customer concentration). Given the generally high degree of customer leverage, customers could well be expected to be price sensitive. However, unique circumstances in the cases of Firms 9 (auto repairs), 13 (holiday tours) and 61 (theatrical props) seemed to moderate this anticipated price sensitivity. Specifically, these new firms were able to impress their main customers of their products' high value-added. Also, it was often the case that their primary customers ran profitable businesses. They regarded the new small firms' products as contributing an insignificant cost relative to their total costs and hence as having little effect on their profitability. Of course, given their strong bargaining leverage, if any of these positive factors were notably altered, customers would be likely to adjust quickly to these new circumstances, increasing rapidly their sensitivity to price variations.

3.   MEDIUM CONCENTRATION

The new small firms operating in medium concentration markets recognize and greatly respect the market dominance of much larger and more established firms. Indeed, new firms in the 'competitive fringe' are content to play the role of niche players, thereby gaining a fair degree of immunity from the competitive pressures the dominant firms could in principle exert. They are largely ignored by the dominant firms, provided there remains a willingness to satisfy small and specialized ('bespoke') volume demands. These firms have higher capital and proprietary knowledge requirements than those firms in the low concentration cases. These create barriers to entry of a particularly tangible variety, given the manufacturing base of these new firms. A combination of entry barriers and the fringe/dominant firm market structure imply that in medium concentration markets firms tend to achieve better competitive advantage (as indicated in Table 1). They are clearly benefitting in some measure from the market power exerted by the dominant firms.[5]

Unlike the generally positive influence of suppliers on new firms operating in low concentration markets, these firms' suppliers have a mixed influence. Firms 25 (electronics) and 52 (fencing manufacturing) viewed their suppliers as a positive influence on competitive advantage, because of the low concentration of suppliers and virtually non-existent switching costs. Also, their respective suppliers treated Firms 25 and 52 well because of the large orders they usually placed. Despite having a recognized ability to 'play-off' suppliers against one another, this was typically more of a threat than an actual choice of strategy. These firms tried to enhance suppliers' loyalty with repeat purchases, thinking this was a better means of achieving optimal pricing and service. On the other hand, Firms 11 (food manufacturing), 17 (computer software), 34 (bulk bags manufacturing) and (to a lesser extent) 54 (printing) admitted to being rather dependent on particular suppliers. They felt that forward integration on the part of suppliers was a genuine threat. Suppliers recognized how important their products were both to these new firms' own products in particular and to the healthy growth of their markets in general. This enabled them to limit, in some measure, the pursuit of competitive advantage by the new firms they supplied.

The threat of substitutes was considered negligible, if not entirely absent, due to either pro-active policies on the part of the firms to counter the threat or the conservative nature of customers. Some customers expressed a consistent preference for traditional materials used in the manufacture of the products (*e.g.*, chestnut for fencing). Firms 17 (computer software), 25 (electronics) and 34 (bulk bag manufacturing) were, by contrast, acutely aware of their customers' changing needs, and even tried to anticipate them. These firms competed for market share and technical excellence and what Porter (1990) graphically describes as 'bragging rights'. They win these rights by a willingness to change constantly, be it painfully, to achieve competitive advantage. The changes they undertake often involve mundane and incremental innovations - but with just enough novelty to maintain a competitive 'edge'. As a result, they tended to thrive on actually *creating* substitutes. Firms 11 (foods), 52 (fencing) and 54 (printing), however, provided basic, traditional high-quality products which over time had consistently been proved to provide a higher value-added/price ratio as compared to substitutes, if and when they presented themselves.

The extent of significant customer bargaining power is less for new small firms in medium concentration markets compared to those in low concentration markets. Indeed, no firm in medium concentration markets confronted customers who both exerted strong bargaining leverage *and* displayed high price sensitivity. Firms 17 (computer software), 25 (electronics) and 34 (bulk bag manufacturing), in fact, are successful at providing products which enhance the quality and profitability of their customers' products to the extent of reducing

---

[5]Typically, the fringe competitors - if they continue to operate in the market - will enjoy an average revenue above minimum average cost. The more efficient this fringe competitor is, the greater the mark-up. Entry into the fringe will tend to diminish this wedge between average revenue and average cost, but barriers to entry will limit this tendency. See Reid (1977) for a complete mathematical analysis of the dominant firm/competitive fringe model covering these and other results.

price sensitivity and limiting bargaining power on the part of customers. Close customer relations, flexibility in meeting precise product demands and 'quick turnaround' on delivery are important contributory factors. Consequently, switching costs tend to be high and the threat of backward integration by customers is minimal. Regarding Firms 11 (food manufacturing), 52 (fencing manufacturing) and 54 (printing), the competitive pressure exerted by customers is mixed. Consider, for example, the case of Firm 11 (foods). Whilst enjoying a low level of customer concentration (with no dependence on any one customer firm), customer switching costs tend to be low and customers are sensitive to different product aspects (*e.g.*, quality, delivery and, of course, price). In short, Firm 11 finds it difficult to be 'all things to all customers'.

4.   HIGH CONCENTRATION

Firms 2 (security blankets), 15 (cosmetics) and 32 (acrobatic aircraft) are all considered to compete in high concentration markets. This is largely due to fortuitous and perhaps exceptional circumstances.[6] These firms compete directly with a few very large and established firms by targeting certain market segments. Entry and exit barriers (*e.g.*, patent protection, absence of channel access, highly technical knowledge and significant strategic stakes) exist to such an extent that a 'competitive fringe' is apparently absent (or at least ignored). Despite these considerable (and very telling) structural attributes, extended rivals nevertheless further illuminate (if not dictate in the case of Firm 32) the extent of competitive advantage in these firms. Firms 2 (security blankets) and 32 (acrobatic aircraft) face extremely concentrated suppliers because of the very specialized nature of their products. They require highly technical (sometimes even prototype) inputs from their suppliers. Both firms admitted to relying on just one supplier for some inputs. On the one hand, firm 32, in fact, after experiencing a six-month stoppage in production due to the inability of key suppliers to deliver, seriously considered backward integration. Such delays ultimately forced the firm to cease operations altogether. On the other hand, Firm 15 (cosmetics) purchased 70 per cent (by value) of its retail products, by agreement, from its franchisor. Furthermore, this firm enjoyed a low concentration of suppliers for the remaining 30 per cent of its retail products. In fact, Firm 15 in conjunction with other franchisees could exert a powerful influence on suppliers, thus limiting the influence of suppliers, as 'extended rivals', on the pursuit of competitive advantage.

All three firms supplied products or services that maintained superior value-added/price ratios compared to substitutes. Firm 15 (cosmetics), although recognizing close substitutes, offered similar products at the high-quality end of the market, but at a considerably lower price. Moreover, it had been a market innovator in emphasizing the use of natural ingredients and committing a share of its profits to the support of environmental concerns, thus creating a first-mover advantage in reputation which proved significant in enhancing its compe-

---

[6]Firm 15 is a special form of new firm, being a franchise operation. Franchising has been a particularly popular, and successful, vehicle for the 'entrepreneurial event' of new firm inception. See Dnes (1992) for a modern economic analysis.

titive advantage. To a lesser, but nevertheless important, extent the emphasis on natural or traditional inputs to the production processes by Firms 2 (security blankets) and 32 (acrobatic aircraft) were considered necessary in staving-off the negative influence of substitutes on competitive advantage. As might be expected of high concentration markets, customers are very insensitive to price and lacking in bargaining power. To a large extent this leads to a form of dependence which is reflected in customers' attitudes. Their perception is typically that alternative products have significantly lower value-added/price ratios. Moreover, in the cases of Firms 2 (security blankets) and 15 (cosmetics) the products' costs relative to the customers' total costs are insignificant, which helps in sustaining price insensitivity. Firm 2, however, did admit that losing just one major customer could be problematic in the sense of denting its current significant competitive advantage. It was hoped, however, that as long as its customers regarded its supplier's products as 'indispensable', they would not realize, let alone attempt to exert, their potential for bargaining leverage.

V.   Final Remarks

Common sense and observation alone may be enough to at least suggest that focusing on the strategic behavior of the new small firm holds some promise of understanding its performance. However, to go beyond this, it is vital for the researcher to examine first-hand (and often) the complex reality of the new firm and its environment.[7] Reid (1990: 276), has argued that there is a genuine ignorance about what makes small firms tick, compared to large firms. Therefore, overcoming the paucity of data on *individual* small firms must be a research priority. This chapter aims to advance that research agenda. Of course, the way in which one uses theory must be modified from the parsimonious, aesthetically elegant, but simplified models of positive economic theory to the complex, sometimes inelegant, but more realistic models of *grounded* economic theory. It was found, following the suggestion of Teece and Winter (1984), that Michael Porter's competitive strategy framework provides a suitable vehicle for this exercise in grounded economic theory. Specifically, it was possible to identify and to 'fill' the categories of *extended rivals* (be they suppliers, producers of potential substitutes or customers). Furthermore, it proved possible to use these categories to provide what we believe to be a convincing account of the pursuit and accomplishment (to a greater or lesser degree) of competitive advantage by these new small firms.

Our findings are that the most successful pursuit of competitive advantage

---

[7]Oskar Morgenstern (1963), in his provocative (yet inspiring) classic *On the Accuracy of Economic Observations*, persuasively argues for economists to be wary of data and 'observations' in terms of their collection and treatment. Hence, economists are urged to be directly and closely involved in the design of field work instrumentation, if not the field work itself. Only then can the data be properly assessed and merit any genuine trust. Morgenstern (1963: 304) himself states that the economist "ought to be in intimate touch with the 'facts', 'get his hands dirty', in order to appreciate the very great difficulties encountered even with routine measurements. The difficulties vary from case to case... . Therefore his [*i.e.*, the economist's] contact ought to be a continuing one".

occurs in small-numbers competition in significant fragmented markets and the least successful in atomistic, imperfectly competitive, insignificant niche markets. An intermediate case exists in which unique features dictate the success with which competitive advantage is achieved. In the method employed one weighs up the evidence more as one would in clinical medicine as opposed to, say, laboratory physics. But given that economics is a behavioral science in which laboratory methods are rarely available, we hope that our 'grounded' approach reaches new conclusions and provides novel insights which are not possible with more traditional research methods. Of course, the theoretical approach adopted must sacrifice the aesthetic advantages of simplified models in favor of greater flexibility and diversity.[8] Finally, it is hoped the cross-site analysis of primary data in this chapter has served to identify some discernable general tendencies concerning the interaction of the new small firm and its extended rivals. And, as a result, a richer insight and appreciation of the new small firms's quest for competitive advantage has been proffered. Further analysis of the evidence as it pertains to other aspects of the Porter framework (*e.g.*, value chain analysis and defensive strategies) remains the consideration of future work.[9]

References

Berle, A.A. and Means, G.C. (1933) *The Modern Corporation and Private Property*, New York, Mac-Millan.

Dnes, A.W. (1992) *Franchising: A Case-Study Approach*, Aldershot, Avebury.

Jacobsen, L.R. (1986) *Entrepreneurship and Competitive Strategy in the New Small Firm: An Empirical Investigation*, Ph.D. Thesis, Department of Economics, University of Edinburgh.

Jacobsen, L.R., Reid G.C. and Anderson M.E. (1992) 'Industrial Concentration and Competitive Advantage in the New Firm', *Atlantic Economic Society* (Best Paper Proceedings) **2**, 143-147.

Morgenstern, O. (1963) *On the Accuracy of Economic Observations*, Princeton, N.J., Princeton University Press.

Porter, M. (1980) *Competitive Strategy*, New York, Free Press.

Porter, M. (1985) *Competitive Advantage*, New York, Free Press.

Porter, M. (1990) *The Competitive Advantage of Nations*, New York, Free Press.

Reid, G.C. (1977) 'Comparative Statics of the Partial Monopoly Model', *Scottish Journal of Political Economy* **24**, 153-162.

Reid, G.C. (1987a) *Theories of Industrial Organisation*, New York, Basil Blackwell.

Reid, G.C. (1987b) 'Applying Field Research Techniques to the Business Enterprise', *International Journal of Social Economics* **14**, 3-25.

Reid, G.C. (1990) 'The Research Agenda for Small Business Economics', *Journal of Economic Surveys* **4**, 275-85.

Reid, G.C. (1991) 'Staying in Business', *International Journal of Industrial Organization,* **9**, 545-556.

Reid, G.C. (1993) *Small Business Enterprise*, London, Routledge.

Reid, G.C. and Jacobsen, L.R. (1988) *The Small Entrepreneurial Firm*, Aberdeen, Aberdeen University Press.

Reid, G.C., Jacobsen, L.R. and Anderson, M.E. (1993) *Profiles in Small Business*, London, Routled-

---

[8]Teece and Winter (1984) made this very argument about Michael Porter and his competitive strategy framework.

[9]A more complete assessment of the primary source data as it pertains to the Porter (1980, 1985 and 1990) competitive advantage/competitive strategy framework is found in a forthcoming volume by the authors (Reid, Jacobsen and Anderson, 1993).

ge.

Teece, D. (1984) 'Economic Analysis and Strategic Management', *California Management Review* **26**, 87-110.

Teece, D. and Winter, S. (1984) 'The Limits of Neoclassical Theory in Management Education', *American Economic Review* **74**, 116-21.

PART IV

COMPETITION OVER TIME

Entry and Exit Processes

Part IV focuses on empirical studies into the dynamics of firm behavior in industries. So, the studies in Part IV contribute to answering the question how competition evolves over time. Particularly, Chapters 14 to 17 deal with the issue of entry and/or exit processes. On the basis of longitudinal datasets the contributions focus on explaining the rates of success - and thus failure - of (new) firms in the face of dynamic competition in Germany (Chapter 17), Portugal (Chapter 16), The Netherlands (Chapter 15) and the U.S. (Chapter 14). Here, Chapters 14 and 16 are on the level of the national manufacturing sectors as a whole, whereas Chapters 15 and 17 concentrate on a specific industry (retailing) and specific regions, respectively.

CHAPTER 14

The Post-Entry Performance of New Firms

DAVID B. AUDRETSCH and TALAT MAHMOOD[1]
Wissenschaftszentrum Berlin für Sozialforschung, Berlin, Germany

Abstract. The purpose of this chapter is to analyze what happens to firms subsequent to their start-up. We propose a model suggesting that new firms typically start at a sub-optimal scale level of output. Their ability to survive is then determined by the gap existing between their start-up size and the Minimum Efficient Scale level of output. Based on a large longitudinal data base tracking more than 11,000 new manufacturing start-ups in the United States, we find considerable evidence supporting the dynamic view of the selection process of new firms which is at the heart of industry evolution.

I. Introduction

Nearly thirty years ago, Edwin Mansfield (1962: 1023) made a plea for a greater emphasis on intra-industry dynamics: "Because there have been so few econometric studies of the birth, growth, and death of firms, we lack even crude answers to the following basic questions regarding the dynamic processes governing an industry's structure. What are the quantitative effects of various factors on the rates of entry and exit? What have been the effects of successful innovations on a firm's growth rate? What determines the amount of mobility within an industry's size structure?". Industrial organization economists responded to Mansfield's plea with a wave of empirical studies attempting to fill this gap of knowledge in the literature about the process by which firms, plants and entire industry structures evolve over time. For example, Geroski and Schwalbach (1991) recently compiled a collection of systematic studies identifying the determinants of industry entry rates across a broad spectrum of countries. One of the more striking empirical results to emerge from a number of the country studies contained in the Geroski and Schwalbach (1991), volume was that the entry of new firms into an industry is apparently not substantially deterred in industries where capital intensity and scale economies play an important role.[2]

This relatively new finding may, in fact, be related to one of the most prevalent and consistent findings in the entire field of industrial economics - the pervasiveness and persistence of an asymmetric firm-size distribution predominated by small enterprises. Empirical studies, dating back at least to the seminal

---

[1]We would like to express our appreciation for detailed comments and suggestions from Steven Klepper, Bruce Kogut, Paul Geroski and Dennis Mueller. We are also grateful to Jianping Yang for his dilligent computational assistance. All errors and omissions remain our responsibility.

[2]Audretsch (1995), Acs and Audretsch (1989 and 1990: chapter five), Evans and Siegfried (1992) and Austin and Rosenbaum (1991), similarly find that the entry of new firms into an industry is not substantially deterred in industries where capital intensity and scale economies play an important role.

study by Simon and Bonini (1958) have identified such a skewed firm-size distribution to exist across a wide range of industries, nations and time periods. The pervasiveness of an asymmetric firm-size distribution is consistent with the observation by Weiss (1964 and 1976), Scherer (1973) and Pratten (1971) that most firms in virtually every industry are operting at a sub-optimal level of output. For example, Weiss (1991: xiv) observed that "In most industries the great majority of firms is suboptimal. In a typical industry there are, let's say, one hundred firms. Typically only about five to ten of them will be operating at the MES (minimum efficient scale) level of output, or anything like it".

Why are most firms small and why is entry not substantially deterred in the presence of scale economies? The purpose of this chapter is to resolve these seeming paradoxes. By examining the post-entry performance of new firms it is possible to shed light on the overall process of firm selection and industry evolution. In Section II of this chapter, a theory of firm selection and industry evolution is presented. At the heart of this theory is an explanation of why entrepreneurs decide to enter an industry, even when confronted by scale disadvantages. In Section III the longitudinal data base for new-firm startups in U.S. manufacturing is introduced. The post-entry performance of those new startups and their ability to survive over time is then analyzed using the hazard duration model in Section IV. Finally, Section V provides a summary and conclusion. In particular, we find considerable evidence supporting the dynamic view of the selection process of new firms which is at the heart of industry evolution. The persistence of an asymmetric firm-size distribution skewed towards small enterprises presumably reflects a continuing process of entry into industries. However, this does not at all imply that such new firms survive over a long period of time. Rather, new firms are typically engaged in the selection process, whereby the successful enterprises grow and ultimately approach or attain the optimal size, while the remainder stagnate and may ultimately be forced to cease operations. Thus, although the skewed size distribution of firms persists with remarkable stability over time, it does not appear to be a constant set of small and sub-optimal scale firms that is responsible for this skewness.

II.   Firm Selection and Industry Evolution

Why should entrepreneurs start a new firm? The traditional model in industrial organization offers one answer: entry occurs because profits in excess of the long-run equilibrium profit rate prevail in the industry. That is, as Geroski (1989) characterizes the underlying motivation for entry,

(1) $E = a[\Pi - \Pi^*(BE)]$,

where E represents entry; a is a rate parameter, Π represents the actual profit rate realized by firms in the industry, and Π^* represents the long-run equilibrium rate of profit, after controlling for the extent of barriers to entry BE. According to this model, the product, production technology, inputs and input prices all remain constant. Entry is about business as usual - it is just that the entrants provide more of it. Thus, entry serves an equilibrating function in the market, in that the additional output offered by the new firms restores the levels of price and profitability back to their equilibrium levels.

A different answer was provided by Schumpeter (1950) who argued that new firms may be the result of an inherent *subjectivity of knowledge*. Schumpeter (1950: 132) observed that "the function of entrepreneurs is to reform or revolutionize the pattern of production by exploiting an invention or, more generally, an untried technological possibility for producing a new commodity or producing an old one in a new way. To undertake such new things is difficult and constitutes a distinct economic function, first, because they lie outside of the routine tasks which everybody understands, and secondly, because the environment resists in many ways."

That is, entrepreneurs may start new firms not merely to replicate the incumbent firm, but rather to do something different. In this sense, new firms can be viewed as *agents of change*. If there were not subjectivity of economic knowledge, there would be no need for new firms, because both managers of the incumbent firms and the inventor of an idea would reach the same valuation of the economic value of that idea. The inventor would merely transfer the idea to the incumbent firm for roughly the value of that idea. However, the greater the subjectivity of information, the greater the gap is likely to be between the evaluation of a potential innovation by the incumbent firm and by the inventor. Acs and Audretsch (1989 and 1990, Chapter five) argue that if this gap becomes large enough, entrepreneurs will tend to start a new firm rather than transfer their ideas to the incumbent enterprises. The emprical evidence clearly shows that start-up activity tends to be greater in those industries characterized by the entrepreneurial regime, or where the conditions of technological knowledge are the most subjective.

Entrepreneurs will start new firms when the gap between the expected value of their potential innovations by themselves and the incumbent firms tends to be the greatest.[3] However, because knowledge is subjective, not all inventions, or potential innovations actually become successful innovations. What happens to those new firms whose potential innovations do not materialize? The answer is, "it depends". Subsequent to entering an industry, a firm must decide whether to maintain its output (Q_{it}), expand, contract, or exit. The probability of a firm remaining in business in period t, or $P(Q_{it} > 0)$, is essentially determined by the extent to which a firm is burdened with an inherent size disadvantage, and the probability of actually innovating, a. Then,

$$(2) \ P(Q_{it} > 0) = f[a_{it}, c(Q_{it}) - c(Q_i^*)],$$

---

[3] A slightly different approach is undertaken by Jovanovic (1982) who proposes that new entrants face random costs which differ across firms. A central feature of his model is the assumption that a new firm does not know what its costs that is, its relative efficiency will be, but rather discovers this through the process of learning from its actual post-entry performance. In particular, Jovanovic (1982) assumes that entrepreneurs are unsure about their ability to manage a new start-up and therefore their prospects for success. For further extensions see Pakes and Erikson (1987) who argue that firms can actively accelerate the learning process by investing in knowledge-generating activities, such as R&D.

where $c(Q_{it})$ is the average cost of producing at a scale of output Q_i, $c(Q_i^*)$ is the average cost of producing the MES level of output or the minimum level of production required to attain the minimum average cost Q_i^*. Thus, in deciding whether to remain or exit from the industry, a firm will weigh the extent to which it is confronted by a scale disadvantage against the likelihood of innovating or otherwise growing to attain scale economies. As the firm size grows relative to the MES level of output, the more likely the firm is to decide to remain in the industry. This suggests that either an increase in the start-up size of the firm or a decrease in the MES level of output should increase the likelihood of survival. The firm's actual level of output in period t is determined by its innovative activity, A_{it}, plus some factor of its output in the previous period, $\overline{Q}_{it}$,

$$(3)\ Q_{it} = \overline{Q}_{it} + Q(A_{it}),$$

where

$$(4)\ \overline{Q}_{it} = \lambda(Q_{io} + Q_{it-1})$$

and Q_o is an autonomous level of output and λ is a factor representing the portion of the previous period's output that can be maintained in the market. Factors such as market growth presumably influence the value of λ. That is, if market growth is sufficiently high, a new firm may be able to grow enough so that $Q_{it} = Q_i^*$, even in the absence of innovative activity.

An important implication of the above process is that firms are more likely to be operating at a sub-optimal scale of output if the underlying technological conditions dictate a higher subjectivity of knowledge. If firms successfully innovate, they grow into viably-sized enterprises. If not, they will be doomed to stagnage and ultimately to exit from the industry. This suggests, just as some empirical studies have recently found that, entry and the start-up of new firms is not greatly deterred in the presence of scale economies. As long as entrepreneurs perceive that there is some prospect for growth and ultimately survival, such entry will occur. Thus, in industries where the MES is high, firms not able to grow and attain the MES level of output would presumably be forced to exit from the industry, resulting in a relatively low likelihood of survival. In industries characterized by a low MES, neither the need for growth nor the consequences of its absence are as severe, so higher survival rates would be expected. In industries where the subjectivity of knowledge is particularly high that is, in highly innovative industries, more entrepreneurs may be motivated to start a new firm. In such industries the likelihood of the firm surviving would presumably be lower.

We analyze the post-entry performance of new firms through the lens of the hazard duration model, which was first proposed by Cox (1972 and 1975) and later by Kiefer (1988). The partial likelihood model has the advantage of compensating for censored observations in the estimation procedure and of not imposing any parametric form on the precise time to failure.

III.   Measurement Issues

The greatest constraint in analyzing the post-entry performance of firms has been the lack of longitudinal data sets consisting of individual plants and firms that identify the actual start-up and closure dates. While Dunne, Roberts, and Samuelson (1988 and 1989), Audretsch (1991), Evans (1987), Hall (1987) and Phillips and Kirchhoff (1989) all had access to such a longitudinal data set, none of these studies explicitly estimated the hazard rate model. One reason why the U.S. Bureau of Census data employed by Dunne, Roberts, and Samuelson do not lend themselves to estimation of the hazard model, is that while observations over time are available, they are identified only at five-year intervals. Thus, we employ a data set which provides bi-annual observations on firms and plants - the U.S. Small Business Administration's Small Business Data Base (SBDB). The data base is derived from the Dun and Bradstreet (DUNS) market identifier file (DMI), which provides a virtual census on about 4.5 million U.S. business establishments every other year between 1976 and 1986.

While the raw Dun and Bradstreet data have been subject to considerable criticism (FitzRoy, 1989), the SBDB data have been adjusted by the U.S. Small Business Administration to clean up the raw data in the original DMI files. Several important studies have compared the SBDB data with analogous measures from the establishment data of the U.S. Census of Manufactures (Acs and Audretsch, 1990: Chapter two) and from the establishment and employ-ment records of the Bureau of Labor Statistics (Brown and Phillips, 1989) and have concluded that the SBDB data are generally consistent with these other major data bases providing observations on firms and plants. The essential building block of the SBDB is the establishment, which is defined as as particu-lar economic entity operating at a specific and single geographic location. While some establishments are legally tied to parent firms through either a branch or subsidiary relationship, other establishments are independent and therefore are firms (enterprises) in their own right. The data base links the ownership of all establishments to any parent firms, thereby enabling the performance of establishments which are independent firms to be distinguished from those which are branches and subsidiaries of parent firms. Besides a detailed identifi-cation of the ownership structure of each establishment, the USELM file of the SBDB links the performance of each establishment within two-year intervals beginning in 1976 and ending in 1986, thereby tracking each establishment over what constitutes a ten-year longitudinal data base.

As Table 1 shows, the mean size of the cohort of new firms in 1976 was about eight employees, with a fairly large standard deviation.[4] The mean size of new start-ups was somewhat larger for those firms still existing in 1982, 1984, and 1986 than for those firms ceasing to exist within the first four years of being established. That is, those firms surviving for a longer period of time tend to exhibit a larger initial start-up size than those firms ceasing operations within

---

[4]It should be noted that there are actually more new-firm start-ups in 1976 recorded in the SBDB, but only those records containing full information about firm size in all of the years could be used.

Table 1.   Evolution of mean firm size (employment), according to survival status of cohort (standard deviation in parentheses)

Cohort	N	Year					
		1976	1978	1980	1982	1984	1986
New-firm start-ups in 1976	11314	7.63 (11.68)	--	--	--	--	--
Firms still existing in 1978	8266	7.51 (11.74)	10.70 (19.61)	--	--	--	--
Firms still existing in 1980	6165	7.27 (11.68)	10.57 (19.74)	12.68 (23.69)	--	--	--
Firms still existing in 1982	4045	7.92 (12.45)	11.80 (20.29)	14.65 (25.05)	15.95 (28.02)	--	--
Firms still existing in 1984	3099	7.98 (12.53)	12.15 (20.22)	15.63 (26.69)	17.23 (29.74)	19.27 (34.99)	--
Firms still existing in 1986	2509	7.94 (12.48)	12.01 (19.76)	15.32 (25.91)	17.05 (29.13)	19.32 (34.64)	20.95 (37.23)

several years subsequent to establishment. Table 1 also suggests that the mean size of firms in existence throughout the sample period tends to be greater than those not surviving. For example, in 1978 the group of firms surviving throughout the entire sample period exhibited a mean size of 12.01, which is considerably greater than the mean size of 10.70 for all firms still in existence as of 1978. In fact, firms that survived until 1984 and 1986 were noticeably larger

Table 2.   Mean firm growth rate (%) over time, according to survival status of cohort[a]

Cohort	N	Period					
		1976-78	1976-80	1976-82	1976-82	1976-84	1976-86
New-firm existing in 1978	8266	12.48	--	--	--	--	--
Firms still existing in 1980	6165	45.39	74.42 (19.61)	--	--	--	--
Firms still existing in 1982	4045	48.99	84.97 (24.15)	101.39 (8.87)	--	--	--
Firms still existing in 1984	3099	52.26	95.86 (28.64)	115.91 (10.24)	141.48 (11.84)	--	--
Firms still existing in 1986	2509	51.26	92.95 (27.56)	114.74 (11.29)	143.32 (13.31)	163.85 (8.44)	--

[a] Growth rate (%) from previous period listed in parentheses.

than those ceasing operations before 1984 in every year for which a comparison is possible. Not only does the initial start-up size of surviving firms tend to be larger, but as Table 2 shows, the growth rate also tends to be higher. That is, between 1976 and 1980 the employment growth of all firms averaged 74.42 percent. However, for those firms that survived throughout the entire sample period (1976-1986), the mean growth rate between 1976 and 1980 was substantially greater, 92.95 percent. There are two important trends which should be emphasized in Table 2. First, the growth rate in each sub-period of time tends to be greater for those firms surviving the longest. Second, the growth rates tend to diminish over time for each cohort of firms still in existence. Taken together, Tables 1 and 2 suggest two important features that are common among firms still surviving a decade subsequent to establishment - they tend to be slightly larger when they start and they tend to grow faster, particularly within the first few years subsequent to establishment (Audretsch and Mahmood, 1995).

IV. Empirical Results

The semi-parametric hazard duration model is used to test the hypothesis that the exposure to risk of new establishments is shaped by the extent to which scale economies play a role in the relevant industry, the initial start-up size of the establishment, market growth, and the technological environment. Measurement of the MES has proven to be challenging at best. Here we adapt the standard Comanor-Wilson (1967) proxy for measuring MES, which is defined as the mean size of the largest plants in each industry accounting for one-half of the industry value-of-shipments in 1977. This measure is derived from the Census of Manufactures of the U.S. Bureau of the Census. While the Comanor-Wilson measure is crude, it has proven in numerous studies to at least reflect the extent to which scale economies play an important role in an industry (Scherer and Ross, 1990). This MES measure is expected to exert a positive influence on the rate of hazard confronting new establishments.

The most reliable and consistent measure of the size of the establishment when it was founded is the number of employees. As already explained, a larger start-up size is expected to reduce the hazard rate. Market growth is measured as the percentage change in the total sales of the four-digit standard industrial classification (SIC) industry within which the establishment operated between 1976, the year that all of the establishments were founded, and 1986, which is the final year of analysis. This measure is derived from the annual Survey of Manufactures of the U.S. Bureau of the Census. Market growth is expected to increase the growth potential of new establishments, and therefore should increase their ability to survive. That is, all boats should be lifted by a rising tide. To measure the degree to which new technological knowledge in an industry is subjective, the innovation rate - defined as the number of innovations in 1982 divided by industry employment - is used.[5] The innovate rate is em-

---

[5]The total innovation rate was introduced by Acs and Audretsch (1987, 1988 and 1990). It is based on a direct measure of innovative output.

ployed rather than the absolute number of innovations in order to standardize the amount of innovative activity by the size of the industry. Presumably, an industry with more innovative activity can be characterized by higher technological uncertainty and therefore greater subjectivity.

Using the 7070 manufacturing establishments founded in 1976 for which compatible industry characteristics could be matched, the hazard duration rate was estimated using the semi-parametric model described previously. The first equation in Table 3 shows the regression rates for the estimated hazard function based on all new plants established in 1976. The hazard rate is estimated only for new firms in the second equation. In the third equation the hazard function for new branches and subsidiaries opened by existing enterprises is estimated. The empirical results indicate that, as expected, the likelihood of survival tends to be reduced in industries where ecnomies of scale play an important role. By contrast, a larger start-up size serves to elevate the likelihood of survival. New plants and firms in highly innovative industries tend to be confronted with a lower likelihood of survival, although the t-ratio is not high enough to be considered statistically significant.

Table 3.   Regression results for hazard duration model: 1976-1986[a]

Independent Variables	All Plants (1)	New Firms (2)	Branches & Subsidiaries (3)	All Plants	
				High-Tech (4)	Low Tech (5)
Minimum Efficient Scale	0.0051 (3.480)	0.0053 (3.500)	-0.0002 (-0.028)	-0.0017 (-0.674)	0.0158 (4.390)
Start-Up Size	-0.0014 (-3.780)	-0.0027 (-3.753)	-0.0007 (-1.617)	-0.0006 (-0.685)	-0.0016 (-2.910)
Growth	0.1273 (0.622)	0.1727 (0.828)	-0.9561 (-0.890)	-1.2840 (-1.270)	-1.0900 (-1.600)
Total Innovation Rate	0.0325 (1.125)	0.0401 (1.338)	-0.0343 (-0.302)	-	-
# of Obs.	8109	7717	392	881	3474
Chi-Square	32.5	35.6	3.89	2.6	30.3
Log of likelihood	-46783.	-44364.	-1417.	-3945.	-18428.

[a] T-statistics in paranthesis.

The results also indicate that, just as the likelihood of survival confronting new branches and subsidiaries opened by existing firms is not influenced by the extent of scale economies in the industry, there is little evidence suggesting that an increase in their start-up size facilitates the ability to survive.

The hazard rate confronting new establishments in high-technology industries is estimated in the fourth equation and that for low-technology industries is estimated in the last equation in Table 3. High-technology industries are defined as those four-digit standard industrial classification (SIC) industries where the R&D/sales ratio exceeds five percent. By contrast, low-technology industries are defined as those four-digit SIC industries where the R&D/sales ratio is less than one percent.[6] The likelihood of survival confronting new establishments in low-technology industries is apparently lower in the presence of substantial scale economies. Similarly, a higher start-up size tends to reduce the hazard rate. However, in high-technology industries, neither the Minimum Efficient Scale measure nor the initial start-up size significantly influences the likelihood of survival for new establishments. These results suggest that the greater subjectivity of knowledge found in high technology tends to spur the start-up of new firms, even in the presence of high scale economies.

V.   Conclusion

The results of this chapter shed at least some light on the seeming paradox posed by the findings in the industrial organization literature that (1) the bulk of firms in an industry are not only very small, but also sufficiently small so that they are operating at a sub-optimal scale of output in most industries, and (2) entrepreneurs are apparently not deterred from starting new firms even in industries where scale economies play an important role. A dynamic view of the process of firm selection and industry evolution is that new firms typically start at a very small scale of output. Because this level of output may be sub-optimal, the firm must grow in order to survive. The empirical evidence presented in this chapter supports such a dynamic view of the evolutionary nature of industries, because the propensity for new firms to survive tends to be shaped by the extent to which there is a gap between the MES level of output and the size of the firm. As this gap increases, the likelihood of any new firm surviving tends to decrease.

Lucas (1978) and Jovanovic (1993) attempt to explain the pervasiveness of small enteprises in the firm-size distribution with a static theory. But viewed through a dynamic lens, the often-observed asymmetric size distribution of firms becomes more understandable. According to this view, the frequent observation of industries dominanted by small firms does not mean that it is the same set of small firms being observed over time. Rather, new firms are engaged in the process of selection, whereby only the successful enterprises are able to grow and ultimately survive. That is, the persistence of an asymmetric firm-size distribution skewed towards small enterprises presumably reflects a continuing process of entry into industries and not necessarily the surivival of such small and sub-optimal enterprises over a long period of time.

---

[6]The classification of industries by R&D/sales is from the National Science Foundation (1987) for the year 1980.

References

Acs, Z.J. and Audretsch, D.B. (1993) *Small Firms and Entrepreneurship: An East-West Perspective*, Cambridge, Cambridge University Press.
Acs, Z.J. and Audretsch, D.B. (1990) *Innovation and Small Firms*, Cambridge, MA, MIT Press.
Acs, Z.J. and Audretsch, D.B. (1989) 'Small-Firm Entry in U.S. Manufacturing', *Economica* **56**, 255-265.
Acs, Z.J. and Audretsch, D.B. (1988) 'Innovation in Large and Small Firms: An Empirical Analysis', *American Economic Review* **78**, 678-690.
Acs, Z.J. and Audretsch, D.B. (1987) 'Innovation, Market Structure and Firm Size," *Review of Economics and Statistics* **69**, 567-575.
Audretsch, D.B. (1991) 'New-Firm Survival and the Technological Regime', *Review of Economics and Statistics* **60**, 441-450.
Audretsch, D.B. (1995) *Innovation and Industry Evolution*, Cambridge, MIT Press.
Audretsch, D.B. and Mahmood, T. (1995) 'New Firm Survival: New Results Using a Hazard Function', *Review of Economics and Statistics* **64**, forthcoming.
Austin, J.S. and Rosenbaum, D.I. (1990) 'The Determinants of Entry and Exit Rates into U.S. Manufacturing Industries', *Review of Industrial Organization* **5**, 211-223.
Brown, H.S. and Phillips, B.D. (1989) 'Comparison Between Small Business Data Base (USEEM) and Bureau of Labor Statistics (BLS) Employment Data: 1978-1986', *Small Business Economics* **1**, 273-284.
Cable, J. and Schwalbach, J. (1991) 'International Comparisons of Entry and Exit', in Geroski, P. and Schwalbach, J. (eds), *Entry and Market Contestability: An International Comparison*, Oxford, Basil Blackwell, 257-281.
Comanor, W.S. and Wilson, T.A. (1967) 'Advertising, Market Structure, and Performance', *Review of Economics and Statistics* **49**, 423-440.
Cox, D.R. (1975) 'Partial Likelihood', *Biometrics* **62**, 269-275.
Cox, D.R. (1972) 'Regression Modells and Life Tables', *Journal of the Royal Statistical Society* **34**, 187-220.
Dunne, T., Roberts, M.J. and Samuelson, L. (1989) 'The Growth and Failure of U.S. Manufacturing Plants', *Quarterly Journal of Economics* **104**, 671-698.
Dunne, T., Roberts, M.J. and Samuelson, L. (1988) 'Patterns of Firm Entry and Exit in U.S. Manufacturing Industries', *Rand Journal of Economics* **19**, 495-515.
Evans, D.S. (1987) 'The Relationship Between Firm Growth, Size and Age: Estimates for 100 Manufacturing Industries', *Journal of Industrial Economics* **35**, 567-581.
Evans, L.B. and Siegfried, J.J. (1992) 'Entry and Exit in United States Manufacturing Industries from 1977 to 1982', in Audretsch, D.B. and Siegfried, J.J. (eds), *Empirical Studies in Industrial Organization: Essays in Honor of Leonard W. Weiss*, Boston, Kluwer Academic Publishers.
Fitzroy, F.R. (1989) 'Firm Size, Efficiency and Employment: A Review Article', *Small Business Economics* **1**, 75-80.
Geroski, P.A. (1989) 'The Interaction Between Domestic and Foreign Based Entrants', Audretsch, D.B., Sleuwaegen, L. and Yamawaki, H. (eds), *The Convergence of International and Domestic Markets*, Amsterdam, North-Holland, 59-83.
Hall, B.H. (1987) 'The Relationship Between Firm Size and Firm Growth in the U.S. Manufacturing Sector', *Journal of Industrial Economics* **35**, 583-605.
Jovanovic, B. (1993) 'Entrepreneurial Choice When People Differ in Their Management and Labor Skills', *Small Business Economics* **5**, forthcoming.
Jovanovic, B. (1982) 'Selection and Evolution of Industry', *Econometrica* **50**, 649-670.
Kiefer, N.M. (1988) 'Economic Duration Data and Hazard Functions', *Journal of Economic Literature* **26**, 646-679.
Lucas, R.E. Jr. (1978) 'On the Size Distribution of Business Firms', *Bell Journal of Economics* **9**, 508-523.
National Science Foundation (1987), *Science & Engineering Indicators - 1987*, Washington, D.C., U.S. Government Printing Office.
Pakes, A. and Ericson, R. (1987) 'Empirical Implications of Alternative Models of Firm Dynamics', Unpublished, Department of Economics, University of Wisconsin-Madison.
Phillips, B.D. and Kirchhoff, B.A. (1989) 'Formation, Growth and Survival: Small Firm Dynamics in

the U.S. Economy', *Small Business Economics* **1**, 65-74.

Pratten, C.F. (1971) *Economies of Scale in Manufacturing Industry*, Cambridge, Cambridge University Press.

Scherer, F.M. (1973) 'The Determinants of Industry Plant Sizes in Six Nations', *Review of Economics and Statistics* **55**, 135-145.

Scherer, F.M. and Ross, D. (1990) *Industrial Market Structure and Economic Performance*, Third edition, Boston, Houghton Mifflin.

Schumpeter, J.A. (1950) *Capitalism, Socialism and Democracy*, Third edition, New York, NY, Harper and Row.

Simon, H.A. and Bonini, C.P. (1958) 'The Size Distribution of Business Firms', *American Economic Review* **48**, 607-617.

Weiss, L.W. (1991) *Structure, Conduct, and Performance*, in Audretsch, D.B. and Yamawaki, H. (eds), New York, New York University Press.

Weiss, L.W. (1976) 'Optimal Plant Scale and the Extent of Suboptimal Capacity', in Masson, R.T. and Qualls, P.D. (eds), *Essays on Industrial Organization in Honor of Joe S. Bain*, Cambridge, MA, Ballinger, 126-134.

Weiss, L.W. (1964) 'The Survival Technique and the Extent of Suboptimal Capacity', *Journal of Political Economy* **72**, 246-261.

CHAPTER 15

Profitability and Number of Firms: Their Dynamic Interaction in Dutch Retailing

MARTIN CARREE and ROY THURIK[1]
Centre for Advanced Small Business Economics, Erasmus University Rotterdam and Department of Fundamental Research, EIM Small Business Research and Consultancy, Zoetermeer, The Netherlands

Abstract. High profitability attracts new firms, whereas a rise in the number of firms creates a pressure on profitability. The purpose of this study is to investigate this dynamic interaction between profitability and number of firms in the Dutch retail sector. A two-equation error-correction model is developed and tested using a panel data set of 36 Dutch shoptypes covering the 1978-1988 period.

I. Introduction

Dynamic market modeling has received broad attention in industrial economics (see Nelson and Winter, 1982; Eliasson, 1984 and 1991; Geroski and Masson, 1987; Carlsson, 1989; Schmalensee, 1989; Klepper and Graddy, 1990; and Mueller, 1990). This study is concerned with a central theme in this literature: the development of market structure and performance over time. In fact, we investigate the growth, or decline, of both profit levels and number of firms over time in the retail sector. We seek to provide answers to questions like: What is the effect of an increase in the number of firms on profitability? What is the effect of high or increasing profitability on the growth of the number of firms? What is the effect of demand growth on profitability and on the entry and exit flows in the industry? Does unemployment lead to an increase in the number of firms as unemployed are forced into entrepreneurship?

This study stands out from other studies in that it deals with the retail sector. There are several justifications for this choice.[2] First, retailing contributes strongly to the economy: for instance, in the Netherlands it accounts for about 23% of the total number of economically active enterprises and about 13% of the total labor force in the private sector in 1988 (Bode, 1990). There has however been scarce attention in industrial economics for non-manufacturing industries, let alone for the retail sector. Second, retailing is a comparatively simple entrepreneurial activity to which there are only limited entry and exit barriers. This implies that adjustment processes generated by entrepreneurs discovering and exploiting profit opportunities can be expected to have a direct

---

[1]The authors are grateful to Kees Bakker and Herman van Schaik of the EIM Small Business Research and Consultancy for providing and elaborating the data. Financial support from the Netherlands Organization for Scientific Research (NWO) is acknowledged.

[2]Clearly, the accessibility of some extensive panel data sets which have been merged for the purpose of the present analysis plays an important role in this choice.

effect in the sense that, for instance, the setting up or closing down of stores occurs within only a limited time period. Interesting evidence on the speed of the competitive and entrepreneurial process in the Dutch economy may be derived from such a low-barrier industry. Third, retailers can be expected to react in a more predictable and direct way to market incentives and disincentives than entrepreneurs in manufacturing industries. This is a consequence of the more clearly structured market environment in retailing, where elements of innovation, complex and time-consuming decision-making procedures and international competition generally play a limited role compared to manufacturing.

In an earlier study (Carree and Thurik, 1994), we used a similar dynamic market model to empirically investigate distinct competitive forces (like actual competition among incumbents, new firm competition and potential competition) and various inflationary processes (such as cost, demand and wage inflation) in the retailing sector. This study provides additional information on the speed and empirical relevance of the adjustment processes in retailing. Our model is discussed in Section II. Section III is used for a description of the data set of 36 shoptypes for the period 1978-1988. Section IV presents the empirical results. Section V is a conclusion.

II. The Dynamic Interaction between Profitability and Number of Firms

Entrepreneurial activity is a vital but elusive concept in theories of economic development and market dynamics (see Hébert and Link, 1989). The entrepreneur is the key figure both for Schumpeterians and for Neo-Austrians. There is however a fundamental difference between the Schumpeterian notion of entrepreneurship and the Neo-Austrian (that is, Kirznerian) ideas on entrepreneurship. Schumpeter takes the entrepreneur to be the innovator and thus the creator of disequilibria. For Kizner, however, the role of the entrepreneur is to discover and exploit profit opportunities leading to the kind of adjustment processes necessary to move markets toward the equilibrium state (see Kirzner, 1973 and 1979). In this study, we concentrate on entrepreneurial activity as a competitive force to adjust profits towards their long-run equilibrium levels. Hence, our model of the dynamic interaction between profitability and number of firms in retailing is based on the Kirznerian notion of entrepreneurship. This implies that we have to specify profit opportunities (market incentives) and the ways of their exploitation. For Kirzner the efficiency of the market system depends crucially upon the degree of success with which entrepreneurs discover and exploit these profit opportunities.

Two fundamental indicators for profit opportunities in an industry are the prevailing level of profitability and the market growth. Profitable and growing markets generally provide more opportunities for entrepreneurs to act successfully than declining markets with many firms experiencing losses. The exploitation of these profit opportunities can be achieved either by incumbents or by entrants into the market. Incumbents may try to enhance their competitive position by decreasing prices or increasing advertising efforts or level of service.

Entrants may find market niches or may profit from the lack of ability of incumbents to adjust to developments in market demand. Many of these entrants may use entrepreneurship as an escape out of unemployment (see Storey, 1991). High unemployment may, therefore, stimulate potential independents to enter and discourage incumbents to exit.

The model which is presented in equations (1) and (2) is of an error-correction mechanism type (see Salmon, 1982; and Gilbert, 1986).[3] Shoptypes which provide entrepreneurs high profitability are assumed to be *in error* - *i.e.*, in disequilibrium. As the entrepreneurs in this study are mainly small independents for whom profits generally equal their income (before taxes) we define excess profit (*i.e.*, the market *error*) as the difference between this profit and gross modal wage. So,

(1) $\Delta\Pi_{it}-\Delta MI_t = a_0 + a_1(\Pi_{i,t-1}-MI_{t-1}) + a_2(\Delta\Pi_{i,t-1}-\Delta MI_{t-1}) + a_3\Delta NOF_{it} +$
$a_4\Delta NOF_{i,t-1} + a_5\Delta CS_{it} + a_6\Delta\Delta CS_{it} + a_7(\Delta K_{it}-\Delta Q_{it}) + \epsilon_{1it},$

and

(2) $\Delta NOF_{it} = $ $\beta_0 + \beta_1(\Pi_{i,t-1}-MI_{t-1}) + \beta_2(\Delta\Pi_{i,t-1}-\Delta MI_{t-1}) + \beta_3\Delta CS_{i,t-1} +$
$\beta_4\Delta CS_{i,t-2} + \beta_5 UN_{t-1} + \beta_6\Delta UN_{t-1} + \beta_7\Delta NOF_{i,t-1} + \epsilon_{2it}.$

In these equations, ϵ_{1it} and ϵ_{2it} are possibly correlated random errors and the variables are *logarithms* of Π_{it} (average profit in shoptype i in year t in 1980 prices), MI_t (gross modal wage in year t in 1980 prices), NOF_{it} (number of firms in shoptype i in year t), CS_{it} (consumer spending for the product package sold in shoptype i in year t in 1980 prices), K_{it} (average value of total costs in shoptype i in year t in 1980 prices), Q_{it} (average value of sales in shoptype i in year t in 1980 prices) and UN_t (number of unemployed in 1,000 persons in year t).

Eight hypotheses concerning the signs of the parameters incorporated in this model are discussed.

HYPOTHESIS 1: $a_1 < 0$ and $a_2 > 0$.

An excess profit situation is one of instability, which attracts entrepreneurial activity not only from within the shoptype but also from diversifying firms in other shoptypes or vertically integrating wholesalers or manufacturers. This activity brings profits down: we expect a_1 to be negative.[4] We have no strong

---

[3]In Carree and Thurik (1994), the dependent variable of the profitability equation is $\Delta\Pi_{it}-\Delta Q_{it}$. Influences of distinct competitive forces on retail pricing practice and the role of retailing in the inflationary process were the major topics in that study.

[4]Empirical studies in the literature on the persistence of profits (see Mueller, 1990) usually find this effect of excess profitability on the development of profitability to be negative. There are however different opinions about the extent of this effect. Geroski and Masson (1987) find a small effect and regard the competitive process to be extremely slow, while Levy (1987) reports a strong effect with adjustment to long-run equilibrium levels in only five years.

a priori reasons to expect the lagged endogenous variable to have any effect in equation (1). Nevertheless, we incorporate this variable to allow for sustained growth or decline of profits *vis-à-vis* modal wage. Such a structural shift may be a consequence of slowly evolving revaluation of the entrepreneurial activity of shopkeepers - for example, by growing or declining managerial responsibilities. This could be a reason for a positive a_2.

HYPOTHESIS 2: $a_3 < 0$ and $a_4 > 0$.

As the number of firms grows competitive forces are expected to increase. This implies that a_3 is expected to be negative. Earlier experience with increases in the number of firms would, however, make a shoptype less sensitive to such new firm competition. A positive a_4 would be consistent with this view. An extreme situation is the one in which $a_3 = -a_4$: changes in the growth of the number of firms ($\Delta\Delta NOF_{it}$) have an effect on the development of profits *vis-à-vis* modal wage and not so much the growth of the number of firms (ΔNOF_{it}). However, we hypothesize that $a_3 < -a_4$ because we expect less recent changes in the industry structure to have a more limited effect than recent ones.

HYPOTHESIS 3: $a_5 > 0$ and $a_6 > 0$.

Growing consumer spending on retail services is assumed to lift the pressure on increases of retailers' profits: a positive a_5 is expected. We also incorporate $\Delta\Delta CS_{it}$ as indicator for unexpected demand shocks: temporary deviations from demand growth over time for specific retail services may facilitate profit increases even more. This indicates a positive value for a_6.

HYPOTHESIS 4: $a_7 < 0$.

Rises in the cost-output ratio are likely to endanger a favorable development of profit as cost shifts are likely to be passed on only partially to customers (in the same period).[5] So, we expect the parameter a_7 to be negative. In the long run, cost changes are entirely passed on in the case of a negative a_1 due to the elimination of disequilibrium by the error-correction mechanism.

HYPOTHESIS 5: $\beta_1 > 0$ and $\beta_2 > 0$.

High profits will encourage entry into a shoptype and discourage exit. The parameter β_1 is expected to be positive. Growing profits *vis-à-vis* modal wage ($\Delta\Pi_{i,t-1} - \Delta MI_{t-1}$) may also provide an incentive to enter a shoptype. This implies a positive β_2.

HYPOTHESIS 6: $\beta_3 > 0$ and $\beta_4 > 0$.

---

[5]Nooteboom, Kleijweg and Thurik (1988) using 16 Dutch shoptypes for the period 1976-1983, find that deviations from *normal costs* are passed on to customers for about fifty percent only.

Growing consumer demand provides opportunities for new entrants. Viable sub-market niches may emerge or incumbents may simply lack the ability to expand quickly enough. As speed of perception and exploitation of these opportunities for entry is unknown both $\Delta CS_{i,t-1}$ and $\Delta CS_{i,t-2}$ are incorporated. We expect both a positive β_3 and a positive β_4.

HYPOTHESIS 7: $\beta_5 > 0$ and $\beta_6 > 0$.

High and growing unemployment discourages shopkeepers to exit as both variables are indicators for poor job opportunities. It also implies that there are a large number of potential entrepreneurs: unemployed may try to become self-employed in retailing to improve upon their financial situation. Evans and Leighton (1989) present evidence that unemployed workers are more likely to enter self-employment than employees. Retailing may be an especially attractive sector for new business start-ups as financial and knowledge barriers are low. Thus, both β_5 and β_6 are expected to be positive. The change in unemployment may very well be a more adequate measure of the tension on the labor market than unemployment, because of the sustained high unemployment level in the Netherlands. Those who are already unemployed for several years may be expected not to have the same amount of entrepreneurial ability and perseverance to become self-employed as workers who have become unemployed only recently. Storey (1991) provides a survey of the studies on the effect of unemployment on new business start-ups.

HYPOTHESIS 8: $\beta_7 > 0$.

Gort and Konakayama (1982) argue that perceptions of profit opportunities are positively related to the successful experience of others in the market. This implies that entrepreneurial activity may tend to be autocorrelated: successful entry may demonstrate the attractiveness of a shoptype to entrepreneurs: a positive β_7 is expected. One might argue that some new entrants already disappear after a one-year period due to inadequate preparations and too optimistic expectations. This could disturb interpretations on the parameter β_7 as representing the demonstration effect, because a lower value for this parameter could be the result of such a correction.

III.   Data

In this study, a data set of 36 Dutch shoptypes for the period 1978-1988 is used. The source of the data is an ongoing panel of independent, mainly small Dutch retailers called *Bedrijfssignaleringssysteem* (interfirm comparison system), which is operated by the EIM Small Business Research and Consultancy in Zoetermeer. In Carree and Thurik (1994), we provide an overview of the shoptypes and the observation periods for which data for these shoptypes are available.[6] We have a total of 341 data points, while on average a data point is computed using observations from about seventy individual retail stores. The consumer spending and modal wage data are from the Central Bureau of Statistics (CBS) in Voorburg, unemployment data were retrieved from the UN Monthly Bulletin of Statistics and data on number of firms were gathered by the Central Registration Office (CRK) in The Hague. Summary statistics for the variables used in the model can be found in Table 1.

Table 1.   Summary statistics of the variables used

Variable	MIN	MAX	MEAN	STD
$\Delta\Pi_{it} - \Delta MI_{t}$	-1.13	0.99	0.037	0.262
$\Pi_{i,t-1} - MI_{t-1}$	-1.29	1.09	0.117	0.415
$\Delta\Pi_{i,t-1} - \Delta MI_{t-1}$	-1.13	0.99	0.039	0.276
ΔNOF_{it}	-0.11	0.10	-0.001	0.026
$\Delta NOF_{i,t-1}$	-0.11	0.08	-0.004	0.025
ΔCS_{it}	-0.22	0.21	0.002	0.058
$\Delta\Delta CS_{it}$	-0.29	0.19	0.006	0.062
$\Delta K_{it} - \Delta Q_{it}$	-0.19	0.17	-0.005	0.054
$\Delta CS_{i,t-1}$	-0.22	0.24	-0.004	0.064
$\Delta CS_{i,t-2}$	-0.22	0.24	-0.007	0.062
UN_{t-1}	5.32	6.71	6.262	0.496
ΔUN_{t-1}	-0.08	0.44	0.127	0.202

Note: MIN, MAX, MEAN and STD stand for minimum, maximum, mean and standard deviation.

IV.   Empirical Results

Equations (1) and (2) are estimated using Three Stages Least Squares (SAS-module SYSLIN). We provide estimation results both for *no fixed effects* (a_0 and β_0 are equal for all shoptypes) and *fixed effects* (a_0 and β_0 are allowed to differ across shoptypes). By using fixed effects we allow the long-term equilibrium relation between profits and modal wage to differ across shoptypes. It is likely that profits in shoptypes characterized by high capital requirements, high risks and high managerial responsibilities will tend to have higher long-term equilibrium values than those in shoptypes in which these are low (see Carree and Thurik, 1994). Estimation results are presented in Table 2.

We find confirmation for profit adjustment to excess profits ($a_1 < 0$). The adjustment rate (the extent of the effect of $\Pi_{i,t-1} - MI_{t-1}$ on $\Delta\Pi_{it} - \Delta MI_{t}$) is rather slow, about 10% in a one-year period, in the case shoptype-specific effects are excluded. This would imply an almost complete profit adjustment in about 30 years. However, the adjustment rate increases substantially to about 50% in a one-year period at their inclusion. This implies an almost complete profit

---

[6]Data are available for 14 shoptypes during the 1978-88 period, for 19 shoptypes during the 1982-88 period, for two shoptypes (electrical appliances, more than 25% repairs and electrical appliances, mixed assortment) during the 1982-87 period and for one shoptype (supermarkets without butcher's shop) during the 1978-83 period.

Table 2.   Estimation results

Parameter	Variable	No FE	FE
α_0	constant	0.053	
		(3.2)	
α_1	$\Pi_{i,t-1}\text{-}MI_{t-1}$	-0.107	-0.492
		(2.4)	(4.3)
α_2	$\Delta\Pi_{i,t-1}\text{-}\Delta MI_{t-1}$	-0.020	0.081
		(0.3)	(1.2)
α_3	ΔNOF_{it}	-8.208	-4.055
		(1.7)	(0.8)
α_4	$\Delta NOF_{i,t-1}$	5.527	2.150
		(1.6)	(1.0)
α_5	ΔCS_{it}	1.049	1.468
		(1.9)	(3.1)
α_6	$\Delta\Delta CS_{it}$	-0.661	-0.671
		(1.1)	(1.2)
α_7	$\Delta K_{it}\text{-}\Delta Q_{it}$	-1.993	-1.530
		(7.7)	(5.9)
β_0	constant	-0.015	
		(1.1)	
β_1	$\Pi_{i,t-1}\text{-}MI_{t-1}$	0.0053	0.0198
		(1.9)	(3.5)
β_2	$\Delta\Pi_{i,t-1}\text{-}\Delta MI_{t-1}$	0.0023	-0.0076
		(0.5)	(1.6)
β_3	$\Delta CS_{i,t-1}$	0.129	0.120
		(6.0)	(5.4)
β_4	$\Delta CS_{i,t-2}$	0.002	0.008
		(0.1)	(0.4)
β_5	UN_{t-1}	0.0022	-0.0017
		(1.0)	(0.7)
β_6	ΔUN_{t-1}	0.0174	0.0178
		(2.6)	(2.6)
β_7	$\Delta NOF_{i,t-1}$	0.674	0.387
		(14.7)	(6.3)
System-R^2		0.439	0.545

Note: Estimations results are for no fixed effects (no FE) and for fixed effects (FE). Numbers in parentheses are t-statistics.

adjustment in about 5 years, which is consistent with the empirical evidence found by Levy (1987) for US manufacturing industries. It is most interesting to find the speed of adjustment to be roughly the same for different sectors, retailing *versus* manufacturing, in different countries, the Netherlands *versus* the United States. The parameter estimate of α_2 is not significant at a 5% level. There is no indication of change in profits *vis-à-vis* modal wage to have any effect on this change in the next period.

Considering the dynamic interaction between profitability and number of firms results are that $\hat{\alpha}_3 < 0$, $\hat{\alpha}_4 > 0$ and $\hat{\alpha}_3 < -\hat{\alpha}_4$, as expected. However, none of these results is statistically significant. Entry and exit may have only a limited direct effect on industry profitability because they are most widespread in the group of relatively small firms who make up the competitive fringe (MacDonald, 1986). Increases of retailers' profits appear to be facilitated by demand growth

($a_5 > 0$) but not by changes in this variable. A favorable development of their profits is however endangered by rises in the cost-output ratio ($a_7 < 0$). Presumably, this results from firms' market positions preventing cost shifts to be entirely passed on to customers within a one-year period or from limited awareness of cost changes during such a period.

Excess profits and growing consumer demand appear to be key incentives to new firm formation in retailing, since both the parameter estimates of β_1 and β_3 are positive and significant. This is consistent with empirical evidence in most studies on entry in manufacturing industries (Acs and Audretsch, 1989). The effect of excess profit ($\Pi_{i,t-1}-MI_{t-1}$) rises strongly at the inclusion of fixed effects. This is not surprising because entrepreneurs will confront expected profits with capital requirements, risks and managerial responsibilities when considering entry and exit. Entrepreneurial reaction, in setting up or closing down stores, to changes in consumer demand seems to be quick: $\Delta CS_{i,t-2}$ has no significant effect on ΔNOF_{it}. The parameter estimate of β_2 is also not statistically significant, indicating that entrepreneurs are not too impressed by short-term profit changes.

The level of unemployment (UN_{t-1}) appears to have no effect on changes in the number of stores. However, an increase in the number of unemployed does seem to be followed by an increase in the number of retail firms: the parameter estimate of β_6 is positive and significant. One is tempted to conclude that people who have become unemployed only recently have a higher propensity of using self-employment, in the retail sector, as an alternative to being unemployed than people who have had no working experience for a longer period. The parameter estimate of β_7 is positive and strongly significant. The demonstration effect appears to have empirical relevance in the retail sector.[7]

V. Conclusion

Measuring entrepreneurial activity is a daring venture as many different theories on the nature of entrepreneurship exist (see Hébert and Link, 1989). In this study, we concentrate on the Kirznerian notion of entrepreneurial activity as a competitive force to adjust profits to their long-term equilibrium levels. An error-correction model of the dynamic interaction between profitability and number of firms in retailing is developed and tested on a panel data set of 36 Dutch shoptypes for the period 1978-1988. One would expect entrepreneurial activity to be high in the retail sector because financial entry and exit barriers are low and starting and running a store is a comparatively simple entrepreneurial activity. Some evidence for this is found in the effects of excess profits and demand growth. The fact that excess profits vanish within a five-year period

---

[7]Robertson and Symons (1992) argue that biases arise when parameters vary across panels, shoptypes, while this is not allowed for in estimation. In the case of few time periods and many panels they find that dynamic properties tend to be over-estimated - *i.e.*, the coefficient of a lagged dependent variable is overstated. The decline of our parameter estimate of β_7 from 0.674 to 0.387 when fixed effects are included is consistent with the Monte Carlo results presented in Figure 4 of their paper.

demonstrates that excess profits arouse fierce competitive action. Excess profits also stimulate entry of new stores (entrepreneurs). Demand growth is followed by an increase in the number of stores already within a one-year period. Recently unemployed workers appear to exploit opportunities of becoming self-employed in the retail sector as increases in unemployment have a positive effect on the change in the number of stores. Profitability and number of firms are two important market phenomena which deserve detailed attention. There are however more elements of market structure and performance, like growth and survival rates of firms, evolving horizontal and vertical (dis)integration, adoption of organizational or technical innovations. We are just beginning to understand the causes and effects of market processes.

References

Acs, Z.J. and Audretsch, D.B. (1989) 'Small-Firm Entry in US Manufacturing', *Economica* **56**, 255-265.

Bode, B. (1990) *Studies in Retail Pricing*, Ph.D.-thesis, Erasmus University Rotterdam.

Carlsson, B. (ed.) (1989) *Industrial Dynamics: Technological, Organizational, and Structural Changes in Industries and Firms*, Studies in Industrial Organization **10**, Boston, Kluwer Academic Publishers.

Carree, M.A. and Thurik, A.R. (1994) 'The Dynamics of Entry, Exit and Profitability: an Error Correction Approach for the Retail Industry', *Small Business Economics* **6**, 107-116.

Eliasson, G. (1984) 'Micro Heterogeneity of Firms and the Stability of Industrial Growth', *Journal of Economic Behavior and Organization* **5**, 249-274.

Eliasson, G. (1991) 'Modeling the Experimentally Organized Economy: Complex Dynamics in an Empirical Micro-Macro Model of Endogenous Economic Growth', *Journal of Economic Behavior and Organization* **16**, 153-182.

Evans, D.S. and Leighton, L.S. (1989) 'Some Empirical Aspects of Entrepreneurship', *American Economic Review* **79**, 519-535.

Geroski, P. and Masson, R. (1987) 'Dynamic Market Models in Industrial Organization', *International Journal of Industrial Organization* **5**, 1-14.

Gilbert, C.L. (1986) 'Professor Hendry's Econometric methodology', *Oxford Bulletin of Economics and Statistics* **48**, 283-307.

Gort, M. and Konakayama, A. (1982) 'A Model of Diffusion in the Production of an Innovation', *American Economic Review* **72**, 1111-1120.

Hébert, R.F. and Link, A.N. (1989) 'In Search of the Meaning of Entrepreneurship', *Small Business Economics* **1**, 39-49.

Kirzner, I.M. (1973) *Competition and Entrepreneurship*, Chicago, University of Chicago Press.

Kirzner, I.M. (1979) *Perception, Opportunity, and Profit: Studies in the Theory of Entrepreneurship*, Chicago, University of Chicago Press.

Klepper, S. and Graddy, E. (1990) 'The Evolution of New Industries and the Determinants of Market structure', *RAND Journal of Economics* **21**, 27-44.

Levy, D. (1987) 'The Speed of the Invisible Hand', *International Journal of Industrial Organization* **5**, 79-92.

MacDonald, J.M. (1986) 'Entry and Exit on the Competitive Fringe', *Southern Economic Journal* **52**, 640-652.

Mueller, D.C. (ed.) (1990) *The Dynamics of Company Profits: An International Comparison*, Cambridge, Cambridge University Press.

Nelson, R.R. and Winter, S.G. (1982) *An Evolutionary Theory of Economic Change*, Cambridge, Harvard University Press.

Nooteboom, B., Kleijweg, A.J.M. and Thurik, A.R. (1988) 'Normal Costs and Demand Effects in Price Setting: a Study of Retailing', *European Economic Review* **32**, 999-1011.

Robertson, D. and Symons, J. (1992) 'Some Strange Properties of Panel Data Estimators', *Journal of Applied Econometrics* **7**, 175-189.

Salmon, M. (1982) 'Error Correction Mechanisms', *Economic Journal* **92**, 615-629.

Schmalensee, R. (1989) 'Inter-Industry Studies of Structure and Performance', in R. Schmalensee and R.D. Willig (eds), *Handbook of Industrial Organization* **2**, Amsterdam, Elsevier Science Publishers.

Storey, D.J. (1991) 'The Birth of New Firms - Does Unemployment Matter? A Review of the Evidence', *Small Business Economics* **3**, 167-178.

CHAPTER 16

Sunk Costs and the Dynamics of Entry in Portuguese Manufacturing

JOSÉ MATA[1]
Banco de Portugal, Departamento de Estudos Económicos, Lisboa, Portugal and Universidade Nova de Lisboa, Faculdade de Economia, Lisboa, Portugal

Abstract. This chapter studies entry dynamics in Portugal in the period 1982-86. The findings are that (i) entry and exit are deterred by economies of scale and product differentiation and (ii) sunk costs are only important to the displacement process in which less efficient firms are replaced by more efficient ones. Long-run industry structure appears to depend on the number of efficiently scaled plants that markets can accommodate, whereas the speed of convergence towards the long-run equilibrium depends on past profits and the degree of cost sunkness. Speed of convergence, long-run profits and market volatility are found to be correlated significantly.

I. Introduction

It was more than one decade ago that the concept of sunk costs entered the economics terminology (Baumol and Willig, 1981). Since then, the theoretical analysis of their effect on entry has developed thoroughly, and became an established part of the theory of industrial organization.[2] However, the empirical analysis of the effect of sunk costs on entry is still scarce. The purpose of this chapter is to reduce this gap, by proposing a measure of the extent of cost sunkness and employing it to analyze the entry flows that have occurred in Portuguese manufacturing in the early eighties. The term entry can be employed in a variety of ways and, over thirty years ago, Mansfield (1962: 1024) noted two of the possible meanings for it: 'Entry can be defined as the net change in the number of firms in an industry. Alternatively, it can be defined as the extent in which new owners of productive facilities become established in an industry either through the construction of new plants or the purchase of existing firms. Each concept has its own set of uses. The first concept is useful in analysing problems regarding market structure and industrial concentration, since the number of firms in an industry is a significant factor in such problems. The second concept is useful in measuring the ease with which new entrepreneurs can become established in an industry and the extent to which they do so". These two concepts have not, however, been kept clearly separate in most empirical studies dealing with entry. The source of such a confusion goes back

---

[1]I am grateful to Luís Cabral, Paul Geroski, António Leite and Max Pinheiro for helpful talks and to participants in seminars at the Universities of Oporto, New of Lisbon, Technical of Lisbon, the 18th EARIE Conference in Stuttgart and the VIII Jornadas de Economia Industrial in Madrid for their comments. The usual disclaimer applies, however. This study was started while the author was at the University of Ninho and was partially supported by a grant provided by the Instituto Nacional de Investigação Científica.

[2]See, for example, the treatment of this issue in the well-known textbook by Tirole (1988).

to the seminal work by Orr (1974), who uses simultaneously, and in a certain way ambiguously, the gross and net entry concepts. Following Orr, economists concerned with the entry issue have typically tried to find answers to the two following questions: what are the sectoral determinants of the entry flows that occur in the economy, and what are the profit levels that can be sustained in the long run in each industry?[3] In this discovery, the two concepts of entry have sometimes been indistinctly employed. In this chapter, we argue that each one of these questions requires the use of a different concept of entry. We assert that net entry is the relevant concept to determine long-run profits and that, by contrast, the role of barriers to entry on entry flows is better appraised using gross entry measures. We suggest that the negative influence of entry barriers on entry, found in studies that used net entry measures, may be in part due to different speeds in the adjustment process to long-run equilibrium, and propose to model these differences explicitly.

This study of entry and exit dynamics is performed with data on Portuguese manufacturing in the period 1982-86. During several decades until 1974, new firm entry and incumbents capacity expansion were severely regulated in most industrial markets by being subject to the discretionary approval of the regulatory authority[4], and this regulatory policy is often deemed to be responsible for creating a quite inefficient industrial structure. Subsequent relaxation of regulatory impediments, making profit opportunities accessible to many potential entrants, combined with prospects of both new profit opportunities and increased competitive pressure resulting from imminent adherence to the EC, may be the main causes of the very high flows of entry and exit that recently occurred in the Portuguese economy. In the sample this study deals with, entrants are about 43% of the total number of plants in operation in 1982, and attain an employment share of about 23%. Exitors are about 31% of the initial number of establishments, and were responsible for 21% of total employment.[5] These very high entry an exit flows probably reflect an intense substitution of more efficient plants for less efficient ones, and a situation of wide re-organization of the industrial structure, constituting an additional motive of interest for the study of competitive processes.

The chapter is organized as follows. First, Section II briefly reviews previous studies based on Orr's model, highlighting what we believe is an inconsistency of the model. In Section III we present a structural model of entry and exit, focusing on entry and exit determinants. Apart from the commonly employed proxies of economies of scale and product differentiation, we use a measure of the degree of cost sunkness to explain entry and exit. We find that, unlike economies of scale and product differentiation, sunk costs are mainly important

---

[3]See Geroski, Gilbert and Jacquemin (1990) and Geroski (1991b) for an overview on recent work on entry.

[4]See Confraria (1991) for a description of some case studies.

[5]The appendix describes the sample and the procedures used to compute the entry and exit measures.

to inhibit the displacement process by which less efficient plants are replaced by more efficient units. From a reduced form of this model, we derive the profit levels which are sustainable in the industry when, although important levels of entry and exit may exist, they mutually compensate. In Section IV, we use partial adjustment and error correction models to estimate the market's speed of convergence. We find that markets differ in the speed they adjust to the long-run equilibrium, and that differences in these speeds depend on sunk costs and on the pre-entry profit levels. In Section V, long-run profits and speed of convergence are compared with a measure of the ease of entry and exit: we find that these measures are significantly correlated, which seems to suggest that all these variables are measuring different aspects of the same phenomenon. We finally conclude by summarizing the most important findings, highlighting the most relevant shortcomings and suggesting some possible extensions in Section VI.

II.   Previous Studies

Modern analysis of entry started with the work by Orr (1974), and his model, which is still the basis for most of the current empirical work in the area (see the papers in Geroski and Schwalbach, 1991), can be generically described through a two-equation system:

(1) $E = \gamma(\pi - \pi^*)$;

(2) $\pi^* = f(BTE)$.

In the first equation, entry (E) depends on expected profitability (π) and the long-run profit rate (π^*) which, in the tradition of Bain's (1956) limit price, is the highest profit rate that does not attract new entry.[6] Note that π is a non-observable, and is usually replaced by past profitability, often complemented with a growth variable to account for industry dynamics. Additionally, π^* is a non observable as well, and it depends on the height of industry entry barriers. In the second equation, π^* is modeled as a function of entry barriers (for ease of exposition we will consider a single barrier to entry, BTE). Assuming a linear form $(\pi^* = a_1 + a_2 BTE)$ for (2), equations (1) and (2) combine to yield

(3) $E = a_1 + a_2 \pi + a_3 BTE$,

which is entirely expressed in terms of observables. There is not, however, one only way to measure E and, although authors' choice is greatly constrained by data availability, it is sometimes possible to choose among competing measu-

---

[6]This is sometimes called the limit-profit rate. Jeong and Masson (1991) argue that the *limit-profit* expression should be saved to describe situations in which incumbents deliberately act to impede entry, and that the *entry-forestalling profit* expression should be used instead.

res.[7] Among the decisions that must be made with respect to this issue, a crucial option is the choice between gross and net entry measures.

Most empirical work that employed variants of this model preferred, following Orr's indication, the use of gross entry measures. The reason for preferring gross measures is that entry and exit are probably symmetric, at least in regard to some of their determinants. It has been suggested that *entry barriers are exit barriers* (Eaton and Lipsey, 1980) and, therefore, that an industry with high entry (and exit) barriers may have quite a small number of entrants and exitors, while in another one with very low barriers substantial flows of entry and exit may simultaneously exist. However, in both industries, the magnitude of these flows can be of the same levels, so that in using net entry measures these two industries would appear to be similar. Then, it would seem that barriers do not influence actual entry. Empirical studies have confirmed the hypothesis of symmetry, concluding that the majority of the entry deterrents are exit impediments as well (Shapiro, 1983; MacDonald, 1986; Shapiro and Khemani, 1987; Dunne and Roberts, 1991; and Sleuwaegen and Dehandschutter, 1991). It is not, however, easy to reconcile a model like the one described above, in which entry depends on long-run profits, with a gross entry measure. If the entry flow generates a corresponding exit flow, just because entry and exit are components of the same competitive process in which less efficient plants are replaced by more efficient ones, then entry will occur if current profits are below the limit level, and even below the competitive one. The measure of entry, in a model that makes a clear appeal to the long-run profit concept, must necessarily be a net measure. Net measures were intentionally employed by Masson and Shaanan (1982 and 1987) in order to derive these long-run profit rates[8], but they have also been used in a number of studies without such a concern, mainly due to the lack of better data.[9] These studies, however, attempted to infer from their models the role of entry barriers in determining entry flows, and this step may suffer from two potential drawbacks. The first is that, although in Orr's formulation y in equation (1) was meant to be a generic function $y(.)$ to be used with a gross entry measure, it can also be interpreted as a parameter measuring the speed at which markets converge to equilibrium, if a net entry measure is employed (see Geroski, 1991a). In this case, in equation (3) we would have $a_1 = -ya_1$, $a_2 = y$ and $a_3 = -ya_2$; OLS estimates of standard errors of equation (3) would not be adequate to make inference on the parameters of

---

[7]At least, six decisions can be made (see von der Fehr, 1991).

[8]Geroski (1989) also studied the entry phenomenon intentionally employing a net measure, but most of his interest was in comparing the effects of entry by different entrants rather than in investigating the determinants of these two entry flows. Kessides (1991) used an entry determinants model with a net entry meaure, basing his arguments on the long-run equilibrium nature of his model.

[9]Acs and Audretsch (1989), Duetsch (1984), Gorecki (1975), Hirschey (1981), MacDonald (1984) and Yamawaki (1991) employed net entry measures. Even Orr (1974), who argued that gross entry should be used, was not able to obtain gross measures and used in his work a rather imperfect substitute.

interest γ, a_1 and a_2.[10] The second is the aforementioned problem of symmetry between entry and exit barriers. With regard to this issue, it is important to recognize that the scale and the irrevocability aspects of entry and exit barriers have different effects, and must be isolated.

When we think of, for example, the relationship between economies of scale and the number of entrants, there are two things to be considered.[11] First, in industries where economies of scale are important, less plants will be attracted by a given positive profit signal and, since the average incumbent in the industry will be larger than the average incumbent in other industries, less plants will be driven out of the market in response to a negative profit signal. If sunk costs are not important, the number of entrants that actually goes into the market may be much larger than would be necessary to eliminate excess profits, and a large amount of exit may be induced. Nevertheless, given sunk costs and profits, the greater the importance of economies of scale, the lesser the number of plants that will attempt entry. The same applies to exit (the greater the importance of economies of scale, the smaller the number of exitors) and also net entry. A given profit level, in excess of the industry long-run level, will generate a net addition to the number of plants in the industry, which will be smaller if economies of scale are important. The second effect is the sunk cost effect. For a given level of profits and importance of economies of scale, the greater the degree of cost sunkness, the lesser the displacement: *i.e.*, the lesser the movement of exit induced by entry and, *ceteris paribus*, the lesser the amount of both entry and exit. Net entry, however, will not be deterred by sunkness of costs. The net addition to the number of plants in the industry in the long-run depends on the room created for new plants, and this varies positively with the level of excess profits and negatively with the importance of economies of scale, but not with the degree of cost sunkness. It can be argued that sunk costs may increase the long-run equilibrium number of plants in the market, implying an increase of net entry. This may be so not because sunk costs create room for more plants, but because the existence of sunk costs can make exits that would otherwise occur unprofitable.[12] Therefore, if we obser-

---

[10]It is, notwithstanding, paradoxical that the only work that seems to have noticed this problem (Khemani and Shapiro, 1988) employed gross measures.

[11]The following discussion also applies to other elements normally listed as entry barriers. Take product differentiation, for example. Product differentiation is normally seen as an entry barrier, due to (i) the existence of economies of scale in the differentiation activities (advertising, R&D), (ii) the exacerbating of technical economies of scale due to market segmentation, but also (iii) the irrecoverable nature of the associated investments. With product differentiation the case is however less clear, since it can also be argued that advertising is a means of entry rather than an entry deterrent and that, in differentiated markets, small-scale entry may be possible if entrants are able to find market niches which could be served even with some cost disadvantage.

[12]Cabral (1993) argues that with sunk costs the long-run equilibrium number of firms is no longer uniquely determined by technical considerations, but depends on the entry mistakes committed in the early phases of the adjustment process. In this sense, net entry would be a random variable, and expected net entry would increase with sunk costs (see also Dixit and Shapiro, 1986).

ve two long-run positions, net entry may not vary negatively with sunk costs. However, we do not normally observe long-run positions, at least we do not observe them for all markets. If markets differ in the speeds at which they converge to long-run equilibrium, and these speeds depend on sunk costs, we can again observe a relationship between net entry and sunk costs, but this relationship is not necessarily monotonic.[13] We have then three different problems: the factors that determine the ease that new competitors experience in establishing in an industry, the profit levels that are sustainable in an industry in the long-run, and the speed at which industries adjust to these long-run positions. We will address these three issues in the remainder of the chapter.

III.   Modelling Entry and Exit

We start with a simple structural model of industry entry and exit to highlight their determinants. We model gross entry (ENT) and exit (EX) in a two-equations system described by equations (4) and (5):

(4) $\text{ENT} = \beta_1 + \beta_2 \pi + \beta_3 \text{BTE};$

(5) $\text{EX} = \delta_1 + \delta_2 \pi + \delta_3 \text{BTE} + \delta_4 \text{ENT},$

We expect $\beta_2 > 0$, $\beta_3 < 0$, $\delta_2 < 0$, $\delta_3 < 0$ and $1 > \delta_4 > 0$. Equation (4) predicts that for a given level of the representative barrier to entry BTE, more entry will occur in industries experiencing higher profit levels, and that given the pre-entry profit levels, less entry will occur in those industries with higher entry barriers. These are the standard hypotheses about the effects of profits and barriers to entry on entry flows, and this equation is formally analogous to equation (3) with $a_1 = \beta_1$, $a_2 = \beta_2$ and $a_3 = \beta_3$.[14] The exit equation (5) predicts that *ceteris paribus* less exit will occur with higher profits and higher barriers. ENT is included as an explanatory variable to model the displacement effect caused by the substitution of

---

[13]Consider, for example, a situation in which we observe two different markets, which simultaneously experience similar exogenous changes that create room for the same number of new plants in each market. Assume that both makets adjust smoothly to the new situation, and that complete adjustment is faster in the first market because entry and exit are easier (sunk costs are lower) in the first. If we observe them again later in time, but before complete adjustment had taken place in both markets, we will record a greater net entry figure in the first market - the market in which sunk costs are lower. If, however, both markets had experienced a similar exogenous contraction, faster adjustment would imply greater net exit: *i.e.*, lesser net entry. The observed relationship, in each case, would therefore depend on which (entry or exit) is more important in each particular sample. If, moreover, adjustments are not smooth, different patterns may emerge depending on the observed equilibrium path and the specific point in time where observations are taken.

[14]Nevertheless, they are different in that equation (4) was not developed from a long-run profit model and that, unlike in long-run profit models, there is no room in equation (4) to interpret the coefficients β_i as interaction terms between the speed of adjustment y and the "true" entry barrier coefficients.

more efficient plants for less efficient ones[15], and the coefficient δ_4 is an estimate of the proportion in which entry induces exit.[16] The model can be viewed as describing the following: in the beginning of each period, there are I incumbent plants in the industry, with different efficiency levels. The industry is not in its long-run equilibrium and it can accommodate more NE new plants. This departure from long-run equilibrium generates profit signals and, observing these signals, ED (ED>NE) new plants, also with different degrees of efficiency enter the market. There will then be a pool of I+ED plants in the industry, from where only the I+NE more efficient can survive in the long run. Some of the entering ED plants (the less efficient D) will not manage to survive until the end of the period (that is, they will die before the end of the period) and will not even be recorded in our data. We only observe the ENT=ED-D surviving new plants and, if ENT>NE, some of the less efficient incumbents (EX) will be driven out of the market. Substituting (4) into (5), we obtain a reduced form for the exit equation:

(6) $EX = \delta_1 + \delta_4\beta_1 + (\delta_2 + \delta_4\beta_2)\pi + (\delta_3 + \delta_4\beta_3)BTE.$

Subtracting (6) from (4), gives the expression for net entry (NETENT) as a function of π and BET:

(7) $NETENT = \beta_1(1-\delta_4)-\delta_1 + (\beta_2(1-\delta_4)-\delta_2)\pi + (\beta_3(1-\delta_4)-\delta_3)BTE.$

Estimating (7) amounts to estimating (3) with a net entry measure, where $\beta_1(1-\delta_4)-\delta_1 = \alpha_1$, $(\beta_2(1-\delta_4)-\delta_2) = \alpha_2$ and $(\beta_3(1-\delta_4)-\delta_3 = \alpha_3$.

The OLS estimates of standard errors of equation (3) will not, however, be adequate to infer on the statistical significance of the parameters δ_i and β_i. Besides, the expected sign of the α_3, the coefficient attached to the BTE variable is not easy to predict. The role played by entry barriers in determining net entry flows depends on the relative magnitudes of β_3, δ_4 and δ_3. Barriers to entry will have a negative effect on entry if $1-\delta_4 < \delta_3/\beta_3$, and a positive effect if $1-\delta_4 > \delta_3/\beta_3$. Reasonable values for δ_4 are encompassed within the interval [0,1], a value of 0 meaning that no exit is induced by entry and a value of 1 implying that each entrant will provoke the exit of a previously installed plant. The predicted signs of both β_3 and δ_3 are negative, which implies that both sides of the preceding inequalities will be positive, and therefore we cannot really predict the effect of entry barriers on net entry. The effect of profits on entry is positive if

---

[15]The possibility of simultaneity between entry and exit was not discussed. There is little rationality in expecting that entry may be determined by the exit of plants that spontaneously leave the market. Khemani and Shapiro (1987) and Rosenbaum and Lamort (1992) tested the possible simultaneity, but found no evidence of such relationship in Canada and U.S.

[16]This is a simplification, since it (i) assumes that industry dynamics are entirely due to entry and exit and (ii) ignores the role that market share turnover among incumbents may have on exit. However, Mata (1993) found that the determinants of installed firms expansion do not differ from the determinants of new firm entry, concluding that the two phenomena seem to be good substitutes.

$1-\delta_4 > \delta_2/\beta_2$, which, given the assumptions on the signs of β_2 and δ_2, is always true. In order to estimate the model (4)-(5), we need to specify the proxies for π and BTE. As a proxy for π, the price-cost margin in the pre-entry period (PCM) is usually employed. Different price-cost margins can however reflect the same entry incentive if industry risk or capital intensity are also different and, to discard these effects, the proxy employed (PROFIT) is the series of the residuals of a regression of PCM on a constant and on measures of industry risk (RISK) and capital intensity (KO). Fitted values of this regression give the normal levels of price-cost margins in the industries, given their capital intensity and risk, and the departures from these levels (the residuals) are the true economic incentive for entry.[17]

The BTE vector includes product differentiation (PAT), economies of scale (LMES) and a measure of the degree of sunkness of machinery and equipment capital (SUNK). To control for different industry sizes, the logarithm of the employment in the industry in 1982 (LSIZE) is included in the list of explanatory variables. Economies of scale were measured by the logarithm of the proxy of the minimum efficient scale (MES) suggested by Lyons (1980). The effect of economies of scale as a barrier to entry is twofold: it depends on the ratio between MES and industry size, since in industries where this ratio is higher, the effect of an efficiently scaled entrant on incumbents is greater than in industries with lower ratios; it also depends on the absolute value of MES, as it may determine the amount of capital required to operate an efficient plant in the industry regardless of the number of efficient plants that the market can accommodate (which, due to the imperfections in the capital markets, may constitute an entry barrier). Entering both industry size and MES in logarithmic form allows to implicitly capture these two effects. Product differentiation affects entry since (i) in segmented markets the role of economies of scale as a barrier to entry can be exacerbated and (ii) the capital requirements barrier can be increased through the additional expenses required to differentiate products (advertising, R&D). Product differentiation was measured by the ratio of patents and trademarks to production (PAT), averaged for 1981-2. That sunk costs can impede entry and exit is well known since the work by Baumol and Willig (1981), but empirical studies analyzing this effect are still scarce (see Kessides, 1986 and 1991; Mata, 1991; von der Fehr, 1991; and Rosenbaum and Lamort, 1992). Cost sunkness depends on capital durability and specificity. Durability was measured by the logarithm of the expected life of machines and other equipment in the industry (DURAB). Capital durability affects cost sunkness since, if capital lasts longer, the proportion of unrecovered capital (and therefore the losses) in the case of exit will be greater. Durability, however, only affects cost sunkness if capital is somehow specific to the particular committed use. If capital assets could be easily resold without losses, they would not be sunk, no matter how durable they could be. As a proxy to the ease of reselling capital goods, we used the importance of the second-hand market for machinery and

---

[17]See Duetsch (1984) and MacDonald (1986) for similar measures. PCM was computed as the average price-cost margin and RISK as the standard deviation of PCM, both across 1979-82. KO was also difined as the average capital/output ratio.

other equipment. The measure employed to measure capital specificity (NEW) is an inverse measure of the ease of selling capital goods, being defined as the average value (1979-82) of machines and other equipment bought new, expressed as a percentage of total expenditures with machines and equipment (figures are net of second-hand market sales).[18] To capture the interaction between durability and specificity, SUNK was defined as the product between NEW and DURAB.

Simple specifications of equations (4) to (7) were estimated. The model (4)-(5) is recursive and, since the exogenous variables are the same in both equations, techniques for estimating seemingly unrelated equations would not improve efficiency. Both equations were therefore estimated by OLS, correcting for heteroscedasticity by White's (1980) method. Equations (6) and (7) were also estimated by the same method. The results are displayed in Table 1.

Table 1.   Determinants of entry and exit

	Entry	Exit	Exit	Net entry
Constant	-66.6	-26.3	-54.7	-11.9
	(-0.982)	(-2.122)	(-1.529)	(-0.348)
PROFIT	311.5	71.5	204.2	107.3
	(2.271)	(1.676)	(2.301)	(1.642)
LSIZE	62.1	13.8	40.3	21.8
	(3.355)	(3.386)	(5.063)	(1.804)
LMES	-44.8	-11.9	-31.0	-13.9
	(-3.206)	(-2.079)	(-3.690)	(-1.487)
PAT	-26.9	-7.2	-18.7	-8.2
	(-2.564)	(-2.120)	(-2.878)	(-1.452)
SUNK	-56.6	-3.6	-27.7	-28.4
	(-1.678)	(-0.952)	(-1.992)	(-1.332)
ENTRY	-	0.43	-	-
	-	(5.379)	-	-
$R^2/\bar{R}^2$	0.42/0.37	0.90/0.89	0.55/0.52	0.20/0.14

Note: t values corrected for heteroscedasticity (White, 1980 and 1982) are in parentheses. Critical t values for a one-tailed test with 60 degrees of freedom are 1.296, 1.671 and 2.390 for the 10%, 5% and 1% significance levels, respectively.

Obtained results for equation (4) confirm the hypotheses made about the determinants of entry. All variables carry the expected sign and are significant, at least at the 5% level. Results for the exit equation also confirm that economies of scale and product differentiation are important in the determination of the exit levels, even after the importance of entry is taken into account, while sunk costs become statistically insignificant when the ENTRY variable is included. This seems to suggest that sunk costs are especially important to inhibit the replacement process, in contrast with economies of scale and product differentiation. Economies of scale and product differentiation are

---

[18]The only type of capital goods we consider here are machinery and equipment. It seems reasonable to expect that buildings (not to mention vehicles) are far less specific than machinery. Kessides (1990) tested and found empirical support for this conjecture.

important in the determination of the number of plants that may efficiently operate in an industry: they therefore play a role in determining the number of plants that, given market size and profit levels, will be attracted into (expelled from) the industry. Cost sunkness does not influence the number of plants that may co-exist in the industry in the long run, but merely affects the ease of displacement. After this effect is taken into account, sunk costs do not affect the exit flows. The PROFIT variable has the wrong sign in the exit equations, although its t-value is substantially reduced when the displacement effect is taken into account.[19] This effect is estimated by δ_4 revealing that, *ceteris paribus*, each new entrant would, on average, make 0.43 established plants leave the market.

In equation (7), the entry barriers variables attracted a negative sign, but t-values are quite low, allowing rejection of the null hypotheses at the 10% level only for each one of the variables other than LSIZE. This agrees with our previous discussion on the effects of entry barriers on net entry. Although we cannot infer from equation (7) the role of entry barriers in determining entry flows, this equation is not useless. Specifically, since equation (7) is a reduced form of the (4)-(5) model, and since this model describes rather well the entry and exit movements, it can be used to estimate the entry-forestalling profits - that is, the profit levels at which entry and exit compensate exactly. By simply making NETENT = 0 and solving for PROFIT, we obtain π^* - *i.e.* the level of profits which are compatible in each industry with the zero net entry position. The π^* average in our sample is -0.15, which cannot be interpreted unless compared with the average for the PROFIT variable, which is zero by definition. This is not surprising, since it reveals that (i) profits are on average well above the entry-forestalling levels and (ii) overall net entry should be positive.

Two sorts of reasons suggest, however, some care in interpreting our estimates of π^*. The first is a general remark about using past profits as a proxy of expected profitability. This may clearly be an incomplete specification, since it (i) assumes that potential entrants would mantain the naive expectation that their entry would not affect market equilibrium at all[20] and (ii) ignores other market dynamics effects. For example, a market experiencing a period of rapid growth may offer profit opportunities and induce entry, even if past recorded profits are not above average. This could be captured by including a measure of industry growth among the regressors, which was attempted but with deceiving results. We employed, alternatively, measures of past industry production, value added and employment growth, but these variables always attracted the wrong signs. Therefore, we excluded them from the reported results. The second reason is that the PROFIT variable did not perform exactly as expected, attracting a positive sign in the exit equation, which may cast some doubts on the

---

[19]PROFIT was employed instead of PCM on *a priori* grounds, but the same equations were also estimated with PCM. Results did not change very much, but PCM becomes statistically significant only at the 10% level in equation (5) and significant at the 5% level in equation (7).

[20]It has been argued that forecast profits should be employed instead of past profits (Highfield and Smiley, 1987; and Geroski, 1991a) but this approach is clearly beyond the scope of this chapter.

accuracy of the π^* estimates. In spite of our discussion on the effect of entry barriers on net entry, in Table 1 all the entry barriers variables attracted negative signs, albeit with reduced t-statistics.[21] One could possibly interpret these results as reflecting the fact that markets are observed before all adjustments have taken place and, as suggested above, that we observe more entry in those markets that adjust faster.[22] In the next section, we present a model of net entry in which these differences in the speed of adjustment are explicitly modeled. In this model, net entry depends on the variables commonly employed as proxies for entry barriers, and we suggest that previously reported models could be seen as incomplete specifications of such a model.

IV. A Model of Net Entry

The model developed in this section is a model of N_t^*, the long-run equilibrium number of plants in the industry. The proposed model is of a partial adjustment type[23], in which the difference between N_t (the number of plants in operation in the industry in period t) and N_{t-1} (the number of plants in the industry in period t-1) is a given proportion (λ) of the difference between the number of plants in the market in the period t-1 (N_{t-1}) and the long-run equilibrium number of plants (N_t^*) in period t. In symbols,

$$(8) \quad N_t - N_{t-1} = \lambda(N_t^* - N_{t-1}).$$

The model says that if markets are out of their long-run equilibria, there will be movements in the number of plants towards equilibrium, but it recognizes that equilibrium is not necessarily achieved immediately. The parameter λ measures the speed at which markets converge to equilibrium, a value of 0 implying complete absence of convergence and a value of 1 complete adjustment. N_t^* is a non-observable and must be replaced, for purposes of empirical estimation, by variables which can be observed. If cost curves are U-shaped and products are homogeneous, N_t^* will be exactly equal to $SIZE_t/MES_t$, denoted by $NESP_1$ (Number of Efficiently Scaled Plants). Allowing for product differentiation and

---

[21]There are also a number of studies in the literature that reported statistically significant relationships between net entry and entry barriers, although this evidencee is not really consistent across studies. Acs and Audretsch (1989) found negative effects for capital intensity, R&D and concentration, and no effect for advertising or scale economies. Duetsch (1984) only confirmed the negative effect for capital intensity, while Gorecki (1975) found a contradictory effect of advertising and reported evidence of a deterrent role played by economies of scale. Economies of scale were found to induce entry by Hirschey (1981) who also reported a positive effect on R&D expenditures. MacDonald (1984) encountered a positive effect of advertising, while Jeong and Masson (1991) found that advertising and economies of scale deter entry. Yamawaki (1991) reported a quite unstable relationship between net entry and the entry barriers variables.

[22]This would be a consequence of the fact that in our particular sample the number of entrants is far more important than the number of exitors.

[23]Partial adjustment is a special case of the error correction models as extensively employed in the macroeconomics literature (see Salmon, 1982; and Nickell, 1985).

including a constant term to keep flexibility, we have

(9) $N_t^* = w_1 + w_2 NESP_t + w_3 PAT_t.$

If we allow for incomplete adjustment, it seems natural to admit that industries differ in the speed at which they converge to long-run equilibria and therefore to model λ as a function of market structure variables, as in Geroski, Masson and Shaanan (1987) did in their concentration model. The speed of convergence was modeled as a quadratic function of past profitability and of the degree of sunkness of costs, reflecting that the higher (lower) the profits are, the larger the incentive to enter (exit) is and the greater speed with which markets will converge. Finally, the presence of sunk costs inhibits entry and exit movements, and slows down the convergence process:

(10) $\lambda = (\Theta_1 + \Theta_2 SUNK_{t-1} + \Theta_3 PROFIT_{t-1})^2.$

Substituting (9) and (10) into (8), and noting that $N_t - N_{t-1} = NETENT$, we get the net entry equation

(11) $NETENT = (\Theta_1 + \Theta_2 SUNK_{t-1} + \Theta_3 PROFIT_{t-1})^2 (w_1 + w_2 NESP_t + w_3 PAT_t - N_{t-1}),$

which can be estimated by non-linear least squares, leading to the results presented in Table 2.

Table 2.   Determinants of net entry: partial adjustsment model

Θ_1	Θ_2	Θ_3	w_1	w_2	w_3	R^2/R^2
2.11	-0.69	2.06	-35.24	4.45	-19.10	0.92/0.91
(5.500)	(-4.254)	(1.921)	(-3.857)	(8.574)	(-5.222)	

Note: t values corrected for heteroscedasticity (White, 1980 and 1982) are in parentheses. Critical t values for a one-tailed test with 60 degrees of freedom are 1.296, 1.671 and 2.390 for the 10%, 5% and 1% significance levels, respectively.

Results in Table 2 show that the number of efficiently scaled plants that may co-exist in an industry and the degree of product differentiation constitute a benchmark to which the actual number of plants operating in the industry converges, which seems to confirm that economies of scale and the extent of product differentiation are important in determining long-run industry configurations.[24] The specification adopted here greatly improves upon specifying λ as a parameter (compare the two R^2). A more formal comparison between the two specifications can be done by testing the null hypothesis $\Theta_2 = \Theta_3 = 0$, using a

---

[24]For comparative purposes, the same equation was estimated modeling λ as a parameter, leading to the following equation: $NETENT = 0.18(-111.73 + 5.60 NESP_t - 2.10 PAT_t - N_{t-1})$ with t values of 1.585, -2.337, 3.898 and -0126, respectively ($R^2/R^2 = 0.70/0.68$). This confirms the importance of economies of scale to the determination of long-run industry structure, but does not confirm the role of product differentiation.

likelihood ratio (LR) test. The computed LR is 93.20, well above the critical χ_2 at any conventional significance level, confirming the hypotheses that industries converge to these yardsticks at different speeds with the actual speed being faster in industries where profits are higher and where the degree of cost sunkness is lower. From (10) we can calculate the different speeds at which markets adjust to long-run equilibrium. Estimates are between 2.7×10^{-6} and 1.84, with an average of 0.13. By construction, λ is bounded by zero, and the maximum of 1.84 implies that all industries eventually converge to their long-run equilibria. Still, both the mean value of 0.13 as well as the estimated value of λ if modeled as a parameter (0.18) seem to indicate that this convergence is rather slow.[25]

An alternative way of modeling net entry within this framework is to use an error correction model in which $N_t^*-N_{t-1}$ is decomposed into two elements: $N_{t-1}^*-N_{t-1}$, the error actually committed in period t-1, and $N_t^*-N_{t-1}^*$, the change in the long-run equilibrium position between t-1 and t. This allows these two elements to be affected by different speeds of convergence. We can rewrite (8) as

(12) $N_t-N_{t-1} = \lambda_1(N_t^*-N_{t-1}^*) + \lambda_2(N_{t-1}^*-N_{t-1})$.

Modelling λ_1 and λ_2 similarly to λ and using the operator Δ for increases, equation (11) becomes

(13) NETENT $= (\Psi_1 + \Psi_2 \text{SUNK} + \Psi_3 \text{PROFIT})^2 (\omega_2 \Delta \text{NESP} + \omega_3 \Delta \text{PAT}) +$
$(\phi_1 + \phi_2 \text{SUNK} + \phi_3 \text{PROFIT})^2 (\omega_1 + \omega_2 \text{NESP}_{t-1} + \omega_3 \text{PAT}_{t-1} - N_{t-1})$.

Non-linear least squares estimates of the parameters in equation (13) appear in Table 3 and, once again, a likelihood ratio (LR) can be computed and used to perform a test of equality between Ψ_i and ϕ_i (i=1,2,3). If λ_1 and λ_2 are equal, equation (13) is equivalent to equation (11), and therefore estimates of the constrained model are given in Table 2. The computed LR-statistic is 86.76, which implies rejection of the null hypothesis of equality between coefficients.

Table 3.   Determinants of net entry: error correction model

Ψ_1	Ψ_2	Ψ_3	$\varnothing_1$	$\varnothing_2$	$\varnothing_3$	ω_1	ω_2	ω_3	$R^2/\overline{R}^2$
1.72	-0.50	2.84	1.13	-0.37	1.23	-35.69	5.86	13.52	0.97/0.97
(7.442)	(-5.702)	(3.850)	(4.936)	(-4.700)	(2.379)	(-2.695)	(5.655)	(1.031)	

Note: t values corrected for heteroscedasticity (White, 1980 and 1982) are in parentheses. Critical t values for a one-tailed test with 60 degrees of freedom ar 1.296, 1,671 and 2.390 for the 10%, 5% and 1% significance levels, respectively.

From the estimates of Ψ_i and ϕ_i, we can compute the values for λ_1, and λ_2. Mean values of these two variables are 0.18 and 0.04, thus revealing that

---

[25]Levy (1987) found similar results for a concentration model, which however failed to hold when industry-specific dummies were introduced. We cannot pursue the same strategy in this chapter, since we have only data for two points in time, but there is clearly room here for further investigation.

industries adjust faster to changes in long-run equilibrium than to past departures from long-run positions. Nevertheless, both speeds are significantly
dependent on the same variables, namely the past profit levels and the degree
of cost sunkness. One, somewhat striking, result is the positive sign attracted
by PAT in this specification. The estimated coefficients of this variable are quite
unstable, perhaps reflecting the fact that if it is true that product differentiation
can act as a barrier to entry, it is also true that in differentiated markets it may
be easier to find niches where small new firms can operate in spite of their cost
disadvantage (see Bradburd and Ross, 1989, for a recent test of this hypothesis).

V.   Measures of Industry Competition

In the preceding sections we addressed three issues which are important to
assess the degree of competition in the industry. We discussed the factors
determining the ease of establishing new productive facilities in an industry,
calculated the profit levels which industries can sustain in the long run without
attracting new competitors, and estimated the speed at which industries
converge to these long-run positions. These are different but related questions,
and we might wonder how they are related. It could be presumed that those
industries in which entry and exit impediments are low, are also those which are
unable to sustain high profits in the long run and are more quickly led to their
long-run positions. From the models presented in the preceding sections, we
were able to derive two different types of measures of the intensity of competition in the industry (entry-forestalling profits and speed of market convergence).
The other element discussed in the text (the ease of establishing new plants in
an industry) cannot be estimated from our models, but it can be measured
directly from our raw data.

The procedure we will adopt here assumes that entry and exit will occur in a
greater extent in industries where entry and exit are easier.[26] When measuring
the ease of entry, one should recognize that net entry will occur if markets are
out of their long-run equilibrium, regardless of how easy entry and exit can be,
and that ease of entry and exit will mainly influence the amount of turnover
(gross entry plus gross exit) that occurs for reasons other than departures from
long-run equilibrium. A good way to measure this is to use the market volatility
indicator suggested by Dunne and Roberts (1991: 196) which "attempts to
summarize the rate of turnover in excess of that resulting from overall growth or
contraction of the market". Volatility is defined as $VOL = ENT + EX - |NETENT|$,
and can be computed using entry/exit rates and employment shares.[27] The
mean values of these shares and rates are 0.32 and 0.51, and their maximum

---

[26]This is not a necessity. Note that in a perfectly contestable market, zero entry and exit is
compatible with complete absence of entry impediments.

[27]A somewhat similar measure (the Grubel and Lloyd index) has been extensively used to
measure the extent of intra-industry trade (see Greenaway and Milner, 1986: 62). VOL is always 2
times ENT or 2 times EX, depending on whether EX or ENT dominates. It can be seen as a measure
of the importance of exit in industries where net entry is positive, and *vice versa*.

values 1.14 and 1.20, respectively. These values are quite high, specially considering that their net entry counterparts are -0.60 and 0.10 and that the results obtained in the previous section revealed a rather low average speed of convergence to long-run positions. The high mean values for the volatility measures thus seems to indicate that a great share of these entry and exit movements is directed to feeding industry turbulence rather than to driving industries towards their long-run positions.

Table 4.   Correlations between measures of industry competition

	π^*	λ	λ_1	λ_2	Volatility share	Volatility rate
π^*	1.00	-0.25	-0.26	-0.25	-0.32	-0.25
λ		1.00	0.86	0.99	0.34	0.09
λ_1			1.00	0.89	0.31	0.08
λ_2				1.00	0.34	0.10
Volatility share					1.00	0.50
Volatility rate						1.00

Nevertheless, these different measures are significantly correlated, indicating that they may be capturing different aspects of the same phenomenon. Correlations in Table 4 suggest that the absence of market share turnover due to entry and exit, in excess of turnover required by changes in industry's structural conditions, may reflect high levels of incumbents' protection, which may result not only in higher sustainable profits in the long run but also in a slowing down of the speed at which industries adjust towards long-run positions.

VI.   Conclusion

Competition is an eminently dynamic process in which new competitors challenge (and sometimes replace) old established firms' positions. This chapter addressed the study of entry dynamics in Portuguese manufacturing in the early eighties, and investigated the determinants of the entry and exit flows. Special attention was paid to the distinction between gross and net entry, and to the modeling of the competitive process in which less efficient plants are replaced by more efficient ones. This displacement effect was found to be significant and our estimates suggest that each new entrant displaces, on average, 0.43 incumbents. Both entry and exit were found to be deterred by economies of scale and product differentiation. Sunk costs, however, proved to be significant only when the interaction between entry and exit is not explicitly accounted for, suggesting that they may be important mainly as a deterrent of this displacement process. We also modeled net entry as a partial adjustment process towards long-run equilibrium. The latent long-run industry configuration was modeled as a function of economies of scale and product differentiation, and the speed of adjustment to this configuration as being determined by the level of past profits and the degree of cost sunkness. All the variables proved to be significant and robust, except the variable measuring product differentiation.

Our results seem to suggest that, in spite of the huge amount of entry and exit, the adjustment process is quite slow. This conclusion should be regarded as tentative and very preliminary, chiefly because we could only work with two observations separated by a four-year period. Estimation of the speed of the market process from cross section data has been the current practice, but it is not likely that these estimates are very accurate. Cross-section data may well be the source to explain the differences in the market's speed of adjustment, as we did here, but more comprehensive time-series analysis seems to be required to obtain proper estimates of these speeds. Also, work along the lines of Gort and Klepper (1982) and Klepper and Grady (1990), exploring the relationship between the extent of industry turbulence and the industry's life cycle, seems warranted. An interesting avenue for further research would be to combine these two perspectives and to investigate how the markets' speed of convergence varies along the industry's life cycle. Entry and exit are important components of the competitive process, but they definitely do not tell the whole story. Post-entry survival and market penetration may be as difficult as entry itself, and market share turnover among incumbents may be as important as entry and exit to explain market dynamics. Work integrating these aspects is still needed to improve our knowledge of the dynamics of competition.

Appendix

The sample used in this study consists in 73 industries from Portuguese manufacturing, meeting the requirements of data availability and excluding all the *miscellaneous* industries in which the public sector has a predominant position or which were judged to have essentially local markets. Entry and exit measures employed here were computed by the author from unpublished data obtained from an yearly inquiry of the Ministry of Employment, described in some detail in Mata (1992). This source is quite accurate for firms with at least five people employed, but not for smaller ones. Accordingly, plants with fewer than five people were not considered in the study. For each one of the terminal years of the study, a file with all plants primarily classified in manufacturing was obtained, and entry and exit figures were computed by comparison of the two files. We identified *entrants* by finding those plants which were in the industry in 1986, but not in 1982. Conversely, plants were classified as *exitors* if they were in the industry in 1982, but not in 1986. These definitions correspond to *industry* entry and exit, and they clearly overestimate plant creation (entry from the whole economy perspective), since those plants which were already operating in industry i in 1982 but changed their main activity to industry j between 1982 and 1986 are both classified as entrants in industry j and exitors in industry i.

References

Acs, Z. and Audretsch, D. (1989) 'Small Firm Entry in U.S. Manufacturing', *Economica* **56**, 255-265.
Bain, J. (1956) *Barriers to New Competition*, Cambridge, MA., Harvard University Press.
Baumol, W.J. and Willig, R.D. (1981) 'Fixed Costs, Sunk Costs, Entry Barriers and Sustainability of Monopoly', *Quarterly Journal of Economics* **96**, 405-431.
Bradburd, R.M. and Ross, D.R. (1989) 'Can Small Firms Find and Defend Strategic Niches? A Test of Porter Hypothesis', *Review of Economics and Statistics* **71**, 258-262.
Cabral, L. (1993) 'Experience Advantages and Entry Dynamics', *Journal of Economic Theory* **59**, 403-416.
Confraria, J. (1991) 'Entry and Exit in a Small Closed Economy: Dilemmas and Inconsistencies of Portuguese Industrial Policy', *Paper presented at the 18th EARIE Conference*, Ferrara.
Dixit, A. and Shapiro, C. (1986) 'Entry Dynamics with Mixed Strategies', in L.G. Thomas III (ed.), *The Economics of Strategic Planning,* Lexington, Lexington Books.
Duetsch, L. (1984) 'Entry and the Extent of Multiplant Operations', *Journal of Industrial Economics* **32**, 477-487.

Dunne, T. and Roberts, M. (1991) 'Variation in Producer Turnover Across US Manufacturing Industries', in Geroski, P. and Schwalbach, J. (eds), *Entry and Market Contestability: an International Comparison*, Oxford, Basil Blackwell.

Eaton, B. and Lipsey, R. (1980) 'Entry Barriers are Exit Barriers: The Durability of Capital as a Barrier to Entry', *Bell Journal of Economics* 11, 721-729.

Geroski, P., Gilbert, R. and Jacquemin, A. (1990), *Barriers to Entry and Strategic Competition*, London, Harwood.

Geroski, P., Masson, R. and Shaanan, J. (1987) 'The Dynamics of Market Structure', *International Journal of Industrial Organization* 5, 93-100.

Geroski, P. (1989) 'The Interaction Between Domestic and Foreign Entrants', in Audretsch, D., Sleuwaegen, L. and Yamawaki, H. (eds), *The Convergence of International and Domestic Markets*, North-Holland.

Geroski, P. (1991a) 'Domestic and Foreign Entry in the UK', in Geroski, P. and Schwalbach, J. (eds), *Entry and Market Contestability: an International Comparison*, Oxford, Basil Blackwell.

Geroski, P. (1991b) *Market Dynamics and Entry*, Oxford, Basil Blackwell.

Geroski, P. and Schwalbach, J. (eds.) (1991) *Entry and Market Contestability: an International Comparison*, Oxford, Basil Blackwell.

Gorecki, P. (1975) 'The Determinants of Entry by New and Diversifying Enterprises in the UK Manufacturing Sector 1958-1963: Some Tentative Results', *Applied Economics* 7, 139-147.

Gort, M. and Klepper, S. (1982) 'Time Paths in the Diffusion of Product Innovations', *Economic Journal* 92, 630-653.

Greenaway, D. and Milner, C. (1986) *The Economics of Intra-Industry Trade*, Oxford, Basil Blackwell.

Greene, W. (1990) *Econometric Analysis*, New York, MacMillan.

Highfield, R. and Smiley, R. (1987) 'New Business Starts and Economic Activity: an Empirical Investigation', *International Journal of Industrial Organization* 5, 51-66.

Hisrchey, M. (1981) 'The Effect of Advertising on Industrial Mobility, 1947-72', *Journal of Business* 54, 329-339.

Jeong, K.-Y. and Masson, R. (1991) 'Entry During Explosive Growth: Korea during Take-off', in P. Geroski and J. Schwalbach (eds.), *Entry and Market Contestability: An International Comparison*, Oxford, Basil Blackwell.

Kessides, I. (1986) 'Advertising, Sunk Costs and Barriers to Entry', *Review of Economics and Statistics* 68, 84-95.

Kessides, I. (1990) 'Towards a Testable Model of Entry: a Study of the U.S. Manufacturing Industries', *Economica* 57, 219-238.

Kessides, I. (1991) 'Entry and Market Contestability: The Evidence from the US', in P. Geroski and J. Schwalbach (eds.), *Entry and Market Contestability: An International Comparison*, Oxford, Basil Blackwell.

Khemani, R. and Shapiro, D. (1988) 'On Entry and Mobility Barriers', *Antitrust Bulletin*, Spring, 115-134.

Klepper, S. and Grady, E. (1990) 'The Evolution of New Industries and the Determinants of Market structure', *RAND Journal of Economics* 21, 27-44.

Levy, D. (1985) 'Specifying the Dynamics of Industry Concentration', *Journal of Industrial Economics* 34, 55-67.

Levy, D. (1987) 'The Speed of the Invisible Hand', *International Journal of Industrial Organization* 5, 79-92.

Lyons, B. (1980) 'A New Measure of Minimum Efficient Plant Size in U.K. Manufacturing Industry', *Economica* 17, 19-34.

MacDonald, J. (1984) 'Diversification, Market Growth and Concentration in the US Manufacturing', *Southern Economic Journal* 50, 1098-1111.

MacDonald, J. (1986) 'Entry and Exit on the Competitive Fringe', *Southern Economic Journal* 52, 640-652.

Mansfield, E. (1962) 'Entry, Gibrat's Law, and the Growth of Firms', *American Economic Review* 52, 1023-1051.

Masson, R. and Shaanan, J. (1982) 'Stochastic-Dynamic Limit Pricing: An Empirical Test', *Review of Economic and Statistics* 64, 412-422.

Masson, R. and Shaanan, J. (1987) 'Optimal Oligopoly Pricing and the Threat of Entry: Canadian Evidence', *International Journal of Industrial Organization* 5, 323-339.

Mata, J. (1991) 'Sunk Costs and Entry by Small and Large Plants', in Geroski, P. and Schwalbach, J. (eds.), *Entry and Market Contestability: An International Comparison,* Oxford, Basil Blackwell.

Mata, J. (1992) 'Concentration and Competitive Dynamics', in Amaral, J., Lucena, D. and Mello, A. (eds.), *The Portuguese Economy Towards 1992,* Norwell, Kluwer Academic Publishers.

Mata, J. (1993) 'Firm Entry and Firms Growth', *Review of Industrial Organization* 8, 567-578.

Nickell, S. (1985) 'Error Correction, Partial Adjustment and All That: An Expository Note', *Oxford Bulletin of Economics and Statistics* 47, 119-129.

Orr, D. (1974) 'The Determinant of Entry: A Study of the Canadian Manufacturing Industries', *Review of Economics and Statistics* 56, 58-66.

Rosenbaum, D. and Lamort, F. (1992) 'Entry, Barriers, Exit, Sunk Costs: An Analysis', *Applied Economics* 24, 297-304.

Salmon, M. (1982) 'Error Correction Mechanisms', *Economic Journal* 92, 615-629.

Shapiro, D. (1983) 'Entry, Exit and the Theory of Multinational Corporation', in Kindleberger, C. and Audretsch, D. (eds.), *The Multinational Corporation in the 1980s,* Cambridge, MA., MIT Press.

Shapiro, D. and Khemani, R. (1987) 'The Determinants of Entry and Exit Reconsidered', *International Journal of Industrial Organization* 5, 15-26.

Sleuwaegen, L. and Dehandschutter, W. (1991) 'Entry and Exit in Belgian Manufacturing', in Geroski, P. and Schwalbach, J. (eds.), *Entry and Market Contestability: An International Comparison,* Oxford, Basil Blackwell.

Tirole, J. (1988) *The Theory of Industrial Organization,* Cambridge, MA, MIT Press.

Von der Fehr, N.H. (1991) 'Domestic Entry in Norwegian Manufacturing Industries', in Geroski, P. and Schwalbach, J. (eds.), *Entry and Market Contestability: An International Comparison,* Oxford, Basil Blackwell.

White, H. (1980) 'A Heteroskedastic-Consistent Covariance Matrix Estimator and a Direct Test for Heteroskedasticity', *Econometrica* 48, 817-838.

White, H. (1982) 'Maximum Likelihood Estimation of Misspecified Models', *Econometrica* 50, 1-25.

Yamawaki, H. (1991) 'The Effect of Business Conditions on Net Entry: Evidence From Japan', in Geroski, P. and Schwalbach, J. (eds.), *Entry and Market Contestability: An International Comparison,* Oxford, Basil Blackwell.

CHAPTER 17

Determinants of New Firm Formation in West German Regions 1986-1989: An Empirical Analysis

MICHAEL FRITSCH

Faculty of Economics and Business Administration, Technical University Bergakademie Freiberg, Freiberg, Germany

Abstract. The chapter presents results of an empirical investigation into regional differences in the formation of new firms in West Germany in the period 1986-89. Some of the findings are quite consistent with the results of similar analyses undertaken for other countries. There is a large positive correlation between the rate at which new firms are founded and the share of the regional labor force that is employed in small companies. Many founders seem to have had experience working in small firms and seem to have developed an above-average level of skill. A high unemployment rate does not promote a rise in the formation of new firms in West Germany, but an increase of unemployment is associated with a relatively high birth rate, especially in the service sector. All in all, a regional environment conducive to start-ups is characterized by low unemployment, high earnings and a well-trained labor force.

I. Introduction[1]

At least for some countries, new businesses seem to be an important source of new jobs.[2] The factors that determine the founding of new firms or establishments have been analyzed quite frequently for the United Kingdom and some other countries [see, for example, Brock and Evans (1986), Cross (1981), Evans and Jovanovich (1989), Evans and Leighton (1989), Gudgin (1978), the contributions in Keeble and Wever (1986), Moyes and Westhead (1990), Storey (1982), Storey and Johnson (1987 and 1990), O'Farrell (1986) and Reynolds and Maki (1990)]. Until recently, such an analysis has been impossible for Germany because there was no appropriate information available about the number of new businesses by sector or by region. Drawing on a new source of data, this chapter reports on the regional dimension in the formation of new firms in the period 1986-89 and investigates what determines regional differences in Germany.

Section II summarizes hypotheses and the empirical evidence provided by earlier studies on regional differences in the founding of new firms. Section III gives a description of the data base, and Section IV contains reflections on adequately measuring new firm formation on the basis of available new establishment data. Section V provides an overview of regional differences in the activities of founding establishments, and Section VI reports the results of

---

[1]This chapter is a revised and slightly extended version of Fritsch (1992). While the earlier version only analyzed start-ups in 1986, here new firms of the period 1986-89 are under study.

[2]The empirical evidence for West Germany is summarized in Fritsch, 1993.

empirical analyses of the factors that determine regional differences in the formation of new firms in West Germany. The data relate to the period 1986-89 and so include no information on the former German Democratic Republic. Section VII concludes the chapter.

II.   Hypotheses and Empirical Evidence[3]

One main result of empirical studies that have analyzed regional differences in the formation of new businesses is that a high level of such activity corresponds to a high proportion of employment in small firms. This finding is commonly interpreted to imply that small firms have a role as a *seedbed* for entrepreneurship, an argument based largely on the fact that many founders had been working in small firms before they decided to start their own business and that they developed entrepreneurial qualifications there (*cf.* Gudgin, 1978; Johnson and Cathcart, 1979a-b; Storey, 1982; and O'Farrell, 1986). The correlation between a person's employment in a small business and the probability of that person founding a new firm is also explained by the presumption that employees of small firms or establishments recognize a much closer connection between their own activity and the development of *their* establishment than do people working in large businesses. In the overwhelming majority of cases, the new business is located rather close to the founder's residence, implying that the founders represent an important part of a region's *endogenous* economic potential (*cf.* Cross, 1981; Gudgin, 1978; and O'Farrell, 1986).

It appears highly plausible that low barriers to entry into the market are conducive to the formation of new establishments. The assets belonging to a person, especially real estate, can be used as a proxy for the ability to meet the capital requirements of getting a business started: if an individual's capital limits the availability of additional external funds (*e.g.*, bank loans), then a high wealth level should contribute to a high birth rate (*cf.* Storey, 1982; and Evans and Jovanovich, 1989). The propensity to start a business is probably also influenced by an individual's skill level and career experiences (O'Farrell, 1986). The higher the skill level; the easier it may be to overcome the human-capital barriers to successfully operate the new business.

It is unclear how much influence the labor market and demand-side features have on the founding of new businesses. Fore one, several authors argue that the danger or experience of being unemployed may often be the final incentive to start a business (see Storey, 1991, for a critical review of the empirical evidence). One would therefore expect a positive correlation between the regional unemployment rate and the level of new firm formation. Additionally, the setup of new businesses may be stimulated by prospering demand (Storey, 1982; and Reynolds and Maki, 1990). Since a high level of demand also induces low unemployment, then a negative correlation between the unemployment rate and the level of start-ups is to be expected. Another line of argument

---

[3]For a more detailled discussion of the main hypotheses see Storey (1982) and Keeble and Wever (1986). A short overview of the factors that are supposed to influence new firm formation is provided by Moyes and Westhead (1990).

states that not being unemployed but *becoming* unemployed may induce entrepreneurship (*cf.* Ashcroft, Love and Malloy, 1991). Therefore, a change in the number of unemployed should have an impact on the number of births of firms in a region, with an increase in unemployment leading to higher birth of firms rates. The likelihood that a new firm will be founded is probably also influenced by several individual characteristics of the founders (*cf.* O'Farrell, 1986) as well as by the line of business. Other factors to be considered when explaining regional differences in the number of new establishments concern what may be called the *local milieu*.

III. The Data Base

Until recently, lack of data on the regional (and sectoral) distribution of start-ups has frustrated empirical analyses of regional differences in the founding of new firms in Germany. A newly developed data base that uses social insurance statistics provides such information including data of a regional breakdown of, for example, the level of skill attained by each employee, his/her position within the business and the size of the establishment.[4] Social insurance statistics are gathered at the level of individual employees, not for establishments or firms. Since the data for individuals contain an identification number for the establishment at which (s)he is employed, the statistics can be transformed to an establishment basis. Hence, new establishments can be identified from each new identification number (*i.e.*, a number that appears in the social insurance statistics for the first time). However, the interpretation of new identification numbers as new establishments may be problematic: the statistics can contain errors, a new number might be (but must not be) assigned to a takeover, and in rare cases the identification number may change for other reasons (*e.g.*, a re-organization of the ledgers that has nothing to do with the economic condition of the establishment). The exact incidence of such questionable cases is unknown, but there are many indications that it is negligible in relation to the total number of new establishments captured in the statistics each year.

To generate information on the number of start-ups it was first necessary to identify all numbers that were new to the data set in a given year (*i.e.*, which were not in the data set in the preceeding year). The social insurance statistics contain several cases in which a particular identification number arises for one year only. These cases simply represent typographical errors or new establishments that failed shortly after being founded. In order to avoid large distortions caused by errors or establishments that fail during their first few months of existence, only new identification numbers that also appeared in the data set for the following year were taken as start-ups. Most of these new establishments were very small: more than 80% had fewer than ten employees and more than

---

[4]The social insurance data are limited to the establishment level. The data base covers far more than 90% of private sector employment. Not included are civil servants, the self-employed, family workers and persons working fewer than the minimum number of hours required for compulsory insurance contributions. For a more detailed description of the data base see König and Weisshuhn (1990) and Fritsch, König and Weisshuhn (1993).

90% had fewer than fifty. But there were also several establishment-numbers new to the data set in a certain year with more than 100 employees, and it can be assumed that these establishments were either new branch plants of large firms, errors in the social insurance statistics or cases in which the identification number changed for noneconomic reasons. Because the investigation did not focus on new branch plants but rather on new firms, which usually start off as relatively small establishments, new identification numbers representing establishments with 50 or more employees were not considered to indicate the founding of an enterprise. In the present study, new firms are thus represented by those identification numbers that (i) were traced in the data sets for two subsequent years but not in the respective preceeding year and (ii) were assigned to establishments having fewer than 50 employees in the second year in which the number is reported in the social insurance statistics. Analyzed in this chapter are the start-ups in the four years 1986-89. Although the data base is limited to the establishment level, the new units are here referred to as *firms* to indicate that the focus is on business formation.

The data base contains only those establishments that have at least one employee working the minimum number of hours required for compulsory insurance contributions: *i.e.*, it comprises no businesses based entirely on self-employment, family labor and/or marginal workers. Establishments enter the social insurance statistics as soon as they begin to create, non-marginal, jobs for persons other than the founder or his/her family.[5] Data on such factors as the sectoral employment structure in the regions studied, the pattern of the size of establishment and the level of skill used in the analysis were also taken from social insurance statistics. Information on unemployment rates and salaries per employee are based on publications of the Federal Statistical Office (*Statistisches Bundesamt*). The regional basis for the analyses are the 75 planning regions (*Raumordnungsregionen*) of West Germany. Figure 1 shows the commonly used classification of West German planning regions into agglomerations, moderately congested regions and rural areas.

IV. Measuring the Founding of New Firms

Regional differences in the founding of new firms can be described by different indicators. The absolute number of start-ups is of only limited value in the present context because it does not account for regional differences in economic potential. Relating the number of start-ups to the number of existing

---

[5]Therefore it is possible that an establishment is already in existence for some time before it enters the statistics. Only rough estimations are possible about the proportion of new establishments that are not covered by the social insurance statistics. According to the 1987 Census of Business (*Arbeitsstättenzählung*), establishments with only one person (in most cases: the founder) working there accounted for 25.9% of all establishments (but only for 2.6% of all private sector employment). Since new businesses tend to start small, the proportion of new establishments that are not covered by the social insurance statistics (at least at the time they are founded) might even be higher. Unfortunately, the comparability of the social insurance statistic and the Census of Business is limited because both reporting systems operate with quite different definitions of what is an *establishment*.

Figure 1.   Geographical distribution of West German planning regions

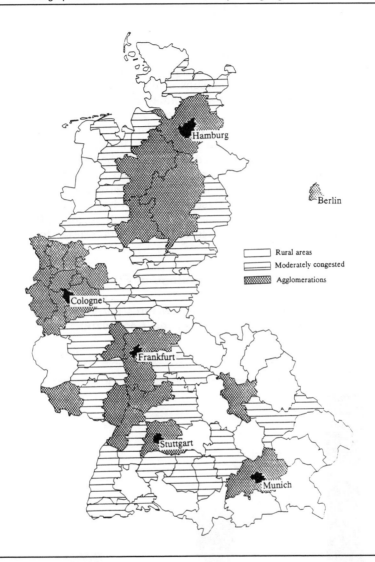

enterprises tells something about the extent of market entry. A severe disadvantage of such an indicator is that small and large establishments are accorded
the same weight. That is, the indicator obscures differences in the economic
potential of already existing establishments. For an analysis of regional variation
in the propensity to found a new business: the number of potential entrepreneurs can be considered an adequate base. Because start-ups are usually
located near the founder's residence, the regional labor force can be seen as an
appropriate measure of the number of potential founders. This view is based on
the assumption that every individual able and willing to work is faced with the

decision either to be a dependent employee or to start a business of his/her own (for a comparative analysis of both kinds of indicators see Audretsch and Fritsch, 1993).

In the analyses reported here, the number of new firms in the different sectors is related to the total regional labor force: in other words, the employees in all sectors in addition to persons registered as unemployed. This relation (number of new firms per 1,000 persons in the regional labor force) is referred to as the rate at which new firms are founded or, for short, the founding rate. To relate the number of start-ups in a given sector to the labor force of that sector would be problematic for two reasons. First, there is the problem of how to define the labor force specific to a sector (*e.g.*, the data provide no information on the sector in which unemployed persons had been working before losing their job). Second, such a unit of measure would not make much sense if many founders had worked in a different sector before starting their own businesses. Nevertheless, in the regression analyses reported in below the influence exerted by the percentage of the labor force employed in each sector on formation rates of the respective sector is tested. Note that all figures refer to *gross* market entry alone.[6]

V.   Overview of Regional Differences in Founding New Firms

Figure 2 shows the average number of new firms per year in different sectors by types of region (*cf.* Figure 1 for the regional framework).

Figure 2.   Average number of new firms per year by type of region - West Germany 1986-89

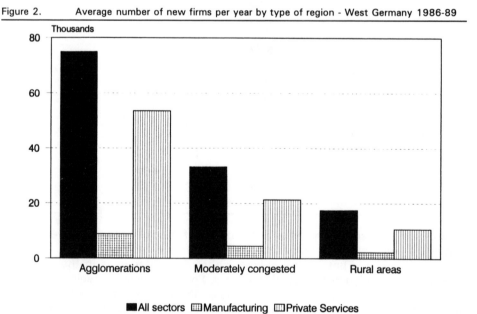

6The present form of the data set contains no information about exits. It is hoped that such information will be available in the foreseeable future.

In West Germany as a whole, about 126 thousand establishments (according to the definition used here) were founded per year in the 1986-89 period. This amounts to 8.6% of all private sector establishments. More than half of these foundings (59.7%) took place in agglomerations; only 14% were in rural areas. About 68% of all new firms were in the service sector. The service sector's share of all new firms was highest in agglomerations (71.4%) and was relatively low in rural areas (60.6%). Just over 62% of the new service firms were located in agglomerations, whereas about 12% were in rural regions. Note that manufacturing includes craft firms.

Although most start-ups take place in the agglomerations, the rates at which new firms are founded in the manufacturing sector were highest in rural areas and lowest in agglomerations (see Figure 3).

Figure 3.   Formation rates by type of region - West Germany 1986-89

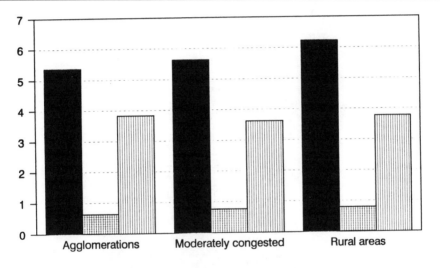

For the service sector the founding rate in agglomerations was nearly as high as in rural areas and was lowest in moderately congested regions. Figure 4 depicts the regional distribution of founding rates for all sectors. The regions with relatively high founding rates are concentrated at the northern, western and southern border, whereas the level of founding activities is relatively low in most regions in the east.[7]

---

[7]The founding rates were classified in such a way that each category contains about the same number of planning regions. The pattern of founding rates shown in Figure 2 also holds approximately for start-ups in the indiviual sectors. One main exception is that the founding rates in manufacturing at the northern border are relatively low.

Figure 4.   Regional distribution of formation rates, all sectors

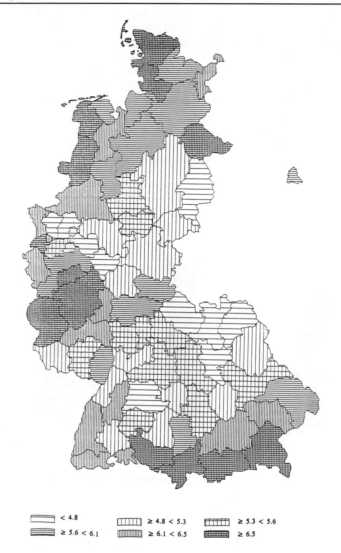

	< 4.8		≥ 4.8 < 5.3		≥ 5.3 < 5.6
	≥ 5.6 < 6.1		≥ 6.1 < 6.5		≥ 6.5

VI.   Determinants of Regional Differences in the Propensity to Found a Business

1.   FOUNDING RATE, SIZE OF ESTABLISHMENT, AND THE IMPORTANCE OF OTHER INFLUENCES

Univariate analyses have been conducted to investigate the reasons underlying regional differences in the rate at which businesses were founded in Germany during the years under study. These analyses are the basis for multiple regressions which allow for conclusions about the relative importance of the different influences on the founding of businesses. The data for West Germany confirm one of the main results of studies pertaining to other countries: a high share of employment in small businesses coincides with a high level of start-ups. Table 1 shows correlation coefficients for the relation between the founding rate and the shares of employment accounted for by different sizes of enterprises.

Table 1. Correlations between founding rate and regional pattern of size of establishment [*]

Share of all persons working in establishments having ... employees in 1985	All sectors	Manu-facturing	Services	Other sectors
Less than 5	0.90[a]	0.54[a]	0.63[a]	0.87[a]
5 - 9	0.78[a]	0.56[a]	0.47[a]	0.82[a]
10 - 19	0.70[a]	0.56[a]	0.35[a]	0.81[a]
20 - 49	0.53[a]	0.55[a]	0.19[c]	0.67[a]
50 - 99	0.33[a]	0.59[a]	0.05[c]	0.42[a]
100 - 199	-0.19[c]	0.40[a]	-0.32[a]	-0.13[c]
200 - 499	-0.24[b]	0.21[c]	-0.31[a]	-0.19[c]
500 - 999	-0.10[c]	-0.10[c]	0.05[c]	-0.22[c]
1,000 and more	-0.53[a]	-0.65[a]	-0.21[c]	-0.59[a]

[*] Pearson coefficients of correlation.
[a] Coefficient significant at the 1% level.
[b] Coefficients are significant at the 5% level.
[c] Coefficient not significant at the 5% level.

Looking first at the results for all sectors one sees that the relation between the founding rate and employment in certain size classes was strongest for employment in establishments with fewer than five employees. The values of the correlation coefficients decline as establishment size increases, and the relation between the founding rate and the share of the total regional labor force accounted for by enterprises with 1,000 or more employees is strongly negative. This pattern basically holds for each of the three economic sectors. In the service sector, it was only employment in very small establishments, those with up to 19 employees, that seemed to influence the founding rate. The correlation coefficients expressing the relation between employment in small businesses and the founding of new firms are highest for the 'other' sectors.

Many of the other variables under study were correlated to a considerable degree with the size of establishment. Table 2 therefore contains not only the Pearson coefficients of correlation expressing the relation between these variables and the founding rate but also partial correlation coefficients that control for the influence exerted by the share of the labor force accounted for by establishments with fewer than 100 employees. As can be seen from Table

2, there was a remarkably strong relation between the founding rate in the service sector and the percentage of the labor force employed in that sector. This indicates that a considerable share of the founders of businesses in services had previously worked within the service sector. This kind of relationship can also be found for start-ups in manufacturing and in 'other' sectors, but is much weaker there. Looking first at the results for all sectors, no relation appears between the founding rate and the level of unemployment. However, there was a significant correlation between the percent change of the number of unemployed in the 1984-86 period and the founding rate, being positive except for the start-ups in manufacturing. This suggests that people just becoming unemployed have a relatively high propensity to start their own business in the service sector or in the 'other' sectors. The indicator *salaries per employee in manufacturing* was negatively correlated with the share of overall regional employment accounted for by small establishments, a fact that may stem from a lower average level of skills and/or lower pay for equal skills in small establishments. The partial correlation coefficient expressing the link between the *salaries per employee in manufacturing* and the founding rate turned out to be statistically significant, indicating that a high average level of skills and/or a high wage level in a region may be stimulating for start-ups. The finding for the indicator *income tax per capita* was quite similar (see Table 2). Remarkably, the founding rate for the industrial sector was *negatively* correlated with the unemployment rate as well as with the change in the number of unemployed.

The percentage of owner-occupied housing (*Statistisches Bundesamt*, 1989) can be seen as a proxy for the capital endowment of the regional labor force. There was a large positive correlation between this variable and the size of establishment as well as the sectoral structure, a relation probably due to differences between central locations and rural or peripheral areas. The negative partial correlation coefficients that control for the influence exerted by the regional pattern of size of establishment indicate that the percentage of owner-occupied housing has a moderately inverse relation to the founding rate. The detailed breakdown of the social insurance statistics on levels of skill was condensed into six categories, an arrangement that proved meaningful in several analyses. These categories are apprentices (*Auszubildende*), unskilled/semiskilled workers, skilled workers (*Facharbeiter*), foremen (*Meister*), skilled clerical employees (*Büroangestellte*) and managers (*Führungskräfte*). As can be seen from Table 2, there were marked correlations between the share of the regional labor force in a certain skill category and the founding rate. The share of skilled workers and foremen, for example, seemed to be important for founding rates in the industrial sector, and the share of skilled clerical employees and managers was positively correlated with the founding rate in the service sector.

2. MULTIPLE REGRESSION ANALYSES

Several of the variables that may explain regional differences in the founding of new firms showed a considerable degree of correlation, which is in some cases simply due to the fact that the measures are related conceptually (*e.g.*, regional income tax per capita and salaries per employee in manufacturing are both indicators for regional wealth). To extract those explanatory variables that provide the best multivariate explanation for regional differences in the founding

Table 2.   Correlations between founding rate and explanatory variables[*]

	All sectors	Manu-facturing	Services	Other sectors
Share of employment in manufacturing 1985	-0.36[a] 0.10[c]	-0.30[a] 0.10[c]	-0.07[c] 0.23[c]	-0.55[a] -0.12[c]
Share of employment in services 1985	-0.14[c] 0.29[a]	-0.39[a] -0.12[c]	0.19[c] 0.50[a]	-0.39[a] 0.01[c]
Share of employment in *other* sectors 1985	-0.20[c] 0.30[a]	-0.44[a] -0.14[c]	0.12[c] 0.50[a]	0.42[a] 0.05[c]
Unemployment rate 1985	0.12[c] 0.03[c]	-0.30[a] -0.38[a]	-0.00[c] -0.05[c]	0.34[a] 0.24[a]
Change in unemployment 1984-86	0.44[a] 0.42[a]	-0.22[c] -0.25[a]	0.50[a] 0.48[a]	0.36[a] 0.33[a]
Regional income tax per capita 1985	-0.29[b] 0.18[c]	-0.11[c] 0.36[a]	0.03[c] 0.36[a]	-0.58[a] 0.18[b]
Salaries per employee in manufacturing 1985	-0.07[c] 0.48[a]	-0.16[c] 0.26[b]	0.21[c] 0.60[a]	-0.33[a] 0.16[c]
Share of owner-occupied housing 1987	0.24[b] -0.31[a]	0.44[a] 0.12[c]	-0.12[c] -0.55[a]	0.47[a] -0.01[c]
Share of apprentices 1985	0.55[a] 0.02[c]	0.33[a] -0.33[b]	0.17[c] -0.27[c]	0.79[a] 0.47[a]
Share of unskilled and semiskilled workers 1985	-0.22[c] -0.27[a]	0.19[c] 0.16[c]	-0.32[a] -0.35[a]	-0.11[c] -0.17[b]
Share of skilled workers 1985	-0.01[c] -0.27[a]	0.25[b] 0.06[c]	-0.26[b] -0.43[a]	0.22[c] -0.04[c]
Share of foremen 1985	-0.15[c] -0.21[b]	0.55[a] 0.50[a]	-0.31[a] -0.35[a]	-0.09[c] -0.16[b]
Share of skilled clerical employment 1985	0.07[c] 0.39[a]	-0.36[a] -0.15[c]	0.39[a] 0.61[a]	-0.22[c] -0.09[c]
Share of managers 1985	-0.18[c] 0.53[a]	-0.44[a] -0.07[c]	0.20[c] 0.81[a]	-0.46[a] 0.11[c]
Population density 1985	-0.24[b] 0.18[c]	-0.34[a] -0.03[c]	-0.01[c] 0.26[b]	-0.38[a] 0.05[c]

[*]   First row: Pearson coefficients of correlation; second row: partial correlation coefficients that control for the influence exerted by the share of overall regional employment accounted for by establishments with fewer than 100 employees.

[a]   Coefficient significant at the 1% level.

[b]   Coefficients are significant at the 5% level.

[c]   Coefficient is not significant at the 5% level.

rate various combinations of variables have been tested in regressions. These tests showed that the percentage of owner-occupied housing in a region, regional per capita income taxes and the share of apprentices in the total regional labor force were not statistically significant when included together with a size-structure indicator and the share of employees with certain skill levels. Therefore, these indicators were excluded from further analyses. The respective share of skilled, unskilled and semiskilled workers were not statistically significant or showed a negative influence on the founding rate. Since these figures are complementary to the share of employees in the higher skill categories and are largely correlated with these indicators, they were also omitted.

Table 3 shows results of multiple regression analyses (OLS) intended to explain regional rates at which new firms are founded in the different sectors.[8] It contains the beta coefficients, which can be interpreted as measures of the relative importance of the different explanatory variables. The pattern of size of establishment had the greatest impact on the founding rate.[9] The salaries per employee in manufacturing also had a statistically significant influence. The share of foremen in the regional labor force had an impact on the founding rate in manufacturing; the share of managers and of qualified clerical employees seemed to be conducive to the founding of establishments in the service sector. These results may be interpreted as an indication that the founders of firms have acquired a high level of skill. The share a regions's labor force employed in manufacturing or services is not statistically significant, implying that many founders moved across sectoral boundaries when they started their own businesses. In the estimations for all sectors the unemployment rate was not statistically significant. The equations for manufacturing and for services show a slightly significant negative sign for the influence of the unemployment rate, whereas in the estimations for the 'other' sectors the impact of the unemployment rate is positive. A rise of unemployment seems to be conducive to new firm formation except in the manufacturing sector.

The often observed large positive correlation between employment share in small establishments and the founding rate is commonly explained by arguing that employees in small establishments are apt to start a new business, suggesting that the influence of the different levels of skill defined above varies according to the size of the establishment. Perhaps foremen employed in small, as opposed to large, establishments are the ones most likely to start a new firm. To get a clearer picture of the potential entrepreneurs, the relevant qualifications were differentiated by size of establishment with the skill variables being expressed as the share of people in the regional labor force who possess a

---

[8]All equations were linear and the variables are as in Table 4. Since the residuals showed (more or less) the desired properties, there was no need for more sophisticated models.

[9]The variable for the pattern of size of establishment for a certain sector was based on the results of univariate analyses (see Figure 3). For the service sector, it is the share of regional employment accounted for by establishments with up to 19 employees; for manufacturing, it is the share of regional employment accounted for by establishments with fewer than 200 employees. In the equation for all sectors, the indicator for the size pattern is the share of total regional employment in establishments with fewer than 100 employees.

Table 3.   Regressions to explain the regional rate at which new firms are founded (I) *

Variable	All sectors	Manufacturing (I)	Manufacturing (II)	Services	Other sectors
Employment share in establishments with fewer than 20 employees	...	...	...	0.93 (9.90)	...
Employment share in establishments with fewer than 100 employees	0.93 (13.17)	...	...	...	0.84 (11.49)
Employment share in establishments with fewer than 200 employees	...	0.69 (8.02)	0.60 (8.47)	...	...
Salaries per employee in manufactoring	0.44 (6.70)	0.16^c (1.76)	...	...	0.30 (3.30)
Share of foremen	...	0.39 (5.16)	0.39 (5.09)	...	-0.21 (2.51)
Share of skilled clerical employment	...	...	...	0.23 (2.32)	...
Share of managers	...	...	...	0.44 (3.67)	...
Population density	0.14 (2.16)	...	...	0.18 (2.46)	...
Unemployment rate	...	-0.15^c (1.83)	-0.2 (2.63)	-0.18 (2.14)	0.18 (2.08)
Change in unemployment 1984-86	0.33 (5.94)	...	...	0.23 (2.33)	0.29 (3.37)
Adjusted R^2	0.790	0.653	0.643	0.732	0.754

* Beta coefficients with t values between brackets. All coefficients (except the ones marked 'c') and all equations are significant at the 5% level.

given skill and work in establishments of a given size. Keyed to the number of employees, the size categories used in the analysis were *fewer than 20, 20 - 199, 200 - 999*, and *1,000 or more* employees.

Table 4 shows the regression estimates. The variable for the regional pattern of size of establishment was omitted because it correlated closely with the variables expressing skills by size of establishment. If the variable for the regional pattern of size of establishment is included in the regression structure, it leads only to a slight increase of the R^2 at best. The results are consistent with the hypothesis that members of the labor force who possess a given skill and work in small establishments are the ones most likely to found a business of their own. In the manufacturing sector, the founding rate was influenced most by the share of the total regional work force employed as foremen in

Table 4.   Regressions to explain the regional rate at which new firms are founded (II) *

Variable	Manufacturing	Services (I)	Services (II)
Salaries per employee in manufacturing 1985	0.10ᶜ (1.32)		0.31 (2.51)
Share of foremen 1985 in establishments with			
- fewer than 20 employees	0.62 (5.94)		
- 20-199 employees	0.26 (2.05)		
- 200-999 employees	0.12ᶜ (1.21)		
- 1,000 and more employees	0.06ᶜ (0.71)		
Share of skilled clerical employees 1985 in establishments with			
- fewer than 20 employees		0.97 (7.70)	
- 20-199 employees		-0.33 (2.84)	
- 200-999 employees		0.22 (2.00)	
- 1,000 and more employees		0.39 (3.47)	
Share of manager 1985 in establishments with			
- fewer than 20 employees			0.61 (4.02)
- 20-199 employees			0.17ᶜ (1.05)
- 200-999 employees			-0.57 (3.73)
- 1,000 and more employees			-0.21ᶜ (1.79)
Unemployment rate 1985		-0.19 (2.09)	
Change in unemployment 1984-86		0.29 (2.69)	0.41 (4.33)
Adjusted R²	0.674	0.665	0.524

*   Beta coefficients with t values in brackets. The coefficients marked with 'c' are not significant at the 5% level. All other coefficients and all equations are significant at the 5% level.

establishments with fewer than 20 employees. The next most influential factor was the share of the total regional work force employed as foremen in establishments with 20 to 199 employees. The coefficients for the share of the total regional work force employed as foremen in larger establishments were too low to be statistically significant. Quite similiar results were found for the importance of managers working in small and large establishments for the start-ups in the service sector. A rather different pattern of skills by size of establishment emerged for the influence of skilled clerical empoyees on the founding rate in the service sector, where the founding of new firms seemed to be positively influenced only by the share of skilled clerical employees working in establishments having fewer than 20 or more than 199 employees. It is somewhat surprising that skilled clerical employment in large establishments had a positive impact on the founding of establishments. A possible explanation is that skilled nonmanagerial office employees working in large firms are relatively often frustrated by their work environment and expect favorable prospects from starting their own businesses.

VII. Concluding Observations

The results of this investigation into the factors determining regional differences in the founding of establishments in Germany are consistent with the findings of studies pertaining to other countries - namely, that the small-business sector functions as a kind of *seedbed*. There is a large positive correlation between the founding rate and the share of the regional labor force that is employed in small establishments. Obviously, many of the new entrepreneurs had skills that were specific to their occupation and had worked in small establishments before starting their own businesses. All in all, the results indicate that the level of unemployment did not promote the founding of establishments in West Germany, at least during the year under study. Nevertheless, a rise in unemployment seems to have had a positive impact on the founding rate in the service sector and in 'other' sectors, but this influence was negative for the start-ups in manufacturing. This might indicate that people that are *becoming* unemployed have a relatively high propensity to start an own business in services or in 'other' sectors and that they are not very likely to found a firm in manufacturing, where barriers to entry are normally relatively high. It cannot be completely precluded that the stimulating effect of a high demand overruled a possible *push effect* of unemployment. But this does not seem to be very likely since the above analyses strongly indicate that founders of new businesses tend to have a high skill level: it is well known that such persons normally face a relatively low danger of being unemployed.[10]

---

[10]Other studies for West Germany confirm this view. It has been shown in several analyses that the share of businesses that are founded by formerly unemployed persons in West Germany was far below 10%. An empirical investigation into the personal background and the career history of West German founders by Klandt (1984) comes to the conclusion that unemployment is of only minor importance in explaining new firm formation and that the founders of fast growing start-ups have had good carreer prospects in their former occupation.

References

Ashcroft, B., Love, J.H. and Malloy, E. (1991) 'New Firm Formation in the British Counties with Special Reference to Scotland', *Regional Studies* **24**, 395-409.

Audretsch, D.B. and Fritsch, M. (1993) 'Measuring the Entry of New Firms in Germany', *Discussion paper FS IV 93-9*, Wissenschaftszentrum Berlin für Sozialforschung, March 1993.

Brock, W.A. and Evans, D.S. (1986) *The Economics of Small Businesses: Their Role and Regulation in the U.S. Economy*, Holmes and Meier, New York.

Cross, M. (1981) *New Firm Formation and Regional Development*, Gower, Farnborough.

Evans, D.S. and Jovanovich, B. (1989) 'An Estimated Model of Entrepreneurial Choice under Liquidity Constraints', *Journal of Political Economy* **97**, 808-827.

Evans, D.S. and Leighton, L.S. (1989) 'Some Empirical Aspects of Entrepreneurship', *American Economic Review* **79**, 519-539.

Fritsch, M. (1992) 'Regional Differences in New Firm Formation: Evidence from West Germany', *Regional Studies* **25**, 233-241.

Fritsch, M. (1993) 'The Role of Small Firms in West Germany', in Acs Z.J. and Audretsch D.B. (eds), *Small Firms and Entrepreneurship: An East-West Perspective*, Cambridge University Press, Cambridge, MA, 38-54.

Fritsch, M., König, A. and Weisshuhn, G. (1993) 'Die Beschäftigtenstatistik als Betriebspanel - Ansatz, Probleme und Analysepotentiale (The social insurance statistics as an establishment panel)', in Hochmuth, U. and Wagner, J. (eds), *Firmenpanelstudien in Deutschland - Konzeptionelle Überlegungen und empirische Analysen (Firm-Panel Studies in Germany)*, Francke, Tübingen.

Gudgin, G. (1978) *Industrial Location Processes and Regional Employment Growth*, Westmead, Saxon House.

Johnson, P.S. and Cathcart, D.G. (1979a) 'The Founders of New Manufacturing Firms: A Note on the Size of their "Incubator" Plants', *Journal of Industrial Economics* **28**, 219-224.

Johnson, P.S. and Cathcart, D.G. (1979b) 'New Manufacturing Firms and Regional Development: Some Evidence from the Northern Region', *Regional Studies* **13**, 269-280.

Keeble, D. and Wever, E. (1986) 'Introduction', in Keeble, D. and Wever E. (eds), *New Firms and Regional Development in Europe*, Croom Helm, London, 1-34.

Klandt, H. (1984) *Aktivität und Erfolg des Unternehmensgründers (Activity and Success of Founders of New Businesses)*, Eul, Bergisch Gladbach.

König, A. and Weisshuhn, G. (1990) 'Changes in Enterprise Size and Employment Levels in the Branches of the Federal Republic of Germany 1980 to 1986', in Schettkat, R. and Wagner, M. (eds) *Technological Change and Employment*, De Gruyter, New York, 111-132.

Moyes, A. and Westhead, P. (1990) 'Environments for New Firm Formation in Great Britain', *Regional Studies* **24**, 123-136.

O'Farrell, P. (1986) *Entrepreneurs and Industrial Change*, Irish Management Institute, Dublin.

Reynolds, P.D. and Maki, W.R. (1990) 'Business Volatility and Economic Growth (Final Project Report)', *Unpublished manuscript*, Minneapolis.

Statistisches Bundesamt (1989) *Bautätigkeit und Wohnen, Gebäude- und Wohnungszählung vom 25. Mai 1987* **5**, Poeschel, Stuttgart.

Storey, D.J. (1982) *Entrepreneurship and the New Firm*, Croom Helm, London.

Storey, D.J. and Johnson, S. (1987) *Job Generation and Labour Market Change*, MacMillan, London.

Storey, D.J. and Johnson, S. (1990) 'A Review of Small Business Employment Data Bases in the United Kingdom', *Small Business Economics* **2**, 279-299.

Storey, D.J. (1991) 'The Birth of New Firms - Does Unemployment Matter: A Review of the Evidence', *Small Business Economics* **3**, 167-178.

PART V

POLICY ISSUES

Integration of Europe and Development of
the Third World

A key element of IO is the assessment of society's welfare and the need for governmental intervention. Here, the large literature on antitrust and regulation policy is illustrative. Part V deals with three policy issues that will be, for obvious reasons, at the heart of the political scenery in the decades to come: the restructuring of Eastern Europe (Chapter 18), the integration of the European Union (Chapter 19) and the development of the Third World (Chapter 20). The three chapters reveal that IO has something to say on such issues of global interest.

CHAPTER 18

Problems of Restructuring in Eastern Europe

ERHARD KANTZENBACH
University of Hamburg, HWWA-Institut für Wirtschaftsforschung, Germany

Abstract. The breakdown of communism in Eastern Europe raised fundamental new problems for economic policy as well as economic theory. In economic science there has been developed a fairly sophisticated theory of comparative economic systems but no theory of the transformation process from a planned to a market economy. This chapter describes some of the characteristics of the transformation process and some of the methodological problems of the development of a corresponding theory.

I. Introduction

The problem of restructuring Eastern Europe is a fascinating topic in two different respects. The *first* thing which is so interesting about it, is its political relevance. There is nothing which has captured the attention of economists quite as strongly in recent years as the transformation of the economic systems in the former communist countries. That is equally true for both American and European members of the profession. However, for reasons which will be obvious, it has been a special focus of interest for economists in Germany. If the countries of Eastern Europe do not manage to establish market economic systems capable of functioning properly within a matter of years, this will not just be a threat to living standards and political stability in those countries alone. In the event of failure, Western Europe too would be confronted with insoluble social and political problems as a wave of refugees swepts towards it. Thus it is in Western Europe's own vital interests to be concerned with transformation problems in Eastern Europe. The *second* point about these problems is that they are also particularly interesting from a scientific point of view, since we have not even attempted, as yet, to formulate a comprehensive theory of transformation. This deficiency has been alluded to in a wide variety of published work, and is especially striking in situations in which economists are called upon to present a scientific judgment of the transformation policies being pursued by individual countries. Projects of this nature are increasingly being entrusted to empirically oriented economic research institutes. This is both a good thing and a necessary one. Nevertheless, we realize again and again just how little we are really able to provide a reliable analysis of the complex interrelationships involved. It is therefore a truly challenging scientific task to develop a theory of transformation and then also, on that basis, to go on to devise a theoretically sound transformation strategy.

At present, though, this chapter has only a humble contribution to make towards that quest. The chapter points out a number of problems associated with the transformation process which would appear to be particularly important in the light of the experience so far. In methodological terms, we are currently still at the stage of proposing intuitive hypotheses on the strength of subjective observations. The plan of the chapter is as follows. Section II briefly summarizes the key two-sided dilemma of capitalism *vs* communism and democracy *vs* dictatorship. Section III describes the current state of the transformation process in Eastern Europe. Section IV confronts the 'big bang' with the gradual approach to this transformation process. Section V gives an impression of the political dilemma that goes along with transforming former communist into capitalist economies. Section VI discusses the issue of policy coordination. Section VII elaborates on the experiences in Poland, Hungary and (former) Czechoslovakia, and Sections VIII and IX deal with the special position of former East Germany. Section X concludes the chapter.

II.   Capitalism *vs* Communism and Democracy *vs* Dictatorship

The main reason why we are unable to rely on secure theoretical knowledge in order to assess transformation processes, lies in the complexity of the process itself. This involves both a transition from communist dictatorship to parliamentary democracy and one from a planned to a market economy. Historical experience shows that these two aspects - the political and the economic - are mutually determined. Other theoretically conceivable combinations have indeed occurred as transitory phenomena in real life. However, such combinations have not proved stable over the longer term. The same applies to attempts to embark upon a *third way* between capitalism and socialism by combining elements of market and planned economies. A large number of theoretical models and political experiments with this intent has been designed. However, the only systems to have proved implementable on a sustainable basis have been those in which one or other of the two possible coordination mechanisms - market or hierarchy - occupied a dominant position in determining how the system basically operates.

We are currently witnessing the breakdown of the socialist system of organizing societies in Central and Eastern Europe. Evidently, then, the democratic market-economy system has proved superior under modern technical and economic conditions. There is no historical precedent for the process of total transformation this has unleashed, and hence no source to turn to for useful experience. Experiential knowledge of particular economic processes, which is available in abundance, is always based on the premise that the surrounding political framework will remain constant. This, of all premises, simply cannot be met in the complex overall process occurring today. All this means that we are left to gather experience, and put forward initial hypotheses derived from it, in a process of interdisciplinary cooperation between political scientists and economists.

III.   Current State of the Transformation: Eastern Europe

This section presents a brief survey of the present stage reached in the transformation process in the various countries of Eastern Europe (*Sachverständigenrat*, 1991: 48; and Schneider, 1992: 3). As an initial, superficial impression, it can be said that the farther west the countries are located, the more advanced the process now is. The transformation process is at its most advanced stage in Poland, Czechoslovakia (now separated, but treated here as united) and Hungary. All three countries now have stable parliamentary democracies in which non-communist parties hold the majority.[1] Although the initial situations in the three countries were very different, they have all set about establishing a market economy system with considerable energy. Since it is thus in these three countries that most experience has now been gathered, subsequent sections concentrate on these countries. In the political sense, the situation in the three Baltic countries is similar to that in Poland, Czechoslovakia and Hungary. They too have completed the change to parliamentary democracy. However, economic transformation is especially impeded by the fact that, owing to their histories as Soviet republics, their economies are particularly closely interwoven with the rest of the former Soviet Union. Rumania, Bulgaria and Albania have so far made less progress than their counterparts to the north and west, both in terms of the political and the economic transformation processes. Here too, though, freely elected parliaments have now undertaken the first legislative steps towards creating a market economic order. However, it is still too early to assess the political stability of these countries, or the success of the economic reforms they have so far embarked upon. What paths will be taken in the future by the successor states of the former Soviet Union and former Yugoslavia is still an open question. Neither the geographical borders of these countries nor their political or economic systems can be foretold with any degree of certainty. Finally, former East Germany occupies a special place amongst the transforming countries. On the one hand, re-unification with former West Germany has ensured that the conditions for political and economic transformation are now absolutely secure. On the other hand, the fact that income levels for those in employment have been rapidly catching up with those in the west, has also created considerable growth and employment problems. Below we shall, in due course, look rather more closely at this problem.

IV. Big Bang *vs* Gradual Approach

As the scientific discussion began, the most prominent issue was one of *how quickly* the transformation process ought to take place. The question was: should it be pushed through as abruptly and rapidly as possible, the *big bang* approach, or should allowance be made for a longer period of adjustment, gradualism (Lösch, 1992)? The method of *piecemeal social engineering* developed by Karl Popper (1969), and generally accepted in economic theory, would have favored the second, gradual approach. By proceeding on a step-by-step, partial basis it is possible to review the outcome of the previous stage of reform before beginning with the next, and to make course corrections where necessary. This strategy is appropriate in stable and generally accepted societal systems where the success of implementing reforms in particular areas is uncertain. The

---

[1]Note that in recent elections former communist parties are gaining power again. Formally, however, these parties are now non-communist (social democratic).

method has the advantage that the steps taken can be reversed if the results prove disappointing.

However, the original starting situation in the Central and Eastern European reforming countries was fundamentally different - in the eyes of liberal reformers at least. A stable societal system capable of consensus was precisely what they did not have; instead, there was a revolutionary situation in which the liberal reforming forces had just assumed power. Their objective was, of course, one of pushing ahead very rapidly with the system transformation so as to reach a point of no return. The intention was to rule out any possibility of relapse into the old, dictatorial, planned economy system. One had to avoid giving any opportunity to the *nomenclatura*, just removed from power, for regrouping to sabotage the reforms and then to return to power if temporary setbacks occurred.

In contrast to the gradualist type of reform carried out within democratic systems, the ultimate target of the transformation undertaken in Central and Eastern Europe was quite clearly democracy and the market economy. On the strength of experience in the West there was no doubt as to the desirability of such a system in the eyes of the liberal reformers. Where there was uncertainty, however, it involved the course the transformation process should take and what level of transitional welfare losses would arise. If the latter were to turn out to be very great and to last a considerable time, the reforming forces faced the prospect of losing public support. They therefore very quickly needed to be able to show some initial success. These considerations all generated a preference for the *big bang* approach.

V. The Political Economy of Transformation

The first attempts are now being made to use the theory of political economy to interpret the transformation process for policy-makers, and to derive recommendations for political strategy from the analysis (Roland, 1992; Apolte and Cassel, 1991: 140; and Leipold, 1991: 228). The theoretical assumption is that each stage of transformation has certain benefits and certain costs for the general public, which will be unevenly distributed over different groups. The overall nature of the resulting strategy recommendations is that individual stages need to be designed and combined so that the winners within society are in the majority over the losers. Provided that this condition is met, the theory goes on to argue that the transformation process will indeed receive the political support from the public it needs.

However appealing this approach may be in fundamental terms, it runs into two serious problems. Firstly, the political frame conditions change fundamentally during the transformation process itself. In the initial situation under dictatorship, for any individual to express an opposing opinion may lead to substantial personal disadvantages, or even threaten his/her very existence. Such disadvantages tend to decrease, and indeed to approach zero, as democratization proceeds. To express this in theoretical terms: like in the market process, in the process of political decision-making different levels of transaction costs will arise, which will influence the workability of the system and which therefore have to be properly taken into account.

Secondly, previous experience shows that the transformation process general-ly leads in the first instance to significant welfare losses. These arise because output and performance fall off as the old institutions collapse much more quickly than the new institutions can be developed to their full potential. The consequences are drops in production, employment and real income, even to the extent of generating severe supply shortages. Under such circumstances, it is hard to conceive of the *winners* being in the majority. Hence, the only way political support can be obtained in this situation, is through strength of the public's future expectations. Yet, such expectations are unstable, susceptible to manipulation by propaganda, and virtually impossible to ascertain empirically.

The economic approach to policy analysis, then, hardly leads to any other conclusion than plain common sense. Before the Central and Eastern European transformation processes could be triggered off, the general public first had to build up a widespread, intensive rejection of the ruling socialist systems. However, the process can only be sustained if there is a similarly widespread feeling that there is the prospect of a lasting improvement in the people's circumstances.

VI. Policy Coordination

1.   SEQUENCING

As indicated earlier, the transformation process in Poland, Hungary and Cze-choslovakia has so far made most progress. A parliamentary system has evidently managed to establish itself in each of these countries. Parliamentary majorities were or still are held by *centre-right* parties. Current governments are seeking to introduce market economic systems. Thus, the will to transform the system is not cast into doubt in these countries, but what is open to intense discussion is the concrete form the transformation ought to take. At least in these three countries, then, the question of optimal timing must now be answered rather differently than five years ago, when the changes first began to unfold. The *point of no return*, which initially was essential to be reached as quickly as possible, has indeed been passed by now. The main challenge now is one of implementing the transformation process as smoothly and harmoniously as possible. The key concern is to keep supply shortages, inflation, unemploy-ment and *unjust* distribution effects to the minimum. Thus, maximum speed has given way to the optimal coordination of individual steps, or to what is known as sequencing, as the dominant problem (Apolte and Cassel, 1991: 121; and Lösch, 1992). In the context of sequencing the wide variety of individual economic policy measures necessary to transform the economy can be grouped into three main problem complexes (Apolte and Cassel, 1991: 115): (i) creating a suitable institutional framework; (ii) establishing workable market-economy microstructures; (iii) sustaining macroeconomic stabilization.

2.   INSTITUTIONAL FRAMEWORK

It is a trivial observation in theoretical terms that a market economic system requires an appropriate institutional framework (*Sachverständigenrat*, 1991:

48). Yet in practice, constructing such a framework is running into substantial difficulties in countries such as Poland, Hungary and Czechoslovakia which have spent more than forty years living under a legal system deliberately intended to impose an opposite framework. Of course, the problems confronting the other former communist countries are much greater, since seventy years ago they were led straight out of a feudal, absolutist order into the communist system. As a result, they did not have the chance to gain any experience with liberal economic systems.

Vertical planning and command hierarchies now have to be replaced by private property rights over autonomous enterprises, and contract law appropriate to organize the wide variety of exchange and cooperative relations between such enterprises has to be designed. Unless these rules are in place, free prices will be unable to fulfil their macroeconomic guiding functions. A monetary regime needs to be set up which includes a two-tier banking system, a financial regime incorporating both high-yielding general taxation and rigid budgetary restrictions, and a properly functioning system of competition controls. Because the transition to a market economy initially involves the shedding of a large amount of labor, it is a matter of utmost priority to establish a system of unemployment support. In addition, measures need to be taken to cushion the effects of price rises upon socially weak groups in society. Before any of these institutions can be developed, the countries involved need a civil service and independent courts capable of functioning, both occupied by well-trained, loyal staff or judges. Experience in former East Germany shows that this is a serious bottleneck for further development, even in the relatively favorable circumstances prevailing in Germany.

3.   MICROECONOMIC STRUCTURES

In addition to these basic institutional provisions, steps have to be taken to create workable market-economy microstructures by breaking down the highly vertically integrated, monopolistic state enterprises into separate, competitive firms (Apolte and Cassel, 1991: 129). This is the only way in which properly functioning markets can develop at all the different stages of production. In countries like Poland, Hungary and Czechoslovakia, with relatively small economies, a conflict arises in certain industries between the objective of creating enterprises sufficiently large and technically efficient and the wish to create market structures which are sufficiently decentralized and will thus enhance allocative and dynamic efficiency. The only way of alleviating this conflict is to allow foreign competition to enter into domestic markets and to export one's own products.

Even for reasons relating to the underlying policy regarding the economic system itself it is important to liberalize foreign trade. However, this liberalization ought to be introduced stepwise in order to allow enterprises to adjust gradually to the new competitive conditions. In this process, completely different industry structures will develop at the level of the macroeconomy, for the state-controlled foreign trade of the past often had little to do with comparative cost advantages. Temporarily, the economic and legal autonomy of individual enterprises may in itself create a substantial boost to efficiency. However, all available experience shows that it is also essential to transfer the majority of the firms to private ownership. Only then will lasting incentive structures be created that can encourage efficient entrepreneurial behavior. With this in mind, all of the reforming countries have now begun to privatize their state enterprises (Apolte and Cassel, 1991: 118; and *Sachverständigenrat*, 1991: 52).

To date it is clear from experience that so-called *minor privatization*, creating family businesses in wholesaling and retailing, craft trades and services, can be implemented relatively rapidly and easily. *Major privatization*, however, of large-scale industrial enterprises is a more controversial affair. Two alternative concepts for carrying out the latter are at the center of discussions. First, a plan which can be realized relatively quickly is the distribution of rights of ownership at little or no charge to broad segments of the general public - *e.g.*, through the voucher system used in Czechoslovakia. The main advantage of this method is distributional: it prevents a *sell-out of the nation's wealth* to foreign interests. However, this leaves the unsolved problem of how to exert effective monitoring control over an enterprise's management. Second, an alternative approach, adopted in former East Germany, is to sell off enterprises in the open market to the highest bidder, generally representing Western interests. This has the advantage of making additional capital and management knowledge available to these economically run-down firms: experience in Eastern Germany has proved that these assets are especially important in order to gain access to Western markets.

4.   MACROECONIMIC STABILIZATION

In most of the reforming countries the necessity for macroeconomic stabilization arises out of the pent-up demand within these economies (Apolte and Cassel, 1991: 116). For the most part, this demand accumulated during the planned economy era, as government expenditure was financed by printing money. The underlying problem was subsequently exacerbated during the transformation process since production cutbacks led to further supply shortages.

Three methods of reducing the amount of pent-up demand are proposed. The first suggests a currency reform in which the stock of money in circulation is converted into a new currency, reduced by a certain ratio. By allowing a certain basic fixed sum per person to be exchanged at a more beneficial rate, it is also possible to simultaneously pursue a distributional policy goal. Moreover, this presents an opportunity to check whether or not money has been legitimately obtained. The second, apparently a particularly elegant solution, is to combine the process of reducing pent-up demand with the privatization of state-owned businesses. However, a precondition for this to work is that it is possible to carry out the privatization within a short timespan, and furthermore that the sale proceeds will not only be at least equivalent to total pent-up demand but will subsequently be taken out of circulation as well. There is reason to doubt whether these conditions can be fulfilled. If neither of the above routes can be taken for lack of administrative efficiency, the third alternative is that of adjustment inflation. Although, in theory, one cannot rule out the possibility that such inflation will remain confined to a one-off movement to adjust to the new conditions or that it will be neutral in its effect on the distribution of income and wealth, the chances of this being the case are slight in practice. There is a real danger that such price movements will trigger off a wage-price spiral.

Events in Poland, in particular, show how difficult it is to apply the brakes to an open inflationary process. Even worse, a rigorous stabilization policy induces severe drops in production and employment and distributional losses to societal groups which are less able to assert their positions, (*e.g.*, pensioners). There is therefore considerable political pressure to pursue a more expansionary policy. Yet, it is absolutely essential to reduce pent-up demand and attain stable price levels if the market economy is to be capable of functioning as it should. This, in turn, requires a central bank able to pursue its policies independently of the government, and pledged exclusively to the task of creating monetary stability. These central bank policies, however, can only assert themselves if parliament and government alike are constrained by strict budgetary discipline as well.

5.   TIMING OF INTERDEPENDENCIES
A central problem for transformation policy is to coordinate the timing of the three different complexes of measures described. The reason why this is so important, is that the measures are mutually dependent in their success. This complicates matters considerably, as each individual measure requires a certain minimum period to be put into effect. It is self-evident that an appropriate institutional framework is a precondition for operating a market economy. This, therefore, has to be put in place at the beginning of the transformation process. However, discussing and passing laws or setting up administrative authorities and courts with trained staff all take a long time. During that time, however, the previously existing planned economy institutions suffer a loss of authority, which calls into question their ability to maintain production and supply of goods and services to the public. This is the trend we are currently witnessing in Russia. The implication is that *ad hoc* measures to maintain production and supplies need to be taken before the new institutional framework has been established.

However, the focal point for scientific discussion is how to coordinate micro- and macroeconomic reform measures (Lösch, 1992). For example, even with properly functioning competition the freeing of prices would inevitably create a rush of inflation, unless the pent-up purchasing power had first been reduced. Conversely, any macroeconomic stabilization policy would not achieve the desired effects on prices and employment, unless the signals it sends out could be responded to by market competitive structures and profit-oriented entrepreneurial behavior. Policy-makers, therefore, frequently need to rely on an *ad hoc* approach if the conditions for measures conforming to a market economic order cannot yet be fulfilled. For example, there will be a tendency to initially exclude sensitive goods such as rents, basic food and energy whilst other prices are freed, preferring to adjust the former gradually in order to restrain the adverse distributional effects of the inevitable boost to inflation.

VII. Real-World Experiences

1.   FOUR EXAMPLES
In the real world the transformation process has proceeded very differently in the four furthest advanced countries of Poland, Hungary, East Germany and

Czechoslovakia. In Poland and Hungary the planned economy system had gradually been shot through with various holes during the past ten years, which is in stark contrast with the histories of Czechoslovakia and East Germany. This section subsequently deals with Poland, Hungary and Czechoslovakia. The next section focuses on the former German Democratic Republic.

2.   POLAND

In terms of its regulatory framework *Poland* was notable for the fact that most of its agricultural sector had remained under private ownership, with the exception of the territories which had previously belonged to Germany, and the fact that employees in the state-owned industrial enterprises had substantial co-determination rights. Poland's macroeconomic policy had been *stop-go*: whenever steps were taken towards political liberalization, these invariably led to increased wages and consumption, thus accelerating inflation and bringing the balance of payments into disequilibrium. To impose more modest wage demands and stabilization, repressive political measures regularly were deployed subsequently.

Poland embarked upon its policy of deliberate system transformation during a phase of hyper-inflation. In 1989 the combination of the freeing of agricultural prices, wage increases and a government budget deficit brought about a 244% increase in consumer prices, which even doubled in 1990 (*Forschungsinstitute*, 1992a: 9). In January 1990 the first freely elected government adopted the Balcerowicz Plan with its radical program of stabilization (Apolte and Cassel, 1991: 122). Its main ingredients were restrictive monetary and fiscal policies coupled with the devaluation of the zloty. Accompanying microeconomic changes were the release of prices and reduction of subsidies.

On the one hand, the government did succeed in reducing the rate of price inflation to 70% in 1991. However, the price of that success - as was to be expected - was a drastic fall-off in production and employment. Gross domestic product declined by 12% in 1990 and by another 9% in 1991 (*Forschungsinstitute*, 1992a: 9). The cuts in income suffered by large parts of the public as a result of this rigorous stabilization policy were almost bound to have political consequences. They have contributed to the fact that four governments have fallen in Poland since 1990. In contrast with the *shock therapy* implied by the macroeconomic stabilization program progress with microeconomic structural reforms has been very slow. Privatization has been sluggish and incomplete so far, with the state retaining substantial shares of capital. The management and employees of the enterprises affected are given preference when new shares are allocated. Foreign interests are restricted to a 10% participation (Apolte and Cassel, 1991: 125). Because of the inadequacies in this structural reform the restrictive monetary policy has also been deprived of some of its effectiveness. Neither the banks nor industrial enterprises are managed solely according to criteria of profitability, and they are not subject to tough budgetary restrictions. As a result, there is hardly any institutional constraint on credit expansion (Apolte and Cassel, 1991: 119 and 125; *Frankfurter Institut*, 1992: 47; and Heinrich, 1991: 150).

3.   HUNGARY
In contrast to Poland, *Hungary* has been pursuing a policy of gradual transition
to the market economy. Initial priority was given to establishing the necessary
institutional frame conditions. A two-tier banking system was introduced as
long ago as 1987, although the commercial banks were not privatized. In 1988
the taxation system was adapted to suit market economic conditions (Heinrich,
1991: 154). Prices were freed stepwise from controls, before being completely
released in 1991 (Apolte and Cassel, 1991: 133). Since 1989 import restrictions, too, have been eased in a series of steps (Heinrich, 1991: 154). During
this gradual liberalization process Hungary's level of pent-up demand was lower
than in Poland. The inflation rate in 1989 was only 17%, but it did increase to
29% and then to 35% in the following two years (*Forschungsinstitute*, 1992a:
9). Gross domestic product did not go into decline until 1990, when it fell 5%
before dropping another 8% in 1991 (*Forschungsinstitute*, 1992a: 9). The
deterioration in the country's economic situation can substantially be attributed
to the collapse of its old COMECON markets.
    State-owned enterprises are being privatized according to the provisions of a
privatization law adopted in 1989. Some enterprises select their own purchasers
- in a process known as spontaneous privatization - while in other cases the
businesses are placed in the market *via* a government assets agency, without
there being any discrimination against foreign purchasers (Apolte and Cassel,
1991: 132).

4.   CZECHOSLOVAKIA
The case of *Czechoslovakia* differs from those of Poland and Hungary, and
resembles East Germany in one respect, in the sense that its political and
economic systems remained relatively rigid until late 1989 or early 1990,
without any appreciable liberalization before that time. On the favorable side,
this also meant that the country's macroeconomic stability was relatively high
(Apolte and Cassel, 1991: 126). The transformation of the economic system
took place abruptly, as in Poland, but not until the turn of the year 1990 -
1991. Privatization began in December 1990. The *minor privatization* to form
family businesses was relatively swift and unproblematic. The *major privatization* of large industrial enterprises has largely been conducted as a process of
open sale to both domestic and foreign investors. A small proportion of the
stocks has also been distributed evenly, at virtually no cost, among the domestic population, under what is known as the voucher system.
    Prices were freed abruptly in January 1991, while a severely restrictive
monetary and fiscal policy was introduced simultaneously. The currency was
devalued by 65%, and internal convertibility was established for current transactions. This *shock therapy* transformation induced a price inflation of 58% in
1991, and the gross domestic product declined by 16% (*Forschungsinstitute*,
1992a: 9). The fact that such a radical policy is not uncontroversial in political
terms became apparent in the elections staged in June 1992. On the one hand,
at the policy's initiator, the finance minister Klaus, did nevertheless gain a
majority to become prime minister in the Czech republic. In Slovakia, on the
other hand, he had to accept defeat by the *socialist* Meciar. Admittedly, the
split in the country this precipitated is primarily due to the tension between

nationalities. However, opposing views on transformation policy can be assumed to have also played their part.

5.   COMMON DENOMINATOR

These few observations on the three countries which have, to date, progressed furthest with their transformation may suffice to draw attention to what are probably the most important problems relating to the process: all three countries scored initial successes in macroeconomic stabilization. However, owing to the drastic fall-off in production and employment and the effect on the distribution of income and wealth, it proved politically impossible to sustain the policy. This suggests that a more gradual and reticent approach ought to be taken to macroeconomic policy and structural adjustment. To a considerable degree, the adverse employment and distributional effects generated by stabilization are attributable to insufficiently flexible markets. The regulatory conditions for economic action, the microeconomic structures, or patterns of behavior compatible with the new system could not be implemented quickly enough. In this respect, therefore, one ought to push ahead more energetically with the transformation, and to accelerate the process.

VIII. German Democratic Republic

The transformation process was quite a different one - by virtue of the different initial circumstances - in the former *German Democratic Republic* (GDR), which now forms the Eastern part of the enlarged Federal Republic (Kantzenbach, 1990 and 1991; *Sachverständigenrat*, 1991: 65; Siebert, 1992; and Sinn, 1991). In October 1989 the sudden collapse of the political and economic system manifested itself. The *iron* curtain against the West caved in. In February 1990 the Federal Republic offered a monetary union to the GDR, and this came into force on July 1, 1990. Finally, the constitutional reunification of East and West Germany took place on October 3, 1990.

Within the shortest period of time the German monetary union and reunification completely changed the regulatory frame conditions in the Eastern part of the country. The first free elections had created a political mix of parties similar to the one prevailing in West Germany. The unification treaty between the two states envisaged, therefore, the adoption *in toto* of the former West German legal system and administrative structure. It was only in setting up the administrative authorities that problems and delays occurred. To a considerable extent, it was necessary to transfer civil servants from West Germany in order to alleviate bottlenecks generated by a lack of trained staff. Even today businesses wishing to invest still complain of the inefficiency of the public administrative services.

Once the monetary union came into force, all impediments to trade between Western and Eastern Germany were removed. This meant that all raw materials, inputs and end products from the West were suddenly available in the Eastern German market. At the same time, of course, enterprises in Eastern Germany were now subject to unfettered competition from Western companies. Given the conditions under which they had to operate - which we shall refer to in more detail shortly - businesses in Eastern Germany were not able to stand up against this sudden competitive pressure, the only exceptions being companies serving locally defined markets (such as local transport and utility undertakings, and newspaper publishers). The result was a fall of more than 50% in industrial production and a corresponding drop in employment. Karl-Otto Pöhl, the then president of the *Deutsche Bundesbank*, spoke of a disaster.

IX.   Currency Reform in East Germany

Neither politicians nor economists had foreseen the sheer scale or the duration of the collapse in production and employment in Eastern Germany. The problem has three essential causes (Kantzenbach, 1993): (i) the dramatic decline in demand for capital goods from the former Soviet Union and other COMECON countries; (ii) the totally inadequate quality of most industrial products for exporting to Western countries; and (iii) a drastic increase in unit wage costs as a result of the currency reform and subsequent pay agreements. By way of illustration we now turn to the latter of these sources of trouble as it relates to the problem of macroeconomic stabilization.

The formation of the unified currency zone made the *Deutsche Mark* the official circulating currency in Eastern Germany. The problem which had to be faced was how to find an appropriate conversion rate from the *Ost-Mark* to the *D-Mark*, both for financial assets (stocks) and for current payment obligations (flows). The key question, as far as financial assets are concerned, was to convert at a rate which would not give rise to a monetary overhang and hence to excess demand, thus boosting inflation. Even though the population of East Germany was about one quarter of West Germany's population, the growth in productive potential as a result of re-unification was estimated at about 10% only, because of the low productivity of labor. This was still an overestimation. Accordingly, effective aggregate demand could only safely increase by 10% following the currency re-organization, which called for a conversion rate of approximately 1.8:1. There is a general agreement that this problem was solved appropriately and smoothly by the *Deutsche Bundesbank*, without any substantial inflationary pressure being created. A much more difficult issue was setting an appropriate conversion rate for current payments, of which wages and salaries are a major element. Two different aspects had to be taken into account here. On the one hand, wages could not be permitted to unduly exceed labor productivity if businesses in Eastern Germany were to remain competitive. On the other hand, the wage differential with Western Germany could not be so large that it would generate social unrest and mass migration.

In view of the fact that there was a productivity differential of about 1:10,[2] it was impossible for these two objectives to be reconciled directly. The only way out of this dilemma would probably have been to detach wage *costs* from wage *incomes* by means of transfer payments from the west. Two years ago a working group at Berkeley headed by George A. Akerlof (Akerlof, 1991) actually

---

[2]This estimation takes the quality differences between Western and Eastern products into account.

worked out a wage subsidy model in which transfer payments were not necessary. The actual conversion carried out for current payments done at a one-for-one parity, which led to a wage differential of approximately 1:3. This change alone was therefore equivalent to a revaluation of approximately 300% for the former GDR. Moreover, the trade unions set the target of achieving standards in Eastern and Western Germany within a matter of years. They therefore pushed through disproportionately high wage increases in the east of the country, with the result that the current wage differential is approximately 1:2. This, in turn, has further curtailed both production and employment capacities in the east. The collapse in production and employment is currently requiring transfer payments of about DM150 billion per annum out of public funds from the west, most of which then goes into private or government consumption. Although the low-point for production does now appear to have been reached, productive conditions can still hardly be expected to equal those in the west within fifteen years.

X.   Final Remarks

To sum up, the chapter began by endeavouring to show that the transformation now under way in Central and Eastern European countries is an extremely complex political and economic process for which there is no comprehensive theoretical explanation currently available. As a result, we lack a reliable scientific foundation, both for forecasting and for making recommendations to policy-makers. For those countries which have already established a stable democratic constitution by now - particularly Poland, Hungary and Czechoslovakia - the greatest problems appears to be associated with the coordination of micro- and macroeconomic reform measures. The chapter has attempted to show the differences between the paths chosen by those three countries, and what their common problems are. To finish off, the chapter focused on developments in the former GDR, now the eastern part of the re-unified Germany. This political re-unification established ideal conditions for creating the regulatory frame conditions for the market economy and a stable currency. However, political re-unification also led to the levelling of incomes to an extent which could not be justified by the productivity differential. The collapse in production and employment which this has exacerbated, will continue to pose serious problems for German economic policy for many years to come.

References

Akerlof, G.A. et al. (1991) 'East Germany in from the Cold: The Economic Aftermath of Currency Union', *Brookings Papers on Economic Activity* 1, 1991.

Apolte, T. and Cassel, D. (1991) 'Dezentralisierung durch kapitalistische Marktwirtschaft: Radikaler Systembruch', in Hartwig, K.H. and Thieme, H.J. (eds), *Transformationsprozesse in sozialistischen Wirtschaftssystemen*, Berlin, 111.

Forschungsinstitute, Wirtschaftswissenschaftliche (1992a) 'Die Lage der Weltwirtschaft und der deutschen Wirtschaft im Frühjahr 1992'.

Forschungsinstitute, Wirtschaftswissenschaftliche (1992b) 'Wirtschaftsreformen in Mittel- und Osteuropa: Beihefte zur Konjunkturpolitik', Heft 40.

Frankfurter Institut für wirtschaftspolitische Forschung e.V. (1992) 'Zur Wirtschaftsreform in Osteuropa', Bad Homburg.

Giersch, H. (ed.) (1991) *Towards a Market Economy in Central and Eastern Europe*, Berlin.

Heinrich, R. (1991) 'Gesamtwirtschaftliche Stabilisierungspolitik in Polen, Ungarn und der CSFR', *Die Weltwirtschaft* **2**, 146.

Kantzenbach, E. (1990) 'Ökonomische Probleme der deutschen Vereinigung', *Hamburger Jahrburch für Wirtschafts- und Gesellschaftspolitik* **35**, Tübingen, 307.

Kantzenbach, E. (1991) 'Wirtschaftspolitische Probleme der Systemtransformation in Ostdeutschland und der deutschen Vereinigung', in Jens, U. (ed,), *Der Umbau*, Baden Baden, 35.

Kantzenbach, E. (1992) 'Thesen zur deutschen Wirtschaftspolitik', *Wirtschaftsdienst* **72**, 239.

Leipold, H. (1991) 'Politische Ordnung und wirtschaftliche Umgestaltung: Zu Restriktionen und Refomren in Politik und Verwaltung', in Hartwig, K.H. and Thieme, H.J. (eds), *Transformationsprozesse in sozialistischen Wirtschaftssystemen*, Berlin, 227.

Lösch, D. (1992) '"Timing" als zentrales Problem der Systemtransformation', *HWWA-Report Nr. 99*, Hamburg.

Popper, K.R. (1969) *Das Elend des Historizismus*, Tübingen, 51.

Roland, G. (1992) 'Issues in the Political Economy of Transition', in *The Economic Consequences of the East*, Centre for Economic Policy Research, London.

Sachverständigenrat zur Begutachtung der gesamtwirtschaftlichen Entwicklung (1991) 'Die wirtschaftliche Integration in Deutschland, Perspektiven - Wege - Risiken', *Jahresgutachten 1991/92*, Stuttgart.

Schneider, H.K. (1992) 'Tempo und Schrittfolge des Transformationsprozesses', in Gahlen, B., Hesse, H. and Ramser, H.J. (eds), *Von der Plan- zur Marktwirtschaft,* Tübingen, 3.

Siebert, H. (1992) 'Real Adjustment in the Transformation Process: Risk Factors in East Germany', in *The Economic Consequences of the East*, Centre for Economic Policy Research, London.

Sinn, G. and Sinn, H.W. (1991) Kaltstart, *Volkswirtschaftliche Aspekte der deutschen Vereinigung*, Tübingen.

CHAPTER 19

Principles of Economic Policy in the Common Market

REINHARD BLUM and PETER WELZEL[1]

Wirtschafts- und Sozialwissenschaftliche Fakultät, Universität of Augsburg, Augsburg, Germany

Abstract. The chapter analyzes economic policy in the European Community against the background of recent, often heated discussions about the Community's future. Principles of policy-making are used from both the traditional theory of economic policy and the German concept of a social market economy. Considering issues of the Community's internal and external economic policies, we argue in favor of a rational approach to economic policy as opposed to policy-making merely based on an alleged dichotomy between government and market.

I. Introduction

Currently we observe heated discussions on the European Community's future in general and its economic future in particular.[2] Albeit hidden behind the smoke-screen of *national identity*, the arguments mostly run along familiar lines: it is the old markets *vs* government debate, now intensified by the fear of a super-bureaucracy in Brussels. Against this background, we discuss some principles of economic policy in the EC (now European Union) from the perspective of both the conventional theory of economic policy and what German textbooks of economic policy usually call *Ordnungspolitik* - a policy which defines a framework for the functioning of markets. While it is often noted that a proper translation of this term into other languages is impossible, we shall try to draw upon German experience in order to shed some light on economic policy in the Common Market.

A major point of our reasoning will be that the German concept of a social market economy - often called a third way between central planning and the market - can help us to deal with the alleged dichotomy between centralized and decentralized decision-making, and between governments and markets. Our readers can be assured that we are not going to suggest a "German solution" to the Community's economic problems. Germany's social market economy only serves as an example. Instead, we want to point out that we all live in countries with economic systems containing market and planning elements. If we accept a mixed system at the national level, however, we also have to accept it for the European Community.

Our analysis sets out from some recent observations on the process of

---

[1]This is the written version of an invited lecture delivered by Reinhard Blum at the 19th EARIE Conference, September 4-6 1992, at Hohenheim University, Stuttgart.

[2]After this lecture was given in early September 1992, these discussions were even intensified by the outcome of the Maastricht referendum in France and the partial break-up of the EMS.

European integration and discussions of the role of government (Section II). We ask what we can learn from Germany's experience with a social market economy. Against this background, we shall turn to a more theoretical notion of rational economic policy, concentrating on the general problem of hierarchies of interdependent policy-makers (Section III), and on issues of internal (Section IV) and external (Section V) economic policy in the Community in particular. We conclude with final remarks (Section VI).

II.   On the Role of Government

1.   RECENT DISCUSSIONS ABOUT ECONOMIC POLICY IN THE EC

With the Single European Act and the Maastricht treaty the European Community recently took some major steps forward towards a full economic and political union. At a time, however, when politicians have taken the initiative and European integration has gained new momentum after a period of stagnation, citizens in the member countries and people outside the EC appear to become more sceptical about the prospect of a closer Europe.

- There are fears that surrendering national authority to the European Community will be equivalent to giving up parts of a country's national identity.[3]
- Other critics point to related dangers of an EC bureaucracy which could become - in their eyes - even more ineffective and inefficient than the national bureaucracies they used to condemn. Bavarians, for example, suspect that due to EC regulations they will no longer be allowed to wear their traditional hat decorations from chamois hair.
- At the same time, people outside the EC are afraid of what has often been called a "fortress Europe" - *i.e.*, a European Community which promotes a free flow of goods, services and factors among its members, but impedes the same transactions with outside partners.

To economists some of these fears look rather irrational, especially when they involve national regulations that - from an economic point of view - quite often create entry barriers, distort markets and protect special interests. Nevertheless, politicians have to deal with this growing Euro-scepticism. If they really want to further integrate the EC member countries, they have to convince their constituents of the Community's advantages. To meet the new challenges, principles that guide policy-making have to be re-examined and - if necessary - re-formulated and adjusted to an environment altered by Europe's move towards integration. Since many of the critical issues will almost certainly be found in the field of economic policy, it is the economics profession in particular which has to think about its view on policy-making in the Common Market and the advice it wants to give to policy-makers in the future. In this process, government's role in the economy has been and has to be discussed.

---

[3]It is not only the German Mark and the *Deutsche Bundesbank* that are involved here. National identity sometimes depends on apparently unimportant issues. Think of the purity regulations for German beer or Italian noodles, which already fell victim to the European principle of mutual recognition of national regulations.

2.   GOVERNMENT AND MARKET: A DICHOTOMY?

Throughout the 1980s, governments in a number of industrialized countries were criticized for being too heavily involved in the economy. German election campaigns of that decade were led under the slogan "more market, less government". Tax rates were cut in several countries. Privatization of state enterprises and deregulation of traditionally regulated sectors such as transportation and telecommunication were gaining ground. At the level of the European Community, the "bureaucracy in Brussels" was held responsible for inefficiencies and rising financial needs of the EC. Further European integration was and is seen as carrying the risk of extending this bureaucracy both in scale and scope.

There is nothing wrong *per se* with discussing and reducing the extent of government influence in the economy. More often than not, however, these arguments are merely based on what could be called ideological grounds. The principles of the market economy are upheld for their own sake without using economic reasoning to examine their applicability in the case at hand. In this view, markets and competition are more than instruments to achieve economic goals: they are seen as ends in themselves. This seems to create a fundamental dichotomy between government and market.

There is a logical inconsistency in this debate about the state's role in the economy. Government is reprimanded for bringing bureaucracy and planning to the market economy. At the same time, planning and bureaucracy are part of every single firm. Modern businesses cannot do without strategic planning to deal with long-term issues, and they need hierarchical structures to coordinate the activities of their employees. In our view, incentive theory and transaction cost economics are not satisfactory in resolving this inconsistency. The real debate, therefore, should not be about the need for planning and collective decision-making, but about the question of who ought to do the planning and the collective decision-making. Should it be government conducting economic policy, should it be business designing "global strategies", or should it be government and business in a joint effort to improve society's well-being?

3.   GOVERNMENT IN A SOCIAL MARKET ECONOMY

The German concept of a *Soziale Marktwirtschaft* - a social market economy - strives for a removal of the alleged dichotomy between government and market. It is a particular solution to the problem of finding a third way between the opposing alternatives central planning and decentralized economic decision-making. Based on the principle of subsidiarity, it attempts to connect the principle of economic freedom in the marketplace with the idea of social justice. While the actual extent of government influence in the economy can still be debated, public policy can no longer be dismissed as an element fundamentally alien or even destructive to a market-oriented economy.

There is no standing definition of a social market economy. In the beginning, it was mainly an idea - a *Leitbild* - to preserve Germany's national identity in the economic sphere against US capitalism and Soviet socialism. But it soon led to the implementation of a pragmatic policy, both qualitative and quantitative in nature, which was not only based on market principles but also on democratic principles and values of the traditional German social policy. Since the concept is not tied to one of the *ideal* economic systems - market economy *vs* centrally planned economy -, it can be and has been evolving over time. Let us briefly provide what could be considered an up-to-date interpretation (*cf*. Blum, 1983: Chapter 4). It draws on the concepts of self-organization and strategic management, which both play an important role in today's management theory (see, *e.g.*, Ulrich and Probst, 1984). In this view, the social market economy combines the notion of self-organization in the market with the idea of strategic planning by the government. The latter is used to formulate society's goals and to set up a framework for the functioning of markets in the economy.

The concept of a social market economy underlines the dominance of society's political - *i.e.*, democratic - sphere over its economic sphere. Our claim is that this is even more important at the level of the European Community. This point may seem trivial, but it carries the message that political decisions take precedence over economic decisions reached by market participants - an idea which business people and economists alike are sometimes reluctant to accept. There is a distinction between doing the right thing, which requires a political decision based on value judgments, and doing it the right way, which calls for economic efficiency in reaching the goals. Practitioners of business who use this notion for managing their firms should also be willing to accept this framework as a way to think about the organizational problems of an economy as a whole. Economists should not object either. As we shall see in a moment, the concept is not in conflict with the search for a rational or optimal economic policy. It does away, however, with the economists' alleged right to determine what is good for society.

4.   RATIONAL ECONOMIC POLICY

Economists are trained to use the notion of rationality in a large variety of situations. Striving for the best possible result from a given set of resources can indeed hardly be objected. When economists write about economics, but also about politics, law, sociology or even the family, they apply this so-called economic principle. In the area of economic policy, it calls for using the policy instruments in such a way that the highest degree of success is achieved under a given set of constraints and a comprehensive and balanced system of societal objectives (*cf*. Giersch, 1961: 22-27).

Incidentally, it took rather a long time until this principle, which had been familiar from resource allocation issues, became an integral part of thinking about economic policy. Take trade policy as an example: Corden (1974: 2-5) distinguished three phases in market-oriented economic thinking about trade policy. Based on the idea of *laissez faire* there was a strong tendency towards free trade in the nineteenth century. Preceded by Hamilton's and List's infant industry argument, numerous special cases calling for protection were identified in a second phase, which lasted until the middle of our century and considerably weakened the theoretical support for free trade. These cases can all be traced back to the existence of deviations from ideal markets - either in the form of market failure or as objectives formulated by society. Since market imperfections are quite common in reality, trade policy seemed to be applicable to many situations. It was not until the 1950s and 1960s that economists - in a major third step - took the rationality principle seriously and addressed the question whether trade policy was not only beneficial but even optimal in these situations. This research culminated in the targeting principle for identification of first-best policy instruments (Bhagwati, 1971: 69-90). Trade policy turned out to be rarely the optimal choice for government.

What is important, though, is the fact that the theoretical discussion of rational economic policy is not only relevant for the correction of market failure. It also covers the case of societies formulating objectives which markets will not meet on their own. Economists may despise the efficiency cost of such policies, but based on the notion of rational economic policy they can suggest instruments which keep these costs low.

III.   Interdependence and Economic Policy

1.   LIMITS TO RATIONAL ECONOMIC POLICY

There are undoubtedly several practical difficulties connected to the notion of a strictly rational economic policy. The following pair of questions is illustrative: (i) do policy-makers act rationally?; and (ii) will rational policy decisions always yield desirable outcomes? The first of these two questions deals with the willingness and the ability of policy-makers to design and implement optimal - *i.e.*, rational - economic policies. Even if they do their best in the pursuit of society's well-being, they may be severely restricted by the complexity of real-world situations. Lack of knowledge about choices available, policy effects and future valuations of these effects raise considerable doubt whether rational economic policy is possible. Economists tend to propose economic solutions - a kind of meta-rationality - to these problems: the degree to which rationality is pursued is itself determined by rational choice. If rational policy is not costless (*e.g.*, because information has to be gathered), fully rational behavior will rarely be optimal (Winston, 1989). However, there are suggestions closer to actual human behavior (*cf.* Simon, 1957: Chapter 5), leading to the notion of bounded rationality and satisficing behavior, and a systems-oriented approach (*cf.* Blum, 1983: 190-219) to economic policy similar to ideas in modern management theory.

As for the question of irrational outcomes of rational economic policy, recall the problem of time inconsistency of optimal policies (Kydland and Prescott, 1977; and Wohltmann and Kröner, 1989). The fact that a benevolent - and perfectly rational - government with discretionary power will try to reach a first-best outcome after other - in most cases: private - agents have committed themselves, makes the second-best result impossible to achieve and leads to a third-best situation (*cf.* Persson, 1988). The issue at hand is a strategic interaction between the policy-maker and her environment, the latter expecting the former to re-optimize and acting according to this expectation. Another - increasingly important - area where economic policy is in a situation of strategic interaction arises when governments design policies which also affect other countries. It is well known that policy decisions of national governments which are taken rationally in the best interest of each single country, can result in collectively irrational outcomes. Numerous examples from trade, industrial or environmental policy show that interdependent governments are under the threat of getting caught in collective dilemmas - *i.e.*, prisoners' dilemma-type situations - from which no single rational government can escape on its own.[4]

2.   INTERDEPENDENCE AND RATIONAL ECONOMIC POLICY

Taking strategic interaction into account is crucial to today's economic policy decisions. An increasing number of economic policy decisions is made interdependently, where several decision-makers think about each others' actions and reactions. There is scope for strategic moves, making other agents change their expectations about one's own optimal behavior, which in turn changes their optimal behavior. Until the 1980s, much research on economic policy explicitly or implicitly assumed a passive environment for policy-makers. This can be seen in, *e.g.*, the small-country assumption prevalent in much of the analyses of trade policy. In the last decade, macro and industrial economists took the lead in considering strategic interactions, both between the government and the private sector and among several governments. Research along these lines became even more intensive when the European Community started its project to finish the internal market by the end of 1992.

This does not mean that the concept of rational economic policy is to be abandoned. Instead, it has to be supplemented by the notion of strategic interaction in situations of horizontal and/or vertical interdependence. Finding the best economic policy turns from a static optimization exercise into an analysis of dynamic game situations. This could even be called a fourth phase, adding to Corden's classification mentioned above: economists are now increasingly aware of the fact that internal policy measures such as subsidies or taxes in industrial or environmental policy, which are proposed by the targeting principle as first-best interventions to correct market failure and achieve society's objectives, are not completely innocent. In today's interdependent world in general and in the European Community in particular, they often affect the well-being of other countries' citizens and induce reactions by other governments. Therefore, rational economic policy has to be designed such that international repercussions are taken into account. Macroeconomics and industrial organization provide a number of suitable concepts.

3.   COMPETITION OF POLICIES OR CENTRALIZED DECISIONS?

In the European Community, interdependence has continuously increased over the last decades - an increase being due to both economic factors and political acts. There are currently at least two relevant levels of policy-makers - national governments and the Council of Ministers together with the Commission. How should they share power? Should Brussels dominate, or should national governments retain their power? The question of harmonization *vs* competition of policies, or centralized *vs* decentralized policy-making, has been widely discussed during recent years. It is also important for the process of European integration itself, since it offers a choice between institutional integration - building a unified framework for the workings of economic processes - and a

---

[4]For the basic setup which underlies many situations in, *e.g.*, international trade or environmental policy towards transnational problems see Schelling (1973).

functional integration - creating free markets for goods, services and factors in the EC - the hope that market processes and institutional competition among national governments will lead to more integration.

From our discussion so far, two fundamental questions emerge regarding the conduct of rational economic policy in the Common Market: (i) what - if any - policy instruments should be used (*i.e.*, the standard question familiar from the search for the best way to correct market failure or to achieve goals set by society)?; and (ii) who should be the policy-makers (that is, can we trust upon the existence of an *efficient market* for political decisions with governments as suppliers and their national constituents and special interest groups at the demand side or will there be market failure in this "market for economic policy", creating the need for harmonization and centralization)? We shall return to these questions below when we discuss some aspects of the European Community's internal and external economic policy. In both cases, democratically legitimized political decisions stake out the area for economic analysis. Given these decisions, rationality as opposed to ideological pro- or anti-market principles should guide the search for an answer to our questions.

IV.   Issues of Internal Economic Policy

1.   DELEGATION *VS* CENTRALIZATION
There is very little doubt that further integrating the economies of the EC member states will create aggregate welfare gains for the Community. The removal of a variety of market barriers can be expected to increase efficiency in many sectors of European industry[5]. A monetary union - properly designed - will also yield positive effects for its members. If the desirability of EC integration at the aggregate level is accepted, two practical questions remain to be answered: (1) how should these gains be distributed among member countries?; and (2) what institutional setup for internal policy-making in the European Community is necessary in order to ensure that these potential gains materialize?

As for the first question, sovereign states can be expected to act according to the Pareto criterion: *i.e.*, they only participate if they see a benefit or at least no loss in a project. Casual observation of the bargaining processes in the EC seems to confirm this simple theoretical prediction.[6] Industrial economists - familiar with the idea of exit barriers[7] - might wonder, however, to what extent the Pareto criterion can be violated without provoking exit once a country incurred sunk costs and became a member. In the following, we ignore

---

[5]For estimates of these microeconomic effects see, *e.g.*, Emerson *et al.* (1988).

[6]In fact, this point is not entirely trivial. For some members benefits from European integration may accrue outside the economic sphere. In principle, there could even be a hegemonic power in the sense of political science which provides economic integration as a public good to other countries without generating an immediate or measurable gain.

[7]Compare in particular with the recent models of entry and exit with sunk costs and an uncertain future (*e.g.*, Pindyck, 1991).

distributional issues and focus on the second question. The history of the US provides us with an example of institutional variety at the state level which has been compatible with successful regional economic integration. But what about the risk of Europe's national governments ending up in political cut-throat competition? With the internal market within reach, there were warnings that in areas such as environmental and social policy, competition among national governments for jobs will lead to deregulation races, ending in undesirably low levels of regulation.

Recent theoretical work on competition among national governments points to the role of opportunity costs of deregulation[8], which serve as a device that will prevent total deregulation. A government which relaxes its environmental policy, for example, in order to attract businesses from other countries faces a trade-off between new jobs and more pollution. A lower level of environmental quality hurts the own constituents and might even induce well-educated people - often the most mobile part of the labor force - to move to another country with stricter environmental regulation. From the perspective of theory, competitive policy-making can induce governments to search for an optimal degree of regulation. There will be situations, however, where markets for policy decisions fail. Take externalities as an example: lower environmental standards in one member country can affect people in the other. Adherents to the Coase theorem will point to internalization through bargaining among governments. However, in the presence of more than two agents or information asymmetries, the theorem loses much of its appeal. In addition, the collective dilemma situations mentioned above should limit our enthusiasm for free competition of national policies.

Some degree of centralization could show the way out. We have to think about mechanisms which help national governments escape from collectively irrational situations arising from nationally rational behavior. From the literature on theoretical industrial organization and game theory (cf. Fudenberg and Maskin, 1986), we know that with the use of retaliation and reputation individually rational agents can reach collectively rational outcomes. The feasibility of such solutions in the context of international collective dilemmas is limited by the lack of international organization. EC governments, however, are in a relatively favorable position. Since they are already partners in a supra-national organization, they do not need to design such mechanisms from scratch. The institutions of the Community can be used to avoid collective dilemma situations by deciding on the supra-national level, by policing contracts among member countries, and - if necessary - by administering a retaliation mechanism against members which violate agreements. In addition, delegation of power to the supra-national level makes it easier for governments to avoid the pressure of national interest groups.

Centralization can then be seen as a credible commitment against demands from special interests. Note, however, that policing existing agreements for a given level of delegation of power is the easier part. New agreements and a change in delegation can still be hindered by the problems related to collective

---

[8]See, e.g., for the field of environmental economics Rauscher (1991) and Van Long and Siebert (1991).

dilemma situations.[9] Centralization via delegation of power to Brussels now does not look so bad. It is useful when markets for policy decisions fail. Combine this idea with the modern interpretation of a social market economy presented above. When applied to the European Community, it calls for a co-existence of strategic decisions at the EC level and self-organization by competing national policies. The principle of subsidiarity, which has been inherent to market-oriented economic thinking for a long time, provides a rule for a reasonable division of labor. At the national level, we propagate decentralization, as long as decision-makers one step down the hierarchical ladder generate results desirable or acceptable for society. The same should now hold for the European Community. Central decision-making is favored if both private markets and political competition among national governments fail.

2.   AGRICULTURAL POLICY

Take agricultural policy in the European Community as an example where the two questions proposed above have to be answered. Who should determine agricultural policy in the EC? A Common Agricultural Policy (CAP) was one of the very first ingredients of European integration in the 1950s. National governments delegated their power to the Council of Ministers. Until the late 1980s, however, they still held the right to veto decisions in this body. How should agricultural policy be conducted? Almost nobody doubts that the current system of price support and subsidized sales in the world market imposes a welfare cost on EC member countries. Estimates range from 0.3% to 1.3% of GDP at the aggregate level.[10] Accept for the sake of the argument the idea that the principal goals of this policy - as initially written down in the treaty of Rome - are unquestioned as the right way to go in agricultural policy. That is, it is an objective formulated by democratic societies of the EC member countries to retain an agricultural sector of a certain size with a particular supply-side market structure. Economists familiar with the notion of rational economic policy will then look for the least expensive way to reach this goal. It has been known for a long time that the policy currently used carries a number of side effects and additional distortions, particularly through its consequences for international trade, which imposes welfare costs that could be avoided. Recent moves towards a reform replacing price subsidies by a system of direct income support are in accord with rational economic policy, since they bring up policy instruments which are closer to the objective at hand and can be expected to create less side effects.

As discussed above, however, the ideas of optimal economic policy and targeting are of almost the same age as the EC. Why have these concepts not be used earlier to improve the Common Agricultural Policy? One of the reasons is that agricultural policy in the European Community is one of the hotbeds,

---

[9]For theoretical analyses of (rational) delegation decisions see, *e.g.*, Gatsios and Karp (1991), Lohmann and O'Halloran (1992) and Zweifel and Eisen (1991).

[10]Studies that use more sophisticated methods tend to produce results close to the upper bound of this interval (*cf.* Demekas *et al.*, 1988).

where until very recently ideological positions and special interests prevented to start searching for efficient instruments in order to achieve political objectives. Proponents of the price support system argue that in a market economy producers earn their income from the sale of goods in the marketplace. If prices are so low that - politically undesirable - exit of farmers is induced, government has to step in and support higher prices. The same arguments are still in use. The president of the German farmers' association recently criticized the Community's move towards a system of direct income support as a bureaucratic solution, leading to a system of supervision of farms. (One can feel the threat of socialism re-emerging.) Instead, he demanded a "European price policy". In his view, the existence of self-employed farmers can only be guaranteed by reasonable revenue earned in the market for agricultural products (*Süddeutsche Zeitung*, May 11 1992: 23). Statements of this kind are largely based on a logic that instinctively prefers market solutions - even if they are only pseudo-market solutions - to public policy. They are caught in the market *vs* plan or capitalism *vs* socialism dichotomy discussed above. However, such instinctive positions impede rational analysis to examine whether and how the market mechanism is applicable. Economic policy-making in the European Community has to avoid this ideological trap, which can be found not only in the agricultural sector.

Return briefly to the second question. Is the centralization of policy-making regarding agricultural policy in the EC justified from the perspective of economic reasoning? Recalling the pros and cons of centralizing policy decisions discussed above, there is one argument that appears to be of particular relevance. Delegating power from the national level to a supra-national institution is like a commitment against special interests inside a country. Farmers' votes are a decisive factor in general elections in several countries of the Community. By ceding their power to the supra-national body, national governments avoid political blackmail from this powerful interest group. Note, however, that this commitment could not work as long as national governments still held veto power in the Council of Ministers. It was only after the introduction of majority voting on the EC level that this commitment became credible.

3.   INDUSTRIAL POLICY

Industrial policy is another area of public policy which has been hotly debated in the European Community during recent years. Again we can ask: how should this policy be conducted, and who should be the policy-maker? In the revision of the EC Treaty passed at the Maastricht conference, the terminology of industrial policy was used explicitly for the first time at the European level. The Community and its member countries assume responsibility for a "strengthening of the competitiveness of the Community's industries" (see Art. 3l and Art. 130 III 1 of the Treaty). At the same time, the treaty still includes passages calling for open markets and a system of unbiased competition, confirming the competition principle which dominated previous versions (see Art.3f, Art. 130 I 2, and Art. 130 III 3 of the Treaty). The claim for unbiased competition has usually been interpreted as binding both private and governmental activities. Industrial policy seems to be in conflict with this requirement. The ranking of these two conflicting parts of the treaty is still open to economic, legal and political debate. Some observers like the German *Monopolkommission*, a council of advisors on issues of competition in the German economy, deplore the mere fact that such an extension of *Community* law took place, however (*cf. Monopolkommission*, 1992: 12-15). The recent move towards industrial policy is somewhat surprising, because the principle of mutual recognition of national regulations, which is an integral part of the Single European Act, seemed to express a consensus among EC governments that *national* industrial policy did not work (*cf. The Economist*, July 11, 1992: 9). Do the member countries believe that industrial policy will do better at the *Community* level? The results of the Maastricht conference point in this direction.

We are then back to the issue of competitive *vs* centralized policy-making. In the field of industrial policy there is considerable risk of a collective dilemma arising from national policy decisions. This is due to both external effects of such measures and the temptation of designing policies such that rent-shifting in international oligopolies is induced.[11] If, for example, industrial policy supporting activities in research and development creates considerable external benefits not only to domestic but also to foreign firms, national governments will not carry out the fully optimal policy. Even more important is the fact that centralized policy-making helps to avoid the inefficient outcome of strategic policies where several governments try to support their national producers in markets in which economic rents are earned. Therefore, some additional coordination or centralization will be useful if the case for industrial policy can be made.

However, many economists question the feasibility of industrial policy: that is, they doubt whether private market failure in this area can be corrected by government intervention, irrespective of the governmental level that intervenes. Learning effects and economies of scale and scope can create a potential for beneficial government intervention. But are governments able to use this scope for welfare-improving industrial policy? "Picking the winners" by governmental decree in an uncertain and changing world seems impossible. For practical reasons, therefore, industrial policy will often have to be confined to what German economists would call *Ordnungspolitik* in a broader sense: creating a framework and an environment in which markets can serve as hotbeds for new ideas and new products. Such an industrial policy will rarely be sector-specific, because we rarely know which sector to support.[12] And - given the existence of some basic rules of the game among EC governments - it could even be administered at the national level. But what about the issue of competitiveness in imperfectly competitive world markets? Should the European Community not use industrial policy as an instrument of trade policy to strengthen EC producers in international competition? Is this not the area where the Japanese government had its most admirable successes? We address the community's

---

[11]The collective dilemma is well-known from the literature on strategic policy to shift oligopoly rents (*e.g.*, Brander and Spencer, 1985).

[12]See also the German *Monopolkommission*'s analysis of strategic trade policy (1992: 801-941).

external economic policy in the next section.

V.   Issues of External Economic Policy

1.   FREE TRADE AND THE EUROPEAN COMMUNITY

Traditional trade theory is filled with elaborate proofs of the optimality of free trade. In fact, the development of the European Community has time and again been criticized for violating the principle of free trade in the world economy. Should we consider this violation - through regional instead of world-wide economic integration - to be a problem? Since the 1980s trade theorists have come a long way to learn what practitioners of international trade always claimed to know: not all international trade works according to the standard concepts of comparative advantage and factor proportions theory. Comparative advantage can be influenced, and factor endowments may be only one cause among many. Part of this work is important to understand patterns of trade observed in the real word - for example, in the presence of scale economies or learning effects. Under the label of "strategic trade policy" it also offered new insights into the desirability of trade policy defined in a very broad sense, overlapping with industrial policy.

The conclusion of this line of research has nicely been summarized by Paul Krugman, one of the main contributors: free trade is no longer optimal but is reduced to the status of a "rule of thumb" (*cf*. Krugman, 1987). This goes well with the scepticism against principles expressed several times in this chapter. The effectiveness of trade policy will have to be examined. If free trade is only a rule of thumb, economic policy will be based upon free trade in complex situations where finding the right policy is difficult (for example, due to information problems). The rent-shifting literature sparked off by Brander and Spencer provides a case in point. Since its policy recommendations are highly non-robust with respect to small changes in the model - number of suppliers, type of oligopolistic interaction, *et cetera* - the government would have to gather an incredible amount of information on an international oligopoly to make sure its policy does at least some good (see, *e.g.*, Helpman and Krugman, 1989). But assume that these information problems are non-existent or can be solved. How strong will then be the case for a strategic trade policy in the European Community?

2.   STRATEGIC TRADE POLICY IN AN INTERDEPENDENT WORLD

In today's world of large, internationally active corporations and large trading blocks in the world economy it is almost natural to think that governments should do the same as their large producers do: make a - strategic - plan for trade in international markets. This is what the Japanese allegedly do, and what the management-oriented interpretation of economic policy presented above suggests. The literature on strategic trade policy provides an analytic framework to examine these issues more closely. Producers in imperfectly competitive markets earn profits above the normal level. Strategic trade policy - narrowly defined — aims at re-directing the flow of these profits towards domestic agents (producers, consumers or government). In a broader sense, strategic trade policy is seen as a tool to support sectors which are considered to be of strategic importance for the economy, being essential for its future development.

In both cases, the policy recommended to the European Community would be: create European champions to replace the former national champions. Large European corporations would be able to compete in international oligopolies, earning oligopoly rents for their European owners. Subsidies, reduced levels of regulation and a relaxation of competition and environmental policy are examples of measures that could be used. Economic policy in the United States seems to have followed this course to enhance international competitiveness throughout the 1980s. The results, though, are not very convincing. Michael Porter's recent book on the *Competitive Advantage of Nations* (1990: 117-122) made the important point that intensifying domestic competition is much more favorable to international competitiveness than directly supporting firms, which only works in the short run.

Japan's economic policy appears to be more in line with Porter's recommendation. Japan promotes fierce competition internally and does some strategic planning for the country's course of action in international markets. There were strategic decisions involving, for example, which sectors of the Japanese economy had to expand and which had to contract. Admittedly, this runs the risk of MITI picking the wrong industry, but in many sectors with only a small number of large firms the risk imposed on society by private decisions is not lower. If the German Daimler-Benz group decides to become a major supplier of a new technology but fails to achieve this goal, the outcome to the German economy is not very different from the one that would have resulted under government participation in the initial decision. The attractive feature of the Japanese approach is that business and government seem to join their knowledge in order to formulate a strategy for the country. In accordance with suggestions of modern management theory they combine elements of self—organization with aspects of strategic planning. German industry today claims to be highly competitive in environmental technologies. This is to a large extent due to an understanding among business and government that strict environmental regulations are or will be imposed. If this works, strategic trade policy and industrial policy can also be successful. Currently, however, these policies in the EC can do little more than react. They are mostly driven by the need to support sectors that are or claim to be threatened by international competition. If this kind of - industry-guided - policy is tolerated, we might as well accept a forward-looking policy that gives government some influence over what it will be supporting in the future. Strategic trade policy of this kind is less likely to provoke retaliation and international dilemma situations. The conclusion for the European Community is that it should not pursue an active policy of rent-shifting. However, government can conduct a strategic policy in the sense of creating a suitable framework for self-organization in the marketplace. Improving educational standards, which modern growth theory stresses as a major factor, is one element to consider. Getting business and government together to jointly define some long-term goals, is another.

3.   EUROPEAN COMMUNITY AND INTERNATIONAL TRADE ORDER

The main caveat of an aggressive strategic trade policy or strategic industrial policy to shift rents can be found if international repercussions are taken into account. Other countries - the US and Japan in particular - can be expected to retaliate. The same arguments that induced Europeans to abandon national trade policies within the EC, can be applied at the world level: national governments will end up in a collective dilemma caused by - nationally perfectly rational - trade policies. This raises the question of the European Community's role in the international trade order. The world trading system has changed considerably. After the Second World War, the US served as what political scientists call a hegemon in international trade (see Keohane, 1984; and Kindleberger, 1986). The US took the lead in promoting free trade. As a hegemonic power, it was willing to incur economic costs in order to establish a liberal trading system. Western Europe's role in the old system was that of a beneficiary of US policy. Today it is a different kind of game with at least three influential countries or blocks. Americans demand "fair trade", the French call for "organized trade", and Japan conducts some kind of strategic management for its international trade. As a relevant competitor the EC has to expect, and actually faces, retaliation from US trade policy. There is again the threat of a collective dilemma. Having accumulated economic power, the European Community has to share responsibility for the world trade order.

Both points should limit the European Community's desire to use aggressive trade and industrial policy to improve its own position at the expense of its trading partners. Instead, Europe has to play a constructive role within the GATT, promoting the free flow of goods, services and factors, which has served Europe so well during the last decades, and preventing a further rise in world-wide protectionism. In particular, the EC should not follow the recent American example of using *aggressive unilateralism* (see Bhagwati, 1990; Bhagwati and Patrick, 1990; and Welzel, 1992) to promote free trade in the world economy. Unilateral measures, which circumvent the GATT conflict resolution procedures, are subject to the lobbying efforts of interest groups. They tend to single out particular countries and impose one's own idea of *fair trade* on them.

VI. Final Remarks

Let us summarize in a few sentences. As for principles of economic policy in the Common Market, we would stress the following:

1. Our thinking should not get caught in a market *vs* government, or strategic management *vs* self-organization dichotomy. No matter whether we call it a *third way* or a *mixed system*, we need government intervention at the EC level as we need it in every single member country.
2. European integration creates a new and potentially positive role for economic policy. It can help to correct market failure in *markets for policy*, where national decisions often lead to collective dilemmas. Furthermore, without macroeconomic adjustment mechanisms like exchange rates, the diversity of economic conditions among EC members requires more rather than less

economic policy compared to the time prior to integration.

3. We should be careful to loath the *bureaucracy in Brussels*. For economic policy at the EC level to work, we need supra-national institutions.

4. While some of our arguments were based on German experience with a social market economy, these conclusions are not in conflict with economic theory once the precedence of democratic decisions over economic rationality is accepted.

Since this chapter was prepared for a conference on industrial economics, our examples were drawn from the sectoral or microeconomic rather than macroeconomic level. Several of the ideas discussed above, however, can also be applied to macroeconomic policy.[13]

When aspects of the role of the European Community and its policy in the world economy are considered, the problem of economic development in the Third World cannot be ignored. The German concept of a social market economy could provide some insights one more time, telling us to combine economic freedom in the marketplace with social justice and leading to *social free trade* as opposed to mere free trade (*cf.* Blum, 1981). At the national level it teaches us that government intervention can play an important and constructive role. It resolves the market *vs* plan dichotomy which unduly burdens the search for solutions. Something similar could be imagined for the world economy. Rich industrialized countries should be willing to provide a framework allowing the Third World to participate in the world economy as well. This requires elements of social policy at the world level, but also access to EC markets for Third World countries. The subsidiarity principle could effectively be used to limit this support to those countries who really need it.

References

Bhagwati, J.N. (1971) 'The Generalized Theory of Distortions and Welfare', in Bhagwati, J.N. *et al.* (eds), *Trade, Balance of Payments and Growth: Papers in International Economics in Honor of Charles P. Kindleberger*, Amsterdam, North-Holland, 69-90.

Bhagwati, J.N. (1990) 'Departures from Multilateralism: Regionalism and Aggressive Unilateralism', *Economic Journal* **100**, 1304-1317.

Bhagwati, J.N. and Patrick, H.T. (eds) (1990) *Aggressive Unilateralism: America's 301 Trade Policy and the World Trading Regime*. Ann Arbor, The University of Michigan Press.

Blum, R. (1981) 'Soziale Marktwirtschaft als weltwirtschaftliche Strategie', in Simonis, U.E. (ed.), *Ordnungspolitische Fragen zum Nord-Süd-Konflikt*, München, Schriftenreihe des Vereins für Socialpolitik, 123-151.

Blum, R. (1983) *Organisationsprinzipien der Volkswirtschaft*, Frankfurt a. M., Campus Verlag.

Brander, J.A. and Spencer, B.J. (1985) 'Export Subsidies and International Market Share Rivalry', *Journal of International Economics* **18**, 83-100.

Cooper, R.N. (1985) 'Economic Interdependence and Coordination of Economic Policies', in Jones, R.W. and Kenen, P.B. (eds), *Handbook of International Economics* II, Amsterdam, North-Holland, 1195-1234.

Corden, W.M. (1974) *Trade Policy and Economic Welfare*, Oxford, Clarendon Press.

Demedas, D.G. *et al.* (1988) 'The Effect of the Common Agricultural Policy of the European Community: A Survey of the Literature', *Journal of Common Market Studies* **27**, 113-145.

---

[13]In fact, there is a voluminous literature on international coordination and cooperation in the field of macroeconomic policy (*cf.* Cooper, 1985).

Emerson, M. *et al.* (1988) *The Economics of 1992*, Oxford, Oxford University Press.

Fudenberg, D. and Maskin, E. (1986) 'The Folk Theorem in Repeated Games with Discounting or with Incomplete Information', *Econometrica* **54**, 533-554.

Gatsios, K. and Karp, L. (1991) 'Delegation Games in Customs Unions', *Review of Economic Studies* **58**, 391-397.

Giersch, H. (1961) *Allgemeine Wirtschaftspolitik: Grundlagen*, Wiesbaden, Gabler.

Helpman, E. and Krugman, P.R. (1989) *Trade Policy and Market Structure*, Cambridge, MA, The MIT Press.

Keohane, R.O. (1984) *After Hegemony: Cooperation and Discord in the World Political Economy*, Princeton, NJ, Princeton University Press.

Kindleberger, Ch.P. (1986) 'International Public Goods without International Government', *American Economic Review* **76**, 1-13.

Krugman, P.R. (1987) 'Is Free Trade Passé?', *Journal of Economic Perspectives* **1**, 131-144.

Kydland, F.E. and Prescott, E.C. (1977) 'Rules Rather than Discreton: The Inconsistency of Optimal Plans', *Journal of Political Economy* **85**, 473-491.

Lohmann, S. and O'Halloran, S. (1992) 'Divided Government and US Trade Policy', *Unpublished manuscript*, Stanford University, Graduate School of Business.

Monopolkommission (1992) *Wettbewerbspolitik oder Industriepolitik*, Neuntes Hauptgutachten.

Persson, T. (1988) 'Credibility of Macroeconomic Policy: An Introduction and a Broad Survey', *European Economic Review* **32**, 519-532.

Pindyck, R.S. (1991) 'Irreversibility, Uncertainty and Investment', *Journal of Economic Literature* **29**, 1110-1148.

Porter, M.E. (1990) *The Competitive Advantage of Nations*, New York, The Free Press.

Rauscher, M. (1991) 'National Environmental Policies and the Effect of Economic Integration', *European Journal of Political Economy* **7**, 313-329.

Schelling, Th.C. (1973) 'Hockey Helmets, Concealed Weapons, and Daylight Saving', *Journal of Conflict Resolution* **17**, 381-428.

Simon, H.A. (1957) *Administrative Behavior*, Second edition, New York, MacMillan.

Ulrich, H. and Probst, G. (eds) (1984) *Self-Organization and Management of Social Systems*, Berlin, Springer-Verlag.

Van Long, N. and Siebert, H. (1991) 'Institutional Competition versus Ex-ante Harmonization: The Case of Environmental Policy', *Journal of Institutional and Theoretical Economics* **147**, 296-311.

Welzel, P. (1992) 'Hegemonialmaacht oder *geschrumpfter Riese*? Die Neuere US-Handelspolitik aus Spieltheoretischer Sicht', in Jakobeit, C., Sacksofsky, U. and Welzel, P. (eds), *Die USA zu Beginn der neunziger Jahre. Analyse aus Politik, Wirtschaft und Recht*, Opladen, Leske + Budrich, 177-199.

Winston, G.C. (1989) 'Imperfectly Rational Choice', *Journal of Economic Behavior and Organization* **12**, 67-86.

Wohltmann, H.-W. and Krömer, W. (1989) 'On the Notion of Time Consistency: A Comment', *European Economic Review* **33**, 1283-1288.

Zweifel, P. and Eisen, R. (1991) 'Delegierte Deregulierung auf EG-Ebene: Das Beispiel der Versicherungen', *Discussion Paper No. 9101*, University of Zurich, Institute for Empirical Research in Economics, to be published in *Zeitschrift für Wirtschafts-und Sozialwissenschaften*, 1993.

CHAPTER 20

Output Tradability and the Regulation of a Multinational Firm

RAM MUDAMBI[1]

Department of Economics, University of Buckingham, Buckingham, England

Abstract. While there is a large literature on government policy towards MNCs, the effects of the tradability of the output good have not been addressed. In this chapter, the topic is studied in the context of foreign exchange scarcity. It is shown that it is of crucial importance in ascertaining the effects of government policy toward the foreign firm. The analysis proceeds by obtaining the government's optimal policy under two alternative specifications of the output good. In the first case, the output is produced solely for domestic consumption. In the second scenario, the good may be either sold domestically or exported. The effects of government policy in these two scenarios are radically different. These results suggest that the tradability of the output good is part of the explanation of the differing repatriation and tax policies adopted by various developing countries towards foreign firms.

I.   Introduction

Restrictions on multinational enterprises, MNEs, in developing countries, LDCs, have been explained in numerous ways. One of the earliest is the infant-industry argument.[2] Restrictions have also been interpreted as a means of promoting exports (*e.g.*, Krugman, 1984) transferring profits to domestic firms (*e.g.*, Brander and Spencer, 1984) or both (*e.g.*, Spence 1984).[3] There is also literature on tax-based restrictions.[4] Lately, aided by pressure from institutions such as the World Bank and the IMF, liberalization has become the accepted paradigm for LDC policy makers. In the last few years, restrictions have been substantially eased (see, for example, Dornbusch, 1992; and Rodrik, 1992). But blind faith in any paradigm is usually dangerous. This is no less true of free trade.

This chapter concentrates on foreign exchange restrictions placed on MNEs. Almost all LDCs still use such restrictions.[5] It is shown below that liberalization is

---

[1] I should like to thank Pat Conway, John Logan, Kunal Sengupta, Ed Tower and seminar participants at Rutgers University, the University of North Carolina, Chapel Hill and Duke University for helpful comments. Any shortcomings are my responsibility. Research support from the Martindale Center at Lehigh University is gratefully acknowledged.

[2] A selection from this voluminous literature includes Nurkse (1953), Clemhout and Wan (1970) and more recently Mayer (1984) and Grossman and Horn (1987).

[3] For a recent survey of this literature, see Bhagwati (1988).

[4] See, for example, Batra and Ramachandran (1980), Jones and Dei (1983), Gang and Gangopadhyay (1985) and Conway (1985).

[5] In fact, of the total of 151 countries studied by the IMF in 1990 84 countries had some restrictions on the usage of foreign exchange for current transactions and 121 had restrictions on its usage for capital transactions.

not always a good thing. Optimal policies towards MNEs are sensitive to the nature of the output good and to the LDC objective function. This chapter starts from the basic assumption that LDC policy instruments are set by policy makers who use their control to steer MNEs toward choices which fulfill their government's objectives. The data seem to indicate that policy makers do exercise such control (*e.g.*, Contractor, 1985). The focus of the policy makers is on input use and technology. This approach is different from that of Itagaki (1989), who studies a similar problem but is concerned with the MNE's output choices under the risk of foreign exchange control, and not with the derivation of optimal policy. Typical instruments of control used by policy makers are the firm's profit repatriation (in, *e.g.*, India, Nigeria, Bangladesh and Colombia)[6], foreign exchange quotas for imports of capital and other inputs (in, *e.g.*, Bangladesh, Benin, Brazil, Egypt, Kenya and South Korea)[7] and the corporate profit tax, which is omnipresent. In addition, most LDCs have differential policies towards MNEs depending on whether or not they export their output to the world market (in, *e.g.*, Egypt, India, Indonesia, Argentina and Colombia)[8]. The countries mentioned above are merely illustrative; the actual list of countries where such restrictions are in place is very long indeed.

In this chapter, the MNE takes the LDC's policy instruments as parameters, but

---

[6]In Nigeria such control is exercised through the Indigenization Decree of 1974, as amended in 1976 and 1977. The instrument of control in Bangladesh is the Foreign Private Investment (Promotion and Protection) Act of 1980. In Colombia control is in accordance with Decision Nos. 24 and 103 of the Cartegena Agreement, which govern foreign investment within countries of the Andean Pact; profit repatriations are limited in non-priority sectors. In India such control is exercised under the provisions of the Foreign Exchange Regulation Act (FERA) of 1973, which limits profit repatriation in sectors designated non-priority by the government.

[7]In Bangladesh foreign exchange quotas are set by the Director-General of Industries on the basis of the Annual Import Policy Order, which identifies priority sectors. In Benin the Directorate of External Commerce sets quotas on imported goods, which are on its restricted list. In Brazil the Foreign Investment Law (No.4131) sets ceilings on the inflow of financial loans. In Egypt the Supreme Council for the Planning of Foreign Trade sets annual foreign exchange quotas for each sector of the economy. In Kenya all imports are classified into four schedules - IA, IB, IIA and IIB - in decreasing order of priority as assessed by the government. Imports of items on Schedules IIA and IIB are subject to foreign exchange quotas set by the Director of Internal Trade in the Ministry of Commerce and Industry. In South Korea the Ministry of Finance prepares and administers the Foreign Exchange Supply and Demand Plan, which sets overall ceilings on the amounts of foreign exchange that may be used.

[8]In India exporters are entitled to freely import capital goods upto the value of their exports under the Import Replenishment Scheme (REP). A similar scheme is operative in Argentina for exporters in priority sectors. In Indonesia, as of May 1986, exporting firms have been split into those which export 85% or more of their output and those which export a smaller percentage. Duties and surcharges on capital goods imports by such firms are partially refundable, with the refund proportion being higher if the firm is in former category. In Colombia all of a firm's export earnings may be used to finance capital goods imports under the regulations issued by the Monetary Board. In Egypt proceeds from exports other than rice and cotton may be fully or partially retained by the exporter in Foreign Exchange Retention Accounts.

is the dominant firm within its industry.[9] The effects of LDC policy variables on MNE behavior, with emphasis on its input use, are examined under two specifications of the output good. In the first case, the good has no market outside the host country. In the second scenario, the good is tradable and may either be sold domestically or exported. When the LDC considers the MNE's output inessential (e.g., a luxury good), the effect of the policy instruments on factor use becomes very important. The effects of profit taxes and foreign exchange quotas in these two scenarios are very different. If the output good is not tradable, the policy variables directly affect the capital input, but have an ambiguous effect on the labor input. If the output good is tradable, the policy variables inversely affect both capital and labor inputs. Heuristically, the reason for the change in the effects of policy can be understood through the utilization of output. In the first case output is only useful to the MNE as a means of producing profit, whereas in the second it is also a means of alleviating the foreign exchange constraint. If the output good is tradable, the policy variables inversely affect total exports and the share of total output that is exported. Lowering either of the policy variables increases the country's foreign exchange reserves by more than would be expected by considering only the direct impact.[10] These results suggest that output tradability provides at least a partial explanation of the differing repatriation and tax policies adopted by various developing countries towards MNEs. The answers which emerge are not obvious ones. Using various plausible objective functions for policy makers, it is not always true that an MNE producing a non-tradable good should face more restrictive policies than an MNE producing a tradable one. In Section II the two models are set up, and the comparative static results with regards to the policy instruments are derived. In Section III possible LDC government objectives are specified, and the associated optimal policies are presented. Section IV is a conclusion. Cumbersome derivations have been relegated to the Appendix.

II. The Basic and Extended Models

1.   THE SET UP
The firm referred to as the *MNE* is the local operation of a larger international entity being referred to as the *parent*. It is a supplier of a good or service, the domestic inverse demand for which is $p = p_0(q)$ with $p_0' < 0$. It is assumed that the MNE is the dominant firm in the industry. Price is denoted by p and q is total industry output being the sum of the output of the MNE and a domestic *competitive fringe*,

(1) $q = y + x$,

---

[9]The MNE is the Stackelberg leader in its industry, but a Stackelberg follower of the LDC government. The dominant firm model is used for notational convenience. An oligopolistic model with large domestic competitors, where the MNE is a Nash player rather than a Stackelberg leader, yields the same qualitative results with regard to the effects studied in this chapter.

[10]Some of the results in this chapter are presented in greater detail in Mudambi (1990).

where y is the output of the MNE and x ($=\Sigma x_i$) is output of the domestic fringe. As in the standard dominant firm model, the MNE faces a residual inverse demand curve

(2) $p = p(y)$ with $p' < 0$ and $2p' + p''y < 0$,

being associated with a marginal revenue curve that is downward sloping. Each member of the fringe is a price taker that maximizes a profit function $\pi_i = px_i - c(x_i)$, where c(.) is the cost function; this yields each fringe member's upward-sloping supply function $x_i(p)$. The supply of the fringe is $x(p) = \Sigma x_i(p)$ with $x' > 0$. By construction $y \equiv q - x(p)$ and at industry equilibrium $p(y) = p_0(q)$. The MNE has a well-behaved production function

(3) $y = f(L,K)$ with $f_1 > 0$, $f_2 > 0$, $f_{11} < 0$, $f_{22} < 0$ and $f_{12} = f_{21} > 0$.

All labor employed by both the MNE and the fringe firms is domestic, and is paid a wage rate w that is assumed to be set through some type of migration mechanism. All of the MNE's capital is financed by equity and is held by its foreign parent firm. The results are unaffected as long as the foreign parent's holding represents a controlling interest. Introduction of debt, either domestic or foreign, also does not affect the results. In addition to profit repatriations, it is assumed that the MNE pays fees to its parent, which may be expressed as a rate of return r on the parent's equity. These fees may be in the form of licensing dues, management fees or any general payments for overhead services provided by the parent. These transfer payments remitted to the MNE's parent amount to rK. The MNE pays a tax on profits at the rate t. Its post-tax profits are $(1-t)\pi = (1-t)\{p(.)f(.)-wL-rK\}$. The MNE uses foreign exchange to pay management fees to its parent and to repatriate post-tax profits. As per observed policies in most LDCs, the government controls foreign exchange usage through a quota. This quota may only be a perceived one if, as is often the case, the government allocates foreign exchange on a case-by-case basis. This imposes a constraint on the optimization problem of the MNE. It may be asssumed to be binding, since foreign exchange is scarce. Both the MNE and the domestic fringe of firms treat government policy variables as parameters.

2.   THE BASIC MODEL: A FIXED CONSTRAINT

First consider the case where the MNE produces a non-traded good (*i.e.*, it has no export market). Denoting the repatriation quota by π_0, the MNE's objective function is the Lagrangian

(4) $\mathcal{L}(\mu,L,K) = (1-t)\pi + \mu\{\pi_0 - (1-t)\pi - rK\}$.

The necesssary conditions for a maximum are

(5a) $\mathcal{L}_\mu = \pi_0 - (1-t)\pi - rK = 0$,

(5b) $\mathcal{L}_L = (1-t)(1-\mu)[f_1(p + p'f) - w] = 0$, and

(5c) $£_K = (1-t)(1-\mu)f_2(p+p'f) - r[1-t(1-\mu)] = 0.$

The sufficient conditions for a maximum are always satisfied, subject to the requirements in (1) and (2). The solution to the conditions (5) yields the MNE's Nash best response factor demand functions, $L^*(x;\pi_o,t)$ and $K^*(x;\pi_o,t)$, and the equilibrium value of the shadow price of foreign exchange, $\mu^*(x;\pi_o,t)$, as functions of the domestic firms' output and the policy variables. Using (5b) and (5c) the MNE's equilibrium MRTS is

$$f_1/f_2 = (w/r)\frac{(1-t)(1-\mu)}{[1-t(1-\mu)]},$$

which may be considered a proxy for the capital-intensity of the production process adopted by the MNE. Both π_o and t have the same qualitative effects on all endogenous variables. Lowering π_o directly tightens the MNE's constraint while lowering t does so indirectly by raising the amount of repatriable profits. Encouraging the MNE by lowering t has the same effect as discouraging the MNE by lowering π_o. Total differentiation of (5) yields

(6) (a) $d\mu^*(.)/dt < 0,$

  (b) $dK^*(.)/dt > 0,$

  (c) $dy^*(.)/dt > 0,$ and

  (d) $d(f_1/f_2)/dt > 0.$

Both π_o and t directly affect the input of capital (the restricted input) and capital intensity. They will affect L directly if the production function exhibits strong factor complementarity and/or the output demand curve of the MNE is very elastic.[11] In this case, lowering either π_o or t will cause the MNE to decrease its employment. However, regardless of the effects of the policy variables on labor input, the measures affect output directly. Lowering either π_o or t lowers the MNE's output and raises output price. Note that the higher output price lowers industry output as well, but *raises* the output of the domestic firms. The MNE's market share falls.

3.   THE EXTENDED MODEL: A FLEXIBLE CONSTRAINT
The extended model considers the case where the output good is tradable. The MNE can finance part of its foreign exchange needs by exporting a proportion a of its output, which indicates an import-export linkage. Impose the "small country" assumption that the MNE is a competitor in the world market for its output, and considers the world price (p_w, expressed in domestic currency) to be fixed. Domestic availability of the good is $q = (1-a)y + x$. Domestic price is

---

[11]The effect of the policy variables on L is directly determined by the sign of $f_{12}(p+p'f) +$ $f_1f_2(2p'+p''y)$, which is the effect of K on the MRP of L. If it is negative the factors would be "non-cooperant" in Hicksian terminology. Similarly, if it is positive, the factors would be cooperant.

determined as $p[(1-a)y]$ [equal to $p_0(q)$ at industry equilibrium]. The MNE maximizes the Lagrangian

(7) $f(\sigma,L,K,a) = (1-t)\pi + \sigma[\pi_o + ap_wf(.) - (1-t)\pi - rK]$,

where, again, the constraint is specified to be binding. The necessary conditions for maximum are

(8a) $f_\sigma = \pi_o + ap_wf(.) - (1-t)\pi - rK = 0$,

(8b) $f_L = f_1\{(1-t)(1-\sigma)(1-a)[p+(1-a)p'f] + [1-t(1-\sigma)]ap_w\} - w(1-t)(1-\sigma) = 0$,

(8c) $f_K = f_2\{(1-t)(1-\sigma)(1-a)[p+(1-a)p'f] + [1-t(1-\sigma)]ap_w\} - r[1-t(1-\sigma)] = 0$, and

(8d) $f_a = f\{[1-t(1-\sigma)]p_w - (1-t)(1-\sigma)[p+(1-a)p'f]\} = 0$.

From (8b) and (8c) the technology proxy is

(8e) $f_1/f_2 = \dfrac{(1-t)(1-\sigma)}{[1-t(1-\sigma)]} (w/r)$.

As seen in (8d), the constraint forces the MNE to export more and to cut back on domestic production relative to the unconstrained equilibrium, raising the domestic output price. The sufficient conditions for a maximum are always satisfied, subject to the conditions in (1) and (2). The solution to the system of conditions (8) yields the MNE's Nash best response functions, $L^\circ(\pi_o,t,p_w)$, $K^\circ(\pi_o,t,p_w)$ and $a^\circ(\pi_o,t,p_w)$, and the equilibrium value of the shadow price of foreign exchange, $\sigma^\circ(\pi_o,t,p_w)$. Again, both π_o and t have the same qualitative effects on all endogenous variables. Total differentiation of the system (8) yields

(9)   (a) $d\sigma^\circ(.)/dt < 0$,

        (b) $dK^\circ(.)/dt < 0$,

        (c) $dL^\circ(.)/dt < 0$,

        (d) $da^\circ(.)/dt < 0$,

        (e) $dy^\circ(.)/dt < 0$, and

        (f) $d(f_1/f_2)/dt > 0$.

4.   COMPARISONS

Comparing (6b) with (9b) indicates that the effects of π_0 and t on K in the extended model are the opposite of their effects in the basic model. This reversal occurs because in the extended model the lowering of π_o increases the marginal value of exports. Increasing exports requires an increased use of inputs, including capital, and this increase swamps the direct effect of the constraint. Lowering t has the same effect as lowering π_o, except that it works through repatriable profits. Inequality (9c) indicates that the ambiguous effects of π_0 and t on L in the basic model are resolved in the extended model. Lowering either π_o or t raises the marginal value of exports, causing the MRP of labor to rise. The MNE is led to increase its labor input. Comparing (6c) with (9e) indicates that the effects of π_0 and t on total output are reversed in the extended model. This reversal is based on the input effects above. The effects of the policy variables on industry output and MNE market share are reversed as well. Comparing (6d) with (9f) illustrates that lowering t drives the MNE towards a more labor-intensive technology in both models.

The share of total output that is exported, a, rises as the instruments π_0 and t are lowered, as do total exports, ay. The effects of the policy instruments on domestic sales, $(1-a)y$, are composed of two opposing effects - one on domestic output share and one on output. It can be shown that as either π_0 or t is lowered, $(1-a)y$ falls and the domestic price rises. As p_w (the world output price) rises, one would expect increased supply. This need not occur, since p_w affects the MNE in two opposing ways. The world price is the marginal revenue of export sales. But it also appears in the repatriation constraint and inversely affects the shadow price of foreign exchange. As p_w rises, its direct effect is to increase the marginal value of exports; but its indirect effect is to loosen the foreign exchange constraint, decreasing the marginal value of exports. If the indirect effect dominates, p_w has the same effect on the endogenous variables as π_0 or t. If the direct effect dominates, the reverse is true.

III.   Government Objectives and Policy Effects

1.   GOVERNMENT OBJECTIVES

The government in an LDC typically has many specific objectives which it wishes to address through its policy regarding MNEs. At the most basic level, MNEs are sources of tax revenue to the government and generators of manufactured output. At another level, they are providers of employment in a capital-scarce, domestic labor-abundant economy. These considerations suggest two possible LDC objective functions.[12] One possible objective function for the LDC policy makers could be the conventional sum of consumer surplus and tax revenue (*e.g.*, Brander and Spencer, 1984). In the basic model such an objective function may be written as

$$(10a) \quad U_1(\pi_0,t) = t\pi^* + \int_0^{q^*} p_0(q) \, dq,$$

where $\pi^* = \pi^*(\pi_o,t)$ and $q^* = y^*(\pi_o,t) + x\{p[y^*(\pi_o,t)]\}$. In the extended model, only the consumer surplus generated by domestic consumption enters the government's objective function, which may be written as

---

[12]At this point it is fair to question the need for the presence of the MNE, given the existence of the domestic competitive fringe. The answer lies in the nature of the dominant firm model - the entry of the dominant firm, the MNE, unambiguously lowers output price and increases industry output.

(10b) $\quad U_2(\pi_o, t) = t\pi^o + \int_0^{q^o} p_o(q)\, dq,$

where $\pi^o = \pi^o(\pi_o, t)$, $q^o = (1-a^o)y^o(\pi_o, t) + x\{p[y^o(\pi_o, t)]\}$ and $a^o = a^o(\pi_o, t)$. Often, the output good of the MNE is not deemed socially valuable in the subjective evaluation of LDC policy makers. In this case, surplus associated with its consumption is irrelevant. The only two quantities deemed valuable by policy makers may be the taxes paid and the employment provided by the MNE. Based on these considerations the welfare generated by the MNE is made up of two components. One component is the total tax revenue; the other component is the total employment of the MNE, weighted by the wage it pays. In the basic model, the government's objective function is

(11a) $\quad G_1(\pi_o, t) = wL^* + t\pi^*,$

while in the extended model it is

(11b) $\quad G_2(\pi_o, t) = wL^o + t\pi^o.$

2. THE EFFECTS OF POLICY

The policy adopted by the LDC is sensitive to the subjective and objective evaluation of the good produced by the MNE. The appropriate objective function is selected using Table 1.

Table 1.   Selection of Objective Function

		Objective Evaluation of Output Good	
		Non-tradable	Tradable
Subjective Evaluation of Output Good	Valuable	(10a)	(10b)
	Non-valuable	(11a)	(11b)

So, there are four cases to be analyzed. In the first case, the relevant objective function is (10a), which must be evaluated at the solution to (5). At this solution it can be shown that both $\partial\pi^*/\partial\mu$ and $\partial\pi^*/\partial L$ are zero while $\partial\pi^*/\partial K$ is positive.[13] Thus, $dU_1/d\pi_0$ and dU_1/dt are both always positive, and the optimal policy is to be as liberal as possible with the repatriation ceiling and as restrictive as possible with the tax rate. In the second case, the objective function is (10b), which must be evaluated at the solution to (8). At this solution it is easily shown that $\partial\pi^o/\partial\sigma$ is zero, $\partial\pi^o/\partial L$ is negative and $\partial\pi^o/\partial K$ is positive.[14] It follows that $U_2(.)$ is nonmonotone in the policy variables and may reach an interior maximum. Such a

---

[13]Using (5c), it can be shown that at the solution to (4) $\partial\pi^*/\partial K$ is equal to $[\mu/(1-\mu)]r$, which is positive.

[14]Using (8b), it follows that at the solution to (8) $\partial\pi^o/\partial L = -[\sigma/(1-\sigma)]\alpha p_w f_1 < 0$. Similarly, using (8c), at the solution to (8) $\partial\pi^o/\partial K = [\sigma/(1-\sigma)](1-\alpha)p_w f_2 > 0$.

solution would involve balancing the impact on tax collections with the opposing impact on consumer surplus. The objective function in the third case is (11a), evaluated at the solution to (5). In this case, the effect of the policy variables depends on their impact on the labor input, since it directly enters into the objective. This, in turn, depends on the effect of the policy variables on the MNE's use of labor. It follows that if $£_{LK}$ is negative, the government may have an interior solution, which involves balancing the effects of the policy variables on employment with the opposing effects on tax collections. However, if $£_{LK}$ is positive, the government has no interior solution, since (11a) is always increasing in the policy variables. Then, maximizing (11a) involves raising the repatriation ceiling and the tax rate to the extent possible.[15] Finally, in the fourth case the objective function is (11b). This in the only case where the optimal policies may be different for the two parameters. It may be shown that $dG_2/d\pi_0$ is always negative. The optimal policy is therefore to lower the repatriation ceiling to the extent possible so as to force the MNE to export as much as possible.[16] However, $G_2(.)$ cannot be shown to be monotone in t, and there may exist an interior solution balancing the opposing effects on employment and tax collections. The optimal policies are summarized in Table 2.

Table 2.   Summary of Policy Prescriptions

		Objective Evaluation of Output Good	
		Non-tradable	Tradable
	Valuable	π_0 : Liberal t : Restrictive	π_0 : Interior t : Interior
Subjective Evaluation of Output Good	Non-valuable (Cooperant factors)	π_0 : Liberal t : Restrictive	
			π_0 : Restrictive t : Interior
	(Non-cooperant factors)	π_0 : Interior t : Interior	

IV.   Concluding Remarks

The principal objective of this chapter is to determine whether plausible policy objectives are likely to be served by liberalization. Specifically, an attempt has been made to analyze the optimal profit repatriation and corporate profit tax policies to be imposed on MNEs by a *small* LDC facing a binding foreign exchange constraint.

---

[15]As the government raises the tax rate, it can increase output only upto a point. This is because the rising tax rate will eventually reduce repatriable profits to the point where the firm can import enough capital to reach its unrestricted profit-maximizing output level. Further increases in the tax rate will have no further effect on inputs and hence output.

[16]The critical step is to note that $w + t[\partial\pi^0/\partial L] = f_1\{(1-a)[p+(1-a)p'f]+[a/(1-\sigma)]\} > 0$ by substituting for w from (8b).

The results are sometimes in favor of liberalization, but not always. It is shown that the tradability of the MNE's output is important in determining the effect of such policies on MNE input use. To the extent that input use and technology choice are as such objectives of policy, output tradability is crucial. Further, optimal policy with regard to overall objectives is itself shown to be sensitive to this characteristic of the output good. In particular, it is important to note that objectives are not always reached by favoring MNE exporters with liberal policies. Other policy considerations may be addressed within the current analysis. Restrictive repatriation and liberal tax policies reduce the MNE's domestic market share, and favor domestic producers. Given the current international lending climate, such policies are unlikely to be advertised. The conclusions of any model are only as strong as its assumptions are realistic. It is to be hoped that the current analysis passes this test. If it does, the optimal policies suggested have relevance for a large number of countries.

Appendix

THE BASIC MODEL
The second-order conditions that guarantee that the solution to (4) provides the maximum to the problem (3) require

(A1) $$|H| = \begin{vmatrix} \pounds_{\mu\mu} & \pounds_{\mu L} & \pounds_{\mu K} \\ \pounds_{L\mu} & \pounds_{LL} & \pounds_{LK} \\ \pounds_{K\mu} & \pounds_{KL} & \pounds_{KK} \end{vmatrix} > 0.$$

It follows immediately from observation of (4) that $\pounds_{\mu\mu} = 0$. At the solution to (4), it may be seen that $\pounds_{L\mu} = \pounds_{\mu L} = 0$. Proceed by evaluating the other terms in $|H|$. To start with

(A2a) $\pounds_{LL} = (1\text{-}t)(1\text{-}\mu)[f_{11}(p + p'f) + f_1{}^2 R]$,

where $R \equiv (2p' + p''f)$, the slope of firm's marginal revenue curve. Using (2) and being subject to the requirement that the firm's marginal revenue function slopes downward [i.e., $R < 0$], indicates that (A2a) is negative. Similarly,

(A2b) $\pounds_{KK} = (1\text{-}t)(1\text{-}\mu)[f_{22}(p + p'f) + f_2{}^2 R] < 0$, and

(A2c') $\pounds_{K\mu} = \pounds_{\mu K} = -(1\text{-}t)\{f_2(p + p'f) - rt < 0$.

The value of (A2c') at the solution to (4) may be obtained by substituting from (4b). This yields

(A2c) $\pounds_{K\mu} = \pounds_{\mu K} = -r/(1\text{-}\mu) < 0$, and

(A2d) $\pounds_{LK} = (1\text{-}t)(1\text{-}\mu)[f_{12}(p + p'f) + f_1 f_2 R] = \pounds_{KL}$,

since f(.) is a continuous function. The sign of (A2d) cannot be deduced unambiguously. It is clear that the sign of $\pounds_{LK}$ is dependent on the cross-effects on the factors' marginal revenue product (MRP). Increasing factor 'i' increases the marginal physical product of factor 'j' $(\neq i)$ [factor complementarity being assumed in (2)], exerting a positive influence on j's MRP. However, this increase also raises output, which lowers price and marginal revenue, exerting a negative influence on j's MRP. Using the foregoing analysis and substituting (A2a)-(A2d) into (A1) reveals that

(A3) $|H| = -\pounds_{LL}[r^2/(1-\mu)^2] > 0$,

so that the second-order conditions for a maximum are satisfied. Totally differentiating the system (4) and using (A2) gives

(A4a) $d\mu^*(.)/d\pi_o = -[\pounds_{LL}\pounds_{KK} - \pounds_{LK}^2]/|H| < 0$,

(A4b) $dL^*(.)/d\pi_o = -(1-\mu)\pounds_{LK}/r\pounds_{LL}$,

(A4c) $dK^*(.)/d\pi_o = (1-\mu)/r > 0$,

(A5a) $d\mu^*(.)/dt = -\{\pi[\pounds_{LL}\pounds_{KK}-\pounds_{LK}^2]/|H|\} - \mu(1-\mu)/(1-t) < 0$,

(A5b) $dL^*(.)/dt = -[\pi(1-\mu)\pounds_{LK}]/r\pounds_{LL}$, and

(A5c) $dK^*(.)/dt = \pi(1-\mu)/r > 0$.

Differentiating (4d) and using (A5a) yields

(A6) $$\frac{d(f_1/f_2)}{dt} = \frac{(w/r)(1-t)\,\pi\,[\pounds_{LL}\pounds_{KK}-\pounds_{LK}^2]}{|H|\,[1-t(1-\mu)]^2} > 0\ .$$

THE EXTENDED MODEL
It is convenient to solve out for a in terms of the other endogenous variables by using (8d), and so to reduce the dimension of the system of first-order conditions. This solution is of the form $a^o(L,K,\sigma;t,p_w,\pi_o)$. Define

(A7) $f_o[L,K,\sigma,a^o(L,K,\sigma;t,p_w,\pi_o);t,p_w,\pi_o] \equiv C_o(L,K,\sigma;t,p_w,\pi_o)$.

Similarly, define functions $C_L(.)$ and $C_K(.)$. By substituting (7d) into (7b) and (7c) these two functions may be explicitly written as

(A8a) $C_L = (1-t)(1-\sigma)\{f_1[p+(1-a^o(.))p'f] - w\} = 0$, and

(A8b) $C_K = [1-t(1-\sigma)][f_2p_w - r] = 0$.

By differentiating the system $[C_\sigma,C_L,C_K]'$ the following is obtained:

(A9a) $C_{\sigma\sigma} = -p_w^2/[(1-t)(1-\sigma)^2(1-\sigma)R] > 0$,

(A9b) $C_{LL} = p_wf_{11}[1-t(1-\sigma)] < 0$,

(A9c) $C_{KK} = p_wf_{22}[1-t(1-\sigma)] < 0$,

(A9d) $C_{KL} = C_{LK} = p_wf_{12}[1-t(1-\sigma)] > 0$,

(A9e) $C_{\sigma L} = C_{L\sigma} = p_wf_1/(1-\sigma) > 0$, and

(A9f) $C_{\sigma K} = C_{K\sigma} = 0$.

Using (A9) and the conditions in (2) reveals that

$$\text{(A10)} \quad |\mathbf{C}| = \begin{vmatrix} C_{\sigma\sigma} & C_{\sigma L} & C_{\sigma K} \\ C_{L\sigma} & C_{LL} & C_{LK} \\ C_{K\sigma} & C_{KL} & C_{KK} \end{vmatrix} > 0,$$

implying that the second-order conditions for a maximum are satisfied. Totally differentiating the system (8) and using (A9) gives

(A11a) $d\sigma^{\circ}(.)/d\pi_0 = -(C_{LL}C_{KK} - C_{LK}{}^2)/|\mathbf{C}| < 0,$

(A11b) $dL^{\circ}(.)/d\pi_0 = C_{KK}C_{L\sigma}/|\mathbf{C}| < 0,$

(A11c) $dK^{\circ}(.)/d\pi_0 = -C_{KL}C_{L\sigma}/|\mathbf{C}| < 0,$

(A11d) $d\alpha^{\circ}/d\pi_0 = [(1-\alpha)C_{L\sigma}(f_1 C_{KK} - f_2 C_{LK})]/[f|\mathbf{C}|] + [p_w(C_{LL}C_{KK} - C_{LK}{}^2)]/[f(1-t)(1-\sigma)^2 R|\mathbf{C}|] < 0,$

(A11e) $dy^{\circ}(.)/d\pi_0 = [C_{L\sigma}(f_1 C_{KK} - f_2 C_{LK})]/|\mathbf{C}| < 0,$

(A12a) $d\sigma^{\circ}(.)/dt = -\{\pi - (\sigma/R)[p_w/(1-t)(1-\sigma)]^2\}[C_{LL}C_{KK} - C_{LK}{}^2] + C_{KK}C_{L\sigma}[\sigma p_w f_1/(1-t)] < 0,$

(A12b) $dL^{\circ}(.)/dt = C_{KK}C_{L\sigma}\pi/|\mathbf{C}| < 0,$ and

(A12c) $dK^{\circ}(.)/dt = -C_{KL}C_{L\sigma}\pi/|\mathbf{C}| < 0.$

GOVERNMENT OBJECTIVES

Firstly, take the case with a socially valuable output good. The derivative of (10a) with respect to π_0 is

$$\frac{dU_1}{d\pi_0} = t \left[\frac{\delta\pi^\bullet}{\delta L} \cdot \frac{dL^\bullet}{d\pi_0} + \frac{\delta\pi^\bullet}{\delta K} \cdot \frac{dK^\bullet}{d\pi_0} + \frac{\delta\pi^\bullet}{\delta\mu} \cdot \frac{d\mu^\bullet}{d\pi_0} \right] - q \cdot \frac{dq^\bullet}{d\pi_0} p_0'(q^\bullet).$$

Note that sgn $[dq^*/d\pi_0]$ = sgn $[dy^*/d\pi_0]$, as required by the conditions for industry equilibrium, so that $dq^*/d\pi_0 > 0$. At the solution to (4) it may be seen that $\partial\pi^*/\partial\mu = \partial\pi^*/\partial L = 0$. Further, by using (4c) it can be shown that at the solution to (4) $\partial\pi^*/\partial K = [\mu/(1-\mu)]r > 0$, which by substitution gives

$$\text{(A13a)} \quad \frac{dU_1}{d\pi_0} = t \left[\frac{\delta\pi^\bullet}{\delta K} \cdot \frac{dK^\bullet}{d\pi_0} \right] - q \cdot \frac{dq^\bullet}{d\pi_0} p_0'(q^\bullet),$$

which from (1), (5b) and (5c) is always positive. It also follows that

$$\text{(A13b)} \quad \frac{dU_1}{dt} = \pi^\bullet + t \left[\frac{\delta\pi^\bullet}{\delta K} \cdot \frac{dK^\bullet}{dt} \right] - q \cdot \frac{dq^\bullet}{dt} p_0'(q^\bullet),$$

which is also always positive. The derivative of (10b) with respect to π_0 is

$$\text{(A14a)} \quad \frac{dU_2}{d\pi_0} = t \left[\frac{\delta\pi^0}{\delta L} \cdot \frac{dL^0}{d\pi_0} + \frac{\delta\pi^0}{\delta K} \cdot \frac{dK^0}{d\pi_0} + \frac{\delta\pi^0}{\delta\sigma} \cdot \frac{d\sigma^0}{d\pi_0} \right] - q^0 \frac{dq^0}{d\pi_0} p_0'(q^0).$$

Similarly, the derivative of (10b) with respect to t is

$$\text{(A14b)} \quad \frac{dU_2}{dt} = t \left[\frac{\delta\pi^0}{\delta L} \cdot \frac{dL^0}{dt} + \frac{\delta\pi^0}{\delta K} \cdot \frac{dK^0}{dt} + \frac{\delta\pi^0}{\delta\sigma} \cdot \frac{d\sigma^0}{dt} \right] - q^0 \frac{dq^0}{dt} p_0'(q^0) + \pi^0.$$

Again, note that industry equilibrium requires that sgn $[dq^o/d\pi_o]$ = sgn $[d(1-a^o)y^o/d\pi_o]$, which can be shown to be positive. The same is true for dq^o/dt. At the solution to (8) $\partial\pi^o/\partial\sigma$ is zero. Using (8b) indicates that $\partial\pi^o/\partial L = -ap_w[f_1/(1-t)][\sigma/(1-\sigma)] < 0$; and using (8c) gives $\partial\pi^o/\partial K = (1-a)p_w[f_2/(1-t)][\sigma/(1-\sigma)] > 0$. Thus, while the second term is always positive (since $p_o' < 0$), the first sign of the term is ambiguous, which means that the government may have an interior solution if the impact of the policy variables on K is large enough. In such a case the government's optimal policy would involve balancing the negative impact of policy on tax collections with the positive impact on consumer surplus.

Secondly, take the case with socially non-valuable output good. The derivative of (11a) with respect to π_o is

$$\frac{dG_1}{d\pi_o} = t\left[\frac{\delta\pi^*}{\delta L}\cdot\frac{dL^*}{d\pi_o} + \frac{\delta\pi^*}{\delta K}\cdot\frac{dK^*}{d\pi_o} + \frac{\delta\pi^*}{\delta\mu}\cdot\frac{d\mu^*}{d\pi_o}\right] + w\frac{dL^*}{d\pi_o} .$$

By using the same methodology as that used in simplifying (A13a) this may be reduced to

$$\frac{dG_1}{d\pi_o} = t\left[\frac{\delta\pi^*}{\delta L}\cdot\frac{dK^*}{d\pi_o}\right] + w\frac{dL^*}{d\pi_o} ,$$

Its sign depends on the sign of $dL^*/d\pi_o$, which is determined by the sign of $\pounds_{LK}$, as seen in the discussion following (6). Similarly,

$$\frac{dG_1}{dt} = t\left[\frac{\delta\pi^*}{\delta L}\cdot\frac{dK^*}{dt}\right] + w\frac{dL^*}{dt} + \pi^* ,$$

its sign being determined by that of $\pounds_{LK}$ as well. The derivative of (11b) with respect to π_o is

$$\frac{dG_2}{d\pi_o} = t\left[\frac{\delta\pi^o}{\delta L}\cdot\frac{dL^o}{d\pi_o} + \frac{\delta\pi^o}{\delta K}\cdot\frac{dK^o}{d\pi_o} + \frac{\delta\pi^o}{\delta\sigma}\cdot\frac{d\sigma^o}{d\pi_o}\right] + w\frac{dL^o}{d\pi_o} .$$

By applying the discussion following (A14) this expression may be reduced to

$$\frac{dG_2}{d\pi_o} = \left[t\frac{\delta\pi^o}{\delta L} + w\right]\frac{dL^o}{d\pi_o} + t\frac{\delta\pi^o}{\delta K}\cdot\frac{dK^o}{d\pi_o} ,$$

which may be shown to be always negative. The critical step is to note that $w+t[\partial\pi^o/\partial L] = f_1\{(1-a)[p+(1-a)p'f]+[a/(1-\sigma)]\} > 0$ by substituting for w from (8b). The derivative of (11b) with respect to t is

$$\frac{dG_2}{dt} = \left[t\frac{\delta\pi^o}{\delta L} + w\right]\frac{dL^o}{dt} + t\frac{\delta\pi^o}{\delta K}\cdot\frac{dK^o}{dt} + \pi^o ,$$

whose sign is ambiguous, since π^o is presumably positive.

References

Baldwin, R.E. (1969) 'The Case Against Infant-Industry Protection', *Journal of Political Economy* **77**, 295-305.

Batra, R.N. and Ramachandran, R. (1980) 'Multinational Firms and the Theory of International Trade and Investment', *American Economic Review* **70**, 278-90.

Bhagwati, J. (1988) 'Export-Promoting Trade Strategy: Issues and Evidence', *The World Bank Research Observer* **1**, 27-57.

Brander, J. and Spencer, B. (1984) 'Tariff Protection and Imperfect Competition', in Kierzkowski, H.

(ed.), *Monopolistic Competition and International Trade*, Oxford, Clarendon Press.

Clemhout, S. and Wan, H.Y. (1970) 'Learning-by-Doing and Infant-Industry Protection', *Review of Economic Studies* **37**, 33-56.

Contractor, F. (1985) *Licensing in International Strategy*, Westport, CT, Quorum Books.

Conway, P. (1985) 'The "Obsolescing Bargain": LDC Decision-Making and Direct Foreign Investment', *Unpublished manuscript*, University of North Carolina, Chapel Hill.

Dornbusch, R. (1992) 'The Case for Trade Liberalization in Developing Countries', *Journal of Economics Perspectives* **6**, 69-85.

Gang, I.N. and Gangopadhyay, S. (1985) 'Multinational Firms and Government Policy', *Economics Letters* **17**, 395-99.

Grossman, G.M. and Horn, H. (1987) 'Infant-Industry Protection Reconsidered: The Case of Informational Barriers to Entry', *NBER Working Paper #2159*.

Helpman, E. and Krugman, P.R. (1985) *Market Structure and Foreign Trade*, Cambridge, MA, The MIT Press.

International Monetary Fund (1990) *Exchange Arrangements and Exchange Restrictions - Annual Report*, Washington DC.

Itagaki, T. (1989) 'The Multinational Enterprise Under the Threats of Restriction on Profit Repatriation and Exchange Control', *Journal of Development Economics* **31**, 369-77.

Jones, R.W. and Dei, F. (1983) 'International Trade and Foreign Investment: A Simple Model', *Economic Inquiry* **30**, 449-464.

Krugman, P.R. (1984) 'Import Protection as Export Promotion: International Competition in the Presence of Oligopoly and Economies of Scale', in H.Kierzkowski (ed), *Monopolistic Competition and International Trade*, Oxford, Clarendon Press.

Mayer, W. (1984) 'The Infant-Export Industry Argument', *Canadian Journal of Economics* **17**, 249-269.

Mudambi, R. (1990) 'Government Policy in the Presence of Foreign Exchange Scarcity', *Martindale Center Discussion Paper 3/90*, Lehigh University.

Nurkse, R. (1953) *Problems of Capital Formation in Underdeveloped Countries*, Oxford, Basil Blackwell.

Rodrik, D. (1992) 'The Limits of Trade Policy Reform in Developing Countries', *Journal of Economic Perspectives* **6**, 87-105.

Spence, A.M. (1984) 'Industrial Organization and Competitive Advantage in Multinational Industries', *American Economic Review* **74**, 356-60.

Authors Index

Studies in Industrial Organization

Kluwer Academic Publishers – Dordrecht / Boston / London